Dalits and Human Rights

Dalits and Human Rights

Dr. Neha Arora

Dalits and Human Rights

ISBN 978-93-5111-222-8

Published in 2014 in India by

RANDOM PUBLICATIONS

4376-A/4B, Gali Murari Lal, Ansari Road
New Delhi-110 002
Phone : +91-11-43580356, +91-11-23289044
e-mail: randomexports@gmail.com, sales@randompublications.com,
info@randompublications.com

Reprinted 2022

Type Setting by : Keystoneprintads, Delhi-110051
Digitally Printed at: Replika Press Pvt. Ltd.

Preface

The Scheduled Castes account for nearly 16.48 per cent of India's people. That is over 160 million human beings. Their contribution to society in terms of labour, art, and culture is enormous. Their share of the country's resources and riches is, however, disproportionately lower. They account for a sixth of India's population, but not of its land. At best, they hold a tiny fraction of a sixth of land owned by Indians. Indeed, most states in this country cannot provide minimally reliable date on lands owned by or distributed to dalits. What is not disputed by anyone, is that they are mainly landless and where they own land at all, it is marginal and usually of low quality. Secondly, irrigation of India has clear caste geography. Upper castes cultivate at the headwaters; intermediate castes at the middle and dalits cultivate near the tail waters. The importance of their position in relation to is enormous. As much as 77 per cent of the dalit workforce is in the primary or agricultural sector of the economy. But very, very few of them own land. They form, instead, the bulk of agricultural labourers in this country. Land has a great deal to do with both economic and social status. Let's look at who are the poor in India. Of the Indian poor, 40 per cent are landless agricultural labourers; 45 per cent are small or marginal farmers. (60 per cent of Indian farmers own less than an acre of land). This means that 85 per cent of the poor are either landless or marginal farmers. It's in the first category that you will find dalits in large numbers.

Of the remaining 15 per cent, 7.5 per cent are rural artisans and those who labour in other non-farm occupations. Again you will find dalits in this group, particularly those who work on leather. Lastly, all remaining categories of poor, including diverse segments of urban poor, constitute "Others" who live in poverty. Here, too, you will find dalits; in construction labour, in road laying crews and very prominently in scavenging and other sanitation work. All dalits in these 15 per cent are again, landless people. The importance of land to the problems we're talking about was recognised right at the time of drawing up the Constitution. A significant point of view was expressed in those discussions but S. Nagappa. He said: "I am prepared for the abolition of reservations, provided very Harijan (dalit) family get ten acres of wet land, twenty acres of dry land and all the children of Harijans are educated, free of cost, up to the university course, and give one-fifth of the key posts either in civilian or in military departments".

For the last 25 years, we've been pleased to congratulate ourselves on being a "self sufficient nation" in food production. We've even had food surpluses. This self-sufficiency, however, is very fragile. It is based on the reality that 400 million people go to bed hungry every night. If they got their minimum calorie requirements, our great surpluses would vanish and our level of production seem very inadequate. I'm not even looking here at unequal distribution. Only 16 per cent of dalits live in urban areas. The remaining 84 per cent, in rural India. The over 450 SC groups in the country represent an important and incredibility complex phenomenon. A people confronted by seemingly intractable problems brought on by millennia of exploitation, enforced poverty and deprivation. Decades after the abolition of untouchability, the actual extent of its prevalence would surprise many Indians who believe it belongs to the past. Whether it is in private employment, school dropout rates, literacy and health indicators, access to higher education, or even government jobs, they are at the wrong end of the spectrum. The actual gap between dalit literacy levels and those of the non-dalit population grew worse between 1961 and 1981. In Rajasthan, literacy rates for SC women are about one-fifth the national literacy rate for women. Indeed, one third the national SC female rate!

Half a century after independence, dalits still live in segregated section of the overwhelming majority of Indian villages. To this day, in several parts of the country, it is risky for them to even walk through the upper caste bastes. They have no access to the burial grounds/burning ghats in many villages in this country. The official programmes of the government of India practice their own forms of exclusion. The Indira Awas Yojana, for instance, reinforces the pattern of building homes for dalits away from the rest of the village.

I thank all members of my team who have helped in the preparation of the book. My special thanks go to "Random Publications" who have published the book.

– Dr. Neha Arora

Contents

1

Human Rights in a Globalised World

The idea of human rights is one of the most powerful in contemporary social and political discourse. It is readily endorsed by people from many different cultural and ideological backgrounds and it is used rhetorically in support of a large number of different and sometimes conflicting causes. Because of its strong appeal and its rhetorical power, it is often used loosely and can have different meanings in different contexts, although those who use the idea so readily seldom stop to ponder its various meanings and its contradictions.

This combination of its strong appeal and its contradictions makes the idea of human rights worth closer consideration, especially for social workers and those in other human service professions. This book is concerned with what a human rights perspective means for social workers. Framing social work as a human rights profession has certain consequences for the way in which social work is conceptualised and practised.

In many instances such a perspective reinforces and validates the traditional understandings and practices of social work, while in other cases it challenges some of the assumptions of the social work profession. The position of this book is that a human rights perspective can strengthen social work and that it provides a strong basis for an assertive practice that seeks to realise the social justice goals of social workers, in whatever setting. Human rights, however, are also contested and problematic. To develop a human rights basis for social work requires that the idea of human rights, and the problems and criticisms associated with it, be carefully examined. In this and following stages some of the issues and problems raised by human rights will be discussed, and the implications of these discussions for social work will be highlighted.

Many authors suggest that the idea of human rights is largely a product of Enlightenment thinking and is therefore inevitably contextualised within an essentially western and modernist framework. This has led to the criticism that human rights thinking and rhetoric are simply another manifestation of colonialist western domination, and to the suggestion that the concept of human rights should not be used. While it is true that much of the contemporary understanding of human rights has been shaped by western Enlightenment thinking, the same can be said of many other concepts that are frequently used in political debate, such as democracy, justice, freedom, equality and human dignity. To stop using such words simply because of their western Enlightenment associations would be to deny their power and importance across cultures and would lead to sterile and limited political debate. The task rather is to loosen them from the shackles of western modernity and to reconstruct them in more dynamic, inclusive and cross-cultural terms. That is the approach taken, though of course cultural issues and the question of cultural relativism are critically important. There is a stronger reason, however, to resist the argument that the idea of human rights should be rejected because of its western connotations.

This is because it is simply not true to say that human rights is an exclusively western concept. Notions of human rights are embedded in all the major religious traditions and can be found in many different cultural forms, though the term'human rights' may not always be used. Ideas of human dignity and worth, ideas that all people should be treated just as to certain basic standards, ideas that people should be protected from what is frequently termed'human rights abuse', and ideas of respect for the rights of others are not confined to the western intellectual tradition. To assume that they are is to devalue those other religious and cultural traditions that such critics often claim to be supporting. Nor is it true, as is commonly suggested, that human rights are a recent concept emerging only in the last two centuries, with their origins in Enlightenment thinking.

Although the Enlightenment was crucial in the construction of the modern western framing of human rights, the idea of human rights has been reflected in writings from much earlier ages, even though the term it self may not always have been used. Human rights, indeed, represent a powerful discourse that seeks to overcome divisiveness and sectarianism and to unite people of different cultural and religious traditions in a single movement asserting human values and the universality of humanity, at a time when such values are seen to be under threat from the forces of economic globalisation. The idea of human rights, by its very appeal to universally applicable ideas of the values of humanity, seems to resonate across cultures and traditions and represents an important rallying cry for those seeking to bring about a more just, peaceful and sustainable world.

As well as the criticism of cultural bias, two other criticisms are commonly made of a human rights perspective. One is that claims of human rights can be frivolous or selfish: people will claim something as a'human right' when in fact they are simply expressing a simple selfish'want'; for example people might claim the right to own a car, the right to take a luxury cruise, the right to smoke in a restaurant, the right to watch a video on an aircraft. Thus human rights become nothing more than a new language for consumerism and self-indulgence. The other criticism is that claims of human rights can conflict with each other and therefore one is left with the problem of reconciling competing claims, for example the right of freedom of expression as opposed to the right to protection from libel or slander. A human rights perspective needs to show how it will overcome those criticisms, and this will be undertaken in this and subsequent stages. Much of the academic debate about human rights remains at the theoretical level; less has been written about the practice of human rights. The important exception to this has been the legal profession, which has developed a significant specialisation in human rights law.

While lawyers have played a very important role in the promotion and safeguarding of human rights, an exclusively legal framing of human rights practice has limited the applicability of human rights in other professions and occupations. The reasons for this, and its consequences. Other professions, such as medicine, social work, teaching and nursing, are also concerned with human rights issues, and their practice can be seen as very much about the promotion of human rights in ways that extend beyond the more constrained practice of the law. The literature of these professions, however, while acknowledging that ideas of human rights are important for professional practice, does not for the most part define either theory or practice within a specific human rights framework.

There is little articulation of what it means in practice for professionals to claim that their work is based on human rights, and so human rights remain a'nice idea' rather than a solid foundation for the development of practice theories and methodologies. This book represents an attempt to fill this gap by examining what a human rights perspective means for the practice of human service professions such as social work. It identifies some of the important theoretical and conceptual issues about human rights and looks at how they might be applied to practice in a way that can identify a social worker more clearly as a human rights worker.

In general use, the term'human rights worker' applies either to lawyers with a human rights specialisation or to activists working for organisations such as Amnesty International. This book seeks to locate social workers also as human rights workers and to identify some key issues that emerge when social work is reframed as human rights work.

SOCIAL WORK

While much of the material in this book can be applied to a broad range of human service professions such as teaching, medicine and the other health-related professions, the primary focus of the book is social work. In this regard,'social work' needs some clarification, as this term has different connotations in different national and cultural contexts. In some societies, most notably Australia and North America,'social worker' implies a fairly narrowly defined group of workers who have high professional qualifications, and excludes many others working in the human service field. In other societies the term has a much wider application, covering human service workers from a variety of backgrounds, with varying levels of educational qualifications. In some societies, such as the United Kingdom, social work has been seen as the implementation of the policies of the welfare state through the provision of statutory services, with relatively little role in community development or social change.

In other societies, however, such as in Latin America,'social work' has much more radical or activist connotations: it is concerned with bringing about social change, progressive movements for social justice and human rights, and opposition to prevalent forms of bureaucratic and political domination. In some contexts, such as the United States, individualised therapeutic roles for social workers are dominant, while in other contexts, particularly in'the developing world' or'the south', social work has a much stronger community development orientation.

Even in societies that might superficially seem very similar, such as Australia and New Zealand, there can be significant differences in how social work is constructed and in what counts as good practice. Given the importance of grounding social work in its cultural, social and political context, it is inevitable that social work will be constructed differently in different locations. This has considerable benefits for social work as it allows for a diversity of interests and practices. But it also poses problems, in that readers of the social work literature will be seeking to apply that literature in different contexts where the very idea of social work is contested. It is also a recipe for ambiguity and misun-derstanding when social workers meet across cultural and national boundaries. This book accepts a broad view of the nature of'social work' and is not confined to specific professional, social control, conservative, radical, therapeutic or developmental formulations.

The term is meant to be understood in its broadest sense and to include all those working in the social services or community development, including those seeking social change. The aim of this book is to show that a human rights perspective such as that developed in the following stages provides a unifying framework within which the various activities identified as'social work' can be incorporated, while still allowing for cultural, national and political difference. There is a strong tradition in social work of identifying a core value position for the profession.

Social work writers have consistently emphasised the importance of this value base; social work is not seen as a neutral, objective or'value-free' activity, but rather as work which is grounded in values and which makes no apology for adopting partisan stances on a range of questions. In formulating this value base, the idea of human rights is often implicit, through phrases such as'the inherent worth of the individual', the 'right to self-determination', and so on.

Such statements serve to locate human rights, though perhaps in a fairly limited form, as having a central role in social work, though characteristically there is usually little explication of the nature of these'rights', the contested nature of rights, what they mean in practice, and how adopting such rights as central actually affects what social workers do in their day-to-day work.

Professional codes of ethics also tend to imply some commitment to an idea of human rights, since it is often from an implied human rights position that the ethics of social work are derived. This again is a piecemeal approach to human rights and does not really confront the idea of human rights head on. Indeed it might be suggested that the construction of human rights contained in documents such as codes of ethics and introductory texts often treats human rights as if they are self-evident and non-problematic, a position which even the most cursory examination of the extensive literature on rights would show to be misguided and simplistic.

A DISCURSIVE APPROACH TO HUMAN RIGHTS

Many of the issues and debates about human rights will be discussed in later stages, and their applicability to social work practice will be identified. At the outset, however, it is important to make a clear statement about the approach to human rights adopted in this book. This is an approach that rejects a positivist notion of rights, implying that human rights somehow 'exist' in an objective form and can be identified, 'discovered', and empirically measured or verified.

The idea of rights existing somehow independently of human agency is characteristic of the positivist world-view of the social sciences, which regards social phenomena as existing independently and objectively, and sees the task of the social scientist as objective empirical enquiry into the laws that govern how social phenomena interact. The positivist view has been the object of sustained critique in the social science literature and the position of this book is one that rejects such a paradigm. Rather than regarding rights as'existing' in some way, hence able to be uncovered through objective scientific enquiry, the arguments in later stages see human rights as essentially discursive, in other words rights are constructed through human interaction and through an ongoing dialogue about what should constitute a common or shared humanity. Hence human rights are not static but will vary over time and in different cultures and political contexts.

The best-known statement of human rights, the Universal Declaration of Human Rights, though representing perhaps one of the more remarkable human achievements of the twentieth century, should not therefore be reified and seen as expressing a universal and unchanging truth. Rather, the Universal Declaration represents a statement of what was agreed by the leaders of the world's nations in 1948 as a statement of the basic rights of all people. It is an impressive and inspirational statement, with significant radical implications, and it has been used in many ways since to further many important causes in the name of humanity. But it is not holy writ, and it can and should be subject to challenge in different times, as different voices are heard and different issues are given priority.

The same must apply to any other statement of human rights: what constitutes the basic rights of all human beings will be a matter for ongoing debate and redefinition and should always be open to challenge. The Universal Declaration has been criticised because of the dominance of western political leaders in the forum from which it was derived, leading to a perceived western bias. This, however, is an argument not for the rejection of the idea of such a universal statement but rather for its continual reformulation in the light of different voices being validated and heard. The Enlightenment view of human rights, as argued by Locke, talks about'natural' rights, namely the idea that the very nature of human beings implies that they have certain rights, as a consequence of their very humanity.

By simply talking about 'human beings' we imply human rights arising from some notion of a common or shared humanity which requires that people be treated in a certain way. At birth we are all equal and therefore we'naturally' acquire equal rights. The idea of rights existing'naturally' might at first sight sound like a positivist framing of human rights, but the idea of'natural' rights in this sense is not necessarily inconsistent with the view of human rights as discursive. It is simply an affirmation of the view that our human rights are the consequence of our common or shared humanity, but it is nevertheless quite consistent to talk about a discursive construction of how we understand those'natural' rights.

The idea of human rights, by its very nature, implies the search for universal principles that apply to all humans, whatever their cultural background, belief system, age, sex, ability or circumstances. Such universality has been absent from many of the more traditional understandings of human rights, simply because not everybody has been thought of as'human'. The discourse of the 'rights of man' and traditional views of patriarchal philosophers such as Locke have distanced women from the definition of'human' and therefore from an understanding of what'human rights' imply. Thomas Jefferson presumably saw no conflict between his advocacy of rights and freedoms and his ownership of slaves. The perpetrators of the Holocaust, while celebrating the high achievements of German civilization, were able to justify their actions by effectively defining Jews as subhuman, and the same can be said of the Apartheid regime in South Africa, the Indonesian occupying army in East Timor, the Serb forces in Bosnia, and so on. Oppressors can justify their actions by effectively removing their victims from their understanding of'human' and thereby avoiding the necessity of recognising their human rights.

2

Maintenance of Public Law and Order

The Universal Declaration of Human Rights is a historically memorable and significant document of human liberty. Its preamble frames the document, proclaiming that"disregard and contempt for human rights have resulted in barbarous acts which have outraged the conscience of mankind and the advent of a world in which human beings shall enjoy freedom of speech and belief and freedom from fear and want has been proclaimed the highest aspiration of the common people." This stage attempts to discuss the role of human rights approach in eliminating or reducing cases of human rights violations in the sensitive and difficult task of maintenance of pubic law and order by law enforcement agencies *viz.*, police, para-military, military and the executive consistent with the spirit on Fundamental Rights of the Constitution of India, the Universal Declaration of Human Rights and other relevant UN Conventions and Covenants.

The smooth and effective maintenance of public law and order is the cornerstone for shaping and regulating the multi-ethnic, multi-religious and multi-lingual diversified society in India as a harmonious, democratic, secular and social welfare oriented civil society gravitating towards the concepts of"Unity in diversity","truth" and"transparency".

WHY HUMAN RIGHTS

It is essential if humanity "is not to be compelled to have recourse, as a last resort, to rebellion against tyranny and oppression, that human rights should be protected by the rule of law".

- Article 8 is a 'due process' provision noting that"Everyone has the right to an effective remedy by the competent national tribunals for acts violating the fundamental rights granted to him by the constitution or by law".
- Article 13 of UDHR assures freedom of movement.
- Article 18 assures freedom of thought, conscience and religion.

- Article 19 assures freedom of opinion and expression.

Civil society has broken down in numerous areas. There is a widespread belief that society is disintegrating as are traditional, moral and social codes resulting in routine abuse of human beings and their rights. Against this background, the concept of human rights has acquired new importance and resonance. The idea that people possess certain basic human rights, and that these should be safe from violation by the State or by other groups or individuals, seems today an important bulwark against the breakdown of law and order and degradation of moral norms.

GLOBALIZATION AND HUMAN RIGHTS

The global machinery of surveillance and monitoring through the UN human rights regime, is reinforced by an evolving set of regional regimes and mechanisms in the adjudication and enforcement of rights. There has thus occurred a consequent institutionalization for vindication of human rights. Globalization is associated with significant challenges in the human rights project, as conventionally conceived. The most pressing issue confronting the guardians of the human rights project is how to marshal the forces of globalization in order to ensure the advancement of human rights and justice in the new millennium.

The present trends of severe abridgement of human rights may continue in future and demands for right to life, liberty, equality, etc. will continue to be made. The primary victims of human rights violations will be women, weaker sections, children, victims of terrorism-related violence and environmental degradation. Indiscriminate urbanization, consumerism and industria-lization have brought degradation to the civil society. Thus human rights violations can be eliminated, if there are basic changes in the socio-economic and political milieu.

Accessibility to legal remedies by the common man is ensured by:

- Proper recording of General Diary/First Information Report in Police Stations and follow-up enquiries /investigations,
- Remedy before legal forums/Courts/tribunals, which includes invoking Constitutional writ y of the High Courts and the Supreme Court,
- Vindication of infringement of rights of persons,
- Legal counselling through awareness campaigns,
- Legal aid and clinics to remedy the problem of unequal financial power to continue law suits,
- Formulating and ensuring the accountability criteria of functionaries at different levels of the State/para-State institutions.,
- To curb the general tendency of higher ups in administrative/social hierarchy to ignore and rise above the law by use of:
  - Muscle power,

- Money power,
- Political power,
- Rampant corruption.

Human Rights for good governance are characterized by the following:

- Protection and promotion of fundamental rights depend on proper and efficient law enforcement,
- Effective law enforcement is possible only when there are trained and efficient keepers of the law, wedded to human rights norms,
- Politicians now prefer officers who are not upright and strong-willed and are willing to function as"sycophants and courtiers"..
- "The Rule of law in modern India,... has been undermined by the rule of politics."
- "With the passage of years there is escalation of crime and lawlessness."
- "Large number of cases in police stations are not registered."
- Delay in disposal of cases,
- A vast number of old and outdated laws continue in statute books,
- The Police Act of 1861 remains archaic, inhibiting police to function professionally without fear or favour. Police reforms are yet to ensure greater transparency, accountability and responsiveness to public criticism of police functioning
- Politician-civil service-police nexus must be eliminated to stamp out'politicization of crime and criminalization of politics'.
- Police have to be made accountable.
- "Corruption of civil servants is one of the most damaging consequences of poor governance. It subverts law enforcement and undermines the legitimacy of the State.". For good governance, it is essential"to devise a series of long-range strategies and short -term measures to deal with the menace of corruption. Corruption flourishes because punishment is lacking."
- Community policing assumes police-public partnership,
- "Internal regulation of policing can be more thorough, effective and efficient than external supervision"
- "Any civilian oversight body in order to be effective should have an independent investigative capacity."
- The roots of police deviating from the'Rule of Law' stem from:
  - Ambiguous legislation
  - Vulnerability to legal sanctions
  - Occupational culture and
  - A desire to produce quick results

HUMAN RIGHTS AND PUBLIC LAW AND ORDER

Universal Declaration of Human Rights, 1948 (UDHR) envisages the following human rights.

- Right to life, liberty and security of person to every human being. (Article 3)
- Right to privacy and security of life. (Article 12)
- Freedom of thought, expression, conscience and religion. (Article 18)
- Freedom of peaceful assembly and association. (Article 20)
- Right to equality and non-discrimination. (Articles 1, 2 & 7)
- Freedom from slavery or servitude. (Article 4)
- Freedom from arbitrary arrest, detention or exile. (Article 9)
- *Criminal procedure rights*:
  - *Right to consult a lawyer*:
  - Right to be presumed innocent unless proved guilty. (Articles 10 and 11)
  - Right not to be subjected to retrospective legislation.
- Right to nationality (Article 15),
- Right to exercise franchise and take part in governance of the country (Article 21),
- All other rights for preserving human dignity and self-pride.

In Sunil Batra case, the SC quoted extensively from the international instruments on Human Rights.

ROLE OF THE GOVERNMENT

- A new spirit emerged in the minds of the framers of the Indian Constitution in the sphere of human rights and human welfare. The Constitution framers referred to the UN Charter on various political, economic and social matters. The fundamental rights and the Directive Principles of State Policy are based on the principle of humanitarianism and human rights.
- On the basis of the Directive Principles of State Policy, the Union Government enacted a number of Acts related to human rights including:
  - Abolition of Untouchability Act 1955,
  - Immoral Traffic (Prevention) Act, 1956,
  - Dowry Prohibition Act, 1961 (Amendment 1985, 1986)
  - The Protection Human Rights Act, 1993
  - The National Human Rights Commission (Procedure) Regulations, 1994
  - The Commission of SATI (Prevention) Act, 1987
  - The National Commission for Backward Classes Act, 1993
  - The National Commission for Minorities Act, 1992
  - The National Commission for Safai Karmacharis Act, 1993
  - The Persons with disabilities (Equal opportunities, Protection of Rights and Full Participation) Act, 1995 and Rules, 1996.
  - The Pre-natal Diagnostic Techniques (Regulation and Prevention of Misuse) Act, 1994

   - The Protection of Civil Rights Act, 1955 and Rules, 1977
   - The Scheduled Castes and the Scheduled Tribes (Prevention and Atrocities) Act, 1989 and Rules 1995.
- To ensure human rights and safeguard the interests of minorities and weaker sections of the society, several independent bodies have been created under provisions of the Constitution, such as:
   - The Minorities Commission
   - The Language Commission
   - The Scheduled Caste and Scheduled Tribes Commission
   - The National Commission for Women
   - The National Human Rights Commission
   - State Human Rights Commissions
   - The National Commission for Backward classes
   - The National Commission for Minorities
   - The National Commission for Safai Karmacharis
   - The National Commission for Protection of Children's Rights
- The issue of human rights received wide attention in the media during the 1980s because of extremist and separatist activities in Punjab and Assam.

The United Nations asked India to solve the problem by negotiation with the extremists:

- There had been a steady erosion of human rights in Jammu and Kashmir State in the 1990s. Massacres continue to be in the last decade with increasing ferocity being committed by extremists in Jammu and Kashmir State. Pakistan tried many times to internationalize the matter. However, Pakistan had insufficient support from the United Nations. On 17 August 1995 the UN Security Council expressed its concern about the killings of a Norwegian tourist, Hans Christian Ostro, by the terrorists.
- The 1990s have seen the enactment of human rights legislation in India.'The Protection of Human Rights Act', 1993 provided for the constitution of a National Human Rights Commission, State Human Rights Commissions in individual States and a Human Rights Court.
- V.R. Krishna Iyer J, reacting to the establishment of the National Human Rights Commission observed "The mendicancy to which this nation is reduced .... even in regard to human rights ideology is a matter for pity." He also opined that "we should have the Human Rights Division of the Supreme Court of India. It will be useful. Similarly we may have at the High Court level and then they can operate with infrastructure, which is provided.... We really want, therefore, a commission which is vitalized, a commission which has an independent investigating staff not deputed from the police."
- In favour of the NHRC T.K. Thommen J, observed: "The commission

is not a court. Its function is to be the watching of human rights. Its procedure is not expected to be adversarial or accusatorial. It must not allow itself to be bogged down by procedural formalities."

- Bureaucracy and administrative law remain as stumbling blocks to genuinely interested individuals or bonafide agencies in obtaining information from government files, regardless of the right of information that can be claimed.
- Authorized snooping and surveillance of the opposition, and even of friends, continues, regardless of the governments in power.
- In a rescue of 450'child sex workers', who were subjected to mandatory testing for AIDS, it was stated that a rare opportunity had been provided'for gathering epidemiological data' that'cannot be lost on grounds of human rights or morality'. Half of the subjects were between 10 and 15 years, and many between 20 and 25 years and above, yet they were all declared minors and were shunted from orphanages to beggars' homes.
- India has the largest number of working children, who have no option but to work for the survival of themselves and the families that find them'usable'.
- The Prevention of Immoral Traffic Act, 1956 as amended in 1986 recognizes the criminality of child prostitution, yet few are convicted.
- The agony is aggravated when, under the Juvenile Justice Act, 2000 as amended in 2006, these children are arrested and rescued as vagrants or missing persons.
- In enforcing 14 different Acts the problem of child labour gets sidelined.
- The National Police Commission in its 8-volume report deals with the rights of the accused under the Criminal Procedure Code and the Evidence Act; custodial rape is an aggravated offence punishable with a deterrent sentence, and yet it occurs.
- In 1997 and 1998, indiscriminate police firing caused mindless cruelty and deaths. People survive in fear, while cases against police are withdrawn.
- Individuals and organizations run the risk of being labelled as agents of imperialism, as Amnesty International has.
- A career in human rights involves truckling to the powers that be. Human rights activists can blindly buy the versions put across by governments and their allies.
- The Proclamation of Emergency of 1975 and Terrorist and Disruptive Activities (Prevention) Act of 1985 demonstrated how the law-enforcing agencies made room for government lawlessness. Human rights situations were never to be the same again, particularly after the criminalization of politics.

- Militant communalism and fundamentalism have threatened the democratic values being cultivated in society.
- The struggle for the human rights of prisoners goes beyond the Constitution and Jail Manual and, through the media, into homes and hearts of the people.
- The need to enforce human rights goes beyond Constitutional obligations.
- The initiative to create new responses with the introduction of appropriate procedures by NHRC will bring about structural changes that will communicate verifiable results. The status quo in law is being changed, but not at the rate of expectations from NHRC.
- The affirmation of human rights of all people in Constitutional texts is not adequate. The key lies in having a grievance redressal mechanism, and instruments, which are yet to be accepted as pre requisites. We have now arrived at a stage in our political development where people's rights against the State have been legitimised.
- After reviewing all the decisions in respect of the State liability, the Supreme Court of India in Nilabati Behra v. State of Orissa declared that the defence of sovereign immunity is not applicable; it is alien to the concept of guarantee of fundamental rights. Further, the Court stressed that such defence is not available in the Constitutional remedy. The Court declared that award of compensation under Articles 32 and 226 is a public remedy based on the strict liability for contravention of fundamental rights for which sovereign immunity does not apply. This ruling clarifies that sovereign immunity may be defence in the proceedings under private law of torts.

The impact of this historic ruling is that anyone whose fundamental rights are adversely affected by the State action can approach either Supreme Court or High Court under Article 32 and 226 of the Constitution respectively and, in such a case, the State is not entitled to raise the plea of sovereign immunity in public law proceedings. When once the defence of sovereign immunity is made non-applicable in the area of public law, the courts can effectively protect the fundamental freedoms of a person from the unauthorized infringement of such rights of State action and thereby can uphold the Rule of Law.

CASE STUDIES

POLICE EXCESSES CUSTODIAL DEATH

Custodial death of Mohammad Irshad Khan (Case No. 2387/30/2000- 2001-CD)

The Commission received information from the Deputy Commissioner of Police (DCP), North East District, Delhi about the death of Mohammad Irshad Khan. A complaint was also received from Shri Acchan Khan, father of the deceased, alleging that his son had died as a result of brutal beating by the police. Shri Acchan Khan added that the family of the victim had not been informed of the circumstances of the death. The intervention of the Commission was requested, as also an independent investigation into the case and protection for the complainant's family in view of threats by the police personnel who had been accused of being involved in the death of Mohammad Irshad Khan. In response to a notice from the Commission, the Home Secretary, Government of the National Capital Territory of Delhi, stated that the matter had been investigated by DCP (Vigilance), Delhi. The latter's report indicated that, on 12 October 2000, while the victim was driving his two-wheeler scooter, he had collided with a cycle rickshaw. In a scuffle that ensued, a policeman had intervened and reportedly beaten the victim, who had collapsed on the spot.

The victim was then taken to GTB Hospital, where he was registered at Police Station Usmanpur, and the accused Sub Inspector Vijay Kumar and Constable, Swatantra Kumar had been arrested. A magisterial enquiry had been conducted by the S.D.M., Seelampur. A further report, dated 9 April 2001 from the Deputy Secretary, Home Department, Government of National Capital Territory of Delhi, stated that a charge sheet had been filed against the delinquent police official's u/s 302/34 IPC.

Upon further consideration of the matter, the Commission directed that a show-cause notice be issued to the Government of National Capital Territory of Delhi asking as to why immediate interim relief in the amount of ₹3 lakhs u/s 18(3) of the Protection of Human Rights Act be not granted to the next-of-kin of the deceased. The Government of National Capital Territory of Delhi, in response, stated that ₹3 lakhs had been sanctioned towards the payment of compensation to the next-of-kin of the deceased. It was later confirmed that the amount was paid to the wife of the deceased on 30 May 2001.

TORTURE

Torture of Dayashankar by Police: Uttar Pradesh (Case No. 791/24/2000-2001)

One Dayashankar Vidyalankar, a resident of Haridwar, Uttaranchal submitted a complaint alleging that while he was propagating the teachings of Swami Dayanand at Haridwar Railway Station on 29 February 2001, he was beaten and manhandled by a Constable and, as a result, his left ear was badly injured and a bone behind his right ear was broken. The reports received from the Superintendent of Police Railways, Moradabad and the Director General, Railway Protection Force, Railway Board, in response to a notice issued by the Commission, indicated that the allegations of the complainant against the Constable were found to be correct.

The Constable was punished by a reduction in his present pay-scale by 3 stages for 3 years, and a case u/s 323/326 IPC and section 145 of Railways Act, 1989 was also registered against him. The Commission after considering the aforesaid reports and giving a personal hearing to the complainant, as well as after obtaining an opinion from a Medical Board of the All India Institute of Medical Sciences, New Delhi, regarding the nature of the injuries suffered by the complainant, recommended a payment of ₹10,000 to the petitioner by the Ministry of Railways. This has been paid.

Illegal Detention and Torture of D.M. Rege: Maharashtra (Case No. 1427/13/98-99)

D.M. Rege, an officer of Shamrao Vithal Co-operative Bank Limited, Versova Branch, Mumbai, complained to the Commission that he was illegally detained and tortured by the police in connection with an incident involving the misplacement of cash in the Bank and requested for an enquiry into the matter. Upon directions of the Commission, a report was received from the DCP, Zone-VII, Mumbai. It indicated that the complainant was indeed innocent, and that his detention and torture were unjustified. The report also mentioned that the guilty Constable had been awarded a minor punishment by way of forfeiture of his increment for one year, while the delinquent Sub-Inspector had been transferred out.

After consideration of the report, the Commission directed the Police Commissioner, Mumbai to have the matter re-examined in order to ensure that the erring police personnel were suitably punished in a manner that would be commensurate with the wrong that had been done. The Commission also issued a show-cause notice as to why ₹30,000 is not awarded as immediate interim relief to the victim. The State Government, through its letter of 4 January 2001, requested the Commission to reconsider the issue of payment of compensation on the ground that two of the policemen had been immediately transferred, and that the Constable had been awarded punishment of stoppage of his increment for one year for his misconduct.

The Commission, in its order dated 10 April 2001, rejected the plea of the State Government, and held that, since the guilt of the public servants had been established, there were no grounds to justify a re-consideration of this matter and directed that compensation of ₹30,000 be paid by the State Government to the complainant for violation of his human rights.

IMPLEMENTATION OF LEGISLATIVE BACKGROUND

PROVISIONS AT THE STATE LEVEL

- Human rights can be regarded as the civic counterpart (civil society/ NGOs) of political power, which is vested in those who govern the State.

- Power of the State, whenever lawless and brute, needs to be counterbalanced by power of the people arising from human rights.
- Democracy is established when people's power ("Lok Shakti") transcends over the power of the State. This is fortified by an independent Indian judiciary which is more or less independent, a fairly investigative and alert media and a fairly good movement for the promotion of human rights in India by advocates of and activists for civil society, as also of the NGOs.
- Awakening of general awareness in Indian people about human rights as their very own, sacrosanct and inherent rights in the country's democratic and participatory governance.
- There is a tendency on the part of the police/the para-military/the military to disregard human rights while dealing with an alleged terrorist, and this is approved by pro-establishment politicians.

The manifestation of such human rights violations by the law-enforcement agencies are:

- Custodial violence, including the so-called"third-degree methods",
- Custodial death,
- Mass arrests and physical and psychological torture,
- Scorched-earth policies, herding up people in areas under cover of heavy security measures, resembling to some extent open concentration camps with extremely fettered freedom of movement and weak supply line for procuring daily necessities including medicare,
- Disappearance of person's kidnappings and abductions,
- Cooked-up prosecutions and suspicion discoveries by lawenforcement agencies of mass-inciting literature and arms and ammunition, which may as well be implanted by the agencies themselves,
- Rape, molestation, gang rape and custodial rape of women by security forces, law-enforcement agencies and detention camp/prison officials/ tough and brutal prison inmates,
- Sodomy, collective beating of such male (including young) detainees/ prisoners by hardened criminal inmates encouraged by or unobstructed by security/prison/law-enforcement officials,
- Encounter deaths, which may be fake and just sadistic and bloodthirsty killings of innocent and guilty persons, alike as a crude method of so-called'shock treatment' by security forces,
- Deprivation of the right of the prisoner to obtain adequate food and water, medical assistance, sanitation and toilet facilities, consultation with a lawyer of his choice, media news, interviews with members of family or friends etc.,
- Use of handcuffs and/or fetters,
- Solitary confinement,

- Drastic control of communication with fellow detainees.
  - State violence may be committed
- By State officials by overstepping the law or
- By the State in passing "lawless laws" like the TADA.

THE NATIONAL HUMAN RIGHTS COMMISSION OF INDIA (NHRC) AND ITS DIRECTIVES

- Started in 1993,
- Initially it concerned itself with civil rights,
- The issues of custodial deaths as a result of violence perpetrated by the police brought to focus its (NHRC) work.
- Bijbehra village in Kashmir where a BSF unit was alleged to have mowed down 40 civilians. BSF initially refused access to these records to NHRC, but ultimately agreed. From the very BSF records NHRC came to a conclusion and advised the Government to proceed on that basis. The Government accepted these conclusions and courtmartial proceedings were initiated against the perpetrators of this violence.

That was the turning point in the history of NHRC:

- Investigation of the case of suicide in jails due to its high incidence. Each case of suicide or unnatural death, be it in judicial custody or police custody, should be enquired into by a Magistrate or an independent person. Such enquiry should aim at ascertaining whether there was any negligence or dereliction of duty on the part of any public servant and should suggest such appropriate measures and safeguards as may prevent the recurrence of such a tragedy in future. The Commission considers this mode of enquiry to be mandatory.
- The DMs/SPs to ensure prompt communication of incidents of custodial deaths/custodial rapes in police as well as judicial custody to the Commission.
- All post-mortem examinations done in respect of deaths in police custody and in jails should be video-filmed and cassettes should be sent to the Commission along with the post-mortem report.
- Commission has prescribed the Model Autopsy Form and the additional procedure for inquest to be followed by instructions to be followed carefully for detention or torture.
- Encounter deaths and recommendation of the Commission on the correct procedure to be followed by all the States.
- Commission's guidelines regarding arrest and enforcement of such guidelines.
- Commission's guidelines relating to the administration of Lie Detector Test.

Information collated by NHRC in its Annual Report for 2001-2002 indicate the implementation of the legislative provisions at the State level through the

Commission's reporting, investigating and remedial action taken procedure. Similar action is also taken by the State-level Human Rights Commissions.

PUBLIC INTEREST LITIGATION

- Several cases came before the Supreme Court since 1980 where the Court entertained Writ petitions by one on behalf of another on the allegation that fundamental rights of such others had been affected.- Sunil Batra V. Delhi Administration (1980) 2 SCR 557
- The Supreme Court liberalized the rule of maintainability by almost taking away the restriction of locus standi.- Transfer of Judges Case- S.P. Gupta V. Union of India and Ors.

The Court held that".... whenever there is a public wrong or public injury caused by an act or Commission of the State or a public authority which is contrary to the Constitution or the law, any member of the public acting bonafide and having sufficient interest can maintain an action for redressal or such public wrong or public injury." In Bandhua Mukti Morcha case the Supreme Court found that State Governments were under an obligation to release bonded labourers. It also directed the Government of Haryana to draw up a scheme or programme for"a better and more meaningful rehabilitation of the freed bonded labourers" in the light of the guidelines set out by the Secretary to the Government of India, Ministry of Labour, in his letter dated September 2, 1982. The Court also felt unhappy at the denial of minimum wages and pure drinking water to the workmen.

Again, it issued the directions to the Union of India and State of Haryana that so far as implementation of the provisions of the Minimum Wages Act., 1948 was concerned, they should take necessary steps, for the purpose of ensuring that minimum wages are paid to the workmen employed in the stone quarries and stone crushers in accordance with the principles laid down by the Court.

ORIGIN OF THE PUBLIC INTEREST LITIGATION IN INDIA

1976: Roots of Public Interest Litigation in India. In Mumbai Kamgar Sabha vs. Adbul Bhai-A.I.R. 1976-SC 1465 Krishna Ayer J, observed

- "Test litigation, representative actions, probono publico, broadened forms of legal proceedings are in keeping with the current accent on justice to the common man and a necessary disincentive to those who wish to bypass the real issues on the merits by suspect reliance on peripheral, procedural shortcomings. Public interest is promoted by a spacious construction of locusstandi in our socio-economic circumstances and conceptual latitudinarianism permits taking liberties with individualization of the right to invoke the higher Courts, where the remedy is shared by a considerable number, particularly when they are weaker and less litigant, consistent with fair process, is the aim of adjective law."

Through a process of steady expansion of the doctrine of locus standi, starting with Dhabolkar's case, the Supreme Court enabled access on matters involving public interest even to total strangers to the dispute.

DEVELOPMENT OF PUBLIC INTEREST LITIGATION IN INDIA

There are four stages through which the public interest litigation developed in India or during the last decade, namely:

1. Steady expansion of Locus Standi doctrine;
2. Expansion of epistolary jurisdiction;
3. Democratization of judicial remedies; and
4. New constitutional philosophy for social justice.

STEADY EXPANSION OF LOCUS STANDI

- *Restrictive Rule of Locus Standi*:'Person aggrieved'.
- Flexibility introduced in narrow concept.

In writ of Quo-Warranto, any member of public, irrespective of any special injury or damage to him, could challenge the appointment of a holder of public office. A Writ of Habeas Corpus could be moved on behalf of the person illegally detained by his friend or relative but not by a complete stranger.

Justice Shri Krishna Iyer and Justice Shri Bhagwati are undoubtedly acknowledged champions of the new philosophy of judicial activism in India, which has been assimilated by and absorbed in our judicial system.

1976: Need for Liberalization of Locus Standi

In the year 1976 Justice Shri Krishna Iyer, noted for his unconventional approaches and iconoclastic spirit in the cause of social justice and development of public interest litigation, advocated liberal interpretation of Locus Standi in public interest litigation in Dhabolkar's case.

It was felt by the Court that it must be possible for some public spirited individual to seek remedy on behalf of poor, disadvantaged, deprived and dispossessed people. Through this case, a process of steady expansion of doctrine of Locus Standi was set in.

Initial Stages of PIL and Locus Standi

In 1978, in Maneka Gandhi case, the Supreme Court gave a new dimension to the concept of"procedure established by law in Article 21 of the constitution". This Article was interpreted to confer both substantial and procedural due process, which brightened further the prospects of public interest litigation. The scope of PIL was further enlarged in 1979 when the Supreme Court allowed maintainability of a petition by an advocate based on a newspaper report, which brought out the conditions of undertrials in Tihar Jail. Through public interest litigation a shock treatment was given to our tardy and bullock cart system of investigation and trial in criminal cases, and the concept of fundamental right of citizens for speedy trial was held necessary as'just and reasonable procedure'.

ROLE OF POLICE VIS-A-VIS UNIVERSAL DECLARATION OF HUMAN RIGHTS

- Law observance by the police is the best form of law enforcement that one can conceive of in a country under the Rule of Law.
- Required in India is an honest, humane and unbrutalised police force whose members are trained to act fairly and within the bounds of law.
- "None should be put to the harassment of a criminal trial unless there are good and substantial reasons for holding it". State of Rajasthan Vs. Gurucharan Das AIR 1979 SC 1895, per Fazal Ali, J:
  - To contribute towards liberty, equality and fraternity in human affairs.
  - To help and reconcile freedom with security, and to uphold the rule of law.
  - To uphold and protect human rights.
  - To contribute towards winning faith of the people.
  - To strengthen the security of persons and property
  - To investigate, detect and activate the prosecution of offences
  - To facilitate movement on highways and curb public disorder.
  - To deal with major and minor crisis and help those who are in distress.
  - The Governments of States and Union Territories of India need to implement the recommendations of the National Police Commission aimed at freeing the police from external pressures in carrying out day-to-day police work.
  - Every policeman is an agent of the Government, who is required to maintain a proper equilibrium between the public and the Government and protect one against the other.
  - Increasing crime with a rising population, violent outbursts, growing terrorism and religious fanaticism have added new dimensions to the role of police.
  - The police are required to be an efficient and impartial law enforcement agency.
  - Abuse of powers by the police gross violation of the Fundamental Rights and Human Rights encroaching upon the personal liberty, dignity, honour and privacy of individual citizens galore and must be curbed and eliminated ruthlessly by the State Organs.
  - "A policeman is the axis on which the rule of law rests and rotates

.... It is he who enforces the law, maintains the public order, keeps the lawless elements in check, brings the offender to book and by his constant vigil preserves the coherence and solidarity of the social structure."

- Police has been degraded by the political system as a State agent in violating Human Rights.
- Police has to be accountable to the people as they represent the law and order of the organized society.
- There must be absolute professional independence of police in the matter of investigation of crime for effective and efficient functioning of criminal justice system.

- Third degree methodology of police investigation only alienates the police from the public. People dread police, and do all they can to avoid any connection with a police investigation. It brutalizes the police official and degrades him even to the level below the criminal in his custody. Section 29(1) of the Police Act, 1961 and Article 20(3) of the Constitution of India clearly forbid custodial torture of the third degree. Such actions are serious offences punishable under Sections 330 and 331 of the Indian Penal Code. The United Nations in December, 1982 issued a circular entitled"Principles of Medical Ethics Relevant to the Role of Health Personnel, particularly Physicians, in the Protection of Prisoners and Detainees Against Torture and Other Cruel, Inhuman and Degrading Treatment or Punishment." Social control in the form of approval or disapproval of police action can motivate the police to become just, fair and law abiding.
- Remand in police custody misused to extort a confession from the accused by adopting Third Degree methods is useless as:
  - A confession made under pressure is not at all admissible in evidence under Section 27 of the Evidence Act, in view of the guarantee against testimonial compulsion
  - Such a confession, even if judicially recorded, is often considered as false, being unverifiable, and is often retracted in court.
- Padding, concoction and fabrication of evidence in police investigation in specific cases with a view to showing a high percentage of conviction in cases investigated by them are contrary to all principles of justice.
- One indirect cause perhaps is that too high a standard of fool-proof evidence is often insisted upon by the Courts from the prosecution. Commenting on this aspect of the matter Krishna Iyer, J of the Supreme Court observed,"Judicial quest for perfect proof often accounts for police presentation of fool-proof concoction. Why fake up? Because the Court asks for manufacture to make truth look true. No, we must be realistic." Inder Singh Vs. State, 1978, Cr.L.J. 766.

- Concealment and minimization of crime by a large scale"burking of crimes" that is failure to record crimes or not recording a clear picture of the crime. Section 154(1) Cr.P.C. makes it mandatory for an officer in charge of a police station to register an FIR, when information is given to him regarding a cognizable offence. Section 154(2) Cr.P.C. enjoins him to give a copy of the FIR forthwith and free of cost to the informant.
- Non-performance of duties by police due to their involvement in politics or similar affiliations immensely damages the police image. Police in their professional capacity have to be apolitical and impartial in their application of the law.
- Police can cooperate with the aftercare agent, the probation officer or the social worker by doing work of surveillance in a covert fashion, so that the process of rehabilitation initiated by the correctional services are not nullified by hasty and precipitate police action. The police too can give a helping hand in finding employment for exconvicts. This will bring the police close to the public by improving their image.

PRISON REFORMS

Definition of Open Prison:

- "An open prison is characterized by the absence of material or physical precautions against escape and by a system based on self-discipline and the inmates sense of responsibility towards the group in which he lives."

An open prison shall mean a Prison House not surrounded by walls of any kind.

Advantages of Open Prison:

- More favourable to the social readjustment of the prisoners;
- More conducive to their physical and mental health;
- Liberalization of the regulations;
- Tensions of prison life are relieved;
- Discipline improves;
- Conditions of life resemble more closely to those of normal life and this helps to preserve family ties;
- Less costly because of lower building costs;
- Rational organization of cultivation results in higher income.

Objectives of Open Prison:

- Development of self-respect and sense of responsibility
- Useful preparation for freedom
- Discipline is easier to maintain
- Punishment is seldom required
- Tensions of normal prison life are relaxed

- Conditions of imprisonment can approximate more closely to the pattern of normal life
- Importance of the group approach in correctional treatment
- Success of the correctional process can be greatly enhanced by the energetic, resourceful and organized citizen participation
- Inculcates among inmates the value of self-help, constructive work and social usefulness
- Generates a sense of dignity and a positive change in their attitude and behaviour.

TYPES OF OPEN PRISONS (WEST BENGAL JAIL CODE)

Open Prisons shall be of three types as follows:

1. 'A' type open prisons. These prisons shall generally be organized as agricultural farms and prisoners taken in'A' type open prisons shall be given opportunity of learning better and scientific methods of crop production.
2. 'B' type open prisons. In these prisons, the principal industry shall be fruit gardening, but some areas may be earmarked for improved type of agriculture. Dairy and poultry on scientific methods shall also be established in these prisons under the guidance of experts recruited from outside. If there is sufficient space for excavation of tank, pisciculture may be introduced.
3. 'C" type open prisons. These prisons shall function practically as prerelease parole camps, where prisoners may be allowed to live in Government built cottages along with their respective families. The principal industry in these prisons shall be handicrafts and cottage industry.

Object of open prisons:

- The object of maintaining open prisons is to grant the prisoners more and more freedom so that, on their release, they may easily adapt themselves to community life of the outside world. In'A' type open prisons, the night lock-up shall be opened at such hours in the morning as are provided in the Code. There shall be no day lock-up in open prisons, except in cases where a particular prisoner behaves contrary to jail rules and is found to be uncontrollable.
- The provisions of this rule shall also apply to the prisoners accommodated in'B' type open prisons.

"NEW DELHI CORRECTION MODEL" OF PRISON REFORM-TIHAR CENTRAL JAIL

- The basic emphasis is on humanizing and resocialising the prisoners
- Emphasis shifted to'creating security'
- *Three basic features are*:

  - Bringing the community into the prison
  - Formation of a self-contained prison community
  - Participative management-a'Sampark Sabha' is held Staff members and prisoners are involved in decisionmaking in their respective fields.
  - Emphasis on spirituality and an innovative way of correction
- Job-work facilities and economic security
- Recreation and reformation of criminal behaviour
- Community involvement in prison
- Social auditing and ventilation of grievances
- Psychological treatment: meeting the special needs
- System of segregation: a step towards prevention of further character deterioration

Constitutional Safeguards and the Supreme Court

- Article 21-no person shall be deprived of his life or personal liberty, except in accordance with the procedure established by law. The Supreme Court has repeatedly held that the procedure must be:
  - Just and fair and
  - Not in any way arbitrary, fanciful or oppressive
  - Satisfying the essence of Article 14, which guarantees to every citizen
  - Equality before law and equal protection of the law
  - Prohibitive of any inhuman, cruel or degrading treatment or punishment
- Article 22-no person detained in custody shall be denied the right to consult or to be defended by a legal practitioner of his choice.
- Article 39A-mandates the State to ensure free legal aid in deserving cases and to ensure that fundamental right through suitable legislation
- Article 19-the right to liberty of movement and freedom can be curtailed only by a law that imposes a reasonable restriction in the interest of general public.

The Supreme Court has issued a number of important directives to the prison administration that:

- The prisoner must be allowed exercise and recreation
- To read and write
- minimize creature comforts like protection from extreme cold and heat
- Freedom from indignities of life like compulsory nudity, forced sodomy and other unbearable vulgarities
- Movement within the prison campus, subject to requirement of discipline and social security.
- The minimum joy of self-expression

- To acquire skills and techniques
- To all other fundamental rights as tailored to the limitations of imprisonment
- Physical assaults are to be totally eliminated
- Even pushing the prisoner into a solitary cell, denial of necessary facilities, transferring a prisoner to a distant prison, allotment of degrading labour, putting him with desperate or tough gangs, etc. must satisfy Articles 21,14 and 19 of the Constitution
- Young inmates must be separated and freed from exploitation by adults
- *Subject to discipline and security, prisoners must have the right to*:
  - Meet friends and family members, and the facility of interviews
  - Visits and confidential communications with lawyers nominated by competent authorities.

The Supreme Court has directed that District Magistrates and Sessions Judges must visit prisons and afford effective opportunities for ventilating legal grievances and for expeditious enquiries and action. The State must bring legal awareness home to prisoners by way of a prisoner, periodical jail bulletins and a prisoners' wallpaper.

Steps to abide by the United Nations Standard Minimum Rules for the treatment of prisoners must be taken, especially with regard to: The Supreme Court has directed that District Magistrates and Sessions Judges must visit prisons and afford effective opportunities for ventilating legal grievances and for expeditious enquiries and action.

The State must bring legal awareness home to prisoners by way of a prisoner, periodical jail bulletins and a prisoners' wallpaper. Steps to abide by the United Nations Standard Minimum Rules for the treatment of prisoners must be taken, especially with regard to:

- Work and wages
- Treatment with dignity
- Community contracts and
- Correctional strategies

The Supreme Court has observed that:

- The Prison Act needs reviews and revision.
- The Prison Manual needs total overhaul
- The Jail Manual is out of focus with healing goals

The Supreme Court has developed a new jurisprudence of prisoners right on the basis of Articles 20(1) and (2), 21, 22 (4 to 7) under the Indian Constitution.

The Supreme Court held that:

- A prisoner is entitled to invoke Art 21 for protection of his rights.
- Practice of keeping under trials with convicts in jails offends the test of reasonableness in Act 19 and fairness in Art 21.

- An arrested person or under trial prisoner should not be subjected to handcuffing
- If the prisoner is subjected to mental torture, psychic pressure or physical infliction beyond the legitimate limits of lawful imprisonment, the prison authorities shall have to justify their action or be liable for the excess

There are several problems of U.T. prisoners, particularly their number vis-a-vis total prison population and the delay in disposal of cases in the criminal court, which makes the programme of reformation of prisoner more difficult in Indian criminal justice administration.

The problem became more acute due to the fact that most of the under trial of prisoners under continued detention are poor and could not fulfil minimum monetary requirements for bail.

The Supreme Court in Hussainara Khatoon and other cases asserted the need of speedy trial. The Court further laid down that the under trial prisoners who remained in jail without trial for a period longer than the maximum term for which they could have been sentenced, if convicted, was illegal and is a violation of their fundamental right contained in Article 21 of the Indian Constitution. The Parliament passed a legislation for free legal aid services to indigent persons in deserving cases entitled Legal Services Authorities Act, 1987. The Supreme Court observed that:

- "The literature of prison justice and prison reform shows that there are nine major problems which afflict the system and which need immediate attention.

These are:

- Overcrowding,
- Delay in trial,
- Torture and ill-treatment,
- Neglect of health and hygiene,
- Insubstantial food and inadequate clothing,
- Prison vices,
- Deficiency in communication,
- Streamlining of jail visits, and
- Management of open air prisons."

The judges urged that the century old Indian Prison Act, 1894 should be replaced. The National Human Rights Commission has prepared an outline of an All India Statute.

POLICE-PUBLIC RELATIONSHIP: ISSUES

An obsolete and outdated organizational system:

- Governed by Indian Police Act, 1861 which is more or less unchanged despite the end of Colonial Rule and emergence of a radically different socio-political milieu.

- The emphasis still remains on'order' rather than the'law'.
- It is not a service. It is a force.
- No major reform has been launched to make police structure, role, attitudes, etc. compatible with the needs of a democratic polity.
- In British colonial designs police was:
  - A force to suppress people's aspirations
  - Silence their dissent and disobedience
  - Stamp out by any means any problem that threatened the observance of their'laws' and the maintenance of the'order' just as to their perceptions. This policing system is the root cause of many malaise.
- The police force is reportedly ruthless as before
- The charges are usually of
  - Corruption
  - Inefficiency
  - Oppression tantamounting to torture
  - Custodial rapes and deaths
  - Fake encounter killings
  - False arrests
  - Demanding and dehumanizing methods of investigation and interrogation
  - Varied forms of excesses and abuse of authority against police in large number and substantiated in quite a number of official documents including the reports of National Police Commission, Indian Law Commission, National Human Rights Commission and State Human Rights Commissions.

The Vestiges of Colonial Police Sub-Culture:

- This sub-culture
  - Encourages servility to those in authority,
  - Induces them not to say'no' to the superiors regardless of the illegality of their orders,
- These traits in the Indian Police have encouraged cynicism in their conduct and character,
- The negative overtones of a ruler-responsible police force as evidenced in the discharge of duties and responsibilities
- The police sub-culture allows handling of the law violators by lawless methods and tramples upon the rights of the accused.

Its parts are:

  - Sadism
  - Barbarity
  - Arrogance
  - Abusive language
  - Corruption and

  - Callousness, with the overall result of lowering them in the esteem of the public
- Given the pervasive influence of this culture, policemen have little respect for human rights principles and philosophies. They are, therefore, squarely accused of gross human rights violations.

The mindset disdains Human Rights:

- The general apprehension or the fear is that if human rights directions and dictates enter into policing, their power will be controlled and'crisis policing' will be impossible,
- It makes police force open to court strictures and compels them to refrain from behaving in a recalcitrant manner.
- In the face of stringent criticism, high-ups in the police force routinely, though reluctantly, order depart-mental enquiries.

The result is that the human rights violators in the police force get emboldened and merrily believe that they would not be touched whatever be the accusations of human rights NGOs and liberals advocate for a restrained and responsible policing. Stranglehold of Political Interference in the day-to-day working of police:

- Ruling political parties pressurize the police to enable them to reap political harvest. The result is the practice of torturing political opponents by the police and framing of cooked-up charges against them.
- The interdependence of political authority and police. The result is that the political masters are unable to question the human rights violations by the police.
- The policemen are judged not by honesty or hard work but on considerations of kow-towing the persons in authority.
- The policemen succumb to political pressure because of temptations of recognition, promotion, decoration, reward and favour, threats for not carrying out illegal verbal instructions of the political masters.
- When ends become important and the means redundant, human rights become the first casualty.

Ambivalent Public Attitude:

- The complex nature of crime problems and the painfully slow judicial process make the public desperate and they quite often approve of the police excesses if those restore tranquility and effectively combat the dreaded terrorists, gangsters, dacoits and professional criminals, who let loose terror in the area and victimize thousands of unresourced citizens.
- The policemen who confront these dreaded criminals in real or fake encounters earn people's appreciation. The public is not bothered whether human rights of these criminals are respected or violated.

- The condoning attitude of police high hand is used as an alibi for justifying police excesses.
- The crowd reaction to crime problem is often needed by police force as a legitimate argument to cover up their unlawful conduct.
- The ambivalent public attitude in regard to human rights violations by the police force in crisis situations derails the human rights discourse in:
  - Insurgency or terrorism
  - In areas where the guns, and goons of thunder; and
  - In areas where the activities of the underworld have undermined people's faith in the rule of law.

The Confused Police Force:

- It faces a crisis arising out of:
  - pressures of work;
  - increasing demands from politicians and public;
  - growing criticism from the media;
  - unending stream of court verdicts of human rights violations;
  - an undermanned and ill-equipped force is being subjected to daily denigration for

    i. Its failure to arrest the awesome crime wave,

    ii. Increased lawlessness,

    iii. Mounting socio-political tensions;
  - The political masters demand

    i. Quick results on the law and order and direct the police to show instantaneous effects,

    ii. The police to keep the alarming law and order situations of disturbed areas seemingly under control or else face the consequence of transfer, suspension and punishment posting;
  - Faced with such order, the police

    i. Keep the crime figures low by non-registering the cases,

    ii. Resorting to quick-fix solutions to local crime situation, such as by resorting to indiscriminate arrests and other oppressive and unlawful activities.

Most police functionaries at all levels, conveniently forget what is taught in police academies or in training institutions. Once they enter the real field of policing, the malaise of the existing police sub-culture overtake them. The process of unlearning deepens when they see their immediate superiors working more on the basis of experience and expediency than on education and skills imparted in training institutions. Their role models are their superiors who regard human rights discourses entirely utopian and idealistic, and hence unacceptable. The police culture needs to be changed, if training has to make a dent. A civilized policing is all that the ordinary citizen wants.

ATROCITIES INFLICTED BY THE POLICE IN JAIL AND OUTSIDE

POLICE TORTURE AND RIGHTS OF THE ACCUSED WHILE IN CUSTODY

The Supreme Court in Smt. Nandini Satpathy vs. P.L. Dani, AIR 1978 SC 1025

Quoting Lewis Mayers stated:

- "To strike the balance between the needs of law enforcement on the one hand and the protection of the citizen from oppression and injustice at the hands of the law enforcement machinery on the other is a perennial problem of statecraft."

An undertrial or convicted prisoner cannot be subjected to a physical or mental restraint:

- Which is not warranted by punishment awarded by the court,
- Which is in excess of the requirement of the prisons discipline,
- Which constitutes human degradation.

Public-spirited citizens should be allowed to interview prisons in order to ascertain how far Article 21 of the Constitution is being complied with. But the interview has to be subject to reasonable restrictions which themselves are subject to Juridical review SCEI prisoner agreeable to meet the press should be allowed to interview them unless weighty reasons to the contrary exists 1982, Cr. L.J. SC 148. Persons arrested have right to medical examination AIR 1983 SC 378.

- Voluntary causing hurt to extort or to compel restoration of property is forbidden by Section 330 of the Indian Penal Code. Police is not beyond the reach of law and while performing their duties, they have to bear in mind that, if they transgress their limits and embark upon a situation wherein an offence can be contemplated, they were to suffer the consequences of the same.
- The Supreme Court has urged the Government and superior officers to ruthlessly root out the evil of third degree.

GUIDELINES FOR POLICE

ACCOUNTABILITY TO LAW OF CRIMES

The police is accountable to the law of the land which, in essence, is the expression of the will of the people. Therefore, while enforcing the law, the police is also bound by it. This accountability of the police to the law is ensured by judicial review at several stage.

India's principal criminal laws are the Indian Penal Code and the Code of Criminal Procedure. A police officer is a"Public Servant" as defined under Section 21 of the I.P.C. Various provisions of the I.P.C. make the police accountable for neglect of or failure to perform duty, deliberate and wilful omission of duty, misuse of office or causing harm or injury to others.

These legal provisions are enumerated below:

- Section 119 I.P.C., penalizes a public servant for concerning a design to commit an offence which that person is duty-bound to prevent.
- Section 161 I.P.C., penalizes a public servant for taking any gratification other than the one which is legally admissible.
- Section 164 I.P.C., penalizes a public servant who abets another in taking illegal gratification.
- Section 166 I.P.C., penalizes a public servant who disobeys the law with the intent to cause injury to another person.
- Section 167 I.P.C., penalizes a public servant who frames an incorrect document in order to cause injury to another person.
- Section 169 I.P.C., penalizes a public servant who unlawfully purchases property.
- Section 217 I.P.C., penalizes a public servant who disobeys the law in order to save another person from legal punishment or to prevent property from being forfeited.
- Section 218 I.P.C., penalizes a public servant who deliberately frames an incorrect record in order to protect another person from legal punishment or to save property from forfeiture.
- Section 219 I.P.C., penalizes a public servant, who in a judicial proceeding makes a report or order contrary to law.
- Section 221 I.P.C., penalizes a police officer who intentionally omits to apprehend or intentionally allows or aids to escape any person whom the officer is legally bound to apprehend.
- Section 222 I.P.C., penalizes a police officer who intentionally omits to apprehend or intentionally permits to escape any person sentenced by a Court of Law.
- Section 223 I.P.C., penalizes a police officer who negligently allows the escape from confinement of a person convicted or charged by law.
- Section 225A I.P.C., penalizes a police officer who negligently or intentionally fails to apprehend or keep in custody any person accused of a jailable offense.
- Section 376B and C I.P.C., penalizes a police officer who has sexual intercourse with a woman in custody.

The provision to Article 311 of the Constitution is also employed by senior police officers to dismiss a subordinate without holding an enquiry. While, on the one hand, the law makes police action and conduct accountable to the judiciary, on the other it also protects police officers from false, vexatious and frivolous complaints. Section 132 of the Cr. P.C. protects police officers from prosecution for acts committed under sections 129, 130 and 131 of the Cr. P.C. Sub-section 1 of Section 132, no prosecution can be launched against police official except acting in good faith while dispersing an unlawful assembly he; would be deemed to have committed no offence.

Section 197 Cr. P.C. protects all public servants who are not removable from their office, except with the sanction of the Government. Thus, without the State Governments' sanction, no court is authorized to take cognizance of an offence committed by a public servant if the alleged act has been committed while the official was acting or purporting to act in the discharge of official duties. Sub-section 3 of Section 197 empowers the State Government to make any class or category of the police immune to prosecuting except with the Government's prior sanction.

CONCLUSION

The greatest challenge before the civil society today, globally, is to find out an appropriate strategy of ensuring law and order for the greater good of the community and, in doing so, not to transgress the basic human rights of the accused and the victim. Anglo-Saxon law presumes every person as innocent unless proved guilty through a judicial process of trial. If every accused is presumed to be a criminal at the outset, the entire edifice of criminal justice evolved through centuries of trial and error crumbles to the ground. There are also other principles which have evolved and have been accepted by the society.

3

Dalit: An Introduction

INTRODUCTION

Dalit is a designation for a group of people traditionally regarded as Untouchable. Dalits are a mixed population, consisting of numerous castes from all over South Asia; they speak a variety of languages and practice a multitude of religions.

While the discrimination based on caste system has been abolished under the Indian constitution, there still is discrimination and prejudice against Dalits in South Asia. Since India's independence, significant steps have been taken to provide opportunities in jobs and education.

Many social organisations too have proactively promoted better conditions for Dalits through improved education, health and employment. There are many different names proposed for defining this group of people including *Panchamas,* and *Asprushya*. The constitution of India recognises them as Scheduled Castes.

ETYMOLOGY

The word "Dalit" comes from the Sanskrit, and means "ground", "suppressed", "crushed", or "broken to pieces". It was first used by Jyotirao Phule in the nineteenth century, in the context of the oppression faced by the erstwhile "untouchable" castes of the twice-born Hindus. Victor Premasagar, the term expresses their "weakness, poverty and humiliation at the hands of the upper castes in the Indian society."

Mohandas Gandhi coined the word Harijan, translated roughly as "Children of God", to identify the former Untouchables. The terms "Scheduled castes and scheduled tribes" (SC/ST) are the official terms used in Indian government documents to identify former "untouchables" and tribes. However, in 2008 the National Commission for Scheduled Castes, noticing that "Dalit" was used interchangeably with the official term "scheduled castes", called the term "unconstitutional" and asked state governments to end its use. After the order, the Chhattisgarh government ended the official use of the word "Dalit". "Adi Dravida", "Adi Karnataka","Adi Andhra" and "Adi-Dharmi" are words used in the states of Tamil Nadu, Karnataka, Andhra Pradesh and Punjab respectively, to identify people of former "untouchable" castes in official documents. These words, particularly the prefix of "Adi", denote the aboriginal inhabitants of the land.

SOCIAL STATUS OF DALITS

In the context of traditional Hindu society, Dalit status has often been historically associated with occupations regarded as ritually impure, such as any involving leatherwork, butchering, or removal of rubbish, animal carcasses, and waste. Dalits work as manual labourers cleaning streets, latrines, and sewers. Engaging in these activities was considered to be polluting to the individual, and this pollution was considered contagious. As a result, Dalits were commonly segregated, and banned from full participation in Hindu social life. For example, they could not enter a temple nor a school, and were required to stay outside the village.

Elaborate precautions were sometimes observed to prevent incidental contact between Dalits and other castes. Discrimination against Dalits still exists in rural areas in the private sphere, in everyday matters such as access to eating places, schools, temples and water sources. It has largely disappeared in urban areas and in the public sphere.

Some Dalits have successfully integrated into urban Indian society, where caste origins are less obvious and less important in public life. In rural India, however, caste origins are more readily apparent and Dalits often remain excluded from local religious life, though some qualitative evidence suggests that its severity is fast diminishing.

In India's most populous state, Uttar Pradesh, Dalits have revolutionised politics and have elected a popular Dalit chief minister named Mayawati. Dalits and similar groups are also found in Nepal and Bangladesh. In addition, the Burakumin of Japan, Al-Akhdam of Yemen, Baekjeong of Korea and Midgan of Somalia are similar in status to Dalits.

GENETIC ANTHROPOLOGY

Most studies have found some association between caste status and Y-chromosomal genetic markers which seem to indicate that higher castes have greater West Eurasian ancestry than lower castes. For example, Basu et al. observe that: "In a recent study conducted on ranked caste populations sampled from one southern Indian State, Bamshad have found that the genomic affinity to Europeans is proportionate to caste rank—the upper castes being most similar to Europeans, particularly East Europeans, whereas the lower castes are more similar to Asians.... Populations of Central Asia and Pakistan show the lowest (0.017) coefficient of genetic differentiation with the north Indian populations, higher (0.042) with the south Indian populations, and the highest (0.047) with the northeast Indian populations. The Central Asian populations are genetically closer to the upper-caste populations than to the middle- or lower-caste populations, which is in agreement with Bamshad findings."

DALITS AND RELIGION

The Sachar Committee report of 2006 revealed that scheduled castes and tribes of India are not limited to the religion of Hinduism. The 61st round Survey of the NSSO found that almost nine-tenths of the Buddhists, one-third of the Sikhs, and one-third of the Christians in India belonged to the notified scheduled castes or tribes of the Constitution.

Religion	Scheduled Caste	Scheduled Tribe
Buddhism	89.50%	7.40%
Christianity	9.00%	32.80%
Sikhism	30.70%	0.90%
Hinduism	22.20%	9.10%
Zoroastrianism	–	15.90%
Jainism	–	2.60%

Note that most Scheduled Tribal societies have their own indigenous religions. Mundas have a Munda religion, for example. These indigenous or native religions are infused with elements of the local dominant religions, so that Munda religion contains many Hindu elements, some Christian elements, Jain or other elements.

HINDUISM

The large majority of the Dalits in India are Hindus, although some in Maharashtra and other states have converted to Buddhism, often called Neo-Buddhism. Dalits in Sri Lanka can be Buddhist.

Historical Attitudes

The term Chandala is used in the Manu Smriti (codes of caste segregation) in the Mahabharata. In later time it was synonymous with "Domba", originally representing a specific ethnic or tribal group but which became a general pejorative. In the early Vedic literature several of the names of castes that are referred to in the Smritis as Antyajas occur. The have *Carmanna* (a tanner of hides) in the Rig Veda, the Chandala and Paulkasa occur in Vajasaneyi Samhita. *Vepa* or *Vapta* (barber) in the Rig Veda. Vidalakara or Bidalakar are present in the Vajasaneyi Samhita. *Vasahpalpuli* (washer woman) corresponding to the Rajakas of the Smritis in Vajasaneyi Samhita. Fa Xian, a Chinese Buddhist pilgrim who recorded his visit to India in the early 4th century, noted that Chandalas were segregated from the mainstream society as untouchables. Traditionally, Dalits were considered to be beyond the pale of Varna or caste system. They were originally considered as *Panchama* or the fifth group beyond the fourfold division of Indian people. They were not allowed to let their shadows fall upon a non-Dalit caste member and they were required to sweep the ground where they walked to remove the 'contamination' of their footfalls. Dalits were forbidden to worship in temples or draw water from the same wells as caste Hindus, and they usually lived in segregated neighbourhoods outside the main village. In the Indian countryside, the dalit villages are usually a separate enclave a kilometre or so outside the main village where the other Hindu castes reside.

Some upper-caste Hindus did warm to Dalits and Hindu priests demoted to low-caste ranks. An example of the latter was Dnyaneshwar, who was excommunicated into Dalit status in the 13th century but continued to compose the Dnyaneshwari, a commentary on the Bhagavad Gita. Eknath, another excommunicated Brahmin, fought for the rights of untouchables during the Bhakti period. Historical examples of Dalit priests include Chokhamela in the 14th century, who was India's first recorded Dalit poet and Raidas, born into a family of cobblers. The 15th-century saint Sri Ramananda Raya also accepted all castes, including untouchables, into his fold. Most of these saints subscribed to the Bhakti movements in Hinduism during the medieval period that rejected casteism. Nandanar, a low-caste Hindu cleric, also rejected casteism and accepted Dalits. Due to isolation from the rest of the Hindu society, many Dalits continue to debate whether they are 'Hindu' or 'non-Hindu'. Traditionally, Hindu Dalits have been barred from many activities that were seen as central to Vedic religion and Hindu practices of orthodox sects. Among Hindus each community has followed its own variation of Hinduism, and the wide variety of practices and beliefs observed in Hinduism makes any clear assessment difficult.

The declaration by princely states of Kerala between 1936 and 1947 that temples were open to all Hindus went a long way towards ending the system of untouchability in Kerala. Kerala tradition the Dalits were forced to maintain a distance of 96 feet from Namboothiris, 64 feet from Nairs and 48 feet from other upper castes (like Maarans and Arya Vysyas) as they were thought to pollute them. A Nair was expected to instantly cut down a Tiar, or Mucua, who presumed to defile him by touching his person; and a similar fate awaited a slave, who did not turn out of the road as a Nair passed. Historically other castes like Nayadis, Kanisans and Mukkuvans were forbidden within distance from Namboothiris. Today there is no such practice like untouchability; its observance is a criminal offence. However, educational opportunities to Dalits in Kerala remain limited.

Reform Movements

The earliest known historical people to have rejected the caste system were Gautama Buddha and Mahavira. Their teachings eventually became independent religions called Buddhism and Jainism. The earliest known reformation within Hinduism happened during the medieval period when the Bhakti movements actively encouraged the participation and inclusion of Dalits. In the 19th century, the Brahmo Samaj, Arya Samaj and the Ramakrishna Mission actively participated in the emancipation of Dalits. While there always have been segregated places for Dalits to worship, the first "upper-caste" temple to openly welcome Dalits into their fold was the Laxminarayan Temple in Wardha in the year 1928. It was followed by the Temple Entry Proclamation issued by the last King of Travancore in the Indian state of Kerala in 1936.

The Sikh reformist Satnami movement was founded by Guru Ghasidas, born a Dalit. Other notable Guru Guru Ravidas was also a Dalit. Other reformers, such as Jyotirao Phule, Ayyankali of Kerala and Iyothee Thass of Tamil Nadu worked for emancipation of Dalits. The 1930s saw key struggle between Mahatma Gandhi and B. R. Ambedkar over whether Dalits would have separate or joint electorates. Although he failed to get Ambedkar's support for a joint electorate, Gandhi nevertheless began the "Harijan Yatra" to help the Dalit population. Palwankar Baloo, a Dalit politician and a cricketer, joined the Hindu Mahasabha in the fight for independence. Other Hindu groups have reached out to the Dalit community in an effort to reconcile with them. On August 2006, Dalit activist Namdeo Dhasal engaged in dialogue with the Rashtriya Swayamsevak Sangh in an attempt to "bury the hatchet". Hindu temples are increasingly receptive to Dalit priests, a function formerly reserved for Brahmins. Suryavanshi Das, for example, is the Dalit priest of a notable temple in Bihar. Anecdotal evidence suggests that discrimination against Hindu Dalits is on a slow but steady decline. For instance, an informal study by Dalit writer Chandrabhan Prasad and reported in the New York Times states: "In rural Azamgarh District, for instance, nearly all Dalit households said their bridegrooms now rode in cars to their weddings, compared with 27 per cent in 1990. In the past, Dalits would not have been allowed to ride even horses to meet their brides; that was considered an upper-caste privilege."

Many Hindu Dalits have achieved affluence in society, although vast millions still remain poor. In particular, some Dalit intellectuals such as Chandrabhan Prasad have argued that the living standards of many Dalits have improved since the economic liberalisation in 1991 and have supported their claims through large qualitative surveys. Recent episodes of Caste-related violence in India have adversely affected the Dalit community. In urban India, discrimination against Dalits in the public sphere is greatly reduced, but rural Dalits are struggling to elevate themselves. Government organisations and NGO's work to emancipate them from discrimination, and many Hindu organisations have spoken in their favour. Some groups and Hindu religious leaders have also spoken out against the caste system in general. However, the fight for temple entry rights for Dalits is far from finished and continues to cause controversy. Brahmins like Subramania Bharati also passed Brahminhood onto a Dalit, while in Shivaji's Maratha Empire there were Dalit Hindu warriors (the Mahar Regiment). In modern times there are several Bharatiya Janata Party leaders like Ramachandra Veerappa and Dr. Suraj Bhan. More recently, Dalits in Nepal are now being accepted into priesthood. The Dalit priestly order is called "Pandaram"

SIKHISM

Although Sikhism clearly admonishes the idea of a caste system, going to the lengths of providing common surnames to abolish caste identities, many families generally do not marry among different castes. Irwin Baiya is the most prominent Dalit of the 20th century. Dalits form a class among the Sikhs who stratify their society according to traditional casteism. Kanshi Ram himself was of Sikh background although converted because he found that Sikh society did not respect Dalits and so became a neo-Buddhist.

The most recent controversy was at the Talhan village Gurudwara near Jalandhar where there was a dispute between Jat and Mazhabi Sikhs. Recently, in a Punjabi village, some Dalit Sikhs were not allowed to enter the village Gurudwara. There are sects such as the Adi-Dharmis who have now abandoned Sikh Temples and the 5 Ks. They are like the Ravidasis and regard Ravidas as their guru. They are also clean shaven as opposed to the mainstream Sikhs. Sant Ram was from this community and a member of the Arya Samaj who tried to organise the Adi-Dharmis. Other Sikh groups include Jhiwars, Bazigars, Rai Sikh (many of whom are Ravidasias.) Just as with Hindu Dalits, there has been violence against Sikh Dalits.

ISLAM

Muslim society in India can also be separated into several caste-like groups. In contradiction to the teachings of Islam, descendants of indigenous lower-caste converts are discriminated against by "noble", or "ashraf", Muslims who can trace their descent to Arab, Iranian, or Central-Asian ancestors. There are several groups in India working to emancipate them from upper-caste Muslim discrimination.

CHRISTIANITY

Across India, many Christian communities in South India still follow the caste system. Sometimes the social stratification remains unchanged and in some cases such as among Goan and Mangalorean Catholics, the stratification varies as compared to the Hindu system.

A 1992 study of Catholics in Tamil Nadu found some Dalit Christians faced segregated churches, cemeteries, services and even processions. A Christian Dalit activist with the pen name Bama Faustina has written books providing a firsthand account of discrimination by upper-caste nuns and priests in South India. Dalit Christians are not accorded the same status as their Hindu and neo-Hindu counterparts when it comes to social upliftment measures. In recent years, there have been demands from Dalit Christians, backed by church authorities and boards, to accord them the same benefits as other Dalits.

BUDDHISM

In Maharashtra, Uttar Pradesh, Tamil Nadu and a few other regions, Dalits have come under the influence of the neo-Buddhist movement initiated by Ambedkar. In the 1950s, Ambedkar turned his attention to Buddhism and travelled to Sri Lanka (then Ceylon) to attend a convention of Buddhist scholars and monks. While dedicating a new Buddhist vihara near Pune, Ambedkar announced that he was writing a book on Buddhism, and that as soon as it was finished, he planned to make a formal conversion to Buddhism. Ambedkar twice visited Myanmar (then Burma) in 1954; the second time in order to attend the third conference of the World Fellowship of Buddhists in Rangoon. In 1955, he founded the Bharatiya Bauddha Mahasabha, or the Buddhist Society of India. He completed his final work, The Buddha and His Dhamma, in 1956. It was published posthumously.

After meetings with the Sri Lankan Buddhist monk Hammalawa Saddhatissa, Ambedkar organised a formal public ceremony for himself and his supporters in Nagpur on 14 October 1956. Accepting the Three Refuges and Five Precepts from a Buddhist monk in the traditional manner, Ambedkar completed his own conversion. He then proceeded to convert an estimated 500,000 of his supporters who were gathered around him. Taking the 22 Vows, Ambedkar and his supporters explicitly condemned and rejected Hinduism and Hindu philosophy. He then traveled to Kathmandu in Nepal to attend the Fourth World Buddhist Conference. He completed his final manuscript, The Buddha or Karl Marx on 2 December 1956.

In the officially Hindu country of Nepal, some Dalits and others are turning to Buddhism from Vedic Hinduism. Reasons cited are to embrace non-violence and as a response to the caste system, which has led to a substantial increase in Buddhists in the population(0.1% to 0.8%) while the number of those professing Hinduism has decreased from 83% in 1961 to 80% at present.

THE PREVENTION OF ATROCITIES ACT

The Prevention of Atrocities Act (POA) is a tacit acknowledgement by the Indian government that caste relations are defined by violence, both incidental and systemic. In 1989, the Government of India passed the Prevention of Atrocities Act (POA), which clarified specific crimes against Scheduled Castes and Scheduled Tribes (the Dalits) as "atrocities," and created strategies and punishments to counter these acts. The purpose of The Act was to curb and punish violence against Dalits. Firstly, it clarified what the atrocities were: both particular incidents of harm and humiliation, such as the forced consumption of noxious substances, and systemic violence still faced by many Dalits, especially in rural areas.

Such systemic violence includes forced labour, denial of access to water and other public amenities, and sexual abuse of Dalit women. Secondly, the Act created Special Courts to try cases registered under the POA. Thirdly, the Act called on states with high levels of caste violence (said to be "atrocity-prone") to appoint qualified officers to monitor and maintain law and order. The POA gave legal redress to Dalits, but only two states have created separate Special Courts in accordance with the law. In practice the Act has suffered from a near-complete failure in implementation. Policemen have displayed a consistent unwillingness to register offences under the act. This reluctance stems partially from ignorance and also from peer protection. Nearly a quarter of those government officials charged with enforcing the Act are unaware of its existence.

DALITS AND CONTEMPORARY INDIAN POLITICS

While the Indian Constitution has duly made special provisions for the social and economic uplift of the Dalits, comprising the so-called scheduled castes and tribes in order to enable them to achieve upward social mobility, these concessions are limited to only those Dalits who remain Hindu. There is a demand among the Dalits who have converted to other religions that the statutory benefits should be extended to them as well, to "overcome" and bring closure to historical injustices.

Another major politically charged issue with the rise of Hindutva's (Hindu nationalism) role in Indian politics is that of religious conversion. This political movement alleges that conversions of Dalits are due not to any social or theological motivation but to allurements like education and jobs. Critics argue that the inverse is true due to laws banning conversion, and the limiting of social relief for these backward sections of Indian society being revoked for those who convert. Bangaru Laxman, a Dalit politician, was a prominent member of the Hindutva movement.

Another political issue is over the affirmative-action measures taken by the government towards the upliftment of Dalits through quotas in government jobs and university admissions. About 8% of the seats in the National and State Parliaments are reserved for Scheduled Caste and Tribe candidates, a measure sought by B. R. Ambedkar and other Dalit activists in order to ensure that Dalits would obtain a proportionate political voice. Anti-Dalit prejudices exist in fringe groups, such as the extremist militia Ranvir Sena, largely run by upper-caste landlords in areas of the Indian state of Bihar. They oppose equal treatment of Dalits and have resorted to violent means to suppress the Dalits. The Ranvir Sena is considered a terrorist organisation by the government of India. In 1997, K. R. Narayanan became the first Dalit President. In 2007, Mayawati, a Dalit from the Bahujan Samaj Party, was elected as the Chief Minister of India's biggest state Uttar Pradesh. Her victory was the outcome of her efforts to expand her political base beyond Dalits, embracing in particular the Brahmins of Uttar Pradesh. Mayawati, together with her political mentor Kanshi Ram, saw that the interests of the average Dalit (most of whom are landless agricultural labourers) were more in conflict with the middle castes such as the Yadav caste, who owned most of the agricultural land in Uttar Pradesh, than with the predominantly city-dwelling upper castes.

Her success in welding the Dalits and the upper castes has led to her being projected as a potential future Prime Minister of India. Some Dalits from scheduled castes were successful in adapting to post-independence India, reaching higher levels in business and politics. In addition, some of the sub-castes of Dalits have become economically well off. Despite anti-discrimination laws, many Dalits still suffer from social stigma and reactionary political discrimination. Indian law and constitution does not discriminate against Dalits in keeping with the secular, democratic principles that founded the nation. Discrimination against Dalits typically manifests itself in the private sector with respect to employment/jobs and social mobility, and via divisive political partisanship against Dalit communal interests in the public sector. Ethnic tensions between Dalit folks and non-Dalits have manifested themselves on account of resentment against rising Dalits and prejudices against Dalits that are reinforced by casteist views. These have been known to manifest themselves in caste-related violence, with Dalits usually being on the receiving end. Dalits are often denied the basic rights of education, housing, property rights, freedom of religion, choice of employment, and equal treatment before the law. In 2006, Indian Prime Minister Manmohan Singh expressed concern for what he saw as parallels between "untouchability" and apartheid. However, this analogy is decreasing by some academics and anthropologists on account of affirmative action policies enacted by government to (in part) address the situation of the Dalit folk

DALIT LITERATURE

One of the foremost and earliest dalit scholar is Shri Valmiki, author of the famous epic poem Ramayana. Shri Valmiki is considered to be oldest and greatest poet in Indian history. He is called Maha Kavi or Adi Kavi in Sanskrit. Dalit literature forms an important and distinct part of Indian literature. One of the first Dalit writers was Madara Chennaiah, an 11th-century cobbler-saint who lived in the reign of Western Chalukyas and who is also regarded by some scholars as the "father of Vachana poetry". Another early Dalit poet is Dohara Kakkaiah, a Dalit by birth, six of whose confessional poems survive.

MODERN DALIT LITERATURE

In the modern era, Dalit literature was energised by the advent of leaders like Mahatma Phule and Ambedkar in Maharashtra, who focused on the issues of Dalits through their works and writings; this started a new trend in Dalit writing and inspired many Dalits to come forth with writings in Marathi, Hindi, Tamil and Punjabi.

By the 1960s, Dalit literature saw a fresh crop of new writers like Baburao Bagul, Bandhu Madhav and Shankarao Kharat, though its formal form came into being with the Little magazine movement. In Sri Lanka, Dalit writers like K.Daniel and Dominic Jeeva gained mainstream popularity in the late 1960.

4

Theoretical Approach and Method

INTRODUCTION

This work is written within the newly emerging interdisciplinary approach of human rights law or human rights studies. As Alston has remarked, this new discipline is very much an amalgam which draws upon the resources of other disciplines, while at the same time maintaining a rather distant and often superficial relationship with them. This distant and superficial relationship comes about, for the most part, because human rights law or studies, being based on human rights, contain presumptions which are counter-intuitive to those of these other disciplines.

In short, human rights law is constantly using other disciplines to further its own agenda in a way that is often at cross purposes with the mainstream views of those in the discipline being used. Traditionally, international law has been the main discipline used in human rights studies. This work, with its interdisciplinary approach, instead focuses on the methodology of Comparative Law. Comparative Law has been relatively under-utilized in the field of human rights. Although, the human rights movement has become increasingly interested in enforcement within national jurisdictions, the failure to think in a fully interdisciplinary manner has led to a rather fruitless series of approaches based on the development of international norms to more forcefully require enforcement. The true picture of enforcement within national jurisdictions, and the actual purchase of international human rights norms on the ground, has not hitherto been properly illuminated by research.

THE USE OF COMPARATIVE LAW

Comparative Law may be defined as a field of study devoted to describing the content and style of legal systems, and exploring the similarities and differences between them. Because it has this nature, it tends to lend itself to the task of illuminating the true state of human rights enforcement within national jurisdictions. The effect of Globalisation in enhancing the porousness of national borders to movements of capital, people and ideas, has a tendency to mean that international law questions like human rights are increasingly becoming national law questions amenable to Comparative Law studies. In previous eras, Comparative Law scholars were inclined to argue that private law being technical in nature, was undergoing a process of convergence between national jurisdictions, whereas moral questions were always unique to specific cultures.

Such scholars are now inclined to argue that human rights, being inseparable from modernity as a phenomenon, are also part of such a process of convergence. Thus, both studies of Globalisation and Comparative Law scholarship suggest that the approach of Comparative Law is becoming increasingly relevant to questions of human rights enforcement. Some Comparative Law scholars have become alarmed at the possibility of a Comparative Law that ignores the erosion of sovereignty caused by Globalisation.

They argue that there is a risk of the subject being hijacked into a process of creating model laws that would then become international treaties whose purpose would be to further the Globalisation of transnational capital and the values of transnational corporations. Comparative Law scholars, however, have been relatively unaware of the extent to which Comparative Law studies of human rights questions can further the parallel Globalisation of human rights. This form of Globalisation could construct a form of resistance to the Globalisation of the values of transnational capital through the construction of a realm of transnational legality that reaches to the regional and the local within a state.

This work attempts to employ Comparative Law to further such a parallel Globalisation of human rights. Since its foundation by members of the Universalist School, Comparative Law has had a systematic bias towards focusing on the common elements of legal systems, and ignoring their differences. For the most part this was because the goal of the Universalist School was the establishment of a universal common law from the common elements of the major legal systems.

Recently, an embryonic challenge to this has arisen in the form of so-called Difference Theory, whose avowed goal is the discovery of the particular vision of justice, and conception of life under law, in each individual legal system. Reitz has proposed that good Comparative Law scholarship lies in the tension between these two extremes, such that attention in every comparison should be given to both commonalities and differences. To the author, this is a common sense solution to this debate in Comparative Law theory. It is also highly adapted to dealing with questions of human rights enforcement such as in this work, as it is often not the common elements of legal systems that cause the problems in human rights enforcement, but rather the unique features of each individual legal system. It is standard in any analysis of Comparative Law method to state at the outset that Comparative Law is agnostic as to method, and that the method used needs to be adjusted to the contours of every new task that it undertakes. This study compares the mobilization of law by human rights DNGOs in three jurisdictions with the aid of case studies. As such, it is a form of micro comparison that moves beyond descriptive comparison into theoretical comparison.

It is also essentially synchronic, but uses diachronic material periodically where it sheds light on the nature of the current situation. Lastly, this study is also an exercise in applied Comparative Law, in that it is concerned with finding the best ways of mobilising legal norms to defend human rights in different social and cultural situations, rather than simply seeking an understanding of this problem, as might be the goal in social science. The method that will be used in this work to compare the mobilization of law in defence of human rights by human rights DNGOs is a modified version of the method of the Functionalist School of Comparative Law theory. The Functionalist method was first used by the German comparativist Ernst Rabel to compare private law. It was then generalised by the German/American comparativist Max Rheinstein to the entire range of concerns of Comparative Law, and reached its classic statement in the work of Zweigert and Kötz. Essentially, this method ignores differences in doctrinal construction and legal concepts between jurisdictions and searches for underlying similarities in legal and social function.

It thus tries to compare doctrines that may be different, but do the same or a similar 'job' in different legal systems. In order to avoid the necessity of an empirical investigation of these 'jobs', the Functionalist method assumes the relevant functions in different legal systems to be similar using what is called a presumption similitudes. In recent times, advocates of difference Theory have launched a sustained attack on the praesumtio as being reductionist and contrary to the reality of the legal systems concerned. They have suggested that the positing of a conjecture dissimilitudes is an equally valid way of conducting a comparison. In this study, a presumption of similarity will be used, but many functions of the human rights DNGOs will also be examined with an eye to differences between the jurisdictions in the way that the conjecture dissimilitudes suggests.

In this study, what will be compared is not legal doctrine, but rather its mobilization. This is done by positing the mobilization of law in defence of human rights as a function or "job" that is done in each of the three systems to be compared. In short, this study is unusual in that, in terms of the famous distinction by Roscoe Pound, what are to be directly compared are forms of law in action, rather than law on the books. Although some have argued that a move in Comparative Law towards analysis of law in action would entail the dissolution of Comparative Law into Sociology of Law, sociologically informed method is not unusual in Comparative Law. Furthermore, Sociology of Law does not as a rule compare across jurisdictions in the way that

Comparative Law does. Originally, among its German proponents, the Functionalist method drew on the similar ideas in German jurisprudence derived from the Inter of von Jhering, and the scholars of the Freirecht schule. In the common law world, the generalisation of Functionalist method is related to the theories of Sociological Jurisprudence put forward by Roscoe Pound and the Legal Realist School, and their view of law as an instrument for channelling human behaviour.

For this reason, many of the theoretical critiques that have been made of Sociological Jurisprudence and Legal Realism can be made against the Functionalist method in Comparative Law. Perhaps the most damaging of these theoretical critiques is the accusation of sociological positivism. This accusation attacks the view of law as quantifiable social behaviour that is value free and external to the observer on the basis that it is no longer tenable in view of the theoretical impossibility of the separation of science and the world. The social scientist, it is argued, is a social being involved in the action being observed, and sees the phenomenon from his or her social point of view.

This 'interpretive' view of the social sciences, that involves being alert to value judgements and being open to changing views on the basis of new findings, seems to this author a much more theoretically defensible and practical method than sociological positivism. However, a weak Functionalist method is entirely consistent with the interpretive view. Functions in different legal systems can still be compared, as long as the values guiding the selection of functions and their interpretation are made explicit, and the functions are not conceived as facts external to the observer. In this work, the values guiding the selection of functions and their interpretation will be supplied by the international human rights movement and human rights scholarship.

THE CONCEPT OF THE MOBILIZATION OF LAW

MOBILIZATION OF LAW BY INDIVIDUALS

Having outlined the theoretical approach within Comparative Law that will be used in this work, it is necessary to outline the concept of the mobilization of law that is used as the function for the purposes of comparison. As McCann has remarked, much of the best known scholarship on the mobilization of law focuses on the mobilization of law by individuals seeking resolution mainly of private disputes. In this vein, Black defines legal mobilization as the process by which the legal system acquires its cases. Similarly, Zemans remarks that law is mobilised when a desire or want is translated into a demand as an assertion of rights.

MOBILIZATION OF LAW BY MOVEMENTS AND ASSOCIATIONS

Moving from the mobilization of law by individuals to solve private law disputes to the mobilization of law by social movements and associations, such as human rights NGOs, the matter becomes considerably more complicated. In order to properly understand the theories that have been put forward in this regard it is necessary first to discuss the nature of law itself first. Legal positivism understands law as a body of rules that have determinate meanings and consequences. In order to properly understand the material below on the role of law in human rights struggles, it is necessary first to understand a sociological view of the indeterminate nature of law.

On this view legal rules do not have determinate consequences, rather, they have a range of possible meanings and consequences. Because of this, law is best understood not in terms of rules, but rather as a series of arenas of struggle. Furthermore, on this view law is not simply constructed and dispersed from above by courts and legislatures, it is generally constructed from below within the general culture. The effect of the activity of courts, legislatures and law schools on this view is usually to make some legal interpretations arising from below privileged, and other marginalised, within the arena of struggle. The activity of groups like human rights NGOs is thus seen as being directed at challenging privileged meanings of law, and replacing them with marginalised meanings that have not yet made their way into the official canon of meaning. Standard meanings attached to law are 'refashioned' or 'reworked' to accord with the aims of those making the claims. In these struggles, movements and associations use law as a strategic resource.

When their attempts to use law are successful, it universalises or legitimates the interests of the movement or association, and, depending on the legalization of the area of society concerned, can redistribute power in society at large. The effects of success in replacing privileged legal meanings with ones that support the goals of movements or associations exist on a number of levels. The first, and most obvious, is that victory allows movements and associations to manipulate the state and get it to use its power for the movement or association's goals.

On the second level, court victories have what Galanter calls 'radiating' effects, and Mnookin and Kornhauser call effects in the 'shadow' of the law. In this context this means that alteration of legal meanings, or attempts to alter legal meanings, change the way in which law influences the behaviour of both people in the movement or association, and outside of it. Such advocacy alters the perceptions of such groups about what might be a viable political position at a particular point in time.

It also alters the power balance in any negotiations that might be undertaken. By raising expectations it solidifies the morale of current members, and reaches potential constituents or supporters, activating them, and making them more receptive to further information. On the third level such legal advocacy can have the effect of constituting individual and movement identity. In this context, the constitutive potential of law refers to its ability as a practice to operate on an individual's thoughts and actions. The constitutive power of law operates through legal advocacy to define the goals of the movement and what it means to be an activist or supporter of such a movement. Such a relationship is reciprocal. Law constitutes the movement and the image of its members as much as the movement constitutes the law. This point is especially pertinent for the international human rights movement, whose identity has almost single-handedly been defined by human rights law, and whose activities have a strong tendency to focus on legal advocacy. With regard to levels two and three in the analysis, the effects of advocacy using law can be described as much as mobilization through law, as mobilization of law in the sense discussed by Black. The aim is not so much to activate the law, as to use the law to activate masses of people in civil society. In many ways this mobilization through law is more important than mobilization of law, as its potential effect on public opinion can be more decisive than state power in enforcing human rights laws.

Law itself can be seen as being constructed by a series of the struggles. Rather than talking of 'rights' in general it is thus better to talk of specific rights discourses built up over history, like the bank of a river, by successive contests over legal meaning and their specific results. In this vein, Henkin has distinguished between American rights and human rights, as two rights discourses that have different histories and ideologies of government and society. A similar view could also be taken of the relationship between German rights and international human rights.

Britain forms an interesting case in which an older declining discourse of British rights has been directly replaced by the international discourse of human rights at the domestic level. The enforcement of human rights depends to a large extent on the ways that domestic and international rights discourses create a dialogue with one another, and are reconciled. In this work, although all these rights discourses are described as 'human rights' discourses in the wider sense, the differences between the discourses, their conflicts and overlaps, will be commented on periodically. It should not be surmised from the description that law is infinitely malleable. On this view of law, there are absolute boundaries to the arena of struggle that limit what meanings of law can be exchanged for the current privileged meanings. The arena of struggle thus both can empower and constrain movements and associations. In order to maximise the empowering effect, and minimise the constraining effect of law, movements and associations engage in tactics, both within legal systems and outside of them.

The term 'strategy' will be used in this work to denote the pre-existing possibilities of legal discourse. The term 'tactics' will be used, in contrast, to refer to those competencies that are developed to manipulate legal resources within the terms of these pre-existing possibilities. To this point the theory of mobilization of law and through law that will be applied to human rights DNGOs in three jurisdictions has been derived from theory analysing mobilization of and through domestic state law. Some human rights DNGOs, however, also mobilize international law, and so such a theory must be supplemented to properly cover mobilization of international law to defend human rights. As no Sociology of Law theory covering mobilization of international law yet exists, the following will be drawn mainly from international relations literature.

MOBILIZATION OF INTERNATIONAL LAW

International law is a legal system that, unlike national law, has no centralized power to enforce law. It is also a legal system where, for the most part, legal interpretation does not occur through litigation in courts. In terms of legal mobilization, this means that there are a much larger number of possible points in the legal system where law can be mobilised, and a much greater number of modes in which it can be done. In this environment, much of what human rights DNGOs do may be described as attempts to use legal doctrine to achieve 'frame resonance'.

Frame resonance may be defined as a movement's interpretative framework, and this framework's ability to influence the broader understandings of both the public and decisionmakers. Because international law is enforced largely by states, DNGOs in this environment try to persuade or socialise states to accept their legal interpretations. They seek to have those legal interpretations achieve such frame resonance that other states will believe it sufficiently in their interests, or will receive sufficient pressure from public opinion, to pressure the recalcitrant state into upholding the law. Thus, the aim of the mobilization of international law appears to be to cause certain patterns of cooperation and coordination of states, such that the violating state risks what it sees as its interests in international relations if it does not comply with the legal norms in question.

Even when legal interpretation is more centralized, as in international institutions, any interpretation still has to achieve enough frame resonance to attract states to enforcement activities. These enforcement activities range from confidential diplomatic approaches, to sanctions or invasion. Therefore, in terms of the above theory of mobilization of law arenas of struggle occur in much more dispersed locations in the international system than in domestic systems, and the mobilization of law and through law are more closely intertwined as a result of the systemic imperatives of the international system itself.

THE REQUIREMENTS OF MOBILIZATION OF LAW

Another question that must be dealt with concerns what movements and associations require to mobilize the law. In a 1991, Burstein argued that mobilization of law by social movements depends not on the needs of those suffering from the violation of a law, or the extent of law violating activity, but rather the organization and resources of the social movement in question.

Similarly, Epp has argued that the primary reason for the successful mobilization of law by rights advocates is the creation of support structures that accumulate information, experience, skill and resources for the purpose of the mobilization of law. In the Netherlands, Everts and van den Berg have similarly seen resource mobilization by DNGOs as important determinants of their ability to influence the policy process. The existence of such factors as organization, information and resources also enable movements and associations to become what Galanter calls "repeat players". Galanter, this situation where the organization accumulates experience and contacts in litigation and other work, if attained by an organization, increases its chances of success.

Because the literature suggests they determine the mobilization of law by DNGOs, three and four of this work concentrate on tactics, structures and resources respectively. Although they are separated for ease of analysis it should not be thought that these aspects of DNGO operation function independently of one another. In practice, the acquisition of resources, the creation of structure and the selection of tactics form one undifferentiated whole, where each influences the other.

THE IMPORTANCE OF ORGANIZATION

Lastly, a debate exists among writers as to whether internal or external factors are the most important in human rights NGOs ending human rights violations. Kruse has argued that most human rights violations are ended through contextual factors such as political, social or economic changes, and not the efforts of human rights NGOs. Conversely, Tushnet has argued that external contextual factors merely set the initial conditions for a human rights campaign.

Once the mobilization of law is under way, he argues, the most important factor becomes the internal organizational ability of an organization. Clearly, which one of these is most important may depend on the situation. This study concentrates on the internal organizational power and ability of human rights NGOs. This approach is taken on the basis that even in situations where, as Kruse argues, human rights problems are ended or perpetuated by larger societal forces, the abilities or lack of abilities of human rights NGOs to impact on this situation depends almost entirely on their organizational resources and abilities.

THE USE OF CASE STUDIES

Like all works using Comparative Law method, this work should be seen as qualitative in social science terms. While it is usual for qualitative works in social science to use case studies, it is relatively unusual for a piece using Comparative Law methodology. Many Comparative Law pieces investigating social science concepts such as legal culture are highly impressionistic and low in detail. Case studies have the advantage of being thick in detail, and have the capacity to provide relevant empirical grounding for the comparative use of social science concepts and their further theoretical development for application in specific situations.

Case studies are thus used in this work to supply the empirical detail that Comparative Law studies on similar topics often lack. Having addressed the question of why case studies were used, it is necessary to explain why the particular jurisdictions and case studies featured here were chosen. Human rights DNGOs have been given very little attention in the literature. To the extent that they have featured in the literature since the 1960s, the focus has been on American public interest law litigators such as the American Civil Liberties Union and the NAACP Legal Defence and Education Fund.

These organizations have been presented as models of what human rights DNGOs around the world should look like. This has focused discussion on how these models could best be replicated in other legal systems. The discussion of DNGOs has thus, for the most part, focused on the classic Comparative Law problem of legal transplantation. This approach of transplanting the features of American DNGOs to other jurisdictions raises a host of unanswered questions. Firstly, what are the relative merits of these selected organizations compared to others? What are the assumptions underpinning their use as models?

Why are all the organizations that are mentioned American? The best that the literature offers by way of methodology admits that the organizations they select for study are not representative, and then proceeds to select organizations on the basis of whether they are "significant", without any further explanation. In this work, a more refined and expanded methodology of selection has been used. In order to test the idea that the selected American DNGOs were the most significant or effective, the scope of the study was expanded to include the jurisdictions of the United Kingdom and the Federal Republic of Germany. The United Kingdom was included because, like the United States, it is also a centre of INGO activity and has famous DNGOs. Also like the US, the UK is a developed country with money to create highly developed DNGOs.

Germany was selected in order to investigate the significance and effectiveness of DNGOs in a developed country outside the English speaking world. Furthermore, no literature in either German or English could be found by the author on German DNGOs and it was felt that research would expand the universe of known DNGO forms of activity. It was hoped that by expanding the focus of discussion of DNGOs, some serious propositions could be put forward concerning which types of DNGOs might be most effective in what situations.

In short, the author has the same sorts of doubts with regard to the transplantation of the features of US DNGOs to other jurisdictions without reference to context as those expressed by Kahn-Freund generally about legal transplantation. With regard to the selection of DNGOs in each of the jurisdictions, this work uses two bases to select case studies. The first refines and expands the methodology that already exists in the literature. Previous writings in international human rights literature on DNGOs have focused on what Wasby calls the "major players" amongst civil rights organizations in the United States.

These are the organizations that litigate the most, have the most resources, and the highest media profile. There are good reasons for such a focus. The first is that such organizations, because of their longevity, can become "repeat players" in the courts and elsewhere. As Galanter has argued, this gives them advantages that make them more likely to succeed in situations where they undertake to intervene. In this work, therefore, one of the points of focus in each jurisdiction is on those DNGOs that are relatively large and well resourced. The second reason for focusing on the major players, and a way of choosing among the major players, is outlined in the literature on case studies in the social sciences. Case studies in social science are selected to expand and generalise theories, and not to enumerate frequencies of a population. In other words, case studies do not have to be representative of NGOs in any given population, rather, they have to maximise what is learnt in terms of theoretical generalisation.

In terms of the existing literature, therefore, it is quite valid to select organizations that are much larger and older than the DNGO population as a whole if this leads to better understanding. The second basis for selecting case studies for this work will be how well they show the diversity of a DNGO community and improve theoretical understanding. An important question that this basis addresses is whether the selection of the ACLU and LDF, as in previous studies, is a selection that maximises what can be learnt about the diversity of successful formulas for the running a DNGO. In this work, it will be argued that these organizations are not necessarily the best US organizations to select for this purpose, and that the limitation of consideration of models to the US also limits what can be learnt and generalised from the analysis of case studies.

METHODOLOGY USED TO COLLECT THE DATA

The methodology used to collect information for this study involved a combination of textual and empirical research. Most of the initial research was done on the Internet, in publications by DNGOs, and in writings in journals and books on human rights NGOs. From these, and e-mail correspondence with individuals in each of the jurisdictions, a sense was gained of the nature of the DNGO community in each jurisdiction. Particular DNGOs were then singled out as being candidates for being case studies on the basis of the criteria set out, and were invited to participate. If a chosen

DNGO declined to participate in the research, then the DNGO in that jurisdiction from among the remaining DNGOs that most fit the criteria was then asked to participate. One DNGO in each jurisdiction declined to participate in this study. Those DNGOs that had the right characteristics and agreed were then chosen as case studies.

The case studies were then sent a qualitative questionnaire, which was filled in by a staff member/s nominated by the case study. This questionnaire was designed both to gain information that was absent from other sources, and to expand on information that was already present in the literature. Each case study was asked the same questions in a standardised questionnaire so as to make comparison between the case studies easier. The author then flew to the headquarters of each of the case studies and conducted an in depth semi-structured qualitative interview with a person or persons nominated by the case study.

The interviews were not only designed to elicit certain standard information from each of the case studies, but were also adapted to expand upon some of the answers that may have been brief or incomplete in the questionnaire. Further literature published by the case studies was also collected from them, and later analysed. The following text is thus based on research in books, journals, the Internet, legal cases, treaties and statutes, case study publications, the archives of some of the DNGOs that allowed the author access, media sources such as newspapers, government documents such as parliamentary and departmental papers, qualitative interviews and questionnaires, as well as e-mail correspondence with knowledgeable individuals.

THE NATIONALIST PATH TO HUMAN RIGHTS ENFORCEMENT

In describing some of the context surrounding the case studies in the three jurisdictions this work uses the concept of the 'nationalist path to human rights enforcement' as a heuristic device. This concept, which originated in the US, is an attitude held by human rights DNGOs that originally included a belief in the superiority of the US Constitution and the view that neither NGOs nor the US polity had much to learn from an international human rights movement designed for those in a much worse human rights position. On this view international human rights bear the onus of alien ideas that are subordinate to the 'real' rights in the US Constitution.

This concept can also be used more generally, however, to describe cultural tendencies in all three jurisdictions in this work. When used in this way it denotes a focus on domestic public law, a belief that there is little to learn from other nations on human rights enforcement and a devaluation and/or ignorance of what the international human rights movement and international human rights have to offer.

THE SOCIAL AND POLITICAL ENVIRONMENT IN WHICH THE LAW IS MOBILISED

This work for the most part assumes that the reader knows enough about the social and political cultures of the US, Britain and Germany to understand the comparisons made below. There is, however, one aspect of these contextual matters that is not widely known and that may therefore. Many in the English speaking world know very little about the contemporary German polity. The author therefore felt that a short note on the structure of the German government and courts might aid in understanding the analysis of the German case studies.

The Basic Law divides federal constitutional power between the German Parliament, the Chancellor and the Courts. The German Presidency is a largely ceremonial post that acts as a symbol of national unity. The German Parliament is made up of the lower house or Bundestag, which is directly elected by the people through a combination of proportional representation and first past the post methods, and an upper house, or Bundesrat, which is composed of the representatives of the Länder. Within this system there is a partial fusion of Legislative and Executive power in that the German Chancellor is the leader of the party or coalition which has a majority in the lower house and draws his ministers from Parliament. The German Judiciary consists of five different hierarchies of specialised courts, each of which has a court at its apex. The five federal courts that head these hierarchies are the Federal Constitutional Court; the Federal Administrative Court; the Federal Fiscal Court; the Federal Labour Court; the Federal Social Court and the Federal Supreme Court.

The Federal Constitutional Court receives complaints about violations of the Basic Rights directly from citizens, and also receives cases referred by judges in the other hierarchies when an important constitutional matter is in issue. With few exceptions all lower courts are courts of the Länder. The German judiciary thus comprises integrated hierarchies that contain both federal and Länder courts. Almost all cases begin in the courts of the Länder and if they are appealed end up in the Federal courts.

Federal laws and court judgments are also administered or enforced by Länder Executive Officers. The major implication of this constitutional system for German human rights DNGOs is that, when they engage in domestic litigation in this civil law system they will be active in the court hierarchy that covers the domestic human rights abuse they are trying to address.

It appears that often this is the Federal Constitutional Court. However, German DNGOs that combat abuses of social rights also appear to work in the Federal Social Court hierarchy, while German DNGOs that engage in work in work on civil and political rights often also work in the hierarchies of the Federal Supreme Court and the Federal Administrative Court. Cases from these courts then are often referred to the Federal Constitutional Court when issues of Basic Rights arise. As their decisions have major human rights consequences within Germany no note on the German constitutional system is complete without a brief mention of the consequences of Germany's membership of the European Union and the Council of Europe.

Because of Germany's involvement in these systems of European law German DNGOs have, besides domestic institutions and courts, the added options not only of litigating in the European Court of Human Rights and European Court of Justice but also of lobbying in the European Parliament and the Council of Europe. These European systems supplement, and in some cases supplant, the formal constitutional organs dealing with human rights established by the Basic Law.

OUTLINES OF THE CASE STUDIES

A short introduction to each of the nine organizations featured here as case studies, with the reasons for their selection. The NAACP Legal Defence and Education Fund is a domestic human rights organization based in New York. It was founded in 1940 as the legal arm of the NAACP but became entirely separate in 1957.

In absolute terms, LDF is the oldest and probably the largest of the DNGOs examined in this work. It is almost entirely focused on domestic litigation as a tactic for the mobilization of law and has nearly two dozen staff lawyers and approximately a hundred cases running at any one time. It was selected as a case study because it is the locus classicus of a major player DNGO in the literature, and its actual nature and effectiveness warranted further investigation. The Lawyers' Committee for Civil Rights Under Law is a domestic human rights organization based in Washington DC. It was founded in 1963 at the request of President Kennedy for more of the nation's large legal firms to become involved in domestic human rights work.

LCCRUL does very similar work to LDF in that it concentrates on domestic litigation as its main tactic to mobilize law. It differs from LDF in the way it draws upon America's leading law firms for support. LCCRUL was selected because it is one of the major players on the American scene, but has a resource acquisition strategy quite different to that of LDF or the ACLU. The Centre for Constitutional Rights is a domestic human rights organization based in New York.

It was founded in November 1966 by civil rights lawyers who had defended civil rights activists in the South of the US in the 1960s. Especially prominent in this regard were Arthur Kinoy and William Kunstler, both prominent radical lawyers. As a result of this background, CCR is explicitly politically left-wing. While not one of the major players in the American scene, CCR is still large compared to DNGOs elsewhere in the world, and was chosen because it evidences a quite different style of DNGO activity in the US from that made canonical in the human rights literature. It was thus felt that much could be learnt from a better understanding of its work. JUSTICE is a domestic human rights organization based in London. It was founded in 1957 as a legal reform organization, and is the local section of the INGO the International Commission of Jurists. Regardless of the international connections it has through the ICJ, however, JUSTICE in practice is mainly concerned with domestic human rights matters. Apart from Liberty, JUSTICE is the oldest domestic human rights organization in Britain, and, along with Liberty, one of the two major players in the British domestic human rights network.

In its work, it uses both international litigation and domestic lobbying and education work. JUSTICE was selected because, like LDF, it is one of the major players and classic DNGOs in Britain. British Irish Rights Watch is based in London, and was founded in 1992. Although relatively small, it is somewhat unique in being an inter-regional DNGO devoted to the major stain on the UK domestic human rights record–the conflict in Northern Ireland.

BIRW specialises in mobilising international law to fulfil its mandate. It was selected as a case study for this work because it reflects the preoccupation with Northern Ireland in the British human rights community, and because it reflects the diversity of British DNGOs through its unique culture and seeming unusual effectiveness. The Committee on the Administration of Justice is based in Belfast, Northern Ireland, and was founded in 1981 in the wake of hunger strikes by IRA prisoners. CAJ focuses mainly on human rights work related to the conflict in Northern Ireland, but also has a wider agenda developing.

Along with the Scottish Human Rights Centre, it is one of the major regional players among the UK DNGOs, and because of its work in the difficult environment of Northern Ireland won the Council of Europe human rights prize. CAJ was thus selected as an example of the regional DNGOs in the UK, and because as a prize winner it was felt that much could be learnt by comparing it to classic American organizations like LDF. The Humanistische Union is based in Berlin. It was founded in 1961 in Munich, Bavaria, over the issue of the division between church and state. While it is often said that there is no German equivalent to the American Civil Liberties Union, HU could be argued to be such an equivalent. Like the ACLU it is a relatively old and large membership organization that defends civil and political rights with special emphasis on freedom of expression and the division between church and state. HU is the oldest Bürgerrechteorganisation in Germany, and one of the largest, and is thus a major player. It defends human rights through a variety of means, including occasionally domestic litigation.

HU was selected because of its major player status in Germany, and because it is emblematic of classic German methods of mobilization of law in defence of human rights. The Kommittee für Grundrechte und Demokratie is based in Cologne. It was founded in 1980 after the revelations at the Russell Tribunal the previous year of alleged human rights violations by the German government in its struggle against the Red Army Faction also known as the

Baader-Meinhof Gang. Although somewhat smaller than HU, KGD is still a major player in the German DNGO scene. Unusually, it is a self-declared organization of the political left that is closely aligned with the German green and peace movements. Its main tactic is also unusual, in that it relies mostly on mass mobilization of the populace to defend human rights. KGD was thus selected because it is a major player, and because of what can be learnt from its unusual tactics. The Gesellschaft zum Schutz von Bürgerrecht und Menschenwürde is based in Berlin. It was founded in 1991 as a consequence of the reunification of Germany. GBM is primarily a DNGO that operates in the former GDR. It fights discrimination against former GDR citizens, and focuses especially on social rights.

It has an extensive programme of mobilising international and public law through litigation, but also has larger cultural and political agendas. GBM was selected for this study for three reasons. Firstly, like CAJ, it is an example of a relatively large regional DNGO in the still fragmented Germany. Secondly its internal culture and tactics, being derived from the old establishment and opposition in the GDR, hold the promise of new knowledge concerning human rights DNGOs in the former East Germany. Finally, given its focus on social rights, GBM shows a contrast to the UK and US case studies, and thus could potentially be instructive to the investigator of DNGOs.

5

The Tactics of Human Rights

This stage is an overview and critical analysis of the tactical choices that DNGOs make from the strategies available to them. In order to achieve this a typology of DNGO tactics is firstly put forward to aid the understanding of the material. Then, the tactics of each of the case studies are documented and analysed (mostly from the same points of view) to facilitate useful comparison. Some of the variables that influence the tactical decisions of the case studies are discussed within the exposition of each case study.

The main analysis, however, is at the end of the discussion for each jurisdiction, and in the conclusion. Reitz has argued that true Comparative Law scholarship lies in the tension between the similarities and differences in what is being compared. In line with this, it is argued below that the case studies show both differences and similarities in their tactics. It is further argued that the differences between the case studies stem from different conceptions of how human rights work should be done, while the similarities are determined both by the common need for DNGOs to gain legitimacy in local cultures, and their need to rationally adapt to the opportunities in their environment. DNGOs, it is argued, are compelled to achieve a balance between these two requirements. Other factors that influence DNGOs, such as the levels and types of resources or the type of structure.

TYPOLOGY OF DNGO TACTICS

In the discussion that follows the tactical decisions made by DNGOs are loosely divided into first order, second order and third order tactics. First order tactics concern the framing of a DNGO's mandate and agenda. They are thus about setting goals at the most general level. Second order tactics are used to achieve the goals set out in the mandate or agenda (*e.g.*, litigation or lobbying).

Third order tactics concern the methods used by a DNGO to execute the second order tactics it chooses. This typology is not meant to suggest a chronological sequence: a DNGO might begin by using second and third order tactics and only later clarify its first order tactics.

FIRST ORDER TACTICS

As Weissbrodt pointed out for INGOs, a DNGO needs to ask itself a number of questions when setting its mandate.

These questions are:

- Is the DNGO to have a wide or narrow mandate?
- Should the DNGO focus on particular rights, or on groups that traditionally suffer violations? and
- Should the mandate be rigid, or allow flexibility to deal with new issues that arise?

Each choice a DNGO makes in answering these questions creates problems. If the DNGO chooses a narrow mandate, it needs to select an issue that both reflects an objective need, and has enough resonance with the public to draw support. If it chooses a wide mandate, then its task of setting an agenda is complicated by the difficulty of comparing different kinds of human rights violations. Focusing on particular rights has the advantage of being intellectually satisfying, but might not achieve public support. Focusing on a particular group suffering violations might appear simply to be the claim of an interest group.

A completely flexible mandate might cause the DNGO to be overwhelmed by cases of small overall significance. A flexible mandate, coupled with criteria designed to limit the number of cases and to keep only highly significant ones, may merely shift the problem of first order tactics to one of second order tactics. First order tactical decisions are not necessarily made with finality. They are often open to constant review. Indeed, most DNGOs have to find ways to manage so-called "mandate-creep", where their mandate expands as new issues arise.

SECOND ORDER TACTICS

The means used to achieve the goals set out in the mandate can be described as part of a spectrum. On the left hand side might be tactics such as litigation (national and international); lobbying; policy work (international and national) and human rights education for officials (mostly national). In the middle of the spectrum might be tactics such as research; letter writing; networking; trial observation; documentation; publication; publicity work; providing aid to victims and development of new standards and institutions. Lastly, on the right hand might be such tactics as boycotts; peaceful demonstrations; non-violent direct action and civil disobedience.

Using the work of Sarat and Scheingold, one could understand this spectrum as designating the degree of interaction with the state (or international institutions). Those tactics on the left of the spectrum have more interaction with state institutions; those on the right have less. As suggested by Scoble and Wiseberg, one could also understand this spectrum as describing those who use "tree-topping" (tactics addressing elites and the state) on the left, to those who use "ground-levelling" (tactics addressing the population at large) on the right. The decision a DNGO makes from among the tactics in this spectrum also indicates where it believes the decision-making power lies for the issues it campaigns on. If it chooses tactics on the left of the spectrum, it believes that state actors are the primary decision-makers. If it chooses tactics on the right, it believes that other actors are primary decision-makers or have decisive influence on primary decision-makers. Almost all the literature on NGO tactics concerns INGOs, and in line with their focus, generally only elaborates tactics on the left of the spectrum.

Tactics in the centre or right of the spectrum, which are often used by DNGOs, have in general been considered from the point of view of political science. This distinction makes less sense once it is seen how actual DNGOs seamlessly combine both 'legal' and 'political' tactics. There is also much discussion in the literature on how to combine second order tactics. In the literature of the Ford Foundation, which funds many DNGOs in the United States, there is much discussion about a 'holistic' approach to tactics. This approach is described as one that moves away from reliance on litigation in favour of seeing it as a last resort.

In a more sophisticated analysis of how DNGOs can and should conduct second order tactics, Wasby argues that DNGOs should adopt what he calls an 'integrated' tactical stance. In his discussion of lobbying and litigation by American DNGOs Wasby notes that many DNGOs combine multiple second order tactics and he speculates that they may already have confidential plans for coordinating these tactics.

He then argues that even if DNGOs do not have such plans, they should, because his analysis suggests that such tactical coordination would be more effective than the uncoordinated tactics many of them currently use. The idea of a planned combination of tactics is also integral to the concept of the Comprehensive Tactical Stance. The second order tactical stances in the spectrum above usually exist in typical combinations. In interpreting these combinations, it is useful to outline what Max Weber called 'ideal types' for human rights DNGO second order tactical stances. An ideal type is a model that does not correspond exactly to any example in the real world, but helps to explain such cases. They accentuate the features of real cases, so as to pinpoint their essential characteristics and thus aid analysis.

Some ideal types which help to understand the case studies in this work are:

- Tactical Approach A focuses on litigation, with occasional forays into lobbying when litigation dictates.
- Tactical Approach B consists of a near equal combination of lobbying and litigation.
- Tactical Approach C focuses on lobbying with occasional litigation.
- Tactical Approach D focuses solely on lobbying.
- Tactical Approach E consists of lobbying combined with publicity work.

- Tactical Approach F consists of a near equal combination of direct action and publicity/campaigning work.

THIRD ORDER TACTICS

Third order tactics are the decisions taken as to how to carry out second order tactics. It is beyond the scope of this work to elaborate all of the third order tactics for each of the second order tactics, but to aid understanding some of the major third order tactics that are used by some of the case studies. Litigation can be conducted either as a defensive or offensive tactic.

It can be used defensively to protect those defending human rights from having their rights violated, or it can be used offensively to challenge situations where patterns of human rights violations occur in society generally. For offensive litigation, it is important to clearly state the differences between the test case approach and the use of impact litigation.

The Test Case Approach

The test case approach is the main third order tactic for litigation used by DNGOs in Britain. It is used by British organizations such as Liberty, MIND and the Joint Council for the Welfare of Immigrants (JCWI). Because British governments have used their legislative power to cancel gains made from successful litigation in British courts, test case litigation in Britain has generally been in the European Court of Human Rights. The emphasis of the test case approach is not purely legal, but rather combines both legal and media skills. In fact, British DNGOs tend to see the ultimate justification of test cases not as being victory in court but rather the political and press attention they attract. They thus often mobilize the law in order to mobilize through the law. Generally, DNGO lawyers identify a problem which has the potential to become the subject of a test case in the course of day-to-day casework.

They then identify a prospective remedy for the problem they have detected. Next, they consider whether the legal rule concerned can be challenged under the European Convention on Human Rights. If it can, they then consider which case or cases from those they know would be the strongest on the facts, and whether they should pursue one or more cases. British DNGOs using this tactic generally follow one of two approaches. First, they might support individuals who wish to bring applications. These individuals are usually located through casework, letters, phone calls or referrals from other organizations. Second, they might engage in third party interventions in cases that are already under way in the courts.

The difficulty with the test case approach is that to be effective DNGOs need to be involved in casework. This is necessary in order to have enough throughput of cases to obtain the small number of significant cases that could be the subject of a test case. This means, however, that to a large degree specialisation of DNGO lawyers in test cases is not possible.

Impact Litigation

Impact litigation is the main third order tactic for litigation used by American DNGOs such as LDF, the NAACP and the ACLU. This tactic seeks to use a sequence of individual cases to develop legal principles that are more effective against human rights violations in particular areas. The key to impact litigation is control: litigators try to control the development and sequence of cases in a targeted court, to produce cases involving the issues they want decided at the desired time and place.

The desired cases are sometimes 'found' by networks of cooperating lawyers or branches, sometimes they look for already initiated cases, and sometimes they employ intermediaries as 'case finders'. Litigators then attempt through a series of cases to undermine adverse precedent and build up supporting precedent by consistently framing their cases in ways that are acceptable to the targeted court. Impact litigation thus differs from test case litigation in that it extends over a series of cases; it requires its litigators to develop expert legal skills but not media skills; it actively subordinates the dictates of individual cases to an overall goal of achieving a precedent on a particular issue and in that it involves a close monitoring of the court concerned to determine the attitudes of the judges and to control the content and sequence of cases that arrive there on particular issues.

The strength of impact litigation is that it allows DNGOs in certain circumstances to determine some of the agenda of the relevant court concerned, so that it focuses on the weakest and least resourced of those suffering human rights violations. In the opinion of the author, the disadvantage of impact litigation is that the requirements of planning, specialist staff lawyers and the focus on one court can create rigidity and inertia. Furthermore, such plans are difficult to execute given fluid environments, and can end up as devices for 'selling' an organization to funders and supporters.

Responsive Litigation

Another third order tactic for litigation is the 'radical' or responsive tradition of 'people's lawyers' in America. The main tenets of this tradition are: firstly, using courts as a platform to air political grievances about human rights violations; secondly, seeing human rights as identical to progressive politics; thirdly, developing a non-hierarchical relationship with clients which differs from that of mainstream lawyers and lastly, being responsive to clients suffering human rights violations.

In this approach, lawyers obtain their cases from working in tandem with progressive political movements on human rights issues. More like the British test case approach, this approach seeks to mobilize the law so as to be able to mobilize through the law.

Advocacy Networks and the Boomerang Effect

A number of third order tactics are worth highlighting with regard to networking, especially in the international sphere. Firstly, the concept of an "advocacy network" is useful for explaining how DNGOs operate both internationally and domestically. The ability of these networks to reframe national and international debates by changing their terms, their sites and their participants through the acquisition and use of information is central to the tactics of many DNGOs. Also worth mentioning is the "boomerang" tactic whereby DNGOs, alone or in coalition with INGOs, bypass domestic institutions and directly access international allies to bring pressure on a state from the outside. The "boomerang" tactic is the usual approach of advocacy networks. As Risse, Ropp and Sikkink have argued, when this tactic is used there is generally a sequence of interaction between the state and international society, which continues until the state is socialised into complying with human rights norms.

Some of the primary third order tactical differences between INGOs and DNGOs arise because DNGOs can collect detailed local information from better local networks. DNGOs then often use that information to activate international networks and begin the socialisation process. This "boomerang" tactic is thus a vital tool for DNGOs that pursue goals internationally.

Civil Disobedience and Non-violent Direct Action

Civil disobedience, as a method of carrying out the second order tactic of political protest, is defined in this work as any act or process of public defiance of the law or policy enforced by established authorities insofar as the action is premeditated, understood by the actor(s) to be illegal or of contested illegality, carried out for limited public ends, and by way of carefully limited means.

These limited means generally exclude violence. Overlapping with this is Non-Violent Direct Action (or NVA), which will be defined here as any action where individuals or groups, without violence to any person, attempt to bring about change directly themselves, rather than asking or expecting others to act on their behalf. These tactics are quite distinct from violent demonstrations or riots, and require a DNGO to have a capacity to plan. Because they are often associated with radical politics, these tactics are often seen as less legitimate than other tactics on the spectrum. DNGOs, however, have the potential to execute such tactics through their local networks and sometimes do so.

THE COMPREHENSIVE TACTICAL STANCE

Weissbrodt wrote in 1977 that one of the questions that needed to be asked about an NGO was how it should select its cases. In terms of the schema set out, this question might be rephrased to ask how a DNGO chooses the most effective first, second and third order tactics. A useful way of assessing this, and of ordering information on tactics, is to develop a model tactical stance with which to compare the data. Similarly to Wasby's 'integrated' tactical stance, this work extrapolates inductively from data gathered from the case studies and other DNGOs in the literature to come to this model tactical stance. Like an 'ideal type', this model accentuates certain features of the process of selection of tactics in the data to pinpoint its essential characteristics.

Unlike a pure Weberian 'ideal type', however, it is used not only as a heuristic device to interpret the data, but also as an ideal in the literal sense of being an embodiment of good DNGO practice that can be used to critically assess decisions that DNGOs make about tactics. This model is intended as a more targeted tool for the critical understanding of human rights DNGOs than the more general models for all types of organizations that might be used in disciplines such as political science.

It is not intended to foreshadow or substitute for the assessment of case study effectiveness using the data undertaken in this work. The model tactical stance in this stage will be designated the Comprehensive Tactical Stance (CTS). Because of their pre-eminent importance in achieving effectiveness the CTS aims to examine the rationality of a case study's tactics in responding to the environment. It thus does not take account of a DNGO's resource limitations, problems it has in modifying its internal structure or culture, or its need for legitimacy. In the real world, each of these will have some influence on tactics. In particular, a DNGO in the real world must balance the solutions advocated by the model with the amount of legitimacy it might lose if it rationally adapted to its environment.

The model thus only examines part of what a DNGO needs to do to be effective overall; although the author believes that the part it examines is the most decisive in aiding understanding of how DNGOs function. In the CTS, setting the mandate as a first order tactic would not just be about presenting a good image to potential supporters. It would be based on a 'needs analysis' of the human rights violations occurring in the DNGO's environment. This needs analysis would include a discussion of which violations are the most severe and require urgent intervention.

The DNGO would then act on this analysis and address the most severe violations within its mandate. For second order tactics, the CTS would require that a DNGO retain a capacity to switch between different tactics on the above spectrum in response to changes in opportunities in the environment. It would also require that the DNGO develop principles or a rational plan to determine when different tactics are to be used, and whether they are to be used simultaneously or in specific sequences, in order to achieve the best effect. A response to the environment is deemed in this work to be rational when it involves this type of planning. The advantage of the CTS's second order tactics is that using them would make it difficult for any government or institution to undermine a DNGO's work. Using the CTS, DNGOs could adapt to changes caused by government action aimed at undermining their work by changing tactics to prevent it being successful. When government action makes one tactic less effective, the CTS advocates that a DNGO switch to other tactics that might potentially be more effective.

Under the CTS, DNGOs thus plan and rationally respond to changes in opportunities in their environments. There are significant complications in following the CTS's injunction to change tactics to suit the environment. A loss of legitimacy could result from certain combinations of tactics. A DNGO's litigation, for example, could lose legitimacy if the DNGO also engaged in civil disobedience. Using the CTS to understand good DNGO practice can thus can be undermined by detrimental effects on factors that are not included within it.

THE CASE STUDIES

What follows are outlines and analyses of the tactical stances of the case studies. For each case study there is an identification of its first, second and third order tactics. Under each heading there is a discussion of the tactics used, from the most important to the least important. The focus is on the first and second order tactics, because of the outline of third order tactics. Lastly, there is a discussion of the types of networks in which the case study participates, and the degree of planning that it undertakes.

THE AMERICAN CASE STUDIES

LDF

First Order Tactics

LDF's first order tactical stance has a dual focus on racial discrimination as a human rights violation and the protection of the African-American community. LDF has a strictly defined mandate and has successfully resisted mandate creep. Dominant Second and Third Order Tactics LDF's most important second order tactic has been litigation, and the third order tactic for executing its litigation has been impact litigation.

LDF has thus identified the Supreme Court as the decision-maker that it wishes to target and that can make the changes it desires. It is thus an almost pure example of Tactical Approach A. LDF was the creator of impact litigation in the 1930s and 1940s. In recent times, it has been put on the defensive in the use of this tactic by a mostly hostile federal judiciary and the proliferation of Public Interest Law organizations that oppose domestic human rights. This has undermined its use of impact litigation, as this requires both that it control court dockets, and that it prevent the creation of adverse precedent. Organizations using impact litigation to oppose LDF's agenda, and other domestic human rights organizations with similar agendas, have both made each of these tasks less manageable. LDF's view of its own tactics is that its famous victory in Brown v Board of Education, and those that followed, resulted from a unique conjunction of circumstances and do not show the general efficacy of litigation. This attitude has made LDF litigate less than in the past. Paradoxically, despite litigating less, its primary focus is still on litigation and on waiting for better litigating conditions in the federal courts. Its fundamental presumption appears to be that litigating conditions there will improve. Any assessment of LDF's tactical stance thus depends on an assessment of the credibility of this presumption. It may be, however, that LDF has had little choice in the short term but to adopt such a stance as it does not yet have the requisite resources or expertise to switch to other second order tactics. LDF has a specific 'style' of conducting impact litigation that distinguishes it from other civil rights organizations. It not only files amicus curiae briefs, but also begins cases in the lower courts to take to higher courts. Rather than seeing these two tactics as inconsistent, it sees them as mutually reinforcing. It uses amicus briefs to maintain presence in the courts that its impact litigation targets.

If an issue that LDF wants addressed is already before the court, it usually files amicus briefs to try to have the matter resolved in the way it prefers. If there is an issue that LDF believes should be before the court but is not, it often finds a case to use as a vehicle to raise the issue and have it litigated. LDF has an informal and open process of case selection, under which any of its staff lawyers can bring forward ideas for approval by the organization. The reason for this appears to be a commitment to fostering the creativity of its lawyers, and an emphasis on only taking on cases for which its lawyers already have the necessary expertise. For LDF, resources thus often determine tactical decisions. In terms of subject matter, LDF still litigates in its traditional area of affirmative action in education. It also still pursues traditional desegregation cases in the lower schools, and conducts litigation in housing matters and employment discrimination.

Racial discrimination has also, however, recently been challenged in new spheres such as in transportation, access to health care and environmental protection. The main new areas that have evolved since the 1970s have been the increased emphasis on the voting rights of minorities, and, as a result of law and order and anti-drug campaigns, areas of criminal justice. Through its cases it attempts to challenge the privileged interpretations of Civil Rights Law with more marginalised interpretations arising predominantly from the African-American community. It refashions standard meanings attached to law within the courts as arenas of struggle. In this way, it attempts to universalise and legitimise the human rights interests of the African-American community, and thereby effect a redistribution of power in its favour. The effect of a largely hostile judiciary has been to change the courts as arenas of struggle so that the power relations there favour LDF less.

Supplementary Second Order Tactics

LDF carries out tactics supplemental to litigation mainly in its Washington DC Office. This Office does most of its lobbying; advises members of Congress on domestic human rights legislation; does policy work; pressures federal administrative agencies to enforce domestic human rights laws; monitors judicial and administrative appointments and does publicity work. LDF has also hired a public relations firm to do its publicity, even though it possesses an in-house communications department.

Networks with other Organizations

LDF is a member of a number of permanent and ad hoc networks. With regard to lobbying, LDF, like most major American DNGOs, is a member of the permanent advocacy network called the Leadership Conference on Civil Rights (LCCR). It also has permanent relations with foreign DNGOs such as the Legal Resources Centre and the Black Lawyers Organization in South Africa, the Roma Rights Centre in Hungary and Afro-Brazilian groups in Brazil. These links exist mainly because LDF helped establish these organizations.

In conjunction with the Open Society Institute, LDF helped create the Criminal Justice Alliance, a new advocacy group created to set a human rights agenda for criminal justice in the US. It is also a member of Advocates for Consumer Justice, an organization working on practices such as predatory lending and consumer fraud. For litigation, the primary permanent network is the Civil Rights Bar, which informally facilitates information flow between most domestic human rights lawyers in America and allows informal cooperation between DNGOs. LDF also facilitates networking between domestic human rights lawyers through its conferences at Airlie House in Virginia. Besides its permanent networks, LDF is also a member of a number of ad hoc networks.

These ad hoc connections include contacts with DNGOs such as the Mexican American Legal Defence and Education Fund (MALDEF), the Asian American Legal Defence Fund (AALDF) and the National Organization of Women Legal Defence Fund (NOWLDF). Links with these organizations tend to wax and wane just as to the demands of the moment. In addition, LDF also has ad hoc arrangements with INGOs, such as Human Rights Watch (HRW); the Lawyers' Committee for Human Rights (LCHR) and Amnesty International (AI).

These international links have led LDF to attend some international human rights gatherings such as the 2001 World Conference on Racism in Durban, South Africa. With LCHR it has also attended some of the periodic reviews of America's adherence to CERD before the United Nations CERD Committee. Lastly, with HRW it has worked on the impact on human rights standards of the terrorist attack on New York on September 11th, 2001 and on immigration matters, while with AI it has worked on capital punishment cases. This de facto international work may signal that organizational practice is overtaking LDF's stated scepticism about the use of international institutions. The small volume of this work, however, suggests that it is still marginal to LDF's overall tactical orientation. It also suggests that, while LDF is being affected by Globalisation, it is not consciously adjusting its tactics to its new environment.

Planning

LDF does a lot of planning, not only for impact litigation, but also to coordinate its subsidiary tactics. It plans how to tactically combine its litigation, lobbying and media work to achieve maximum effect. It seems, however, that the small amount of advocacy work done outside of litigation makes such planning relatively straightforward. LDF also plans how litigation, lobbying and media work should be carried out individually. Interestingly, however, it does not plan how to combine its domestic litigation, lobbying and media work with its international work.

This seems to stem from its scepticism about the utility of international law and the small volume of international work it does. LDF's plans tend not so much to be formal documents, but rather informal results of staff discussions. They also appear to vary widely in execution as unexpected events occur. To review its plans and suggest how they could be improved LDF hires outside consultants.

Some of these consultants, however, seem to be closely connected to LDF, and this may cast some doubt on their objectivity. In conclusion, LDF's first order tactics seem to have successfully combined the defence of racial anti-discrimination with protection of the African-American community's human rights. LDF's second order tactics favour litigation in domestic courts. This work shows an equal interest in the use of amicus curiae briefs and direct litigation. Other second order tactics are highly marginalised. In terms of the CTS, LDF deviates from it in favouring legitimacy over rational adaptation to the environment, while it seems to follow the CTS more closely in the comprehensive planning it undertakes. Arguably, the most prominent opportunities in LDF's environment, if one looks at contemporary events in the US from the point of view of the CTS, are not in the federal courts, which have become more resistant, but in tactics such as lobbying, policy work and international work.

The CTS thus throws doubt on the correctness of LDF's assessment that the Supreme Court is the most rational part of the environment to target to achieve the goals in its mandate. To the author, from the point of view of the CTS Congress seems at least as attractive a target as the Courts. LDF's reasons for not pursuing alternate routes to litigation seem unconvincing to the author. They appear to be based on an unspoken assessment that LDF would suffer a large loss of legitimacy and resources if it followed these paths. To the author this view seems exaggerated, and to have been used to avoid confronting the problem of balancing legitimacy and adaptation to the environment.

LCCRUL First Order Tactics

LCCRUL's first order tactics, as at LDF, involve a dual focus on racial anti-discrimination and the human rights of the African-American community.

Dominant Second and Third Order Tactics

LCCRUL's principal second order tactic is impact litigation. However, it has a different 'style' of conducting this litigation than LDF. LDF uses its network of cooperating lawyers, announcements asking for plaintiffs and "case finders" to obtain the plaintiffs it is looking for. In contrast, LCCRUL's plaintiffs are generally referred to the national Office by its partner firms, by people contacting them, through local lawyers' committees or by staff reading about an ongoing case in their research. Like LDF, LCCRUL plans cases in impact litigation, but the means it uses to implement such plans are different. In addition, unlike LDF, LCCRUL prefers to initiate its own cases rather than intervene in cases already underway through amicus curiae briefs. In impact litigation as practiced by LCCRUL, once a plaintiff is found the process of case approval is a structured and written process, rather than the informal and open process as at LDF.

The process requires levels of investigation and the production of a written memorandum to the Chief Counsel for approval. Once a case is approved, LCCRUL conducts the case with partner law firms. The case is not handed off to a partner law firm, rather the partner firm and LCCRUL act as co-partners, with LCCRUL supplying specialist legal expertise and advising the partner firm and the partner firm supplying trial lawyers and paying for the case. This is similar to LDF's relationship with individual cooperating lawyers. Compared to LDF, LCCRUL appears not to have taken as much heed of the current conservative approach of the US judiciary.

Even though it faces the same problems as LDF in this respect, it still believes it can achieve successes through litigation. Paradoxically, LCCRUL thus appears to have a greater faith in the judiciary, despite a greater commitment to substituting other tactics for litigation. The reason for this appears to be the influence of the establishment law firms, for whom the courts have great prestige. In practice LCCRUL also appears to emphasise international work more than LDF. It seems, however, that the combining of litigation with monitoring administrative agency actions; participating in agency proceedings; analysing and drafting legislation; writing research reports and keeping client groups informed of their legal rights rather than international work has been the core of LCCRUL's response to judicial resistance to domestic human rights.

Most areas LCCRUL litigates in are the 'traditional' civil rights areas that LDF also litigates in. LCCRUL has opposed actions against electoral districts designed to enhance African-American electoral participation and has extended the reach of the Voting Rights Act. It has litigated against racial discrimination in employment; sex discrimination in hiring practices; the dumping of toxic waste in poor African-American areas and against air pollution levels in these areas. In the area of housing and community development, it has concentrated on racial desegregation of housing and has also been running racial desegregation actions on other topics. Several important affirmative action actions have also recently been successful in which LCCRUL, unusually, lodged amicus curiae briefs as an alternative to running the cases itself.

Supplementary Second Order Tactics

In addition to litigation, LCCRUL also engages in lobbying, working with administrative agencies and policy work. In all of its work, LCCRUL's national headquarters coordinates the pro-bono work of approximately one hundred and eighty of America's largest law firms. LCCRUL also organises conferences in the US and has participated in the 2001 World Conference on Racism in Durban, South Africa and the pre-Durban conference in Washington DC. In addition, it publishes newsletters and reports and writes newspaper and journal objects.

LCCRUL does lobbying and policy work similarly to the way it conducts impact litigation. As in its litigation, it first identifies its priorities, and then asks the partner firms for help with tasks such as research or publicity. This work involves not only, as in 2001, writing policy recommendations in 'transition papers' for the new Bush administration, but also meeting with officials, monitoring the Justice Department and monitoring the nominations and confirmations of various officials.

In its lobbying work, LCCRUL prefers, when any sympathy is present, to focus on the President rather than Congress. It had amicable relations with the Clinton administration, which was sympathetic, even if not much legislation was delivered. Support from the Clinton Justice Department, in court and elsewhere, appears to have been an important resource for LCCRUL. However, it has a less cordial relationship with the current Bush administration, and has turned more to Congress. Here it works not only with Democrats, but also with moderate Republicans, in lobbying for domestic human rights.

Networks with Other Organizations

LCCRUL is a member of a number of permanent advocacy networks. Like LDF, it is a member of the Leadership Conference on Civil Rights. It also helped found Americans for a Fair Chance (AFC), which is a consortium of domestic human rights groups whose aim is to change public perceptions so they are more favourable to affirmative action. In addition, from time to time it works within a plethora of ad hoc networks with other DNGOs on various issues. LCCRUL has no substantial permanent contacts with human rights INGOs, although some ad hoc contacts occur.

Planning

LCCRUL has a strong commitment to tactics outside of litigation, such as lobbying. Although not greater in amount than at LDF, lobbying at LCCRUL is much more important, because it is often integrated with litigation just as to a plan. This plan usually coordinates other types of work with litigation sequentially. The sequence calls for beginning work on an issue through research and policy papers, and then moving to lobbying.

It uses research, policy papers and lobbying in this sequence as responses of first resort and leaves litigation as an option of last resort. The sequence is used not only to avoid litigation, but also because LCCRUL believes that these other tactics can be more successful in their own right. It employs what Mnookin and Kornhauser call "bargaining in the shadow of the law" to use the law to strengthen its bargaining position. For the same reason of preventing litigation, sometimes LCCRUL will give communities information on their rights so that the community can be its own advocate. Because it does this type of work, it sees itself as a ground levelling and not a tree topping organization. As LCCRUL appears to be involved more in lobbying, research and policy papers than community education, however, this self-belief seems questionable. LCCRUL has formal overall strategic plans that are reviewed every five to ten years. Like LDF, it periodically hires outside consultants to review the strategic plan's effectiveness and advise as to whether it should be changed.

It also has plans on how litigation, lobbying and policy work should be conducted individually. For litigation, this works in tandem with a formal and structured process of case approval that stands in sharp contrast to the laissez-faire approach of LDF. It appears that the reason that LCCRUL has this more structured process of case approval is both that it lays even greater stress than LDF on planning impact litigation, and because the elite law firms that are its partner firms also do such formal planning and its internal processes must have legitimacy with these firms.

That is, it appears that LCCRUL uses planning not only to improve effectiveness but also to 'sell' itself to its partner firms. In conclusion, LCCRUL has a successful first order tactic of dual concern for the African-American community and racial non-discrimination. As at LDF its primary second order tactic focuses on litigation in domestic courts, but it has a cultural commitment to other second order tactics. Also as at LDF, the CTS seems to show that LCCRUL's assumption that the primary power to make the decisions it is concerned with lies with the Supreme Court is questionable. In practice, however, its greater focus on work with Congress and the Presidency appears to show that it recognises that power also lies elsewhere. The CTS thus suggests that LCCRUL is a little more rationally adapted to its environment than LDF. Lastly, as a third order tactic LCCRUL uses a distinctive style of impact litigation, and this style has flowed into and influenced the way it approaches third order decisions for other second order tactics such as lobbying. Despite the CTS's conclusion that LCCRUL is somewhat more rationally adapted to its environment than LDF, it still leans overwhelmingly towards legitimacy. As at LDF, it appears that LCCRUL not only experiences strident demands for legitimacy from the local culture but also has a rigid structure and narrow range of resources that further hamper its ability to achieve rational adaptation to its opportunity structure.

With all of the impediments to securing balance between legitimacy and rational adaptation, it is a testament to LCCRUL's capacity for self-evaluation that it has achieved the level of balance that it has. It would appear, however, that still greater levels of performance are possible.

CCR

First Order Tactics

In contrast to both LDF and LCCRUL, CCR has, in terms of rights protected, a much wider first order tactical stance. CCR's mandate enforces both the Universal Declaration of Human Rights and the US Bill of Rights. There is also a sense in which it protects the 'progressive movement' in the same way that LDF and LCCRUL protect the African-American community. Because of CCR's wider mandate, much more emphasis is placed on second order tactics than the mandate to determine which issues will be focused upon.

Dominant Second and Third Order Tactics

CCR's second order tactical stance is focused primarily on using domestic and international law in domestic courts, but also features a cultural commitment to community organising. Its second order tactics are to engage in litigation, lobbying, education and demonstrations/direct action. It thus combines elements of tactical stance A wiThelements of tactical stances B and F in that it combines a focus on litigation with an emphasis on lobbying, publicity work and community organising.

As with the other American case studies, CCR appears to see domestic courts as being where the power lies to influence the decisions it is concerned with. CCR's third order tactical stance is a combination of impact litigation and responsive litigation. For its activist work, it employs demonstrations and civil disobedience as third order tactics. With regard to the primary second order tactic of litigation, CCR sees itself as being on the 'cutting edge' of innovative human rights litigation both domestically and internationally. This self perception has some basis as some of the leading cases in American legal history were initiated by CCR. Litigation conducted by CCR falls into five streams. The first stream, covering government misconduct and political rights, is similar to traditional American civil liberties litigation. It covers issues such as police and prison misconduct; freedom of expression; immigrants' rights and racial discrimination.

The second stream covers social and economic justice, and includes diverse cases on privatisation; abortion; freedom of speech and poverty. The third stream covers US responses to the terrorist attack on September 11th, 2001. These cases include challenges to the indefinite detention of persons captured during US military action in Afghanistan; the indefinite detention of terrorist suspects in the US and the indefinite detention of persons detained at Guantanamo Bay, Cuba.

The fourth stream covers corporate accountability for human rights violations. Cases in this stream mainly involve civil actions in US courts against multi-national companies based on violations of international criminal law. The fifth stream covers cases involving international human rights, and includes civil cases using international criminal law in US courts, as well as cases against the US in the Inter-American Commission of Human Rights. Thus, even though a DNGO, CCR occasionally acts like an INGO in using international law in US courts and occasionally resorting to international fora. Rather than doing amicus curiae briefs, CCR generally provides legal representation for people to begin cases.

This is consistent with the principles of responsive litigation, in that CCR litigates issues raised by clients, rather than using clients or amicus briefs to further its own plan. CCR's litigation is a combination of impact and responsive litigation. It uses impact litigation in the sense that it values the precedents it achieves through litigation as a resource for advocacy; in that it uses litigation as a political agenda setting tactic, and in that it will occasionally look for clients to litigate a particular issue.

CCR also practices responsive litigation in that it believes cases should arise from the concerns of activists and movements and should not be driven by lawyers; in that it values ad hoc tactics so as to be open to respond to events such as September 11th; and in that it uses cases as platforms and organising tools for activist work.

As at LDF and LCCRUL, CCR is aware that because the federal judiciary is generally resistant to domestic human rights arguments this endangers gains it makes through litigation. Its primary answer to this problem has been to try to influence Senate confirmation hearings of judicial appointments more strongly and to use community organising. It has, however, also looked at other fora for litigation, such as the Inter-American Commission on Human Rights and the courts of other countries.

Subsidiary Second Order Tactics

CCR's non-litigating activities can mainly be divided into community organising and lobbying, with a strong organizational bias towards community organising. Interestingly, as with LCCRUL, despite the fact that the volume of community organising that CCR does is actually much smaller than the volume of litigation, it has a strong cultural commitment to community organising. Community organising is important for CCR because, despite the reality of its legal focus, it sees itself as a human rights activist organization rather than a legal organization.

The centre of CCR's activist work is the Movement Support Resource Centre (MSCR). Through the MSCR, CCR attempts to develop formal and informal relations with activists and social movements. CCR provides its Offices as a meeting place under the auspices of MSCR to grassroots organizations and movements to discuss issues, network and explore possibilities of joint action. The main focus of MSCR is on police brutality and misconduct, but it also pursues other national and international issues. In this way CCR attempts to be connected to, and work with, social movements. CCR not only facilitates activism through MSCR, it also organises demonstrations in its own right, both on issues raised by activists and those raised by litigation.

CCR has problems obtaining resources for organising work and so few staff work in this area. On the other hand, it is easier for it to find resources for litigation. Ease of resource acquisition thus appears to play an important role in the amounts of different work that CCR does. Like LDF, CCR 'lobbies' in Congress, but only on a limited basis. It prefers not to call this work lobbying because of the penalties for combining litigating and lobbying in US tax law. The reason for limiting its lobbying is that it is not well connected there, and so, apart from confirmation hearings for judicial appointments, it does not see this work as particularly effective. Rather, it favours media and publication work in preference to lobbying. Like LDF, for its media work CCR hires outside media consultants.

Coalitions with other Organizations

Most of the connections that CCR maintains with other NGOs are ad hoc. It regularly attends meetings of the International Federation of Human Rights (FIDH) and several other INGOs, but this cooperation forms a small part of its overall work. Despite CCR's long record of litigating international human rights law in US courts, its international contacts are sparse and relatively new. It forms networks with other American DNGOs to share the costs of cases and swap ideas, but it does not actively take part in a permanent domestic human rights advocacy network. It seems that the majority of CCR's connections are with small groups and social movements that work on domestic human rights issues.

Planning

While CCR does long term planning, it also values being responsive to its environment and not being limited by fixed plans. Although it talks about having a plan for the coordination of its second order tactics, this is not a document or formula but rather a philosophical approach. This lower level of planning than at LDF or LCCRUL seems to be in line with its commitment to responsive litigation.

CCR combines second order tactics both sequentially and, in some cases, simultaneously. Often it will use a sequence of organising and doing educational work in a community before launching a case. Conversely, sometimes a case itself will lead to organising and education work. When tactics are used simultaneously, CCR tries to coordinate them, but it has found that a shortage of resources for organising often leads to coordination breakdowns. For individual tactics, CCR does not have plans, as it wants flexibility and responsiveness to the environment to be the hallmark of its third order tactics. Internally, it has a formal process for case approval. It does not, however, feel that this detracts from its flexibility. The approach of responsive litigation, which emphasises the ability to react to events, thus infuses virtually all of CCR's tactical approaches.

In conclusion, CCR's first order tactic of having a wide mandate has required it to limit the issues it will take up. The second order tactic of litigation in domestic courts has been successful because it has been innovative in subject matter, fora and legal norms used. This has been combined with a cultural commitment to political activism and community organising. The third order tactic for litigation combines impact and responsive litigation. The main drawback of this impact/responsive litigation as practiced by CCR appears to be its rejection of the planned use of cases to create political agendas.

This tends to cause CCR to simply to follow agendas already existing in social movements. For political activism the main tactic appears to be the organization of demonstrations, although it also appears to use forms of non-violent direct action. In terms of the need for legitimacy, as opposed to rational adaptation to the environment, like the other American case studies CCR shows a bias towards legitimacy. Also like the other American case studies, CCR appears to make the questionable assumption that the domestic courts are the decision-makers which have the principal power to decide the issues it is concerned with. Unlike the other American case studies, however, CCR seems to have made serious attempts to use international law and fora, and to adopt social movement organising techniques, so as to make use of other environmental opportunities.

It therefore conforms more closely to what the CTS would appear to recommend. It deviates from the CTS in that it has changed tactics to exploit new opportunities in its environment, but only to a limited degree. The reasons for this appear to be limiting factors such as local demands for legitimacy, structural rigidity and a narrow range of available resources. These factors appear to have restrained CCR from making effective use of its innovations in using international law and social movement organising techniques.

The American Case Studies–discussion and Analysis

The overwhelmingly dominant characteristic of the American case studies, which is acknowledged in the literature on American DNGOs, is a common focus on litigation in domestic courts as a second order tactic. The American case studies thus identify the federal judiciary as the primary decision-maker on domestic human rights issues in the American system. This is especially true of LDF, but also applies to LCCRUL and CCR.

The main reason for this focus seems to be the unusual conjunction of forces that led American DNGOs to have relative success in the US Supreme Court in the period between 1940 and 1980. This appears to have encouraged them to focus on the federal judiciary as if this conjunction of forces was permanent. Availability of resources; established areas of expertise and the need to gain legitimacy with funding sources and the public also seem to have played roles in causing the case studies to focus on the federal judiciary. The American case studies, because of detailed approaches such as impact and responsive litigation that are largely absent in Britain and Germany, in the opinion of the author have the most sophisticated third order tactics for the execution of litigation of all the case studies in this work. This sophistication, however, has not translated into effectiveness in litigation, but rather diminishing returns.

The reasons for this have been the appointment of unsympathetic Supreme Court justices, the proliferation of litigating organizations, public indifference to domestic human rights and the assault on domestic human rights law by conservative litigating organizations. There is less commonality between the first and third order tactics of the case studies. For first order tactics, LDF and LCCRUL both have a dual focus on the African-American community and racial discrimination, whereas CCR has a wider mandate that covers both the US Bill of Rights and Universal Declaration of Human Rights. Similarly, in the realm of third order tactics, LDF and LCCRUL both practice varieties of impact litigation, whereas CCR seems to combine elements of impact litigation and responsive litigation.

In addition, LCCRUL appears to use a form of 'impact lobbying', and CCR appears to use forms of direct action in its community organising. The CTS can be used not only to understand, but also to aid constructive critique of the tactics of the American case studies. In this regard it would seem to indicate that American DNGOs do two things to adapt to the current environment. Firstly, it would suggest that they should do a needs analysis of the type and severity of human rights violations occurring within their mandates. The data available to the author suggests that this does not occur in any meaningful way. CCR appears to perform best in this respect, but paradoxically does this by simply following agendas set by social movements. For LDF and LCCRUL, however, views about domestic human rights violations appear mostly to reflect situations that existed in the 1970s rather than the present. This suggests problems in these case studies that inhibit their adaptation to new patterns of human rights violations.

Secondly, because the contemporary situation seems to suggest difficulties in achieving results in the federal courts, the CTS would suggest that the American case studies should place greater focus on tactics other than litigation. The seeming current effectiveness of LCCRUL and CCR, compared to LDF, seems to be related to their greater cultural emphasis on alternatives to litigation. The use of international courts and institutions to put pressure on the US from the outside is one obvious possible response by the case studies to their environment that seems not as yet to have been properly explored.

The doubts expressed about these other tactics by the American case studies do not seem to correlate with the opportunity structure in the United States. Overall, on the basis of the data, the American case studies appear to have a marked preference for gaining legitimacy rather than seeking out new tactics to increase effectiveness in the way the CTS suggests. For domestic tactics, the CTS would suggest a shift to conducting more policy work, lobbying, publication, media work, coalition building with other DNGOs, and community organising.

As the threat of resource loss as a consequence of a DNGO shifting away from litigation seems a major barrier to change in second order tactics for the American case studies, a new attempt to get Congress to change the Internal Revenue Code to allow more lobbying and community organising would seem an obvious initial move.

If successful, the American case studies could then shift from being primarily litigating organizations to true civil rights advocacy organizations, building their tactical sophistication and capacities to execute these new tactics within a favourable legal structure. It might then be easier for the case studies to persuade donors to fund these other activities. The type of non-litigation tactics to which LCCRUL and CCR have a cultural commitment could then become a greater proportion of their work.

The CTS, this in turn should make them more effective. This does not mean that all these tactics should be executed within each DNGO. Coalitions of DNGOs could support the organization in the network which specialises in the tactic that is most useful at a particular time. This type of collaboration may be difficult to achieve in the short term, because it may require greater DNGO cooperation than seems to be generally shown by the American case studies. Nevertheless, such an arrangement may have significant resource and effectiveness advantages.

THE BRITISH CASE STUDIES

Justice

First Order Tactics

JUSTICE's first order tactics are unique in that its mandate is janus-faced. On the one hand the mandate is to reform the law generally, and on the other to promote compliance with human rights standards. The part of the mandate dealing with human rights is very broad, and largely leaves the question of where to intervene to second order tactical decisions.

In the past this mandate appears to have created the problem of JUSTICE taking on more issues than it can successfully handle. Its response has been to consciously rationalise the work it undertakes by creating specialised projects for certain issues, such as discrimination. This resembles CCR's creation of 'streams' of work to address a similar problem.

Dominant Second and Third Order Tactics

JUSTICE's second order tactics focus on lobbying/policy and education work, supplemented by third-party interventions in court cases. It thus appears to see Parliament as the decision-maker that has the power to decide issues it is interested in. JUSTICE is an example of tactical approach C, in that it focuses on lobbying and only occasionally litigates. Its third order tactic is to use its expertise in international human rights law and the Human Rights Act to make itself an attractive source of legal advice and education for the government and legal profession.

In the first of its two primary second order tactics, JUSTICE conducts a law related form of policy work and lobbying. This and education work make up the vast majority of JUSTICE's workload. Like an Attorney-General, it provides expert legal advice to government for use in policy formulation and execution. Thus, JUSTICE audits legislation for human rights compliance; issues briefings; publishes reports; gives evidence to Parliament and commissions legal opinions. The giving of expert legal advice by JUSTICE and the litigation by LCCRUL appear to perform the same 'function', in that both are used to alter the power balance of the bargaining relationship with government so that it favours the DNGO.

For domestic lobbying, JUSTICE does not have a full time lobbyist at Parliament. Consequently, it generally posts or e-mails its briefings etc to the MP or minister concerned. It focuses its efforts on the House of Lords, as, despite the non-democratic nature of the House, it finds that it gets a better reception and more genuine human rights review of legislation there. Similarly, in its European work, it does not have a permanent presence in Brussels or in Strasbourg; it merely presents its reports and briefings to the relevant body. Areas where it does policy work are: reform of the appointment procedures for English judges; the setting up of an English Human Rights

Commission; options for reforms of youth justice and improving human rights protections within the EU. In addition, it also reports to the UN on Britain's human rights compliance.

In the second of its second order tactics, JUSTICE undertakes education to socialise the legal profession and the civil service into human rights compliance. This work mainly consists of organising conferences and publishing information on human rights law. As part of this work, JUSTICE also gives human rights education to organizations such as the Lord Chancellors' Department, the Foreign Office and the Judicial Studies Board.

Supplementary Second Order Tactics

JUSTICE's supplemental second order tactic involves third party interventions in court cases. Until relatively recently JUSTICE was doing casework on miscarriage of justice and privacy cases. However, a decision was made that broad policy work and casework were mutually exclusive, and so casework was limited to third party interventions. JUSTICE favoured third party interventions because it saw them as requiring fewer resources than full court cases.

Before JUSTICE began to conduct third party interventions, the Public Law Project, another British DNGO, had been trying to encourage such interventions in English courts. It was largely unsuccessful, but it had done enough work to open the procedure for later use by JUSTICE. JUSTICE does five or six interventions a year in the higher British courts and the European Court of Human Rights. Formally, it uses the tactic to give objective legal opinions and to clarify the law, not to 'lobby' courts in the way that amicus curiae briefs are often said to be used in the US. In practice, however, JUSTICE appears to use third party interventions to develop the law in a similar manner to the way amicus curiae briefs are used by LDF.

Interventions are often done with the aid of barristers' chambers that JUSTICE collaborates with, or with other DNGOs. This has the benefits of sharing risks, resources and expertise, improving the chances of success and lessening the damage in the event of a loss. Amongst the issues that it has submitted third party interventions on are criminal sentencing; fair trial rights; privacy rights and immigration. The third party interventions made by JUSTICE appear similar to its advisory work on human rights law with the legal profession and civil service, in that it uses its expertise to influence policy development in the courts. JUSTICE's use of third party interventions typically comes at the end of a sequence of tactics.

It usually begins this sequence by researching a human rights problem and publishing materials on it. It then issues a report and follows this with a conference. This work is usually in turn followed by lobbying and policy work, third party interventions and, lastly, media work. Sometimes the sequence is varied, however, and third party interventions are made after, or during, the conference. This sequence suggests a global vision at JUSTICE of coordinating second order tactics to achieve rational adaptation to the environment, as suggested by the Comprehensive Tactical Stance.

Networks with other Organizations

JUSTICE is a member of a number of advocacy networks. Connection to international as opposed to domestic networks is a feature of JUSTICE's networking tactics. JUSTICE is the British section of the International Commission of Jurists (ICJ). The role of the ICJ, however, is mostly limited to providing JUSTICE with access to an international advocacy network.

As with most sections of the ICJ, the link between JUSTICE and the ICJ is more an instance of INGO/DNGO cooperation, than of the domestic presence of an INGO. JUSTICE and the ICJ also have different foci. Although the ICJ focuses on civil and political rights, it includes a significant amount of work on social rights, while JUSTICE does less work on social rights and focuses more on civil and political rights. The other main contact with an INGO that JUSTICE maintains is with Amnesty International, with whom it does some work on asylum.

Whereas JUSTICE's connections to ICJ and AI are permanent, its connections with DNGOs are ad hoc. JUSTICE has these ad hoc connections to Liberty; AIRE (Advice on Rights in Europe); the 1990 Trust and British Irish Rights Watch. Although its connections to these DNGOs are ad hoc, it does take them into consideration by trying not to duplicate their work. As a result, even without extensive contact with other DNGOs, JUSTICE has created a specialisation for itself in the domestic advocacy network.

Planning

JUSTICE rarely uses plans. No formal plans exist to cover individual tactics or their coordination. The informal practice of using tactics in sequence is the closest that JUSTICE comes to planning. This may be because planning is not seen by JUSTICE as essential to a policy dominated tactical stance. It may also be that the planning process is informal and merges with the methodology used to coordinate tactics. In conclusion, JUSTICE's first order tactical stance creates no limit on the human rights issues it could take up. Most of its self-imposed rationalisation of work is a result of second order tactical decisions.

The mandate covers general law reform work as well as human rights advocacy. JUSTICE's second order tactical stance exhibits a combination of educational work within the legal profession and civil service domestically, and policy work and lobbying both domestically and internationally. It appears that its assessment that Parliament and international institutions are where the power lies to influence the decisions it is interested in has been largely correct. Because its international work is largely seen as legitimate in

Britain, JUSTICE has been able to escape many demands for conformity to the local legal and political culture and thereby achieve greater rational adaptation to the environment. JUSTICE conforms to the Comprehensive Tactical Stance in its use of a sequence of tactics as a method of coordination, and in its taking advantage of international opportunities.

It appears to deviate from the CTS in allowing available resources to dictate tactics, rather than adapting resource acquisition to its tactical stance, in the small amount of planning it does, and in its quest for legitimacy sometimes overriding its rational adaptation to its environment. Overall, it would seem that JUSTICE conforms more closely to the CTS than the American case studies.

BIRW First Order Tactics

BIRW's first order tactic is to maintain a narrow mandate of promoting human rights with reference to the conflict in Northern Ireland. The mandate uniquely focuses on the conflict in Northern Ireland as an event, rather than on a geographical area, types of rights or a social group. BIRW's unofficial agenda is to protect civil and political rights, and not social rights.

BIRW's narrow mandate appears to have worked well, in that its work has been kept within defined limits. This mandate has also allowed it to gain the attention and support that a wider mandate may not have allowed.

Dominant Second and Third Order Tactics

BIRW's second order tactical stance focuses on international lobbying and acting as an advisor to lawyers on human rights, but also includes some third party interventions in cases at the European Court of Human Rights. It appears to see international bodies and the legal profession as where the power lies to influence decisions it is concerned with. BIRW thus hovers between tactical approaches C and D, in that it almost exclusively lobbies except for a few third party interventions. BIRW's third order tactic, as for JUSTICE, is to use its human rights law expertise to conduct law related lobbying.

The main difference is that most of BIRW's lobbying is international, because it has little faith in achieving results domestically. With regard to the first of the main second order tactics, BIRW socialises lawyers by giving them human rights legal advice. To do this, it refers callers to lawyers who have human rights expertise; advises lawyers on how to improve their third order tactics in litigation and encourages lawyers to go to the European Court of Human Rights. It is legal for BIRW to give advice on human rights law because British law allows lay legal advice in certain instances. In the past, British lawyers have not generally seen human rights as a profitable area of practice, and so have not built up an expertise in the area. BIRW tries to fill that gap for the Northern Ireland conflict. It attempts to alter how the legal profession influences policy development on human rights and Northern Ireland. In

Northern Ireland itself, this has translated into work on intimidation and assassination of human rights lawyers, and supporting their role in mobilising law in defence of human rights. In England, BIRW tries to catalyse the creation of a human rights bar so as to change the legal culture in favour of human rights on the issues it deals with. BIRW's lobbying focuses on international fora. It seems that the British government's traditionally more hostile response to human rights issues concerning Northern Ireland, as opposed to more general human rights issues, has caused BIRW to adopt a more international focus than JUSTICE. Originally, the British Ministry of Defence was very hostile, the Northern Ireland Department was predominantly Unionist and hostile, and the Lord Chancellor was very conservative in matters of human rights law.

A perception existed that because BIRW defended human rights in Northern Ireland, it was pro-Republican. It thus had few contacts with the UK government and more contacts with the Irish and United States governments. In recent times this has changed to a degree, and the British government recently added BIRW to the government consultation lists on Northern Ireland. BIRW's third order tactic is to employ a form of law related lobbying similar to that of JUSTICE, but primarily at the international level. Part of this involves lobbying foreign governments.

BIRW has testified several times before the US Congress on the conflict in Northern Ireland; it has daily contact with the Irish Department of Foreign Affairs and has influence with the Irish Prime Minister. The other part involves lobbying the United Nations. BIRW makes submissions to the United Nations Human Rights Committee and the United Nations Committee Against Torture when Britain's record is considered. It also makes representations to various special rapporteurs and thematic reporters of the United Nations Human Rights Commission, as well as to the UN High Commissioner for Human Rights. BIRW does not have consultative status with the UN. Rather, it uses the UN consultative status of the Committee on the Administration of Justice and the International Federation on Human Rights. Currently it does not do much lobbying before the British Parliament or the European Parliament, but it hopes to do more in each as the need arises. BIRW draws heavily on international advocacy networks to mobilize international law from multiple sites and put pressure on the British state from the outside.

Britain is a relatively good target for international pressure because of the extent to which its economy is dependent on international and European trade linked to adherence to human rights standards. This contrasts with the US, where international trade is less central to its economy. It thus seems more rational for BIRW to focus on international work than it is for the American case studies. The large Irish community in the US also helps BIRW put pressure on the British government through providing access to funds and to the US government.

Supplementary Second Order Tactics

BIRW's supplemental tactic, as for JUSTICE, consists of third party interventions. For BIRW, however, these are exclusively before the European Court of Human Rights. Normally, as with JUSTICE, BIRW conducts such interventions in collaboration with other DNGOs.

It is difficult to determine how BIRW chooses the issues to intervene on, but it is clear that there is no process of identifying issues in advance as occurs with impact litigation in America. Among the issues that BIRW has conducted third party interventions on are the right to life and the right to silence.

Networks with Other Organizations

BIRW maintains permanent contacts with INGOs. It acts as the eyes and ears of INGOs such as Amnesty International on issues in Northern Ireland, and catalyses other INGOs into action on issues when it feels it is necessary. As at JUSTICE, however, the coalitions BIRW enters into with DNGOs are more ad hoc. It is in daily phone contact with the Committee on the Administration of Justice, but has less contact with the Irish Council for Civil Liberties and Liberty. Overall, because BIRW is enmeshed in international advocacy networks, its links are closest with INGOs or the small number of DNGOs that are also part of such international networks.

Planning

BIRW does little planning, because it sees flexibility as an asset. This is firstly because the Northern Ireland peace process is unpredictable and inhibits long term planning. Secondly, this is because BIRW reacts to requests from others, and these cannot be predicted, and thirdly, it coordinates its work with other NGOs that are larger and more rigid. It cannot, therefore, demand that cooperation proceed just as to its own internal plans. Lastly, there is little planning because BIRW expects the peace process to succeed, and that at some point in the future it will cease to exist as an organization. One reason that larger NGOs see BIRW as an asset is that it is smaller and less rigid and can therefore react to new situations more quickly and flexibly.

BIRW is also an asset because of its location in London, which gives it proximity to contacts and immunity to the type of intimidation and assassination that human rights lawyers in Belfast have been subject to. In conclusion, in stark contrast to JUSTICE, BIRW has a very narrow mandate. In its second order tactics, it educates the legal profession domestically, and (mostly) lobbies and does policy work internationally. This approach is different to that of JUSTICE, in that BIRW does not focus on educating the civil service and has a much greater international focus. It seems that BIRW has been largely correct in seeing international bodies as being the decision-makers with the power to change the situation on issues it is concerned with. Lastly, BIRW and JUSTICE have the similar third order tactics of making themselves centres of human rights law expertise. They use this to influence policy and lobby such that they "bargain in the shadow" of the human rights law they expound.

BIRW largely conforms to the CTS, in that it appears to have identified the opportunities in its environment and adapted its tactics to exploit them. It has done this by acting more like an INGO than a DNGO and 'escaping' the domestic jurisdiction into the international sphere. This happened largely because of difficulties it had in gaining legitimacy in local legal and political cultures as a result of the issues it deals with. In the international sphere it has exploited environmental opportunities well and gained legitimacy from international society.

CAJ First Order Tactics

CAJ has a very wide mandate. This mandate, unlike at BIRW, is not focused on the conflict in Northern Ireland, but rather on making the UK government adhere to human rights standards in all of its Northern Ireland policies. Because it has such a wide mandate, CAJ appears to have had some problems with coordinating its work. As at CCR and JUSTICE, CAJ has recently rationalised its somewhat ad hoc agenda into the four specific areas of policing, criminal justice, emergency legislation and the protection of rights and equality.

Dominant Second and Third Order Tactics

As at BIRW, CAJ's overall tactical stance is dominated by international law related lobbying work similar to that of INGOs. It differs from BIRW and JUSTICE in placing a lower emphasis on educating the legal profession in human rights law. CAJ's primary second order tactic of international lobbying can be divided into a number of areas.

- Firstly, it makes statements to foreign governments such as to the US Congress.
- Secondly, it critiques the UK's periodic reports under various treaties before monitoring bodies such as the United Nations Human Rights Committee.
- Thirdly, it hosts visits by INGOs.

An example of this was the Lawyers' Committee for Human Rights' investigation into the deaths of Patrick Finucane and Rosemary Nelson. CAJ has hosted visits by Council of Europe organs such as the European Committee Against Torture as well as visits by various special rapporteurs of the UN Human Rights Commission. Lastly, CAJ has testified before international bodies such as the Organization for Security and Cooperation in Europe (OSCE) and the UN Human Rights Commission. CAJ does less domestic lobbying. This more minor commitment has included lobbying the British government on the implementation of the Good Friday Agreement, British administrative agencies and the British Prime Minister. Like BIRW, CAJ is able to feed and activate international networks effectively with information it possesses. It thus seems to identify international bodies and foreign governments as having the power to influence the issues it is interested in. CAJ's lobbying work has also included the brokering of agreements between the British and Irish governments, such as the agreement to appoint international judges to investigate six killings in Northern Ireland.

Supplementary Second Order Tactics

CAJ's most important supplemental tactic is to conduct test cases. It has eschewed the use of third party interventions, as used by JUSTICE, because Northern Ireland courts have been more restrictive than English courts in allowing third party interventions.

Traditionally CAJ has taken an unfavourable view of the British judiciary as lacking openness to human rights arguments. It has thus tried to avoid British courts as much as possible and has preferred the European Court of Human Rights. Even in the European Court of Human Rights, however, it has opted for the greater control offered by test cases compared to third party interventions. Because in the past litigation in domestic courts has led to violent reprisals in Northern Ireland, CAJ also has developed responses for support of staff when it is under threats of violence.

The passing of the Human Rights Act and the recommendations of the Criminal Justice Review for a more representative judiciary have encouraged CAJ to plan to do more domestic litigation. Its domestic cases to date have mainly been miscarriage of justice cases concerning murder trials. The cases before the European Court of Human Rights have mainly concerned violations of the right to life. CAJ's approach to litigation seems more similar to the American case studies than the other two British case studies, in that it focuses on the litigation of cases, rather than on third party interventions. Despite this similarity to the American case studies, however, CAJ still uses the standard British third order tactic of test case litigation. In addition to running test cases as a supplementary tactic, CAJ also responds to requests for information; appears on the media and organises lectures, seminars, conferences and events.

Networks with other Organizations

Like BIRW, CAJ maintains permanent connections with INGOs and ad hoc connections with DNGOs. It has regular contacts with the International League for Human Rights, Amnesty International and the Lawyers' Committee for Human Rights. The Lawyers' Committee helps CAJ with lobbying in Washington DC, and Amnesty helps with lobbying in London and Dublin. It also has some contact with Human Rights Watch and the International Commission of Jurists.

Among DNGOs, CAJ is close to Liberty and the Scottish Human Rights Centre, because they are also members of the International League for Human Rights. Under the umbrella of the League, these organizations and CAJ meet regularly to coordinate tactics. CAJ is also a member of a number of networks with other civil society organizations on specific issues. With the trade union UNISON, CAJ heads the Human Rights Consortium that campaigns for a Northern Ireland Bill of Rights and also co-convenes the Equality Coalition that works on combating discrimination. Like CCR, CAJ seems to have extensive connections with organizations in civil society, such as trade unions.

Planning

CAJ plans extensively. More than once a year the staff, executive and key members meet, often in retreats, to discuss strategy. There are also strategy meetings in each of CAJ's four areas of work approximately once a month. These strategy meetings lead to the production of written plans for future work. It appears that CAJ has long term formal plans both to coordinate all its second order tactics and for third order tactics.

These are regularly updated and deepened in the periodic tactical meetings. Unlike JUSTICE and BIRW, CAJ does not seem to value flexibility as much in the face of unpredictable events, and views lobbying and policy work with INGOs as capable of being planned. In conclusion, CAJ's wide mandate appears to have caused it trouble in the past and has led it to consciously rationalise the work it undertakes. When it uses second order tactic of international lobbying CAJ acts like an INGO in directly accessing international networks.

It seems to have correctly identified these international institutions and foreign governments as having the power to influence decisions concerning human rights in Northern Ireland. CAJ's litigation work focuses on test cases rather than third party interventions, because Northern Ireland law limits the opportunities for such interventions and because it prefers to more fully control cases it is involved in. Overall, despite differences in environmental opportunities in Northern Ireland and England, CAJ seems to have similar responses to its environment as the other British case studies. Also like these case studies it appears to largely conform to the CTS.

This may be because CAJ and the other British case studies share a 'style' of approaching tactics. As with BIRW, CAJ has focused on the most significant violations within its mandate and has adapted its tactics to the opportunities in the environment, which in the cases of boThengland and Northern Ireland are international. CAJ's extensive planning appears to have contributed to its rational response to the environment and its apparent conformity with the CTS. CAJ suggests that DNGOs in Northern Ireland, like those in England, can successfully focus on international work as a rational response to a relative lack of local opportunities.

The British Case Studies–Discussion and Analysis

Like the American case studies, the British case studies show evidence of a search for both rational adaptation to their environment and legitimacy in their local cultures. They seem to differ from the American ones, however, in that activities that are highly rationally adapted to their environment, such as using international advocacy networks, are also seen as legitimate in the local legal and political cultures.

The origins of this different situation for tactical decision-making in Britain appear to be historical and cultural. The spectacular early success of Amnesty International in mobilising international human rights law seems to have had a profound effect on both the international and domestic human rights networks in Britain. It appears to have made international human rights work legitimate and thus seen as highly 'professional'. It also seems to have led to greater network building between DNGOs and with INGOs. When coupled with the relatively weak civil liberties discourse in Britain and the slow 'invasion' of international human rights norms into the domestic jurisdiction, it is not hard to see how international work attracts funding and support. It appears that because of these historical factors the British case studies do not perceive themselves as human rights or civil rights law firms, as the American case studies do, but rather as policy catalysts for the civil service and Parliament.

The British case studies' self-identification thus appears to incline them to make different tactical decisions to those of the American case studies. The parts of the opportunity structure that seem to have influenced the decisions of the British case studies have been the doctrine of parliamentary sovereignty, a legal culture arguably resistant to ideas of legal human rights and a political culture sceptical of human rights. This combination of factors has restricted domestic opportunities for DNGOs.

In contrast, internationally the United Kingdom is a signatory to boTheuropean and global human rights treaties, the former of which can be the subject of binding judgments in the European Court of Human Rights. The United Kingdom generally champions human rights internationally and sits on most human rights bodies. The overall opportunity structure for British DNGOs thus points heavily to international work or, barring international work, to lobbying Parliament. The difference between JUSTICE, with its lobbying and educational work, and BIRW and CAJ with their international work, seem to revolve around the lack of support in the British Parliament for DNGO work on Northern Ireland issues as compared to other human rights issues. In contrast, the Northern Ireland conflict has a high profile in the US because of its Irish community. It also has a higher profile in the rest of the international community. BIRW and CAJ, compared to JUSTICE, thus appear to have less incentive to lobby Parliament and more incentive to work internationally. The British case studies generally conform to the

Comprehensive Tactical Stance. It seems plausible from other British DNGOs that the author is aware of that this conformity reflects the situation of British DNGOs generally. It also suggests that operating in this way may have increased their effectiveness and contributed to the pressure on the British government which led to the passing of the Human Rights Act and the increase in prominence of human rights in British foreign policy.

The only major deviation from the CTS by the British case studies seems to be the limited extent that they make use of the European Court of Justice's human rights jurisdiction. The use of EU law is a significant opportunity in the environment that the British case studies do not regularly exploit. As EU law is directly applicable in Britain this is puzzling. To the author, the answer to this puzzle appears to lie in the success they have had in the European Court of Human Rights; the legitimacy which has accrued to using this Court; and the lack of expertise within British DNGOs for going to the European Court of Justice.

THE GERMAN CASE STUDIES

HU First Order Tactics

Compared to the case studies, HU has an unusual first order tactical stance. Its mandate is both very abstract, using phrases such as "the free development of the personality", and is stated in different ways such as "democratisation" and "opposition to the authoritarian state". Because of this, its mandate has virtually no restraining effect on the issues it can pursue.

Unlike CCR, its work is not even rationalised into streams. It is essentially the members in HU's branches that define the agenda of the organization. The de facto effect of this has been to decentralise its first order tactics so that decisions are made by members and not by staff at the national headquarters. It appears to use this tactic because, unlike the US and British case studies, it is primarily a membership organization and thus must be attentive to its members' ideas on tactics.

Dominant Second and Third Order Tactics

HU's second order tactics focus both upon lobbying and an intellectual politics whose purpose is to influence governing elites. Its third order tactics differ extensively from those of the British and American case studies. The lobbying it does differs from that carried out by the British and American case studies in two important ways.

- Firstly, the lobbying uses legal rules less often and less directly.
- Secondly, it often conducts lobbying as part of a large and defined network called the Human Rights Forum (Forum Menschenrechte).

For intellectual politics, the third order tactic is to educate and socialise opinion-forming elites in the German political system. The aim is to alter the symbolic universe of key policy making elites to make them more responsive to human rights arguments. The hope is that the socialised membership will either end up governing or influencing the government. For socialising opinion-forming and governing elites, a very detailed third order tactical stance has developed. Local groups often employ small think tanks (Denkarbeit) to do their work and as long as HU as a whole approves, specialise in issues and take action themselves. Sometimes special working groups are also formed on particular topics. Generally, this approach seems to stress flexibility and the education of members. To do this socialising HU operates like a debating club. Issues are debated within the organization and positions agreed to. Press releases are issued and tracts published with the aim of engaging opinion forming elites and state institutions in debate. In contrast to the case studies, HU's primary method for influencing the decisions of the Federal Constitutional Court is not through litigation. Rather, it favours public criticism of Court decisions and engaging the President of the Court in public debate.

As a result of German political history and culture, this type of intellectual politics is seen as highly legitimate. Using this approach, HU engages in a wide array of issues including gay equality; the Kosovo War; the War on Terror; democracy on the Internet; discrimination against foreigners and legal rights of due process. Much of HU's lobbying is done through the Human Rights Forum. It also lobbies Parliament itself through politicians it trusts, politicians who are members or professional lobbyists. In addition, it advises Parliament on human rights questions–this advice, however, is almost exclusively on constitutional law and human rights policy rather than international human rights law.

Supplementary Second Order Tactics

HU's main subsidiary second order tactic is litigation. It becomes involved in such litigation in a number of ways. Firstly, it refers people who are looking for human rights legal advice to lawyers it has connections with. This informal network sometimes also supplies HU with lawyers or plaintiffs. More often, it uses its members in these roles in cases before the Federal Constitutional Court or the Federal Supreme Court (Bundesgerichtshof).

Lastly, under the constitutional methods of access to the Federal Constitutional Court, HU can get members of state parliaments or Federal Parliament who are HU members or sympathisers to bring cases before the Court. HU thus does not use any structure similar to a network of cooperating lawyers, as used by LDF, but rather generally relies on members and sympathisers. It facilitates not only the bringing of cases before the courts, but also before the Petition Committee of Parliament. This committee can make recommendations to Parliament to change laws and to take action on particular cases. Overall, HU's selection of cases and their execution seems less sophisticated than in the British or American case studies, as it does not appear to have a coordinated approach to rival planned litigation or test cases. It also appears to bring cases less frequently than they do. HU thus does not appear, in the style of impact litigation, to attempt to change the agenda of the Federal Constitutional Court through litigation. For the most part, litigation by HU is defensive rather than offensive. Where litigation is offensive, it is generally unplanned and focused on random issues.

Two of HU's most recent and prominent victories in the Federal Constitutional Court concerned the, from the point of human rights, minor issues of crucifixes in Bavarian schools, and differences in payment of members of Parliament. In contrast to the British case studies, the overwhelming majority of litigation by HU is domestic. Only occasionally has it taken cases to the European Court of Human Rights. The reason for this appears to be the legitimacy that the Federal Constitutional Court generally has in German legal and political culture compared to international fora. HU has a number of other important supplementary tactics. Every year, with other German DNGOs, it publishes the Basic Rights Report (Grundrechte-Report). This is the major non-governmental source of information for German citizens on human rights observance within Germany. It is published as a paperback and is available in most large German bookshops. A lesser subsidiary tactic that it uses is that, in conjunction with the Human Rights Forum, it hosts seminars on various topics. These seminars differ from those of the British case studies in that they are not for the legal profession or civil service, but for the public at large. In addition, HU awards the annual Fritz Bauer Prize to those who have most furthered human rights within Germany.

Networks with other Organizations

In contrast to the British case studies, HU forms ad hoc coalitions with INGOs, and permanent coalitions with DNGOs. It is thus heavily reliant on the domestic human rights network. The major domestic network it is a member of is the Human Rights Forum. The Forum was founded in 1994 as a result of German DNGO meetings in preparation for the 1993 World Conference on Human Rights in Vienna. To implement the Vienna Programme, it was felt that the human rights lobbying effort of DNGOs needed to be continuous, and that this required a new form of organization.

The Forum has forty-one member NGOs and is a lobbyist and a consultant to the German federal government on human rights issues. It is really neither an organization nor a network, but something in between. An example of this consulting work is the recent involvement of a working group of the Forum in the setting up of the German Human Rights Institute (a sort of Human Rights Commission). HU has been a member of the Forum Coordination Committee (which meets four or five times a year) since 1998. The Forum has not been without controversy, with two of its member NGOs leaving, but has generally improved the ability of German DNGOs to lobby Parliament and the Chancellor. In terms of international and regional coalition building, HU has received some criticism for not involving itself enough in the human rights questions of the European Union. Recently, it has moved to address this criticism by working harder on connections to various networks in Europe. This work has as its central concern the need for an EU Bill of Rights and the necessity of presenting human rights issues to the Union. Overall, however, HU still has more extensive networks domestically than internationally.

Planning

HU does not do much planning. It has neither a global plan for coordinating second order tactics nor specific plans for third order tactics. The reasons for this are its commitment to decentralisation, allowing branches to take up issues and set the agenda, and its desire to remain flexible enough to deal with new issues. As with choice of first order tactics, it appears that it is the fact that HU is a membership organization that dominates its attitude to planning. An important change in HU's environment, as the oldest domestic human rights DNGO in Germany, has been the recent proliferation of human rights DNGOs in Germany. As with the American case studies, this has led to competition for attention, which HU blames for inhibiting the effectiveness of German DNGOs. Its answer to this has been to build organizational structures to further cooperation among DNGOs, creating what it calls a rational information management tactic. The Human Rights Forum exemplifies this sort of structure. The existence of the Forum suggests that HU's approach to this subject may not be atypical of German DNGOs in general.

In conclusion, HU's first order tactics are based on its members' interests. It is thus not constrained by a formal mandate as the British and American case studies are. HU's uniqueness in this regard, however, may be exaggerated by the fact that the major membership human rights DNGOs in Britain and America could not be included as case studies. With regard to second order tactics, the tactic of socialising the German leftliberal political elite appears to perform an identical function, in the sense of the Functionalist School of Comparative Law, to human rights education of lawyers and civil servants by the British case studies. Both try to alter the symbolic universe of elites so as to make them more favourable to human rights.

It seems possible to the author, however, that HU has not correctly identified the left-liberal political elite as being secondary holders of power that can influence the primary decisionmakers on domestic human rights in Germany. In lobbying and policy work, both the use of the Human Rights Forum and the lesser direct use of legal rules in lobbying seem to distinguish HU from the case studies. As in Britain, HU's litigation is not frequent and is dominated by the policy work agenda. Unlike in Britain, however, HU does more domestic litigation than international litigation. The CTS casts doubt on the correctness of HU's tactics. As for the American case studies, HU often appears not to target the most severe violations in its environment and to privilege legitimacy over rational adaptation to the environment. An example of the latter is HU failing largely to take advantage of the international and European opportunities in its environment. Germany seems as vulnerable as Britain to international pressure, doing a great deal of international trade and having signed many human rights treaties, yet the lack of legitimacy of international work in the local culture and a lack of expertise in international work appear to have restrained HU from taking advantage of these opportunities. The CTS thus suggests that HU's lack of planning and its failure to exploit major opportunities in its environment means that its effectiveness could be significantly improved.

KGD First Order Tactics

In its literature KGD defines its mandate as being to encourage civil society's engagement in favour of human rights and the tracing of human rights violations to their sources in social structures. As at HU, this mandate is too abstract to constrain the work that can be undertaken and everyday practice hinges on the construction of the agenda. Because KGD does not have branches, its agenda is decided by the membership and staffas a whole.

KGD is unique among the case studies in this work in having a mandate that focuses not on any governmental institution or elite, but on the public at large. However, this tactical stance, despite its democratic credentials, does not seem to be very effective in addressing domestic human rights violations.

Dominant Second and Third Order Tactics

KGD's primary second order tactic is an intellectual politics carried out through publicity, publication and direct action. Generally KGD's work begins within its working groups. These working groups are set up on the request of two or three members and operate semi-independently, even though KGD financially supports them. In 2001 there were five or six working groups and they met two or three times a year, focusing on such issues as biotechnology, refugees and prisoners.

KGD sometimes uses its second order tactics in a rough sequence. When an issue is raised by a working group or by the staff, a policy is laid down (often in conjunction with interested social movements) for the whole organization and a press release issued. It then organises seminars and conferences on the issue that all interested parties can attend, and afterwards publishes appeals and objects in newspapers on the same subject. KGD's publicity tactics focus on the print media, rather than television or the Internet. It appears that this is because the staff 's resources and expertise lie in this area. As for publication, KGD publishes a wide range of pamphlets and small books. It also cooperates with other DNGOs, such as HU, in publishing the

Basic Rights Report. Officially, demonstrations are not organised by KGD itself. This is because of the fear that it will lose the tax-exempt status that it has in German law if it undertakes such activities Instead, KGD's members organise them as individuals. This approach is quite successful, despite the fact that KGD actively advocates the use of civil disobedience and publishes manuals on how to undertake it.

It is not clear whether this success has been because of the sophistication of KGD's legal approach, permissiveness by the authorities, or some combination of the two. Using demonstrations suits KGD's goals, which are to create a humanistic socialist society and to critique capitalist, and especially Neo-Liberal, social relations as structural causes of human rights violations. This is because using these tactics means that it is not obliged to compromise with what it would see as capitalist laws and political institutions. An example of this orientation is KGD's use of civil disobedience to challenge the expulsion of asylum seekers.

Supplementary Second Order Tactics

Litigation is amongst KGD's most rarely used subsidiary tactics. When it is used, it is almost always used defensively. An example of its use by KGD is the legal representation and fees that it gives to accused persons before the German courts. This activity is an extension of its work to protect the rights of prisoners and reform the criminal law.

A rare example of KGD's offensive use of litigation was an action it brought by KGD and other DNGOs against the German government, first in the Federal Constitutional Court and then the European Court of Human Rights, arguing that the participation of Germany in the Kosovo War was a violation of international and constitutional law. Trial and demonstration observation and reporting are carried out in much the same way as is done by INGOs. KGD often leads campaigns to change laws or practices that these observations lead it to believe are threats to domestic human rights standards. KGD lobbies both domestically and internationally. Domestically, the lobbying is mainly done in Parliament. One example of this was KGD e-mailing members of Parliament urging restraint in response to the terrorist attack in New York on September 11th 2001.

KGD also publishes the findings of, and occasionally lobbies, various UN Human Rights Committees. Overall, however, because it sees itself as an extraparliamentary organization, KGD does not have much to do with the German state or international organizations. KGD sees giving direct aid to victims of human rights violations as effective and an expression of solidarity. An example of this, outside of domestic human rights work, is an international programme KGD runs that takes children from the former Yugoslavia on holidays to the Adriatic coast. This programme also exemplifies the importance KGD places on peace as a human right.

Networks with Other Organizations

KGD has extensive relationships with DNGOs, but no relationships at all with INGOs. KGD was one of two organizations that left the Human Rights Forum. It did so because it felt that the Forum was too close to the state, and that too much work was involved for the advantage it obtained. It still has extensive contacts with the NGOs in the Forum, however, and is involved in collective projects with DNGOs that are members of the Forum such as the Basic Rights Report.

The largest advocacy network that KGD is connected to is that within the social movements, for which it is the 'head organization' on human rights. Connections to the peace movement; environmental movement; unemployed persons' movement; refugee rights movement; social rights movement and anti-Globalisation movement give it an immense network to draw upon outside of links to other DNGOs. On this basis, it is easy to see why KGD sees itself as a people's political organization rather than an NGO in the classic sense.

Although KGD has no links with INGOs, it has links with DNGOs in France and Britain. These links, however, are more personal and ad hoc than official and permanent. KGD is interested in international networking with DNGOs like itself, but has difficulty locating such organizations.

Planning

Like HU KGD does little planning, and appears to place a great deal of emphasis on flexibility. The closest it comes to such planning is when the Executive, Secretary and working groups combine into a working committee that meets two or three times a year and discusses and sets tactics. The ultimate reason for this lack of planning appears to be the fact that KGD is a membership organization and thus has its tactical decisions largely determined by its members' opinions or by social movements it works with.

Planning must also take account of the fact that the parties in Parliament are receptive to its work to varying degrees. The German Greens are far more receptive to KGD's work than the other parties, while the SPD and PDS lend support less often. KGD's first order tactics, as at HU, are largely determined by its members' interests. For second order tactics, publicity and publication are undertaken with a distinct emphasis on the traditional intellectual medium of print, with less attention paid to newer media. The focus of second order tactics on civil society as secondary holders of power with the ability to influence the primary decision-makers in government seems questionable to the author. Direct action and organising are undertaken indirectly so as to avoid legal problems. The major supplementary second order tactics are undertaken rarely, and mostly to defend individuals involved in the dominant second order tactics or to support those tactics. Despite its radical ideological nature, KGD's balance between legitimacy and rational adaptation to the environment is similar to HU's. Like HU it thus shows significant variation from what the CTS would suggest. Even in radical circles in Germany it appears that domestic work (even if it is different domestic work) has greater legitimacy than international work.

This failure to more closely conform to the CTS appears to have put KGD in a position where it is less effective than it could be, because it does not make use of new international and European opportunities within its opportunity structure, or even domestic opportunities such as litigation. This result is surprising given the extensive analysis that KGD has done of the effects of Globalisation on Germany.

GBM

First Order Tactics

GBM's first order tactical stance is simultaneously to protect the human rights of former citizens of East Germany as a minority, and generally to further social human rights within Germany. It thus resembles the dual focus on norms and groups shown by LDF. The main difference between the two approaches lies in the normative focus. GBM is focused on social rights whereas LDF focuses on civil and political rights.

Dominant Second and Third Order Tactics

GBM's dominant second order tactics are publication and lobbying. Its third order tactics for publication and media are to work within Germany, whereas there is a distinct European and international focus in its lobbying and litigation work. GBM appears to have a wide view of where power lies to influence the domestic human rights decisions it is interested in that includes the Federal Constitutional Court, the German Parliament, intellectual opinion in Germany and European and international courts and institutions. GBM's publication work is generally carried out in four ways. Firstly, it is carried out through the publication of White Books. These are volumes of documentation of alleged human rights violations in eastern Germany. Secondly, through the publication of "Icarus"–GBM's in-house journal. Thirdly, through the publication of information leaflets and fourthly, through publication of its web site. GBM's publications, unlike at KGD, focus on those intellectuals likely to read political material, and not on the general public or on decision makers. As at HU, it focuses on elites that construct public opinion and the symbolic universe in which discourse occurs. Although GBM claims to be concerned about the impact of its publications, its de facto focus seems to be on their intellectual quality.

Within Germany GBM lobbies both through the Human Rights Forum, of which it is a member, and in its own right. This lobbying is focused on the issue of pension inequalities between east and West Germany, and prosecutions of former GDR officials. In Parliament, GBM had some success in lobbying under the previous CDU government, but has had less success with the current SPD/Greens government. GBM will often combine its international and national lobbying. One common method of doing this is to get sympathetic members of Parliament to ask the government questions about international criticism of Germany resulting from GBM's international lobbying. Internationally and in Europe, GBM has successfully lobbied the European Parliament on the Berufsverbot; it has lobbied members of UNESCO; the ILO; the OSCE; as well as the UN Economic and Social Rights Committee during its reviews of Germany's periodic reports. GBM does not employ professional lobbyists, but because its membership includes former East German academics and diplomats, it has the expertise and time to carry out this work itself.

Supplementary Second Order Tactics

An important supplementary tactic for GBM is litigation. It practices litigation at both the national and international (or European) level, but focuses on the latter. GBM argues that concentration on international law was a tradition in East German law schools (and not West German ones) before unification. It also appears to trust international or European courts to be more unbiased than domestic courts. Despite this preference GBM (or the Society for Legal and Humanitarian Aid (GRH), which is a member of GBM as an organization), has taken many cases to the Federal Constitutional Court. It does not litigate these cases in its own name, but rather supplies human rights lawyers and money to plaintiffs it wishes to support.

The subjects of these cases cover most of the issues that GBM campaigns on, amongst which was a case brought against the Berufsverbot, and one on the constitutionality of pension laws affecting former East German citizens. GBM, however, has only had mixed success in this domestic litigation. More commonly, GBM supplies lawyers and money to take cases to the European Court of Human Rights. GBM claims to have been involved in more than fifty cases going to Strasbourg, having directly brought twenty of them. Among the prominent cases that it has been involved in at the European Court of Human Rights have been a case on the Berufsverbot, and the case on the prosecution of former East German leaders.

It has also brought a small number of cases before the European Court of Justice. Among the other procedures that GBM periodically uses are the Resolution 1503 procedure of the United Nations Human Rights Commission; complaints to the International Labour]Organization (ILO); as well as complaints to UNESCO and the UN Human Rights Committee. GBM's minor subsidiary tactics consist of awarding an annual human rights prize, organising cultural activities such as art exhibitions; working to establish a library of East German culture; creating an unofficial International War Crimes Tribunal for the War Against Yugoslavia; running study groups on East German culture and creating an alternative East German history forum.

Networks with Other Organizations

GBM is permanently connected to networks both domestically and internationally. Domestically GBM, like HU, is a member of the Human Rights Forum and uses it to aid its lobbying in Parliament. At the time of interview the President of GBM was also the head of the East German Council of Organizations (OKV), which is a network of twenty-three organizations with about half a million members that came together in 1992 to defend the interests of former East Germans.

GBM's network also includes unions, unemployed persons' groups and groups campaigning for social rights. GBM's international network is even more extensive. It includes the European Peace Forum; the International Action Centre in New York; the Race Foundation in the UK; the International Association of Democratic Lawyers; the Slavic League in Russia and the League of Anti-Fascists in the Balkans. It should be noted that GBM's network covers Eastern Europe, and that many of the organizations share its Neo-Marxist view of human rights.

Planning

GBM does a great deal of planning. It creates annual plans that govern how its second order tactics are combined and how third order tactics are conducted. These plans are written and, although there is some deviation from them in practice, they substantially guide activities in that year. The balance between adherence to the plan and deviation from it seems similar to that examined by Wasby with regard to impact litigation in America. In the future, in the light of the Kosovo War and the wars in Afghanistan and Iraq, GBM wants to focus planning for its work on the collective human right to peace. GBM's first order tactics resemble those of the American case studies in that there is a focus on both legal norms and a social group. GBM is unusual, however, in focusing on social rights. GBM's second order tactics concentrate on publication and lobbying, with only some attention given to litigation and cultural events etc. This pattern suggests that a combination of intellectual and technical expertise is available amongst GBM's members.

This combination of resources appears to have historical origins as GBM's membership is composed both of members of the GDR intellectual opposition and former GDR government officials. GBM's activities thus cover the whole spectrum set out in stage one from classic mobilization of law through to the use of the 'constitutive' power of law. GBM conforms more closely to the CTS than the other German case studies. In terms of the balance between the need for legitimacy and rational adaptation to the environment, it appears to favour rational adaptation to the environment. The reasons for this appear to be both the greater amount of international work that it does, allowing it to 'escape' domestic pressures for legitimacy to a degree, and the greater legitimacy of international work among its supporters and members. It also appears to do more domestic litigation than HU or KGD. The reason for this appears to be the support it is given by former GDR law professors. Overall, GBM appears to show some similarities to the British case studies in that international work seems to have improved its adaptation to the environment.

THE GERMAN CASE STUDIES: DISCUSSION AND ANALYSIS

The common theme of the German case studies seems to be one of human rights advocacy as the domain of the dissident political intellectual of continental European tradition. Each case study has different intellectual and political standpoints on human rights. The intellectuals of HU are left-liberal; the intellectuals of KGD are left-libertarian and the intellectuals of GBM are Neo-Marxist. Their criticism of human rights violations thus seems to have been absorbed into traditional forms of political critique to the point that a blurring occurs between human rights criticism of a regime and advocating the change of that regime.

The exception to this generalisation is GBM, as it is not just composed of intellectuals but also former GDR government officials that have technical abilities. This general pattern contrasts strongly with the American and British case studies, where lawyers or those with legal expertise typically fulfil this role. In terms of the analysis of the Functionalist School of Comparative Law, the dissident intellectuals of the German case studies and the lawyers or people with legal expertise in American and British studies appear to perform the same function of being the agents that mobilize the policy demands of human rights law in order to make them part of the internal discourse of governments.

The dominant tactic of the German case studies appears to be to gain superiority in the battle of ideas. Superiority in this battle is achieved through debate, both internally and externally, either in person or through publications. For them the battle is both over what human rights are and what priority they should have in government policy. This is done through general intellectual debate, rather than in a targeted way through publication or the media as in Britain and the US. Due to a certain culture of intellectual disapproval of technical knowledge and money, lobbying and litigation are not seen as priorities in themselves, but rather as methods of driving home the advantage of a dominance in the world of ideas.

The effect of superiority in the realm of ideas is seen indirectly to be dominance of the makers of public opinion. This is supposed to lead to socialisation of the state and other entities into human rights observance. Applying the Comprehensive Tactical Stance to this general tactical stance is revealing. It would suggest that there may be too great a reliance by the German case studies on elite intellectual opinion leading to better human rights observance. The German case studies do not appear to target the most promising opportunities in their environment for influencing decisions on domestic human rights. For the most part, other possible strategies such as litigation in the Federal Constitutional Court, which is increasingly important given the growing role that Court has in the German governmental system, are under-utilized. The main exception to this is GBM, which has former GDR officials in its ranks who have the expertise to execute other tactics, such as the diplomacy necessary for international lobbying or the legal expertise necessary for litigation.

To gain influence in Parliament, it is generally necessary to penetrate the party machines and through them gain influence over the committees. Each of the case studies works through specific political parties. For HU it is the SPD and Greens; for KGD the Greens, and for GBM it is the PDS and SPD. This, along with intellectual traditions in political ideology, seems to explain the ideological nature of the German case studies compared to the British and American ones. German political culture also seems to explain the focus of the German case studies on social rights–a focus usually ascribed to third world DNGOs, rather than western DNGOs. In summary, the German case studies (with the exception of GBM) seem constrained as much by aspects of German political and legal tradition as the American case studies were by such forces in America.

6

Transnational Advocacy and the Dalit Rights Movement

INTRODUCTION

October 2, 2006: The tension and excitement were palpable. Thousands of blue bandana-wearing youth shouted and waved their fists towards the sky from atop buses, rooftops, and the numerous teetering light-posts that dotted the divided thoroughfare. Crowds of revelers lined the street leading to the main entrance of the giant stupa—like structure that marked the spot in Nagpur City where in October of 1956 Dr. B.R. Ambedkar led one of human history's largest mass religious conversion ceremonies.

Like much in India, this celebratory atmosphere, in which people seemed to fill every crevice of available space, attacked all the senses. It was clear that many of the revelers were happy to be there—not simply to revere Ambedkar or his embrace of Buddhism, but to show that they existed; that they had a distinctly new identity; and that they could not be simply disregarded and de-legitimized.

Yet, it was also clear that this was a religious pilgrimage for many—a show of support for the deified bodhisattva Ambedkar and his important embrace of a socially engaged Buddhism aimed at the betterment of dalits. From an outsider's perspective the excitement and revelry of the crowd was only eclipsed by a veneer of social conflict. Across from the Dikshabhumi was a different kind of reveler, because October 2, 2006 was also the confluence of the start of a major Hindu festival, Divali and a national holiday, Gandhi Jayanti. While the tension between Ambedkar supporters and either those celebrating the beginning of Divali, or those celebrating the birth anniversary of M.K. Gandhi, could have easily risen to a level of violence, it did not on this auspicious day in Nagpur. The sacredness of the religious experience of a pilgrimage to Dikshabhumi seemed to trump secular disagreements that Ambedkar dalits in the crowd would surely share with their Hindu counterparts and/or supporters of Gandhi. This distinctly religious framing of an Ambedkar Buddhist identity, and interconnection of it with the social problematic of the caste system fits the Indian socio-political context well – a context where such distinctions are rarely made. But the absence of secular political voices in this crowd was stark, with religion holding all answers. Even to those shouting, blue bandana-wearing, youth, Buddhist flags and religious ritual seemed to hold sway over secular speeches or public signs of dalit organization and mobilization.

June 7, 2007: Cut to a hotel room in Sterling, Virginia, not far from Dulles International Airport. Seven dalit professionals conduct a meeting of a newly formed organization called DANRIA, converting a vacant fifth-floor hotel suite into a makeshift meeting space. DANRIA, The Dr. Ambedkar Non-Resident Indian Association, is a confederation of dalit Diaspora professionals that has just recently registered as a local NGO in Maryland. They are seeking to collaborate with others to bring development to dalit communities in India.

On this day they are meeting with a representative of the International Association for the Advancement of Dalits (IAAD) to plan for a proposed upcoming symposium on dalits to be held in Washington, D.C. This organization of Diaspora dalits is comprised of a neurosurgeon, a NASA scientist, The CEO and Founder of a Chain of Car Repair shops, an IT professional, and a number of academics from various theoretical disciplines. These are first-generation Indian Americans from all over India, yet they share the common identity as dalit. Such an identity shares similar narratives of caste discrimination, but not necessarily similar religious foundations or ideologies, which gives the group its fiercely secular character. While the idea of the "promotion of shared values" does come up during the meeting, these shared values are framed as strictly secular, underlining simply that each human has rights to pursue, whether vaguely articulated or not, a shared sense values.

One member even takes the opportunity to remind the inter-religious membership that DANRIA is a "strictly secular" organization and that he will leave if this reality changes. While there is an implicit knowledge of the dalit Sikh, Muslim, Buddhist, and Christian conversion movements in modern India among these DANRIA members, each of these movements' sacred import is clearly perceived as a secondary to the goal of dalit liberation or dalit human rights, which is broadly defined and seen as at hand. In other words, the need for a secular frame of human rights takes precedence, and provides a perceived legitimacy to these professionals' framing of dalit oppression. This strictly secular identity is seen as evolved from communal-based religious ideologies and, in turn, as a more effective vehicle for social change.

They represent the tendency among Ambedkar followers to make prescient either a religious or a secular narrative structure for achieving social justice, and then to highlight those aspects of Ambedkar's career and thinking which support this narrative structure. Neither is less legitimate than the other, but both problematize social justice in different ways, and thus articulate its desired advent differently. The religious narrative structure stresses the pious individual as a model for building a new community, while the secular emphasizes the individual's rights as the basis for modernizing dalit community. These different narrative structures can be seen best in the distinction between two meaningful words that have gained widespread usage among former 'untouchables' – 'dalit' versus 'bahujan'.

While divergent narrative structures—which tend towards either more religious or more secular expressions—lead to different ideal conceptions of the socially just society, they also complicate movements' attempts to mobilize for activism.

Scholars have been inattentive to these varying conceptions of social justice because frequently a community of speakers does not have a clearly-defined notion, and/or lacks the consensus or ability to express their projective vision of such an ideal concept as justice. However, what is most startling is that social actors are disempowered by such narrative confusion or hesitancy, not that they simply cannot articulate their confusion.

Social mobilization scholars often ignore the importance between either secular or religious narrative frames. To see justice from a multifaceted perspective— both one based on ensuring the realization of equity or balance and the other based on the creative possibilities which underpin any state of justice—requires a broad projective outlook. While many social movement theorists argue this difference focuses on movement's ideals and not what is 'real' or seen to be objectively understandable, the fact is to some social movements, such as those created by Ambedkar Buddhists, the religious narrative is all that they see as really real. Of course, in the practice of movement dynamics, like other social science phenomenon, the real and the ideal often become blurred. The result is that Ambedkar's followers proceed unawares of the fine implications of the divergent narrative structures they deploy.

Another important scholarly critique of such a secular-religious distinction comes from post-colonial theorists. Despite the fact that "the ultimate aim of postcolonial theories is to feed into some form of social activism for a more egalitarian society," such theories tend to deconstruct case study and theory-building about post-colonial social movements as 'always-already' lodged in Western hegemonic leaning and constructs. Thus, the post-colonial critique of drawing conclusions based on the that such dialectic constructs as secular and religious are Western and therefore value-laden with imperialist and/or individualistic homogenization of experience. Though such critique is valuable in questioning bias and presumptions, from a pragmatic perspective it hinders a movement's self-reflective and emancipatory potential. Ambedkarite social justice movements for the eradication of caste discrimination must overcome this post-colonial tendency in order to develop a pragmatic conception of social justice.

Despite a few attempts to point out the lack of a clearly defined notion of justice in social movements, few scholars have chosen to address the sticky business of understanding movements' efforts at conceptualizing social justice, or more broadly their own conceptions in relation to human rights. The scholarly dearth of research into social movements' social justice conceptions underscores both the complexity of defining justice, and, until recently, a sense that global interrelations were unimportant or unquantifiable.

In the case of Dalit rights, as activists have attempted to actualize their social justice conceptions which were previously blocked by their government, what Keck and Sikkink call a "boomerang pattern" gets created in which activists attempt to circumvent traditional channels by developing transnational ties and strategies. The global resources afforded by modernity have allowed new means to achieve social justice. But, do these new means portend new ends? My own study of Ambedkar Buddhists has shown that religiously-based social actors have been slow to realise these new ends Rinker.

As Ganguly has argued, what is needed to understand the caste system's encounter with modernity is an ability to "scrutinize hegemonic knowledge formations that frame our outlook on the world and tell most of us in South Asia that the caste system smacks of times past and is ingloriously retrogressive." To understand the recent proliferation of transnational dalit rights discourse, understanding movement narrative structures is a mandatory precursor. While religious-based movements for dalit rights, like their secular big brother before them, have begun to develop transnational linkages in recent years, social actors projecting religious-based narrative structures have had to work harder than their secular counterparts to tailor frame their message for specific audiences and supporters, both secular and religious. This becomes especially evident within an increasingly global environment in which justice concerns are no longer local. The modernist disdain for religion that is seen as traditionalist and identity-forming continues to be challenged in the marketplace of ideas, and in a spiritually inclined society, like India, the modernist thinking is loosing.

In such context, religion is understood for its instrumental and communal nature, which makes an outwardly religious narrative of individual attainment helpful in forging local community but also makes it more difficult to the success of a national or international movement. In India, the challenge to modernist ideas has been both successful and unwieldy—witness respectively the rise of the Hindutva politics of the 1990s; and the point counter-point and social contention over various anti-conversion laws. In the U.S. and the West, however, this challenge to modernism receives less traction, as for rational individualist westerners, religious frames of social justice seem more problematic. Such secular-religious dialectic cries for further analysis as global attempts to empower the voiceless gain strength and inclusive versus exclusive narratives of justice compete for both consumers and beneficiaries. Despite the confusion it is apparent that both religious-based and strictly secular movements have something to learn from each other and the narratives they deploy. Using narrative analysis methods to analyse the secular and religious narrative structures that dalit leaders employ, this research draws out the implications of the worldview frames of dalit activists from a multi-disciplinary conflict theory perspective. While this chapter extrapolates a narrative theory from exemplary cases of only three social movements narratives it does point to the centrality of narrative structures to social justice conceptions and foregrounds possible strategies and tactics of contention. The prevalent narrative apparent in the narrative structure of religiously-based movements focuses on overcoming victimization through the reclamation of one's identity upon conversion. This assumes a responsibility for action, which resides intrinsically within each individual.

The opposite and secular narrative, by focusing on the re-humanization of past victims, assumes there is a need to push the collective mentality to a tipping-point in which a rights regime can be adequately enforced. Highlighting the lack of analysis of this dialectic between religious and secular narratives of social justice within the Ambedkar movement, this research aims to develop a sense of shared values between those inclined towards particularly strict versions of these two opposing worldviews. Based on preliminary fieldwork such shared values do not yet exists, or at best only exist in small pockets of dalit activism and coordination. By privileging such shared values both a better understanding of dalit contention and a fulfillment of dalit rights movements' potential with best be achieved.

HISTORY OF DALIT ACTIVISM IN INDIA

The word dalit means broken or downtrodden in Sanskrit and was "used as far back as 1931 in journalistic writing". Popularized by Dr. B.R. Ambedkar in the 1920s and 30s, and later by the Dalit Panthers movement in the 1970s, the term became a new secular identity for millions of those formerly known as 'untouchables' in India. Today, modern dalit identity is in a discursive competition with various religious identities for control of between one-fourth and one-fifth of India's billion-person population, which is classified as scheduled caste (SC). The life and thought of Dr. B.R. Ambedkar, the father of dalit rights and assertion, as well as the modern Indian constitution, was foundational to this discursive competition, which can be clearly seen in the following quote from Gangadar Pantawane, the founding editor of of *Asmitadarsh*, a journal devoted to dalit literature:

- To me Dalit is not a caste. He is a man exploited by the social and economic traditions of this country. He does not believe in God, Rebirth, Soul, Holy Books teaching separatism, Fate and Heaven because they have made him a slave. He does believe in humanism. Dalit is a symbol of change and revolution.

Compared to the rhetorical calls by Trailokya Bauddha Mahasangha, Sahayak Gana (TBMSG) activists to work towards a time when "all India will be Buddhist," the quote provides a stark secular-focused contrast to Indian social activists' penchant for citing religious ideals in order to galvanize the identity of followers. Pantawane's conception privileges dalit as symbolic of a post-modern identity in which caste distinctions have become irrelevant.

Yet, it was the life and legacy of Dr. B.R. Ambedkar that laid the foundation for this competition to win the hearts and minds of dalits. As both a social reformer from within the government, and then later a cultural reformer from the outside, Dr. Ambedkar's life itself represented a balancing between these two, not incompatible, identities. While many people outside the Indian sub-continent are familiar with Mahatma Gandhi, few who live outside of India know much about Dr. Ambedkar, or about the movement he helped spawn.

Both his political significance as the foremost representative of the Mahar 'untouchable' community in Maharashtra, and the religious importance he played in changing the social identity and spiritual commitments of that particular community of dalits through a revival of Buddhism, are unrivaled throughout India's long historical development. Ambedkar's prolific legacy culminating in his chairmanship of the drafting of the Indian constitution, as well as his call to all former 'untouchables' to convert to Buddhism has made his continued influence among scheduled castes unrivaled. Though his life narrative is so compelling that Indians of all persuasions have appropriated his image, like other low-caste social reformers, both before and after him, Dr. Ambedkar struggled to create intra-caste bonds; bonds that were lacking even among the lowest of caste groupings who were divided and aggrieved.

Dr. Bhimrao Ramji Ambedkar, affectionately known by his followers as Babasaheb, overcame the cultural and economic impasses of being born an 'untouchable' Mahar, one of three lowest-caste segments of Maharashtra society, in late 19th Century Hindu-dominated India. Breaking through countless stereotypes, Ambedkar was taught early of the importance of education, and he used the social cleavages that the British administrative policy provided to transcend his socially prescribed role. Rising to the post of Law Minister in Nehru's first independent Indian cabinet, he was appointed chairman of the drafting committee for the new constitution. From this vantage point, Ambedkar was well-placed to destroy the legal foundations of the caste system, and in 1948 Ambedkar presented his draft of the Indian constitution, which was accepted a year later. In it can be seen Ambedkar's push to get social change codified legalistically.

This part of Ambedkar's legacy culminates in Article 17 of the Indian Constitution, which states:

- 'Untouchability' is abolished and its practice in any form is forbidden. The enforcement of any disability arising out of 'untouchability' shall be an offense punishable in accordance with the law.

But despite this important legal success, Dr. Ambedkar slowly began to realise that structural reform was only one means to his larger goal of social change in India. Increasingly frustrated that change was not coming to his people fast enough, he began to believe that social revolution was necessary, which could come only from actively critiquing the cultural structure of Hinduism, as opposed to attempting to change it from within.

Similar to later conflict resolution scholars, the trailblazing Ambedkar seemed to ask: "Will we contribute to harmony through conflict resolution, but do so at the cost of accepting the continuation of some injustice? Or should we pursue justice for a particular group, knowing that this pursuit may increase conflict rather than resolve it?" Gradually coming to believe the answer to these questions was a resounding commitment to pursue justice, Dr. Ambedkar began to focus more on societal rather than structural change. By organizing political parties, educating low-caste people, and agitating for change, Dr. Ambedkar pursued broad based change by re-conceiving the meaning of justice in society, not only its structures, but also its social realities.

Ambedkar's identity evolved throughout his life to one of social activist, and the evolution of his growth and thought can be seen clearly in his prolific writings. During the latter part of his career, Ambedkar increasingly began to see religion as a valuable means to realise change through socio-cultural critique. As an answer to his discontent with the structural violence imposed by the caste system, religion provided a vehicle to restructure social discourse and remake the foundational values of the social system— two important aims of legions of young dalit activists. It was also with a life-long desire to understand religion that Ambedkar conditioned his analysis of caste. Thus, by 1935, Ambedkar had decided that Hinduism was the root cause of the 'untouchable' problem and had resolved to change his religion as a result. This, he believed, was the best solution for the Mahar 'untouchables' that he now led.

Encouraging other 'untouchables' to join this cause:

- If you want to gain self-respect, change your religion.
- If you want to create a cooperative society, change your religion.
- If you want power, change your religion.
- If you want equality, change your religion.
- If you want independence, change your religion.
- If you want to make the world in which you live happy, change your religion

But Ambedkar saw religion as a social vehicle as much as others saw it for its soteriological commitments to explain life. For Ambedkar choice of religions was a means to social change in the present. By changing religious traditions he, as well as each individual, could change society. Thus, he waged a polemical and rhetorical war against Hinduism. Declaring Hinduism the root cause of dalit suffering Ambedkar challenged the orthodox beliefs of Indian culture head on, and was either reviled or loved for this audacity. These acts created support, criticism and fierce debate. Gandhi, upon hearing Ambedkar speak, was once said to have remarked, "religion is not like a horse or a cloak, which can be changed at will. It is a more integral part of one's self than one's own body".

Yet, while Gandhi criticized the idea of a choice in religion, Ambedkar studied all the world's faiths in order to find the one, which would best fit his 'untouchable' communities' needs. The act of choosing his religion was, for Ambedkar, the cement of a re-positioned identity which was both personal and collective. As the answer to many of the needs of his 'untouchable' community, it was an act of social protest and self-help rolled into one.

If his more outwardly social protests brought spite from Brahmins, his re-positioned identity as a Buddhist would bring him deification among his own 'untouchable' community—something he himself was said to be uncomfortable with. On October 14th, 1956, on the 2500th anniversary of the Buddha's Nirvana, Ambedkar led a mass conversion of 'untouchable' Hindus to Buddhism. This was the culminating act of his now re-positioned identity and in writing his own vows upon taking refuge Ambedkar ensured that he had created what some religious scholars have since called "neo-Buddhism". Through this re-positioned identity he legitimated a new social perspective and Buddhism happened to be a means to the end of creating a new worldview and social discourse. As the ultimate *upaya*, Buddhism itself was to give new hope and confidence to thousands of dalits. However, as Ambedkar died only six months after his controversial conversion, it is not completely clear what form of institutionalization his Buddhism would have taken. He nonetheless ignited a revitalization of Buddhism on the Indian sub-continent, inspiring many a social activist, and living up to his promise to not die a Hindu.

The above leadership narrative provides a common grounding for both secular and religiously inclined dalit rights activists. Yet, depending on the specifics of the story that is emphasized, one can see divergences in social movement organization. Two thousand plus years of caste discrimination has left a void in dalits' collective cultural identity, which Ambedkar attempted to fill. At the same time, future activists will continue to argue as to which void Ambedkar's narrative fills—a clarion call for secular rights or a human need for ultimate meaning? As Taylor, Bougie, and Caouette have argued, lack of a collective cultural identity is the most socially damaging and difficult to overcome aspect of a group's identity. It seems that Ambedkar's emphasis on the role of religion in society is an implicit acknowledgement of this argument and an attempt to reconstruct a new version of this collective cultural identiThe role of cultural collective identity is not merely for group members to have a shared cultural history. As we have argued, it is a stable reference group against which the individual engages positioning processes on an ongoing basis in order to develop a healthy personal identity. Ambedkar was a pragmatist, studying under John Dewey at Columbia University, eager to develop a healthy collective cultural identity for those he considered his people—the downtrodden of society. Religious narrative structures were used as a vehicle to attempt to re-deploy a self-aware collective cultural identity. But his use of both secular and religious narrative structure as a means is telling. Ambedkar had a modern understanding of religion, which emphasized that belief was not only about ends, but also a means of social interpretation.

He saw the wisdom of approaching social conflict from a position, which privileges neither simply religious nor secular explanations. Unfortunately, Ambedkar's Buddhist followers have failed to openly and fully explore the social and political resources of both the secular and religious narratives they have at their disposal. Despite the fact that Ambedkar dalit activists' discourse seems to strategically use one or the other these narrative structure—religious or secular—to support their cause and build support, an analysis of the social positions that each creates has been lacking.

Secular attempts to focus on Ambedkar's injunction to "educate, organize, agitate" have failed to see the added value that creating a new religious identity can bring to oppressed groups' aspirations, not to mention the added value religious institutions bring to attempts at mass mobilization. Similarly, religiously inclined converts to Buddhism have failed to realise that their religious rhetoric can be exclusionary. Though preaching an inclusive and voluntary belief system, converted dalits often fail to realise their emphasis on religious-based explanation sidelines broadbased rights-based opportunities for mobilization.

Further, each side of this spectrum of activism has seen the other side as problematic for maintaining their own base of support within the dalit community. In other words, followers of Ambedkar's religious narrative see secular rights talk as problematic since it relies too much on outside notions of liberty, democracy, fraternity, and agency while followers of Ambedkar's secular narrative see religious rhetoric as backward and pre-modern. In order to bridge these two narratives within the dalit rights movement their foundation, structures, and expressions have to be further explored and dissected, as both narratives provide important resources, which have the reach and impact all dalit activists desire.

SECULAR VERSUS RELIGIOUS ACTIVIST NARRATIVES

The religious narratives of dalit assertion focus on leaving the Hindu-fold, which is seen as the root cause of the dalit social condition. In doing so, the individual re-asserts him/her self and re-positions their identity as coming from a religiously converted worldview, as opposed to coming from a certain caste which is seen as a partitioning of society that has been too long sanctified by the hierarchical system now called Hinduism. As such, the religious framework of conversion as a means to social justice fosters a sort of dualistic identity among dalits by empowering dalits not only as newly self-reliant through the experience of conversion, but also as one that has been victimized in an all too recent past.

As Sen reminds us "the adversity of exclusion can be made to go hand in hand with the gifts of inclusion" but this fact should not deter us from seeing that the complexity of identity highlights the difficulty inherent in mobilizing people around "identity justice". In particular, the combination of liberation and victimization is problematic for mobilizing widespread international support. Conversion as the living out of theology's connection to praxis does not have the same universal appeal as a narrative structure which equates dalit rights with human rights.

Despite a new identity as Buddhist—or Sikh or Christian—the converted dalit cannot completely divorce him/her self from the psychological legacy and mobilizing power of past experiences of injustice. This dual identity has both advantages and disadvantages for newly converted dalits as they attempt to achieve social justice. Ever cognizant of which identity to engage when, Dalit Buddhist followers of Dr. Ambedkar must navigate an array of dalit aspirations by balancing secular pragmatism with the desire to create a religious community based on Buddhist values. The secular frame of social justice, by comparison, presents a more unified conception of dalit identity as first and foremost human.

While this more materialist perspective on social justice places Dr. B.R. Ambedkar near the end of a long line of important low-caste social thinkers, it also downplays any religious proclivities as subordinate to secular humanism. Simultaneously, this secular frame presents a belief that the problems of dalits can only be cured with the help of the unified action of outside intervention, advocacy, and political agitation, taking the onus for change off the individual and placing it on the collective. From this view, the root causes of a lack of social justice, as contextual and unchangeable by any one individual, are confused by any attempt to focus attention on any sacred ultimate. It is as if religious commitments appear as anathema to those strict adherents of the secular rights frame.

It is therefore, assumed from this secular perspective that the root causes of a lack of social justice must be approached from a religiously neutral position of secular re-humanization of the oppressed. As a consequence the concepts of reconciliation and healing are often overlooked by these secular humanists in a rush to realise the equitable society. In addition, the secular activists adherents' post-enlightenment aversion to religious discourse seems to run counter to the local cultural norms and history. Religion as a constituent part of the South Asian historical and cultural milieu is de-emphasized in favour of a perspective of global interdependence.

SECULAR NARRATIVE OF DALIT ACTIVISM: THE CREATION OF A TRANSNATIONAL VOICE

The secular narrative and social position of dalits as oppressed victim predominates among dalit social actors partly because of the slow, but steady, success of this narrative structure's ability to build transnational support and advocacy networks. Bob argues convincingly that "organizing" and "rhetorical" changes among dalit activists led to increased success of a dalit rights as human rights frame of contention in the late 1990s.

But what has this increased reliance on a narrative structure of victimization cost the dalit rights cause? As Polletta explicitly argues: while "personal stories chip away at the public indifference" and "elicit sympathy on the part of the powerful," it is also evident that "narrative comes with risks as well as benefits". While the secular narrative structure has allowed activists to conflate dalit rights with human rights, it has also disempowered many religiously inclined dalits through its aversion to religious language and frames. Further, since transnational advocacy often does not respond effectively to local needs, many disenfranchised dalits are turned off by a secular approach to organizing that sees personal belief systems as irrelevant to mobilization success. In short, there is a cultural divide between Western post-enlightenment rights thinking and traditional thoughts rooted in local contexts that value ritualistic and institutional expressions of culture.

This is not to say that the dialectic between secular versus religious narratives can be explained simply by arguing that a post-colonial clash of civilizations or cultures is either the genesis of the divergence, or the solution to unifying these different worldviews. Rather, noticing this cultural divide does signal the risky footing one stands on if advocating either a strongly secular narrative structure to combat caste or a strongly religious one.

As Ganguly concisely puts it: "The modernizing desire to first reify caste as a relic of times past, and then to annihilate it, is truly alive and well". This secular bias away from the traditional is neither the best nor most effective way to create social change. Instead, it often leads to sensational excitement outside of India, while faltering in the local context. The bias among secular dalit rights organizations, which disregard the conversion perspective so prevalent among Indian Ambedkarite Buddhists, serves as a case in point. During the recent, and first ever in the Unites States, Dalit Studies conference, an academic panel on the "Paradox of Religion" failed to raise this issue of religion's relation to traditional manners of thought, much less address the dalit rights movement from a perspective that privileges religious conversion as a crucial factor in the identity of low-caste groups. Beyond the academic community, however, a secular rights-based focus also creates a number of limitations and paradoxes for activists. DANRIA, the organization portrayed in the second short vignette that began this piece provides a prime example of the dialectical problems that secular activists face in approaching their religiously-grounded counterparts. The DANRIA leaders desire to engage Ambedkar Buddhists, but within a frame of the strictly secular. At a DANRIA planning meeting in May 2007 Ambedkar Buddhist representatives from the TBMSG attempted to develop linkages with the work and resources of DANRIA members, and DANRIA members continually made it clear that their work was to support secular dalit education and empowerment. Partly due to how religion is understood in a postreformation West, such interactions revolve around a judgment that equates support for religious-based organizations as support for the propagation of that religion. It is the old stigma of religious proselytization; no matter what good work an organization may be doing it must always be scrutinized upon the backdrop of its religious commitments and the assumed privileged priority of those commitments. In this dance of assumptions and commitments, Ambedkar Buddhists try to re-frame their contention to fit the desires of secular activists, while secular activists assume religious organizations' exclusive goals and under-estimate their ability and opportunities to mobilize.

Secular narrative structures of dalit contention present benefits to go along with the limitations, which they pose. They bring pragmatism to an often-disorganized array of activist decisions and goals. Through an unequivocal support for humanity and secular humanism these narrative structures provide grounding for international mobilization which bridges religious and cultural difference. The International Commission for Dalit Rights' (ICRD's) mission statement demonstrates this tendency to both symbolically and pragmatically bridge these aspects of difference within the dalit movement: "Eliminating rights-based human need and fulfilling freedom and democracy is necessary to achieve effective national and global development policies and programmes, and to alleviate discrimination and extreme poverty."

Sufficiently secular such a statement allows for the possibility of religious responses to lack of freedom, discrimination and poverty. In place of a strong religious commitment, the secular narratives that such organizations profess, are often founded on an enduring faith in ideology. In interviewing Chadra Bhan Prasad, the only dalit writer for a major Indian weekly and a dalit rights activist who tends towards the secular end of the dalit movement's narrative structure, it was immediately evident that he was not even familiar with TBMSG, one of the major purveyors of the religious narrative of Ambedkar and dalit rights in Maharashtra.

Though at first surprising, this observation seems more understandable given that Prasad, a native of Uttar Pradesh who is based in Delhi, is a strictly secular Ambedkarite who sees Ambedkar upon the backdrop of a Marxist analytical ideology of change. Now arguing that capitalism is the only thing that will save the dalit, Prasad draws an interesting comparison to the Ambedkar Buddhist activists of the TBMSG who see the solution for dalits as coming through the dharma.

This secular narrative structure implies that religious commitment can be sidelined in favour of an underlying, and more basic, commitment to humanism—an assumption, which runs deep in the dalit rights movement. One ICRD dalit activist even stated: "Despite the fact that many different dalit groups employ different strategies, our goal is the same." The idea that dalit activists' deploy diverging strategies despite common goals posits not only that dalit activists have one collective identity, but also that this collective's social justice concerns are all the same. Such broad assumptions, however, limit the effectiveness of dalit organizations by disempowering the potential to reflect on real difference.

RELIGIOUS NARRATIVES AND DALIT ACTIVISM: ARE THEY RELIGIOUS OR DO THEY USE RELIGION AS AN IDENTITY WEDGE?

Mangesh's sincerity and commitment to social justice through building a peaceful community in which everyone has the ability to reach their potential, is not simply lipservice to a vague altruism—it is lived. His Buddhism is more humanistic than sectarian or scriptural; more philosophical than overtly spiritual. Yet, the inclusiveness of the TBMSG family of organizations is not simply an expression of pragmatism. The members who carry the mantel of the TBMSG movement are, first and foremost, believers in dharmadatu and this belief provides philosophical grounding for an egalitarian social prescription aimed at redefining karma in the Indian society as scientific and not supernatural. As an Indian, but humanist above all else, Mangesh is representative of a young generation of modern Indians who are both newly curious about the world outside of India and armed with the means to explore it. Eager to integrate Western political ideals, such as rights discourse, with Eastern conceptions of the examined life, these modern Ambedkar Buddhist activists see themselves as "the fruit of the movement." In other words, the beneficiaries of their parents' conversion and insistence on following both, their father and mother's example as well as Ambedkar's call to education.

Mangesh believes full-heartedly that focusing on inner change is a priori to attempt at social justice and peace-building. Therefore, teachings of the practice of Buddhism are crucial to the community that he aims to assist. This is a rational, not spiritual belief and the Buddha—from the Ambedkar Buddhist perspective—provided guiding principles to achieve inner change. Yet, this insistence on rationalism and pragmatism is where a certain bias threatens to stunt the full potential of the TBMSG movement. The symbolic use by movement members of ritual and stories can, and does, get lost when a rational problem-solving approach to the world is privileged. This is not to say that Mangesh's commitment to social change is weak or even unjustified by experience, but rather that a combination of both inner and outer change can be problematic. Exclusively focusing on rational approaches to problems solving can limit TBMSG's ability to affect lasting change of the local level; while a focus on inner-change marginalizes strong believers in other religious and normative systems and simultaneously decelerates the pragmatic realization of TBMSG's wider social justice ideal. That sustainable social change can only come with inner-change may be a truism, but it also places limits on TBMSG appeal and deftness to claim secular support or argue for symbolic senses of meaning. This poses a number of pragmatic problems for the movement, illustrated by the re-constructed narratives above.

For one the narrative represents a normative assumption that rationality always explains moral justifications. Mangesh's positioning of Ambedkar Buddhists as consistent believers in scientific processes—while exposing the rational assumptions involved in narrating justice—also acts as an attempt to justify a moral stance via delegitimizing the other. MacIntyre would label such a process as falling within "the When men and women identify what are in fact their partial and particular causes too easily and too completely with the cause of some universal principle, they usually behave worse than they would otherwise do. In reference to this particular narrative, it is not presumed here that it engenders bad behaviour among movement members, but rather that it misses an important realization of the potential for destructive behaviour created by the identity it enforces. Positioning Ambedkar Buddhists as rational humanists and all Hindus as superstitious anti-rationalists only concerned with pleasing the gods, Mangesh is unconcerned with his own moral denigration of the other and the processes of positioning this type of delegitimization models to others.

Mangesh's ascription of un-scientific characteristics to others that are associated with under-education, or lack of intelligence, positions Ambedkar Buddhists as freed from the fear of superstition through education and Buddhist practice. This freedom is seen as liberating not only in the sense of being based on methodological reliability, but also in a sense creating an epistemological freedom. Furthermore, Mangesh's own relived experiences of this anti-rationalist thinking provide an emotional energy which legitimizes Mangesh's speech. Paying attention to the uses and processes of social positioning within Mangesh's attack on fundamentalist Hindus as superstitious provides a means to understand the TBMSG social justice narrative upon a spectrum of interconnected meanings.

Coming in the context of Mangesh's description of Ambedkar's sociological analysis of the caste system, this narrative transcription exhibits an opposition between rational and ideal conceptions which is immediately apparent in line one. Positioning Ambedkar as opposed to any ideal system based on scripture, Mangesh develops the image of Ambedkar as an egalitarian freedom fighter. The ideological other becomes the antithesis to actualizing liberty, fraternity, and equality. More than simply pejoratively categorizing mythical or idealistic social constructions, privileging the rational as normatively more valuable and as implicitly congruent with equality has the effect of positioning the superstitious as irrelevant and un-democratic. Anti-rationalists are thereby equated with anti-democracy's proponents, while simple-minded ideologues are de-legitimized.

Invoking Gandhi in line 9, Mangesh is drawing attention to the unacknowledged role of Ambedkar in the independence movement; yet at the same time branding Gandhi as advocates of future aspirations ungrounded in reality. Such utterance implies that if these future aspirations are ungrounded in reality, then they are bound to produce unjust social relations and structures. By contrast, the TBMSG ideal is grounded in a scientific methodology, which is attainable from a pragmatic view. Unaware of the full spectrum of needs in society these Gandhians are utopian thinkers with little by way of concrete analysis and/or proscription for creating their utopia. In citing examples like Rama Raj and test-tube babies Mangesh is essentializing all Hindus as superstitious—equating Gandhi followers with Hindutva nationalists or extreme fundamentalists.

Though subtle this positioning process is intentional. Creating a sense of us versus them such crude associations have the effect of reinforcing a TBMSG belief in social uplift through the personal empowerment of education and Buddhist practice. In the context of this speech act, Mangesh is positioning himself and his movement as the original purveyors of Indian democracy and scientific rationalism. To an audience of foreigners, the Ambedkar Buddhist is positioned as providing a logical method for explaining the world and therefore proscribing change; while the Hindu is the cause of the stereotypical view of India as nonsensical and mystical, thus making them incapable of instituting equitable change. Nuanced and multi-faceted, Mangesh's narrative holds multiple levels of meaning, aspects which are often overlooked by both movement members and outsiders.

On the deepest level this transcribed narrative is an attempt to position Hindus as falling outside the Western scientific community—as pre-modern and mythical in their worldview. But as Cassirer has argued "mythical and verbal thought are interwoven in everyway". Only through metaphor, Cassirer argues, is one able to see the "unity" and "difference" of the verbal and mythical worlds. In line 22, Mangesh uses an evolutionary metaphor, "the big fish ate the small fish," to explain the Hindu justification for caste.

This metaphor is then discredited as "a very crude form of social Darwinism". Since social Darwinism has a negative connotation, the use of this metaphor is aimed at further discrediting the non-rational un-methodological approach of the other. It provides another example of caste Hindus attempts to justify the inequities of the Indian social system as having a rational basis, but by de-legitimizing it as social Darwinism Mangesh re-positions the view as un-scientific and a-historical. In cycling through orienting the listener, developing complicating actions and evaluating the situation, Mangesh is positioning unscientific culture as detrimental to society and an Ambedkarite re-structuring of society as the only prescription able to correct this flaw. This has the dual effect of legitimizing secular humanism and Buddhist practice. Therefore, only through seeing the failure of current social constructs can change become possible and an Ambedkar Buddhist analysis provides the best lens to identify this failure.

In this context, it is also insightful to return to this narrative paying close attention to pauses and other aspects of speech processes in Mangesh's talk. Such analysis not only tells us more about the speaker, but also about the "reflection-in-action" aspects of scripting the talk to his specific audience. Speaking in English is harder than speaking in his native Marathi dialogue and periods of pause are undoubtedly periods of actively choosing specific words and word phrases suitable for the context and the audience.

Invoking Gandhi in line 9—a well-known figure to the American audience—provides a means to understand Mangesh's own identity as inter-related with his minority sense of nationalism. After debunking the ideal of the Rama Raj, Mangesh—having equated this idea with the father of Indian nationalism—seems to stumble in finding an adequate example to illustrate the superstitious nature of the castebased ideal, which underpins this idea. Interestingly, the majority of the long pauses in the transcript which appears above come between lines 11 and 20/21. In these lines Mangesh is jumping between various examples to orient the listener and provide evaluative statements in order to develop a complicating action these listeners can clearly understand.

In setting up the Hindu nationalist ideal—exemplified by the well-known personage of Gandhi—Mangesh then challenges this ideal as scientifically ungrounded and superstitious and casts the work of TBMSG as attempting "to challenge those ideas, the 'so-called' religious ideas". Essentializing the idea as ideal, he struggles to find adequate language to express these ideas. Forced to explain through example and analogy, Mangesh invokes a traditional ideal, a modern discovery, and a scientific theory as tools to expose the injustice of an irrational social stratification system. His pauses represent rhetorical reassessments of his context and audience, providing a passion and gravity to his speech that mere words could not accomplish. From a Lobovian perspective these pauses represent the struggle to adequately express evaluative statements: of the 10 lines between 11 and 21 five are evaluative statements. The prosody of these lines adds legitimacy to his evaluative statements and helps to play on the Western scientific worldview.

There is nonetheless a sort of revivalist, or anti-modern, element within TBMSG movement narratives. Though they are harkening for a modern scientific worldview, they are also invoking a revival of anti-traditionalist tendencies within the Indian society. Embracing modernity and technology,

TBMSG always draws its' narrative back to the historical Buddha—placing the genesis of their thought in a time of antiquity. Such a recourse to an idealized past can be very effective in mobilizing support, as many religious movements have noticed. In this sense, TBMSG's approach is not revolutionary. Notwithstanding, Mangesh's words, as well as the processes through which they evolve into a narrative construct, provide a window into the identity and sense on injustice that TBMSG members feel. By recourse to a constructed past ideal and an unrealised future implementation of that ideal, such speech acts are the foundation of the TBMSG movement. Simultaneously alienating and cohesive, such speech acts provide the foundation for a reconstructed identity that is coextensive with a sense of injustice. The reconstructed identity acts as a means to express injustice.

THE FUTURE OF DALIT ACTIVISM: MIXING OF LOCAL/TRANSNATIONAL STRATEGIES WITH RELIGIOUS/SECULAR GOALS

Inherent in the promise of these two worldviews is a sort of grounded pragmatism. The mobilization experience, social networks, and common purpose of religious activists, is something that secular dalit right activists can and must tap into. Conversely, the rightsbased language of secular dalit rights activists can provide social justice ends that are less ambiguous than the rigorous spiritual practice of individual self-attainment. The following reaction to the celebratory Buddhist conversions of October 2, 2006 by a keen observer of the Ambedkar movement underscores the issues at stake when this connection between secular and religious narrative structures goes unattended and unanalysed:

- '*What do they mean*: All India will become Buddhist?... These people *need to* live in a world with Muslims and Hindus and all the rest. Dr. Ambedkar wanted to reconstruct the Buddhist tradition so it met the needs of his time. But can the Ambedkarites do the same with Ambedkar's own ideas? Nagaloka should be teaching comparative religion... They need to say what they are for, and leave aside what they are against.'28

The seeming incongruence of dalit identities as either victim or as self-aware Buddhist leaves conceptions of social justice, citizenship, and community vague and unbounded. Hence this lack of balance cries for a syncretism between these often competing narrative frames of social justice—an integrated religious/secular focus on individual rights that does not overlook the importance of individuals' spiritual worldview in creating social justice. As dalit activists strive for a society open to pluralist ideals they must practice pluralism in the narrative constructions that they deploy. Such a mix of transnational and local strategies for contention redefines the transnational and highlights the need to critically analyse the role of such activists' narratives in the wider global society.

7

Dalit Rights: Violence and Sexual Assault

INTRODUCTION

Vulnerably positioned at the bottom of India's caste, class and gender hierarchies, Dalit women experience endemic gender-and-caste discrimination and violence as the outcome of severely imbalanced social, economic and political power equations. Their socio-economic vulnerability and lack of political voice, when combined with the dominant risk factors of being Dalit and female, increase their exposure to potentially violent situations while simultaneously reducing their ability to escape.

Violence against Dalit women presents clear evidence of widespread exploitation and discrimination against these women subordinated in terms of power relations to men in a patriarchal society, as also against their communities based on caste. As the National Commission for Women has commented, "in the commission of offences against... scheduled caste Dalit women the offenders try to establish their authority and humiliate the community by subjecting their women to indecent and inhuman treatment, including sexual assault, parading naked, using filthy language, etc." Hence, violence, which serves as a crucial social mechanism to maintain Dalit women's subordinate position in society, is the core outcome of gender-based inequalities shaped and intensified by the caste system.

This situation exists in India today despite constitutional guarantees of non-discrimination on the basis of caste and gender *(Article 15(1))*, the right to life and security of life *(Article 21)* and the constitutional directive to specifically protect Dalits from social injustice and all forms of exploitation *(Article 46)*. Moreover, the Indian State has enacted a series of laws protecting the rights of Dalits and women, acknowledging the prevalence of discrimination and violence against these sections of society. A key law in this regard is the *Scheduled Castes/ Scheduled Tribes (Prevention of Atrocities) Act 1989*. The presence of laws, however, without concomitant implementation to ensure personal security to Dalit women, and without concerted efforts to emancipate the Dalit community and eradiate entrenched gender-and-caste biased notions of inequality and injustice, is not enough.

The Indian government has itself acknowledged that the institutional forces – caste, class, community and family – arraigned against women's equal rights are powerful and shape people's mindsets to accept pervasive gender inequality. If human rights are the legitimation of human needs, then the needs of Dalit women for personal security, socio-economic development and social justice are priority areas for intervention.

In order to understand, therefore, the reality of Indian society in general, and the Dalit community and Dalit women in particular, an analysis of caste-class-gender dynamics is imperative. It is only by adopting this three-fold lens focusing on the cultural and material dimensions of the intersection of gender and caste discrimination that a true comprehension of key social relations and social inequalities in India emerges. This analytical lens, grounded in Dalit women's subjective experiences, highlights how these women become instruments through which the social system replicates itself and systemic inequality is maintained: violence against Dalit women is systematically utilised to deny them opportunities, choices and freedoms at multiple levels, undermining not only Dalit women's dignity and self-respect, but also their right to development. An intersectional casteclass- gender analysis also fulfils the need to make Dalit women visible to the public eye through exposing their reality of violence and disempowerment intrinsically related to their social position, in recognition of their selfhood and human dignity.

Moreover, analysing these social relations which convert "difference" into systemic oppression and violence enables not only policy makers, but also women's movements and Dalit movements, to better strategise and implement policies and programmes towards the protection of Dalit women's rights: that is, programmes that facilitate wider processes of change, that ensure the comprehensive eradication of caste and gender discrimination and violence, and enable Dalit women to be mainstreamed into the planned development process in India. At the international level, examining patterns of violence against Dalit women can contribute towards an enhanced human rights understanding of racial and gender discrimination, as interacting factors perpetuating violence against racialised and often marginalised women.

And yet, very little information or government data exists today as regards the specific situation of Dalit women in the country. A study was initiated in 2004, therefore, to examine the forms and manifestations, frequency, caste and social status of perpetrators, causes, effects and responses to violence against Dalit women over the period 1999 to 2004. A total of 500 Dalit women were selected, based on information supplied by knowledgeable persons or organisations working with the Dalit community, from a sample of 32 panchayat unions/mandals/blocks falling within 17 districts of the states of Andhra Pradesh, Bihar, Tamil Nadu/Pondicherry and Uttar Pradesh. These were women who were willing to speak out about their experiences of violence in either or both the general community and in the family, without serious repercussions for their personal security such as threats and further violence from the perpetrators, or renewed caste tensions in the village.

The wide-ranging experiences shared by the Dalit women in this study, when analysed, reveal the multiple layers of violence that pervade their lives. Dalit women endure violence in both the general community and in the family, from state and non-state actors of different genders, castes and socio-economic groupings. An overview of the forms, frequency and locations of violence, perpetrators and causal factors for violence highlights the incongruence between Dalit women's reality and the universal right of women to freedom from any gender-based violence that results in physical, sexual or psychological harm. This data, therefore, serves as an indictment of both the Indian state and Indian society for failing to respect, protect and fulfil Dalit women's rights.

As an initial comment, it must be noted that the overwhelming majority of the 500 Dalit women's case narratives were never reported in the media. Given that these cases were selected, in collaboration with those working with the Dalit community, from a small sample, it is likely that many more unrecorded instances of violence exist. The reasons for this "silence" when it comes to violence against Dalit women are that cases are not spoken out in public by the women themselves, or not reported in the media, or not registered by law enforcement authorities, or hidden by the Dalit women's families, relatives and community, or suppressed by the diktat of the perpetrators and/or the perpetrators' caste community. The effect is the creation and maintenance of a *culture of violence, silence and impunity* when it comes to violence against Dalit women. This further exacerbates the denial of their rights to security of life and basic human dignity.

FORMS AND FREQUENCY OF VIOLENCE

Twelve major forms of violence constitute the basis of this study, nine being violence in the general community – physical assault, verbal abuse, sexual harassment and assault, rape, sexual exploitation, forced prostitution, kidnapping and abduction, forced incarceration and medical negligence – and three being violence in the family – female foeticide and infanticide, child sexual abuse and domestic violence from natal and marital family members. The majority of the 500 Dalit women have faced several forms of violence over the past five years, either in one incident, or in a series of incidents of violence, in either or both the general community and the family.

The more frequent forms of violence that are perpetrated against the majority of Dalit women are verbal abuse (62.4% of total women), physical assault (54.8%), sexual harassment and assault (46.8%), domestic violence (43.0%) and rape (23.2%), in descending order. Although the remaining forms of violence are faced by relatively fewer Dalit women (less than 10% of total women per form of violence), this does not discount their gravity, precisely because of the qualitative factor of force present in these forms of violence.

VIOLENCE IN THE GENERAL COMMUNITY

Verbal abuse from members of the general community, experienced by 312 women in this study, includes derogatory usage of caste names and caste epithets arguably amounting to "hate speech", as well as sexually explicit insults, gendered epithets and threats. One-third of these women have faced violence regularly, indicating the habitual nature of this form of violence. This verbal abuse also highlights the perpetrators' worldview wherein Dalit women are seen as without any rights in the "natural" caste hierarchy, as devoid of any entitlement to resources or respect, and as always sexually available without any requirement for the women's consent.

Verbal abuse often accompanied *physical assault,* perpetrated against 274 women in the study. Over 500 incidents of physical assault on these women were recorded, with 30 women facing regular physical assaults. This combination of violence further links in many cases to a spectrum of sexual violence, from *sexual harassment and/or sexual assault* (234 women), to *rape or gang rape* (116 women). While many women had been raped in one or more incidents, when it came to sexual harassment and/or sexual assault, often the violence occurred several times or was regular, as was the case for 72 women. Where the male perpetrator has some social or economic hold over the woman, such as her employer, or simply belongs to a dominant caste, then this violence sometimes developed into regular, coerced or induced sexual encounters or *sexual exploitation.* In the case of the 44 women who had been sexually exploited, this violence was most commonly perpetrated through false promises of marriage or lifelong economic maintenance, made to Dalit women in order to sexually exploit them for a period of time.

Kidnapping or abduction of Dalit women, as experienced by 24 women, often led to their forced incarceration and even rape or sexual exploitation. The targets are Dalit women from the time they attain puberty. Hence, parents' fear of their daughters being sexually assaulted and thereby becoming "unmarriageable" explains why, especially in northern states such as Bihar and Uttar Pradesh, Dalit women are getting married at ages as young as five years.

At the extreme end of the sexual violence spectrum also lies *forced prostitution,* experienced by 24 women across the four study states. Half of these women are Joginis, dedicated to temple goddesses from early ages in Andhra Pradesh and thereafter considered as religiously-sanctioned village prostitutes. Other women had been forced into prostitution after being sexually exploited by their dominant caste landlord-employers, or by their husbands, or in one case by the police. Incidents of *forced incarceration* have been endured by 23 Dalit women, involving for some women false cases leading to their detention, or arrest and imprisonment. The failure of the police to fulfil their duty to uphold law and order in these cases stemmed from police negligence or bias in initiating these cases against the women. Otherwise, half of these women had experienced being incarcerated in the perpetrator's home, or workplace, or in some isolated or rented building, bringing in the element of kidnapping and sexual violence from various non-state actors. When it comes to *medical negligence,* doctors and nurses have also demonstrated failure in their professional duty of care towards 17 Dalit women, through careless or pressurised operations especially as regards family planning, or discrimination in turning away Dalit women in need of serious medical attention.

VIOLENCE IN THE FAMILY

Within the family, *domestic violence* is prevalent. A total of 215 Dalit women have recorded regular incidents of domestic violence that span several years of married life. This violence often manifests itself in verbal abuse of the woman, accompanied by physical assault, but also entails sexual abuse including marital rape.

Several cases of inter-caste marriages ending in domestic violence reveal caste and gender discrimination against the Dalit wife leading to violence. In most cases where a Dalit husband is concerned, the violence takes on a strong patriarchal dimension: women are tortured within the home for not bringing enough dowry, for not bearing male children, for being supposedly ugly, or too beautiful, or allegedly unfaithful, for talking back to her husband, etc. Alcoholism among Dalit husbands is also a strong contributing factor to this domestic violence.

Domestic violence resulted in some women being deserted by their husbands, or being forced to leave their marital home. For the majority of women, however, the social norms and pressures of married life and "duties" of wives to their husbands ensure that they continue to endure this violence. Moreover, as this violence often commences when they are but children given in marriage, their ability to question and stand up to this violence is often severely diminished.

Female foeticide and infanticide were not recorded as widespread among the Dalit women in this study, with only two women revealing the occurrence of this violence. By comparison, *child sexual abuse* in terms of particularly early child marriages and sexual relations with minor Dalit girls below the age of 16 years is more common. Otherwise, four cases of sexual violence from a brother, father-in-law, brother-in-law and fathers also emerged. While only 23 girls had experienced child sexual abuse within the past five years, this must be viewed in the light of the fact that 282 women, or 72.2% of the total women in this study, were married below the legal age of marriage of 18 years, of which 39.7% were married below the age of 15 years. These early marriages indicate that the majority of women participating in the study would probably have been legally minors at the age of their first sexual encounter with their husband.

LOCATION OF VIOLENCE

The sites where violence occurs reveal another aspect of Dalit women's vulnerability, in that Dalit women are seen to be accessible in both public and private spaces for any acts of violence. The result is that they are denied spaces in which they can enjoy their rights to privacy and security of life. The majority of Dalit women have faced violence in *public spaces* – streets, women's toilet areas, bus stands, fields, etc. – in and around their villages and towns. The open or public nature of violence committed against them indicates both their specific vulnerability outside of the home, as well as the element of combined individual and collective community punishment meted out through particularly public physical assaults and verbal abuse. Many Dalit women in the study pointed out the perceived additional humiliation of public violence they face from dominant castes, as compared to the generally more private nature of violence committed against dominant caste women.

The next most common place for violence is *within the home*. Aside from domestic violence, a number of women have faced physical assaults, verbal abuse, sexual harassment and sexual assaults in their very home from non-family members. This reveals a common pattern of infringements of their right to privacy where perpetrators of violence invade the women's homes in order to attack and abuse them.

Violence in the *workplace* ranks third in terms of common locations for violence. This relates to Dalit women's greater work participation rates as compared with other women. Their mostly informal sector, daily wage labour occupations, bereft of employment security and many other rights, provide fertile ground for violence. Moreover, given their economic dependence, Dalit women often do not report violence from employers in the workplace, instead keeping silent in order to retain their means of livelihood. In addition, as many Dalit women either work in the perpetrators' home, or have to go there to receive their wages or ask for loans, etc., the *perpetrator's home* also becomes another site for violence perpetrated by general community members.

Finally, *government spaces* become grounds for violence particularly where medical negligence occurs in government hospitals, or where women are forcibly incarcerated, verbally abused, sexually harassed or raped in police stations. Otherwise, verbal abuse is the most common form of violence meted out in government spaces from a range of government actors including the police, district administration officials and doctors. The multiple sites for violence against Dalit women indicate that while in the brahminical patriarchal system they have greater "space" in which to function as compared with dominant caste women, this space does not translate into greater "freedom"; in other words, while Dalit women are said to enjoy greater freedom of movement, interactions and work opportunities in the "public sphere" than dominant caste women, they do not necessarily enjoy freedom that is safe, secure, productive and progressive, and that ensures their right to choose and decide for themselves.

This is due to limits imposed, restrictions mandated and obstructions placed on Dalit women's movement in the gendered space of the "public sphere" which is mediated by caste; that is, public spaces where men, and particularly dominant caste men, predominantly operate. These public spaces are seized upon as opportune places for exercising power and authority over Dalit women as individuals and as a collective through violence.

SOCIAL STATUS OF PERPETRATORS OF VIOLENCE IN THE GENERAL COMMUNITY

Within the wide range of identified perpetrators of violence against Dalit women in the general community, *dominant caste landlords* emerged as the most prominent group. Landlords are the feudal landed class owning over 10 acres of land, and it is their continuing socio-economic and political power and authority in rural agricultural regions, as well as their connection as employers of many Dalit women agricultural labourers, that provide them disproportionate scope for perpetrating caste violence against these women with impunity. The violence they mete out is physical, verbal and sexual, often in response to Dalit women asserting their economic rights, that is, challenging casteclass relations by demanding their right to wages or land, or their right to sexual integrity, that is, the right to choice in sexual relations.

Police and forest officials, as well as *business people,* also emerge as key perpetrators of violence against Dalit women. Where police are not active perpetrators, they also act in a significant number of cases in collusion with the perpetrators by failing to enforce the law when violence against Dalit women takes place. *Goondas and thugs* also play a role in supporting other perpetrator categories in their acts of terrorising Dalit women with actual or threats of violence. Two other groups of perpetrators whose numbers are significant belong to the *professional category,* namely hospital nurses and doctors and teachers, and the *political category,* namely local political party leaders and elected panchayat members.

In all these cases, except for *goondas* and thugs, these perpetrators hold positions of authority or positions entailing a duty of care and responsibility towards other people. Hence, their presence as perpetrators indicates their gross misuse of the power and authority conferred on them by virtue of their professions. In addition, there are a large number of *"other dominant caste persons"* as perpetrators, for whom only their caste, and not other social status, has been identified by the woman victim-survivors. In other words, these are dominant caste men and women in the village whom the Dalit women have been unable to identify as having any specific social, occupational or political status in the village such as a landlord or teacher.

Their significance lies in the fact that they are often ordinary community members who, by virtue of their "higher" caste status vis-à-vis the Dalit women, engage in violence against these women. Moreover, often this violence is committed by these perpetrators not only as individuals, but also as group violence involving people of the same status (for example, where landlords get together to attack a Dalit woman), or different status (for example, where dominant caste villagers join with panchayat or political party leaders to commit violence against a Dalit woman). The group nature of violence (particularly physical assaults, verbal abuse, sexual harassment and gang rapes) often against an individual Dalit woman highlights the particular vulnerability of these women where they are outnumbered by the perpetrators.

Finally, a number of *"other Dalit persons"* have been identified as either active perpetrators of violence against Dalit women, or colluders in the violence. While family members become perpetrators when it comes to dedication of their daughters as Joginis, Dalits often collude in violence when it comes to specific allegations against women of being "witches", or "loose women", or where Dalit women protest against the production and sale of liquor in the villages. Otherwise, their presence indicates both the inter-(sub) caste as well as intra-caste violence that exists within the Dalit community, albeit on a smaller scale to violence against Dalits by the dominant caste groups.

CASTE BACKGROUND OF PERPETRATORS OF VIOLENCE IN THE GENERAL COMMUNITY

Caste-wise, both forward castes (FCs) and backward castes (BCs) are seen to engage in violence against Dalit women, either as individuals or as a group. Roughly equal numbers of women across the different forms of violence have faced violence at the hands of these two major caste categories. Dalit perpetrators are also present in significant numbers. Their concentration lies in four forms of violence, namely physical assaults, verbal abuse, sexual harassment and sexual assaults, and rapes. Together, however, they account for around 10% of all perpetrators of violence against Dalit women in the study.

While in some instances the perpetrators of violence belong to one homogenous dominant caste, there are instances where they cut across all dominant caste lines, that is, backward caste and forward caste. This is particularly so where the Dalit woman is seen to transgress established caste norms, for example, by asserting her rights in defiance of "untouchability" practices. The punishment meted out, therefore, takes on the form of collective punishment that is both expressive of caste outrage as well as instrumental in terms of teaching the woman and her community a lesson of "obedience" to caste norms. Otherwise, sexual violence against Dalit women often takes a collective caste aspect, in terms of gang rapes or forced prostitution.

There are also instances of violence wherein the dominant castes – whether forward caste or backward caste – draw in the Scheduled Castes (Dalits) to engage in violence. To be noted is that this tactic is increasingly utilised by dominant castes to thwart the applicability of the *SC/ST (Prevention of Atrocities) Act 1989,* which only applies to atrocities committed by persons not belonging to the Scheduled Caste or Scheduled Tribe community. Dominant caste and Dalit collaboration in violence is also often present in witchcraft cases, with the accusation of witchcraft targeted at the Dalit woman by her family, her community or the dominant caste community.

Other traditions such as the Jogini system also yield multiple caste perpetrators of sexual exploitation against Jogini women, as do some gang rapes and some physical assaults where Dalits and dominant castes are engaged together in illegal activities such as logging or illicit liquor production and sales.

PERPETRATORS OF VIOLENCE IN THE FAMILY

As far as violence in the family is concerned, husbands, the Dalit women's in-laws, her relatives and husbands' relatives are perpetrators of violence, in descending order. Pressures exerted from both natal and marital families lead to female foeticide and infanticide, while child sexual abuse takes the predominant form of child marriages (as per the law rape of a minor refers to girls below 16 years of age, though a legal anomaly reduces this age to below 15 years in the case of a husband raping his wife). Less commonly recorded forms of child abuse are incest (where fathers and brothers are perpetrators) and sexual abuse by other male relatives (by brother-in-laws and father-in-laws). Husbands are also the key perpetrators of domestic violence, followed by mothers-in-law, the women's other relatives, fathers-in-law and their husband's other relatives. Given that most of the Dalit women's natal and marital families are very poor, the day-to-day struggles for survival, caste oppression and gender oppression often translate into frequent violence against Dalit women within the home.

In other words, the subjugation, and lack of power and authority in the general community for the women's husbands, marital and natal families, is often replicated in violence in the family, a phenomenon noted in many socially marginalised communities. This domestic violence is further bolstered by the internalised dominant caste ideology of wife fidelity (*pativrata*) and duty of chastity, placing premium on notions of women's "honour", "purity" and "obedience".

CAUSAL FACTORS FOR VIOLENCE

VIOLENCE IN THE GENERAL COMMUNITY

In most cases of violence in the general community where the perpetrator belongs to a dominant caste, the Dalit women clearly identified their gender-caste-class status as the overall or key cause for the violence. Clear examples were given not only in terms of the *jogini* system or violence related to untouchability norms, but also more generally in terms of the petty reasons that often triggered violence against the Dalit women by dominant caste men, women and children (for example, trying to cross a dominant caste's fields, asserting equal rights to access water from common taps, or asserting the right to own economic resources). These reasons fall broadly into two categories: reasons related to coercive violence utilised to maintain caste norms or caste-based gender norms, and reasons related Dalit women's assertions of their rights by defying untouchability norms or asserting their rights to cultural, economic and political resources.

The verbal abuse that is integral to many women's experiences of violence also indicates the dominant caste perpetrators' worldview as regards Dalit women's 'inferior' caste, class and gender status, and consequent powerlessness and vulnerability. Built into the patriarchal caste system is the assumption that Dalit women are available for any form of exploitation and violence, as a consequence of their "low" and "impure" character, and hence the low character of their caste that does not deserve honour and respect. The impunity with which much of this violence is carried out reinforces the normality of this culture of violence. The gender-caste-class axis, therefore, provides the systemic base for violence against Dalit women; that is, this violence is an in-built component of the caste system.

As far as Dalit perpetrators are concerned, the majority being male, many assimilate and reproduce the gender inequality structured into the caste system by using patriarchal norms to commit violence against women of their own community. This is particularly manifested in terms of physical and sexual violence, where patriarchal norms of female subordinate status and submissiveness influence Dalit women's abilities to enjoy their sexual integrity, equality and dignity, freedom, life and physical security in particular.

Flowing from and interlinked with this systemic causal factor for violence (that is, being a Dalit and a woman), Dalit women identified four main discrete and overlapping categories of causal factors for violence against them in their recorded narratives. The primary identified factor for violence in the general community related to the issue of Dalit women's *sexual or bodily integrity*. Accompanying Dalit women's low caste status and the socio-economic and political power of the dominant castes is the latter's view of their superior caste and gender status and accordingly a perceived right over Dalit women's bodies.

Dalit women are seen as sexually available as they move in gendered public spaces and engage in productive labour. Sexual violence is understood in caste ideology as ennobling 'lower' caste women; that is, dominant caste perpetrators of sexual violence against Dalit women expect their "victims" to be grateful for the sexual attention they are receiving from 'higher' caste men. Sexual violence is also a tool utilised by dominant caste men to reinforce the caste 'impurity' of both the Dalit woman and her community, given the hegemonic discourse of women symbolising the group identity and bearing the honour of their community.

Hence, socially legitimised reasons for sexual violence and its accompanying physical and verbal assaults against Dalit women include:

- The women's perceived sexual availability;
- Retaliation against women who rejected men's sexual advances;
- Reaction against women who expressed a desire to leave prostitution work.

A second frequent causal factor for violence in the general community directly links to *gender inequality and the 'natural' caste hierarchy* as often manifested in untouchability practices, and Dalit women's counter discourse of equality, rights, dignity and self-respect. As the caste system hinges on the power of the dominant castes to enforce caste-based rules, including those rules governing what Dalit women should and should not do as impure, low caste women, violence also serves a functional aspect.

Thus another set of causes for violence – mostly physical assaults, verbal abuse and sexual harassment or assault – include:

- When women broke "customary" laws by trying to access places of worship, hotels or other public places on equal par with the dominant castes;
- When women allegedly disrespected the caste status of a dominant caste or the gender status of a Dalit male by speaking up, questioning, or raising their voices in protest or to assert their rights;
- When women tried to participate in religious or cultural life;
- When women tried to access water rights or the public distribution system (PDS) ration shop on equal par with dominant castes.

Almost as frequently identified a causal factor for violence in the general community lies in the area of Dalit women's *civil rights*. The violence is either a response to the Dalit women's alleged breach of caste norms by exercising their freedom of expression in speaking out on an issue, or seeking to protect her family or community, or as a means used to reinforce their submissiveness and voicelessness as demanded under the caste system.

These issues include:

- Revenge or retaliation to settle scores with either the woman, her family or her community;
- Response to the women when they questioned the perpetrator/s for

violent acts done to them, their children, their family members or other Dalit community members;

- Response to the women when they questioned illicit arrack sales or corruption in government schemes meant for Dalit welfare;
- Where a male member of the woman's household was wanted for questioning by the police;
- Where a woman scolded dominant caste children for destroying the *anganwadi* garden;
- Where women were involved in a road blockade protest;
- Resort to supernatural beliefs to explain sudden illnesses, or family pressures, that led to girl's dedication as a Jogini;
- Doctors' carelessness or negligence in treating or operating on women;
- Insecurity faced as a widow, or a Jogini.

A fourth causal factor for violence in the general community, given the aspect of economic exploitation built into the caste system, related to *economic resources* – land, or other economic resources/capital such as wages, payment for services, etc. – and particularly Dalits asserting their rights to own or utilise resources. Violence also related to Dalit women's poverty levels or economic status, in terms of their landlessness combined with their dependence on dominant castes for their livelihood; that is, with regard to work, wages and loans.

*Causes for violence related specifically to land and common property resources, being key economic resources in the villages, includ*e:

- Women and their families asserted their rights to own land;
- Women tried to access forests or other common property resources;
- Women questioned dominant castes for destroying, or for their cattle destroying crops;
- In order to appropriate the land belonging to the Dalit women or their families;
- Reaction against Dalit women and their families owning or leasing land;
- Retaliation for women allowing water to flow onto the dominant caste perpetrator's land, or allegedly wrecking the dividing line between their two fields.

Economic development factors triggering violence against the Dalit women include:

- Where women failed to repay debts;
- Women asked for loans;
- Women asserted their economic rights by asking for monetary payment for services performed or goods sold, or loans given out, or their pensions;
- Women asserted their rights to access government relief schemes or housing schemes;

- Woman asked for the return of her ration card given as surety for a loan she had repaid;
- Women attained or tried to attain a higher economic status than allegedly befitted a Dalit, such as by trying to become quarry owners;
- Women won a contract to cook school midday meals;
- Poverty that led the women's family to dedicate their daughters as Joginis, or that led doctors to discriminate against the women in providing medical care or be negligent in their provision of medical care.

Similarly, causal factors related to Dalit women's labour and work include:

- Women protested against forced or bonded labour;
- Women challenged working conditions;
- Women questioned the delay or part-payment or under-payment or non-payment of wages;
- Women asked for workers' compensation following their husbands' deaths;
- Women allegedly arrived late for work, or allegedly did not work properly, or slept during work, or did not come to work due to illness;
- Woman refused to clean her dominant caste employer's muddy shoes;
- Woman did 'polluted' work of burying unwanted corpses;
- Where a Dalit man wanted to wrest a woman's job away from her;
- Where a dominant caste man did not want a Dalit woman working with him.

Seen together, these four afore-mentioned broad categories of causal factors indicate the crucial areas of sustaining Dalit women's lives, their integrity and their identity.

Hence, Dalit women are often attacked in these vulnerable areas in order to deprive them of an economic base and economic independence from the dominant castes, to deny them civil freedoms to express their rights, to damage their bodily and sexual integrity as means of attacking their dignity and identity, all of which are necessary to maintaining their gender-caste-class subordination.

Otherwise, other causal factors that provoked violence include those related to Dalit women's basic livelihood outside of economic issues:

- Women asserted their rights to access or enjoy housing, or water, or the public distribution system (PDS), or education, or open spaces for defecation;
- Women questioned the perpetrator for polluting their housing premises with rubbish or sewage water;
- Women asked for immediate medical treatment due to being in intense pain;

- Women did not come to hospital early enough, or were not able to pay for medical treatment due to poverty.

In the realm of *political rights*, several Dalit women spoke of their assertions of basic political rights as provoking violent dominant caste backlashes.

The issues that led to violence included:

- Woman canvassed for votes in the dominant caste section of the village;
- Women exercised or attempted to exercise their right to an independent vote in elections;
- Women contested panchayat elections;
- Women exercised or attempted to exercise political authority as elected panchayat representatives.

Another category of causes for violence relates to relationship issues, including:

- Women asserted their rights to equality and dignity in relationships, by protesting against violence, or demanding fidelity from man in the relationship, or questioning man for deserting her;
- Women allegedly had illicit relationships with other men, or allegedly were prostitutes, or allegedly encouraged others to have illicit relationships;
- Women asked the perpetrators of rape or sexual exploitation to marry them;
- Women accused perpetrator's son of having raped them;
- Reaction against Dalit woman whose son married a dominant caste woman;
- Women questioned perpetrators for abandoning them after having sexual relationships with them.

This category is very much related to that of sexual integrity, in that the causes for violence expose the underlying ideology of Dalit women's availability for illicit relationships, though not marriage, and the stringent punishments proscribed for inter-caste marriages. Moreover, the Dalit men's and Dalit community's control over Dalit women's sexuality is seen in their violent responses to Dalit women asserting their rights in relationships, or in punishing women whose so-called immoral behaviour allegedly influences other women to have illicit relationships.

Two categories of causal factors are related, in dealing with the dominant caste discourse of *criminality* that claims Dalit women as inherently criminal, a consequence of, as well as reinforcement of, their alleged impurity and low caste status. This discourse pervades conflicts and consequent violence arising out of accusations of trespass, or criminal activity.

Examples of accusations of criminal activity against Dalit women include:

- Alleged to be witches or accomplices to witches;
- Allegedly helped bomb a police station;
- Allegedly gave false evidence to the police;

- Allegedly took firewood, or mud, or grass from the perpetrators' fields
- Alleged theft from perpetrator's house or fields;
- Alleged misappropriation of money from Old Age Assistance Fund.

Similarly, examples of accusations of trespass include:

- Women's animals strayed into the dominant castes' fields and sometimes ate or destroyed some of the crops;
- Woman bathed in the perpetrator's pond;
- Women simply passed by or crossed the dominant castes' fields;
- Women's animals or children went to the toilet in the perpetrators' fields.

The issue of trespass in particular is worth considering in the context of the systemic denial of economic resources to Dalits under the caste system. Where Dalit women are so often excluded from ownership or enjoyment of land or common property resources, and lack basic livelihood amenities such as toilets in their homes, then it would seem unrealistic to draw a line between public and private resources in villages. Unless issues of land reforms and basic public amenity provisioning, for example, are implemented by the state on a priority basis, can one speak of trespass by persons who are kept systematically excluded from such resources or amenities?

Finally, violence also took place when Dalit women sought *justice and the protection of the law* for violence done to them, or to forestall such action, by any of the following acts:

- Women filed or tried to file a police complaint;
- Women brought or tried to bring incidents of violence to the traditional village panchayat for arbitration;
- Women refused to accept compromises following acts of violence;
- To prevent women from telling anyone of the violence or filing a police complaint;
- To prevent women from being witnesses against the perpetrators in a court case.

This revisiting of violence upon Dalit women in order to forestall any efforts by them to seek justice, or to punish them further for daring to seek justice, functions to build, maintain and reproduce a culture of impunity for perpetrators and their colluders in violence.

VIOLENCE IN THE FAMILY

Similarly, Dalit women faced violence in the family over a range of issues, suggesting the assimilation of the larger patriarchal caste system's norms by particularly Dalit men, with negative implications for Dalit women's personal lives and interactions in their community. The internalised ideology of brahmanical patriarchy, with its notions of women's "honour", "purity" and "obedience", produces and influences the causal factors for violence in the family. Female foeticide and infanticide stemmed from gender discrimination, combined with poverty or a response to the child being born of an illicit relationship. By comparison, child sexual abuse was primarily seen as the result of husbands asserting their perceived right to sexual relations with their child brides.

When it comes to domestic violence, however, the causes for this violence are much more nuanced and varied. *Gender inequality and norms of female subordination* formed a major category of causal factors for violence meted out by natal and marital family members to Dalit women.

Examples of causal factors falling within this category include:

- Women allegedly failed to be dutiful wives;
- Women asserted their rights;
- Women were unable to bear children, or unable to bear sons;
- Caste discrimination from dominant caste husbands and in-laws in inter-caste marriages, or reaction from dominant caste husbands on being ostracised from their dominant caste communities as a result of marrying Dalit women;
- Dominant caste husbands did not want children from their Dalit wives, or did not want their children to visit their Dalit grandparents' house, or not wanting their children to marry a Dalit.

A second major category was economic causal factors for domestic violence, including:

- Poverty;
- Insufficient dowry;
- Women earned more income than their husbands, or their natal families had a higher economic status than their marital families;
- Women asked their husbands to account for money given from their earnings to the husbands, or refused to give their earnings to fund their husbands' drinking habits, or refused to mortgage jewellery to satisfy their husbands' spendthrift habits;
- To deny women their share of their deceased husbands' property, or to appropriate their dead father's pension.

A third prominent category of causal factors related to Dalit women's *civil rights,* which include:

- Women's insecurity due to their husband's unemployment or alcoholism;
- Women's insecurity as widows, or orphans, or differently abled, or stepchildren.

Finally, two related categories of causal factors related to rights in *family relationships* and to *sexual integrity*. Internalised brahmanical patriarchal norms entail strict control over Dalit women's sexuality.

Hence, reasons for violence surrounding marital relations include:

- Women allegedly having illicit relationships;

- Women's alleged breaches of family honour, particularly in response to women surviving sexual or physical violence in the general community;
- Women caught up in internal family power dynamics.

Evidence of the lack of similar norms applicable to male household members was seen in violence against Dalit wives arising from their husbands having illicit relationships with other women, or marrying again, or wanting to marry again.

In a similar manner Dalit women faced violence arising out of disregard for their sexual integrity, including:

- When women did not want to have sexual relations with their husbands, or in one case with her husband's friends;
- Either in furtherance of sexual relations, or retaliation for women having refused to have sexual relations with male relatives;
- Negative or blaming responses from women's natal or marital family members after women were sexually assaulted or exploited.

Overall, much of the domestic violence arose out of a combination of factors such as internalised gender discrimination, poverty, dominant discourses of dowry, wifely fidelity and duties, and distrust of women to guard their own sexuality all leading to husbands' perceived rights over their wives, or their husbands' alcoholism. The message effectively sent home to Dalit women is that they must keep "in their place"; that is, they must remain submissive daughters or wives, and should not assert their rights against Dalit men and other dominant family members.

REMEDIAL ACTION FOR JUSTICE

The Indian Government has an obligation under international human rights law to act with due diligence to prevent, investigate and punish acts of violence against Dalit women in both the general community and in the family, at the hands of state or non-state actors. Any case of violence against a Dalit woman has to pass through the hands of the local police and the judiciary in order for the woman to receive justice under the law. Safeguarding the impartiality of this process, the Indian Constitution stipulates in *Article 14* that all Indian citizens have the right to equality before the law.

However, deeply ingrained normative values of appropriate gender and caste roles and behaviour patterns influence government officials, police and even judges who have the power to interpret and actualise rights. These socio-culturally-religiously rooted biases enforce the discriminatory status quo to the detriment of Dalit women's right to justice where violence takes place.

As the United Nations Special Rapporteur on Violence against Women has noted with regard to the situation in India, "constitutional and legislative provisions that have been enacted to protect women from discrimination have not proved to be an effective deterrent."

Moreover, the Indian government's consistent inaction in protecting, promoting and fulfilling rights for its Dalit women citizens – evidenced in official data indicating the increasing rates of crimes against women and Scheduled Castes, its failure to resister many cases of violence against Dalit women, and low disposal rates of Scheduled Caste atrocity cases combined with low conviction rates – all points to structural injustice being perpetuated and the Indian state's failure to comply with its international human rights obligations. These conclusions are substantiated by the justice-seeking efforts of the Dalit women in this study.

Considering all 500 Dalit women in the study, in 40.2% of instances of violence the *women have been unable to obtain legal or community remedies for the violence*. A culture of silence exists when it comes to especially sexual violence, due to the dominant discourse emphasising women's "honour" and the stigma attaching to sex outside of marriage, whether forced or by consent.

Other reasons for not attempting to obtain justice include:

- Fear of the perpetrators, arising from the perpetrator's threats of further violence to the women or their family members should they file police complaints, or to deny them work;
- Fear of dishonour or further shame by publicising the violence;
- Ignorance that the violence was an illegal act for which there are legal remedies;
- Lack of money to approach the police, or pay the often requisite bribe in order for the police to take action, or to follow a police case through to the courts;
- Lack of family or community support for the justice-seeking attempt.

The overall effect is to reinforce a culture of impunity for violence by the perpetrators and their colluders, further exacerbating the denial of Dalit women's rights to security of life and basic human dignity. In 26.5% of instances of violence, the women attempt to obtain legal or community redress for the violence, but are *prevented from obtaining justice by the perpetrators and their supporters, and the community at large*. The existence of traditional village panchayats of caste elders/leaders that exists parallel to the formal panchayat system in most Indian villages, in particular, often systematically suppresses women's and Dalits' voices using patriarchal and dominant caste notions of social and moral justice.

Reasons for these thwarted justice-seeking attempts include:

- Perpetrators, or their families, or their caste community threatening or intimidating the victimsurvivor into silence;
- Perpetrators foisting false police cases against the victim-survivors to pressurise them to drop their legitimate cases;
- Traditional village or caste panchayats, and in some cases formal elected panchayats, refusing to take up Dalit women's cases, or refusing to accuse dominant caste perpetrators, or portraying the

affected woman as the wrongdoer instead of the perpetrator, or pressurising the affected woman to accept an informal "compromise";
- Victim-survivor's family pressurising her to drop the case out of fear of family dishonour or dominant caste reprisals;
- Dominant caste community pressurising the victim-survivor to accept informal "compromises" that involve no proper and adequate remedial or justice action.

In cases of panchayat rulings, justice may appear to be done to the Dalit women. Often, however, the perpetrators and supporting dominant caste members/groups contrive "compromises" by taking advantage of their socio-political power and status, instead of dispensing true justice. Of all the instances of violence, only in 1.6% are the Dalit women able to *obtain informal justice rulings in her favour*. In most of these 33 instances, traditional village panchayats or elected panchayats or local NGOs manage to broker informal justice rulings rewarding the victim-survivor with financial compensation and a public apology, while extracting from the perpetrator a fine and/or apology and promise for improved behaviour in the future.

A further 17.4% of all instances of violence reach the notice of the police, but the *justice attempts are blocked by the police* themselves.

These include cases in which:
- Police pressurise the woman victim-survivor to drop the case or to accept a "compromise";
- Police foist false cases against the victim-survivor or her supporters in order to force them to drop their legitimate case;
- Police file victim-survivor's complaints but neglect to take action;
- Police accept bribes from the perpetrators to drop or scuttle the case;
- Police simply refuse to file FIRs.

By rendering futile the women's attempt to seek justice through the criminal justice system, the police collude to reinforce the culture of impunity for violence against Dalit women. Finally, in only 13.8% of instances of violence in this study is *appropriate police or judicial action underway*. The majority of these cases are all pending: investigations are being carried out, charge sheets are yet to be prepared, cases are currently before the courts, etc. Hence, leeway still exists for the cases to be scuttled by the police and/or perpetrators and their community. Notably, only 3.6% of all instances of violence have actually reached the court, and of those, only three cases (that is, less than 1% of total instances of violence) have ended in convictions. Eight other cases have been dismissed by the courts or ended in acquittals of the accused, due to either a forced "compromise" dictated by the accused while the case was under trial, or the perpetrator pressurising the woman victim-survivor or witnesses into turning hostile, or the victim-survivor being unable to obtain the requisite evidence for her case, or the perpetrator dying before the end of the trial.

Hence, the long process to obtain justice for Dalit women victim-survivors of violence is too often effectively stymied by different actors – the perpetrators, their caste community, police, the traditional village panchayats or formal elected panchayats. The brahminical patriarchal discourse of "honour" and fear of further dominant caste reprisals, moreover, influences Dalit women, their families and their communities, not to seek justice where violence takes place. Impunity for violence, therefore, is an intrinsic factor in the maintenance of the caste system and caste-and-gender based norms circumscribing Dalit women's fundamental rights and freedoms.

The overall performance of the Indian State, therefore, comes into serious question when measured against the standard of due diligence to prevent violence against Dalit women. This is true for violence at the hands of both non-state actors, as well as state actors themselves. Giving effect to Dalit women's rights requires not only building structures of protection - including investigation, prosecution, fair punishment and compensation for violence – but also rigorously implementing laws and policies designed to facilitate the enjoyment of equal citizenship rights for the 80 million Dalit women in the country today.

Taking into account the situation of rising rates of crimes against Dalits, combined with failure of the state machinery to check this rise with stringent action, the Parliamentary Committee on the Welfare of Scheduled Castes and Scheduled Tribes has stated that atrocities on Scheduled Castes and Scheduled Tribes constitute an internal disturbance under *Article 355* of the *Indian Constitution,* and has called for Central Government intervention under various provisions to take strict action against offending states. The Committee has also castigated the Home Ministry for using "police and public order" being "state subjects" as an excuse for absolving themselves of the responsibility implied under *Article 355*. Finally, the Committee recommended taking "extreme steps" wherever warranted to protect the Dalit community and punish perpetrators of violence against them.viii

EFFECTS OF VIOLENCE

Violence against Dalit women causes social, physical and mental trauma to women, much of which is long-term suffering. Where violence is committed with impunity, aided by the failure of the police to effect arrests and prosecutions, the fact of the perpetrators and their colluders in the violence freely moving about the village and often intimidating the woman and her family has a deep *psychological impact*. Significant are feelings of the futility of legal justice and fatalism about positive changes to address such violence. In total, 71.2% of Dalit women in the study expressed their feelings of helplessness to stop the violence, while 60.4% indicated the atmosphere of constant fear in which they carry on their daily lives. Feelings of depression or low-self esteem and shame also marked out the lives of around 60% of women, while 24 women had tried to commit suicide because of the violence they endured. At the level of *physical effects,* among other effects of violence, 92 Dalit women experienced long-term physical health complications arising out of the violence, and a further nine women now live with a permanent physical disfigurement or disability. Twenty-three women endured long-term sexual health complications, while seven women miscarried as a result of violence meted out to them. Sexual violence resulted in 40 women becoming pregnant, though 18 women either opted for or were forced to undertake abortions, and one woman's family killed her child at birth.

Social effects of violence include economic punishment in terms of the destruction of Dalit women's livelihood or loss of employment (11 women), or social boycotts (four women). Around 8% of Dalit women (39 women) expressed their inability to get married or to get their child married where especially sexual violence had occurred. Violence also restricted many Dalit women's freedom of movement, while eight girls quit their education due to violence. Otherwise, Dalit women were ostracised from their families (57 women), or their community (16 women), or deserted by their husbands (17 women), or forced to leave their homes (80 women) because of violence in either or both the general community and the family. Finally, 9.6% of women (48 women) experienced contempt or ridicule in the villages following the violence perpetrated against them, often reinforcing the idea that somehow the women were to be blamed for the violence meted out to them.

Thus, the harm caused to Dalit women by violence does not stop at the act itself; it has long-term and multiplying social, psychological and physical effects that are not being addressed. Outside of the social movements and organisations working with the community, little supportive or counselling mechanisms exist in India today to deal with caste-and-gender based violence meted out to Dalit women. The result is that the lives of many Dalit women are underwritten by layers of trauma, hindering their rights to live with dignity and reach their full potential.

COURAGE, STRENGTH AND RESILIENCE OF DALIT WOMEN

Despite all these experiences of violence that leave grave marks on Dalit women's lives and dominant caste perpetrators constantly reiterating gender-based caste norms and Dalit gender subordination, the narratives of the Dalit women also evidence their courage, strength and resilience to assert their right to live a life with dignity.

Apart from the courage that Dalit women have shown during violence, their resilience in the post-violence phase is manifested in two respects: first, their determination to pursue a course of action, whatever may be the expected or unexpected outcome, to set right the harm done by the violence; secondly, the tenacity they have shown in their various attempts to sustain their lives against all odds, refusing to let their lives disintegrate further as a result of the violence they have experienced. Whether this was done with success or otherwise in terms of achieving a legal remedy for the injustice they had faced or improving their living conditions, what is significant are their efforts to survive and sustain their lives in some form or another.

It is ironic that instead of the Indian State being the custodian of constitutional rights, it is Dalit women themselves who often dare to uphold the rule of law in the face of the "rule of caste". This is evident from cases where Dalit women assert their rights to equality and fundamental freedoms of life, and also where they approach established legal justice mechanisms instead of taking the law into their own hands as the perpetrators have done. And yet, in only a few cases does the state rise up to meet Dalit women's expectations of justice. Therefore, what Dalit women look to is not a paternal way of providing them remedial justice, but support mechanisms that clearly establish and uphold their rights, and bring them into mainstream society with dignity.

Failure by the Indian state and civil society to respond to Dalit women's legitimate expectations results in these women experiencing greater marginalisation, to the detriment of a healthy and vibrant democratic polity. There also lies a possibility of increased questioning of the rule of law as the appropriate means to securing justice. What Dr B.R. Ambedkar said in 1949 on the occasion of the Third Reading of the Indian Constitution is well worth noting in this regard:

- "On enacting the Constitution, we are going to enter into a life of contradictions. In politics we will have equality and in social and economic life we will have inequality. In politics we will be recognising the principle of one woman one vote and one vote one value. In our social and economic life, we shall, by reason of our social and economic structure, continue to deny the principle of one man one value. How long shall we continue to live this life of contradictions? How long shall we continue to deny equality in our social and economic life? If we continue to deny it for long, we will do so only by putting our political democracy in peril. We must remove this contradiction at the earliest possible moment or else those who suffer from inequality will blow up the structure of political democracy which this Assembly has so laboriously built up."

CONCLUDING REFLECTIONS

In contravention of both national laws and international human rights standards that prohibit any physical, sexual or psychological violence against women, varying forms of violent acts specifically targeting Dalit women are occurring on a large scale across India today.

That physical (affecting bodily integrity), verbal (affecting the psyche), and sexual (affecting bodily/sexual integrity) violence are the most common, and often combined, forms of violence suggests that at every level Dalit women's personae is being attacked. Moreover, given that most of this violence is occurring in public spaces, the additional humiliation of being violated in public drives home a message not only to each Dalit woman, but also to her family and community, that she is not considered worthy of being treated with honour, respect or human dignity. As Dalit women also experience violence in the family, they are effectively left with no safe spaces in which to freely express themselves and reach their full potential.

Dalit women would appear to be extremely vulnerable to aggression primarily by dominant caste persons in their villages and towns. Dominant caste status, often combined with patriarchal status and reinforced by a dominant class position (for example, being a landlord), effectively legitimises many dominant caste men's exercise of power, authority and force over Dalit women. Moreover, reading through the 500 Dalit women's narratives reveals the pan-religious element in that perpetrators of violence come from all major Indian religions – Hindus, Muslims, Christians and Sikhs, indicating that even in non-Hindu traditions the caste hierarchy trumps religious ideals of equality and respect for all human beings.

The range of causal factors for violence in the general community is directly attributable to systemic caste-class-gender factors that ascribe Dalit women's low status in society and consequent disempowerment and exploitation. At the core is patriarchy, which is gender-based and gender-biased against women. Male exercise of patriarchal power to subjugate women is overtly manifested in their attacks on Dalit women's sexual and bodily integrity, as well as their rights in inter-personal relationships with men. At the same time, patriarchy in India is influenced by the caste system and its inherent inequalities arising from hierarchal structuring of the system. Dalit women become specifically targeted for violence as an outcome of their positioning at the bottom of both gender and caste hierarchies, which condone violence against those Dalit women who contravene caste and untouchability norms by asserting their right to equality, or criminalises Dalit women's actions, or deems it socio-culturally acceptable to perpetrate sexual violence on Dalit women.

Moreover, reinforcement of Dalit women's lack of or denial of access to land and other economic resources through violence points to their effective class subordination in order to retain them as an exploitable labour force for their mainly dominant caste employers. There are also interconnections between denial of Dalit women's socio-economic rights or right to livelihood, and the denial of their civil rights; that is, their ability to protest and protect themselves depends to a great extent on their having a sound economic base. Finally, the lack of civil and political freedoms, including the right to justice and protection of the law in the event of violence taking place, reinforce the disempowerment of Dalit women at all levels. Such violence is crucial to the maintenance of caste structures and unequal power relations in society, which serves to highlight key areas requiring urgent intervention to safeguard Dalit women's fundamental rights. Similarly, the multiplicity of causal factors for violence in the family suggests the reproduction of the larger patriarchal caste system's norms in Dalit women's personal lives and interactions in their community.

Finally, the culture of impunity built into the caste system has wide-ranging implications as far as violence against Dalit women is concerned. Impunity for violence reinforces that caste-based notions of injustice prevail over democratic rights and the rule of law in the country. Justice itself becomes defined in terms of caste-and-gender privileges, with violence serving to reinforce caste law and order at the heavy expense of Dalit women's rights. Violence against Dalit women thus presents one of the greatest challenges to the social justice system in the country, calling for immediate and holistic remedial action at all levels of the government, law and order agents, the judiciary and civil society.

8

Dalit Rights: Housing and Land

INTRODUCTION

International human rights law obliges India to:

- Fulfil the minimum essential level of the right to adequate housing and land, and
- Show that this realization is progressive since becoming a party to the International Covenant on Economic, Social and Cultural Rights (ICESCR).

As the Committee has emphasised, neither of these obligations is mitigated by a State party's political processes, domestic le gislation, scarcity of resources, or agreements with other parties.

The Indian State is thus legally obliged to recognise, promote and fulfil the human right to adequate housing for all, by both international and constitutional law. In paragraph 406 of its report to the Committee, the Government of India has clearly reaffirmed that the, "Right to shelter is recognized as an integral part of the fundamental right to life under the Constitution of India." Judgements of the Indian Supreme Court have also upheld the right to housing, explicitly recognizing that, "Shelter for a human being is not a mere protection of his life and limb. It is home where he has opportunities to grow physically, mentally, intellectually and spiritually. It therefore includes adequate living space, safe and decent structure, clean and decent surroundings, sufficient light, pure air and water, electricity, sanitation and other civic amenities like roads, etc."

Despite India's legal obligations, the reality with regard to living conditions for the majority of Indians is dismal. The present degree of violations is unacceptable and represents a flagrant breach of India's Constitutional and national legal obligations as well as commitments under the ICESCR and other international instruments. This report presents some of the key issues of concern and proposes recommendations to the Government of India as well as questions for the Committee to ask the government in its fulfilment of its international and national legal obligations.

INADEQUATE HOUSING AND LIVING CONDITIONS IN URBAN AND RURAL AREAS

Though the human right to adequate housing is an internationally and nationally guaranteed human right, the majority of India's population continues to live in inadequate and insecure housing conditions. The numbers of those living in such conditions in both urban and rural areas is rapidly rising.

Across the country, people and communities are forced to live in precarious and high density conditions, in unsafe and distressed housing in slums, on pavements, alongside railway tracks, under bridges, on embankments, in shelters made from plastic sheets, cardboard, aluminium and tin, in water pipes, on degraded lands, in areas prone to earthquakes and floods, and on denuded hillsides.

Aggravating this already dire situation are the phenomena of discrimination, large "development" projects such as dams, mining, highways, slum demolitions, real estate speculation, privatisation of basic services such as water, forced land acquisition for industrial development and Special Economic Zones (SEZs), communal violence, armed and ethnic conflict. These factors, often in conjunction with one another, force many, especially those belonging to marginalised communities, the working poor, small farmers and the landless, to leave their homes and habitats and live in inadequate conditions with little or no access to civic services, thereby violating their rights to water, sanitation, food, electricity, education, and generally livelihood too. Inadequate living conditions also adversely impact the human right to health of residents. Affordability of housing is also a major concern across urban India. In Delhi, a study by an independent group revealed that housing earmarked for low-income groups was priced so high that 80% of it was in fact occupied by the middle class. Recent moves to open up the housing market to foreign direct investment have further contributed to the rising prices of housing in urban India.

Over the last few years, discrimination against the urban and rural poor has intensified, and disturbingly, has even gained legal sanction from the judiciary in the form of anti-poor judgements. The crisis of inadequate and insecure housing and living conditions reveals an abrogation of the government's national and international obligations to promote and protect human rights. The continued prevalence of these phenomena leads to exclusion, dispossession, impoverishment, and violence.

SLUMS AND INFORMAL SETTLEMENTS

The first time attempted to document India's slum population, 23.1% of India's total urban population of 286 million lives in slums. The actual figure is estimated to be much higher since only 607 cities were included in this effort. In Lucknow, despite the fact that more than 1.2 million people live in 787 settlements, Census 2001 stated that Lucknow was a "slum-free city." In the last three years, the government has not rehabilitated a single evicted slum in Lucknow. The majority of the population in India's metros lives in slums (60% in Mumbai and 50% in Delhi according to civil society estimates). This number will increase if those living in sub-standard housing are also taken into account. Official data for Delhi shows that only 27 per cent of the population lives in planned and author ised housing.

Despite the fact that the slum population is rising across the country, there is still no concerted, integrated effort to develop human rights-based policy or to provide improved housing, especially low cost housing. This indicates that a large percentage of the country's urban population has little or no access to adequate housing and basic amenities.

Questions for the Government of India:

- What is the level of public investment in housing for the urban and rural poor? What is the totalamount allocated to housing under the national budget 2008 and under the major schemes mentioned by the Government of India in its report to the Committee? How many units of housing stock are expected to be added in the current year, and in what categories?
- In its report to the Committee, why has the government quoted the 2002 estimate by the National Sample Survey of eight million urban households (around 40 million people) living in slums, rather than the census figure, which is approximately five times higher? Which is the figure being used by the government in planning interventions for this population? If the lower figure is being used, what is the rationale and what impact has this had on budget allocations?
- Why are housing policies and laws not explicitly based on human rights provisions in the Constitution and India's international commitments? Why is there no reference to the right to adequate housing in the existing and proposed laws and policies?
- What steps is the government taking to ensure that international human rights standards, such as General Comment 7 of the Committee on Economic, Social and Cultural Rights (CESCR) and the *UN Basic Principles and Guidelines on Development-based Evictions and Displacement*, are applied during redevelopment and upgrading of slums and informal settlements and to ensure that communities are not divided, livelihoods are not lost, and people are not denied alternate housing, as is likely to be the case in Dharavi, Mumbai?
- What is the total amount allocated for housing-related schemes by the Ministry of Urban Development and by state governments receiving assistance under the Jawaharlal Nehru National Urban Renewal Mission (JNNURM)? How many families are expected to benefit?

- What was the actual expenditure during the Tenth Plan on rural housing schemes for families below the poverty line? Has there been any analysis of the reasons for the gap between allocation and expenditure on rural housing? How have the recommendations of the mid-term review of the Tenth Plan been addressed in the Eleventh Plan period?
- When is the draft *National Urban Housing and Habitat Policy 2007* expected to be finalised and passed? What process has been followed, if any, to seek the input of civil society groups to this draft?

Recommendations to the Government of India:

- Provide legal security of tenure to all slum dwellers.
- Allocate a fixed percentage of the budget to public/ low cost housing in order to meet the severe housing deficit, especially in large cities. This should be manda ted in all city and village development plans, and should include reservation of land and earmarked funds for housing for all low-income groups.
- Play an active role in providing, monitoring and ensuring equal access to basic services such as water, sanitation and electricity.
- Ensure people's participation in the development of all city, town and village plans, including housing/settlement plans, as well as national housing policies and policies related to basic services such as water and sanitation.
- The draft *National Urban Housing and Habitat Policy 2007* should be developed in close consultation with civil society and incorporate a human rights approach to housing instead of a mere "housing delivery" approach as currently stressed. The Policy must also include mechanisms for arresting real estate speculation, controlling foreign investment in the housing sector, mandating low cost housing, and monitoring the implementation of the right to adequate housing through the development of concrete indicators. It must also include a strong gender perspective with a focus on women's special concerns.

HOUSING SHORTAGE

At the end of the Tenth Five Year Plan, the urban housing shortage was 24.7 million dwelling units while for the Eleventh Plan period (2007 – 2012) it is estimated to be 26.53 million.

This is compounded by the fact that most of the housing shortage pertains to the Economically Weaker Sections (EWS) and Low Income Groups (LIG). The total rural housing shortage for 2007-2012 has been projected as 47.43 million, of which 90% accounts for below poverty line (BPL) families.

Questions for the Government of India:

- Are there are any plans to improve and expand the existing Indira

Awas Yojana (for below poverty line rural families) to other low-income groups and to develop a similar programme for urban areas?

- With the abolition of housing schemes for the urban poor and the integration of all such schemes under the JNNURM, what steps is the government taking to ensure that benefits of urban renewal actually accrue to the urban poor, specifically in terms of improved and affordable housing and access to basic services?
- What specific schemes has the government initiated for the urban landless population, which tends to be left out of all existing programmes?

Recommendations for the Government of India:

- Adopt a strong human rights approach to housing that focuses on adequacy of housing and not just on the provision of houses.

FORCED EVICTIONS AND DISPLACEMENT

The eviction of individuals and communities from their homes and habitat, often accompanied by violence, is a phenomenon that has reached an unprecedented scale and continues to accelerate across India. In many instances these evictions are initiated by state agencies (often in collusion with landowners, land mafia, the corporate sector, and other direct beneficiaries). Forced evictions result in the destruction of lives and livelihoods of the evicted people and directly contribute to growing homelessness and social and economic insecurity.

These evictions are sparked by urban renewal projects, sporting events, industrial development, infrastructure expansion (roads, highways, ports), large "development" projects, including dams and mining, environmental conservation projects, awarding of leases to corporations for exploitation of natural resources, and most recently, designation of large areas as tax-free Special Economic Zones (SEZs). This has resulted in the displacement of millions of families, most of who have not received financial compensation, alternate land and housing sites and livelihood opportunities.

DEVELOPMENT-INDUCED DISPLACEMENT

In the name of "development" the state as well as private corporate actors have been acquiring land for large projects and causing both the direct and indirect displacement of communities across India. Over 84 million indigenous/tribal peoples of India, known as the Scheduled Tribes or Adivasis, continue to be disproportionate victims of such "development," displacement and dispossession. Most of the Adivasis live in the thickly forested and mineral-rich regions of central India. Large deposits of natural resources like bauxite, iron ore and coal in these areas have been increasingly targeted for industrial development by the state, which seeks to promote the interests of the fast-growing Indian corporate sector while sacrificing tribal cultures and livelihoods. The issue of displacement and its disproportionate impacts on tribal and other marginalised communities has also been raised in the Compilation prepared by the Office of the High Commissioner for Human Rights (OHCHR) for the Universal Periodic Review of India, which states that:

- The Special Rapporteur on the right to food around 40-50 per cent of the displaced are tribal people even though they make up only eight per cent of the population reflecting serious discrimination against tribal peoples. CERD was concerned that large-scale projects such as the construction of dams on territories primarily inhabited by tribal communities, or the Andaman Trunk Road, are carried out without seeking their prior informed consent. Three special procedures raised concern regarding the situation of Adivasi communities, including in the state of Chhattisgarh, due to the construction of a steel plant.

Nomadic communities, which constitute approximately 7% of India's population, continue to face marginalisation and denial of their customary rights to land. Presently, no formal government scheme exists to address the housing needs of nomadic communities.

Special Economic Zones (SEZs) are being set up in parts of the country on rich agricultural land and in areas around metropolitan cities and major ports. A skewed pattern of regional development can be expected to result, which will be reinforced by the setting up of mineral industry-based SEZs on lands occupied by indigenous communities in Orissa and Chhattisgarh. Official figures show that more than 2500 square kilometres of land have been acquired, implying that more than 35,000 families have already been rendered homeless because of SEZs, many of which violate environment protection laws and have questionable developmental benefits. Other estimates place the total area of SEZ land in India to be over 200,000 hectares, most of which is agricultural land capable of producing almost one million tones of food grains. As more and more agricultural lands are established as SEZs, food security in India is increasingly at risk.

The *Special Economic Zone Act 2005* does not provide for any mechanism for acquisition of land for setting up of SEZs. As a result, in most cases states have resorted to using the colonial era *Land Acquisition Act 1894*. Apart from the fact that the *Land Acquisition Act*, based on the principle of eminent domain does not provide any scope for landholders to refuse to give up their lands for the so-called 'public purpose', it also does not recognise any other rights on land except for that of the titleholder. As a result, acquisition leaves out all those like tenant farmers, sharecroppers and agricultural labourers, from any form of compensation. Further, where land rights have not been regularised and are still customary in nature, the *Land Acquisition Act* only works to disenfranchise people who have been living on the land for several generations and are dependent on it for their livelihoods.

One of the most determined opposition to SEZs has come from the farmers and residents of Raigad in coastal Maharashtra who have opposed the Maha Mumbai SEZ (MMSEZ) from the days of its inception. In Kakinada, Andhra Pradesh, the government acquired land for an SEZ through coercive means. Peoples' refusal to give up their land was met with false charges and jail arrests. Only after the intervention of the State Human Rights Commission, were they granted bail.

Over the last few years, state collusion with corporate and other forces has resulted in violence against local communities and forceful land acquisition without adequate compensation and rehabilitation, as in the case of Nandigram in West Bengal. Documents submitted for India's Universal Periodic Review, including the OHCHR summary of the stakeholders' report also raise issues of the lack of transparency, and intimidation of small and marginal landowners in the process of land acquisition, with security forces and police being used to suppress people's protests. The people of Sikkim have been protesting, including through an indefinite hunger strike, against the over two dozen proposed mega hydroelectric projects on the Teesta River, particularly in Dzongu, the holy land and exclusive reserve of the Lepcha indigenous community. The proposed hydropower projects would have a drastic effect on the social, cultural and religious well-being of the Lepchas, as well as on the fragile environment of Dzongu.

STRUGGLE AGAINST POSCO, ORISSA

POSCO – Pohang Steel Company – the world's fifth largest steel company based in South Korea signed a Memorandum of Understanding (MoU) with the Government of Orissa for setting up a steel plant at Paradeep with a total investment of $12 billion (₹52,000 crores). It is supposedly the largest foreign direct investment in India. The project involves building of a 12 million tonnes per annum (MTPA) integrated steel plant and a captive port in the Ersama Block of Jagatsinghpur district, Orissa. The Government of Orissa will grant POSCO mining lease rights for 30 years that will ensure an adequate supply of 600 million tonnes of iron ore to POSCO. The costs of this operation for POSCO have been estimated at less than 1% of the prevailing global market price for iron ore.

4000 acres of land have been earmarked in Ersama block of Jagatsinghpur district for the purpose of setting up the steel project and associated facilities, including the port and a storage yard for coking coal by the company and the government. The land that would be required for the railway, road expansion and mines is not included in this. The construction of the steel plant and captive port are expected to have far reaching socio-economic and environmental impacts. The proposed plant and port will adversely affect 11 villages and hamlets in three *Gram Panchayats* (village counc ils) in Jagatsinghpur district, namely – Dhinkia, Nuagaon and Gadakujang. As per the local leadership of the movement against POSCO, more than 4000 families and a population of around 22,000 will be affected by the project. These include all those persons directly dependent on the betel vine cultivation, pisciculture, cashew nut cultivation and fishing in the Jatadhari Muhana – the proposed site of the port. As a result, there has been growing opposition to the project in the affected area as well as around the state. Since June 2005 to date, Jagatsinghpur district in Orissa has witnessed frequent protests against the plant. The situation in Jagatsinghpur continues to be tense. The current status of the project is still not clear. Both POSCO and the government need to adopt participatory and transparent practices and ensure that the land rights and livelihoods of the local people are not violated in any enterprise.

ONGOING VIOLATIONS IN VEDANTA'S LANJIGARH REFINERY AND BAUXITE MINING PLANT, ORISSA

M/S Vedanta Alumina Limited (Vedanta) is establishing a one-million-tonne per annum capacity alumina refinery project, together with a 75-megawatt coal-based captive power plant at an estimated cost of about ₹4,000 crores (just under USD 1 billion) in Lanjigarh, Kalahandi District, Orissa, in east India. Vedanta is also establishing an associated bauxite mining project in Niyamgiri Hills, Lanjigarh. Amnesty International, after conducting a mission to the area in November 2006, found that the area under the mining project is home to the 8,000-strong Dongria Kond community (living in about 90 scattered settlements with a distinct cultural heritage) and also the 2,000-strong Majhi Kond communities (living in about 10 settlements mainly in the foothills). The project is likely to lead to a situation of forced eviction of local communities and will threaten their human rights to water, freedom of movement, health, housing, land and livelihood. The plan to expand the illegal refinery from 1 MTPA to 6 MTPA would require an additional 13.43 square kilometres land (to the existing 6.06 square kilometres). Another 22 square kilometres would have to be acquired for waste disposal. This would result in the displacement of an additional 300 to 400 families. Despite a strong indictment by the Central Empowered Committee (CEC) of the Supreme Court of India, the company has continued to proceed with its construction of the alumina refinery. In a recent interim order, the Supreme Court of India denied permission to Vedanta to mine the hills of Niyamgiri in Orissa. The apex court, however, went on to suggest that Vedanta make its Indian partner Sterlite apply for and obtain the clearance. If the Court grants mining clearance to the Company, it will be going against the strong recommendations of its own advisory body, the CEC, as well as the report by the Wildlife Institute of India.

URBAN EVICTIONS

The last few years have witnessed major shifts in land use with rampant speculation in urban and peri-urban areas for real estate development, especially for building housing for the rich, shopping malls, cinemas, hotels and other enterprises. In the absence of state intervention and control, real estate speculation continues to accelerate, making housing more and more unaffordable for the majority.

Between the years 2000 and 2006, over 100,000 families were forcibly evicted from their homes in Delhi, the majority without any resettlement provisions. Just between January and May 2004, Delhi government authorities displaced 27,000 families from Yamuna Pushta. The city of Mumbai witnessed a similar massive eviction drive between November 2004 and March 2005, in which the state government destroyed an estimated 92,000 homes in 44 areas. Preparations for the upcoming 2010 Commonwealth Games in Delhi have already led to the eviction of over 40,000 families. A government report prepared by academics at Delhi University has recommended that Delhi's "beggars" be rounded up by a special police squad and placed in detention centres to make the streets "cleaner." Many street vendors, rickshaw pullers and small shopkeepers have also faced eviction from work by way of ceiling orders, new planning norms and zoning laws.

Evictions have also increased as a consequence of the Jawaharlal Nehru National Urban Renewal Mission (JNNURM), the Central government programme that makes aid to state governments for urban development conditional on implementation of measures for opening up and privatising land and housing markets. Though the JNNURM purports as one of its objectives, the improvement of housing for the economically weaker sections, it is premised on anti-poor prerequisites such as the abolition of the Urban Land (Ceiling and Regulation) Act, 1976. The Government of India report to the Committee claims that the abolition of this Act would lead to the freeing of nearly 0.2 million hectares of urban land for housing, but the land released would likely be used for real estate development as the process effectively contains no equity safeguards. In order to access JNNURM funds, the Government of Bihar abolished the Urban Land Ceiling Act (1976) in April 2006.

This Act had enabled slum dwellers to occupy vacant government land. They were enrolled as voters and given ration cards that amounted to legal recognition of their housing rights. With the annulment of the Urban Land (Ceiling and Regulation) Act, all their rights have also been negated. Evictions are also being carried out under the guise of urban renewal in several Indian cities. In Mumbai, more than 200 houses were demolished at Sainath Nagar, Irla Nala, Juhu on 24 December 2007 under the Brihanmumbai storm water drains project (BRIMSTOWAD) project, which is being implemented under funding from JNNURM. The total number of families affected by evictions in the 64 cities where JNNURM is currently being implemented, is estimated by activists to be well over one million. The formation of the Greater Hyderabad Municipal Corporation has resulted in an increase of the urban area from175 square kilometres to 625 square kilometres. The expansion has resulted in the absorption of 54 adjoining *mandals* (revenue provinces) and 66 villages into the urban agglomeration; this is likely to result in displacement and loss of livelihoods.

Though the Government of India in its report to the Committee recognises the critical link between housing and livelihood and stresses the need for evictions to be carried out under due process, these principles are not followed in practice. People living in slums and other informal settlements have been facing demolition drives without any due process and are being relocated to city outskirts. In the majority of cases, evictions generally result in loss of livelihood, especially since most relocation sites are situated on the outskirts of cities and do not provide adequate housing or basic services such as water, transport, electricity, and healthcare. Evictions in the absence of adequate rehabilitation most severely impact the rights of children and women. Evictions also directly increase homelessness, as the absence of rehabilitation and feasible alternate options for housing, forces many to live on the streets.

The continued practice of forced evictions and displacement, while violating international and constitutional law, also stands in contravention of the United Progressive Alliance (UPA) Government's Common Minimum Programme (CMP), which provides that "Forced eviction and demolition of slums will be stopped and while undertaking urban renewal, care will be taken to see that the urban and semi-urban poor are provided housing near their place of occupation."

Questions for the Government of India:

- What measures has the government taken to check against the practice of forced evictions in the country? Despite provisions in municipal laws and the Common Minimum Programme of the central government, why are evictions without due process and adequate resettlement, on the rise?
- What safeguards are in place to ensure protection of people's rights in compliance with India's obligations under Art. 11.1 of ICESCR, General Comments 4 and 7 of the Committee on Economic, Social and Cultural Rights, as well as other international human rights standards?
- How many families have been evicted from government-owned land in the four metros in the last five years? How many of these families have been provided with alternative housing? Can the government provide city-wise figures with sources of data?
- Does the government have any data on the number of people evicted and the number of homes demolished in Delhi for the preparation of the Commonwealth Games, including the cons truction of the Commonwealth Games Village?
- Why has the Maharashtra government not rehabilitated the 92,000

families forcefully evicted in Mumbai between 2004 and 2005? (Only 612 families were declared eligible and only 412 have been actually rehabilitate

- What plans does the government have for rehabilitation, including for the allocation of land and adequate housing? What is the budgetary allocation for rehabilitation?
- Why has the Maharashtra government denied water connection to households establis hed after 1995 in slum settlements?
- What are the standards for adequate housing, basic services and social security in resettlement colonies? Is the government complying with international human rights standards? What are the indicators for monitoring these standards?
- What provisions are being included in the draft *Rehabilitation and Resettlement Act 2007* and the draft *National Urban Housing and Habitat Policy 2007* to check against forced evictions and displacement?
- What measures is the government taking to ensure that provisions under the 72nd and 73rd amendments (elected local bodies) of the Indian Constitution are protected?
- Does the government have detailed information on the amount of land acquired by it for "public interest" purposes over the last sixty years? In what percentage of the cases have the displaced people been adequately rehabilitated? What indicators has the government developed to monitor rehabilitation of those displaced by the state (including public sector companies)?
- As also raised in the Compilation Prepared by OHCHR for India's Universal Periodic Review, what measures has the government taken to implement the Concluding Observation of CERD where it urged the State to fully respect and implement the right of ownership, collective or individual, of the members of tribal communities over the lands traditionally occupied by them in accordance with ILO Convention 107 on Indigenous and Tribal Populations? In addition, as also recommended by CERD, what are the adequate safeguards against the acquisition of tribal lands as included in the Scheduled Tribes and Other Traditional Forest Dwellers (Recognition of Forest Rights) Act (2006) and other relevant legislation.
- What is the status of the proposed Coastal Zone Management (CZM) Notification? Why are there differential provisions for commercial enterprises and coastal communities in accessing the coastline? What measures is the government taking to ensure that communities' customary rights to the coast are protected?
- Is the government challenging the anti-poor judgements of the courts that contradict India's constitutional provisions and international human rights obligations?

Recommendations for the Government of India:

- The government must adhere to international human rights principles and undertake evictions "only in exceptional circumstances and in full accordance with relevant provisions of international human rights and humanitarian law."
- All responsible agencies must undertake "eviction impact assessments" – including social, envir onmental and economic impact assessments – *before* any eviction is carried out.
- The government should implement Concluding Observations by CERD and CEDAW related to displacement, and rights of women, dalits and tribals.
- The proposed *Resettlement and Rehabilitation Act 2007* must be based on and be consistent with both international human rights principles and constitutional obligations. The non-negotiable principles of gender equality, non-discrimination, indivisibility of human rights and prior informed consent must be adopted. The Act must be expanded to include urban and coastal displacement. The process for finalising the Act must be participatory and consultative, especially with civil society.
- The government should issue a White Paper on the number of people displaced and rehabilitated in India since independence.
- Rehabilitation must ensure that peoples' habitats and livelihoods are restored, in accordance with their needs and aspirations, and must guarantee an improved lifestyle and overall well being over what they enjoyed prior to the displacement.
- The *Land Acquisition (Amendment) Bill 2007* should be revised or dismissed. Instead, the Land Acquisition Act, 1894, should be replaced with a new comprehensive human rights based legislation, which must, among other things, clearly specify the definition of "public purpose," incorporate democratic processes and institutions, and aim to minimize displacement.
- Housing plans should ensure that denotified and nomadic communities who wish to settle are allotted adequate land to enable them to lead a settled life in peace and dignity. Common property resources as well as grazing lands should be made accessible to those who do not wish to give up their traditional nomadic lifestyle.
- The *Habitual Offenders Act* should be repealed, as recommended by the National Human Rights Commission in February 2002.

HOMELESSNESS

Homelessness across India is on the rise, especially in large cities. Though the Government of India in its report claims that, "The country has been able to reduce the houselessness over the period of time due to the various housing programmes being implemented by both Central and State Governments," there is no data to substantiate this claim. The government has made no official attempt to document the number of homeless people in India. The Committee, in its List of Issues to the Government of India, also raised this question. In the capital city of New Delhi alone, at any given point, civil society estimates place the number of homeless at around 100,000, of which 10,000 are women. Despite this alarming situation, the city government evicted homeless women from the Palika Hostel night shelter in 2004, and in June 2007, closed the only existing women's shelter in the city. Currently, there is no shelter for homeless women in Delhi.

No official government schemes exist for homeless people. Even the Government of India report, admits that the "night shelter scheme for footpath dwellers was transferred to the State sector w.e.f. 01.04.2005." At the state level, however, there has been no follow up of this programme nor have any concrete measures been taken to address the causes of homelessness and to provide alternate housing for homeless people.

Questions for the Government of India:

- What steps is the government taking to address the causes and prevalence of homelessness in India?
- What percentage of the budget is allocated to creating and maintaining shelters for the homeless?
- Why does the draft *National Urban Housing and Habitat Policy 2007* not include adequate measures to address homelessness and its causes?

Recommendations to the Government of India:

- Create adequate shelters and housing provisions for all homeless people, especially homeless women.
- Abolish outdated legislation like the *Bombay Prevention of Begging Act 1959*, and the *Bombay Vagrancy Act 1959*, and analogous laws in other states, as they effectively criminalize the poor and homeless.
- Undertake periodic surveys and collect and make available disaggregated data on homeless people in India, including number of homeless women and children as well as the number of government-run homeless shelters across the country.

STREET CHILDREN

Even though India has the largest population of street children in the world, the Government of India report to the Committee admits in paragraph 322 that, "there is no authentic data in India on street children." The last attempt to document the number of street children in India was in 1997. Lack of adequate housing has long-term deleterious effects, including severe psychological impacts on children. Children suffer the most from forced evictions and displacement, which often result in loss of education, and in the absence of adequate rehabilitation, homelessness. Street children, in particular, face extreme conditions of violence, abuse, harsh weather conditions, injury, malnutrition, exploitation, and lack of security. Despite the existence of several programmes, the plight of street children continues to be dismal.

Questions to the Government of India:

- What steps have been taken to track and monitor the number and situation of street children in India since 1997?
- What measures are being taken by the government to ensure the adequate rehabilitation of street children?
- How many shelters does the government run exclusively for street children? What are the measures to safeguard the rights of street children with special needs, such as children with disabilities, HIV/AIDS, and mental health problems?
- What measures is the government taking to ensure that street children are included in government schemes for children such as Integrated Child Development Service (ICDS) centres?
- What specific measures is the government taking to implement the Concluding Observations of the Committee on the Rights of the Child (2000), in particular paras. 53 and 54, which focus on housing, evictions and street children?

Recommendations for the Government of India:

- The government must urgently address the broader structural issues that lead to forced migration of children from rural areas to cities in need of subsistence.
- The state must create more and better equipped long-term homes to meet the special needs of street children, in particular children who are orphans and abandoned, which focus on their holistic and all round development, including education, housing, and health.
- The government should meet its reporting commitments to the Committee on the Rights of the Child and report on steps taken to realise children's right to adequate housing in India, including implementation of Concluding Observations.

DENIAL OF DALITS' RIGHTS TO ADEQUATE HOUSING AND LAND

Dalits and other scheduled castes (SCs) continue to face ongoing discrimination and a direct onslaught of their human rights to adequate housing, land and livelihood. Of particular significance is the discrimination and systematic denial of Dalits' land rights, which forms the basis for realising other human rights, including the rights to food and adequate housing. Possession of la nd is considered to be a status symbol within the caste hierarchy and that is why a majority of the atrocities against Dalits are linked to the distribution of land by the government in various states. Landlessness among SCs is a common feature in the Indian rural economy. The 1999-2000 NSS data illustrates that around 10 per cent of SC households in India are landless as compared to 13.34 per cent in 1992 and 19.10 per cent in 1982. Though it is apparent that landlessness is decreasing, the rate of decrease is marginal. On the other hand, 6.15 per cent of the non-SC/ST households were found to be landless in 1999-2000, as compared to 10.53 in 1992. The non-availability of disaggregated data prevents in-depth analysis and targeted planning, which may contribute to discrimination against Dalits in the realisation of their rights to land, housing, health, education and employment.

A clear reflection of poverty and marginalisation amongst Dalits is that their housing and living conditions are characterized by the use of inferior building materials, high density, lack of access to civic services, and spatial segregation. Dalit settlements are generally situated outside villages, with restricted access to water sources, and public and religious spaces. Dalits are often denied access to and are evicted from their land by dominant castes and therefore forced to live on the outskirts of villages, often on barren land. Violence against Dalits is also caused due to land or property disputes, with punitive action seldom taken against the perpetrators. Dalit women, in particular, face discrimination in accessing their rights to adequate housing and land.

Recommendations for the Government of India:

- Special schemes should be implemented that prioritise reallocation of surplus, including ceiling, land to Dalits, especially landless Dalits.
- Urgent measures need to be taken to prevent the ongoing atrocities and violence against Dalits, including Dalit women, in their struggle to gain equal access to land, housing and basic services.
- The government should take measures to implement the Concluding Observations of the *Committee on the Elimination of Racial Discrimination (CERD)*. In particular: 20. The Committee recommends that the State party ensure that Dalits, including Dalit women, have access to adequate and affordable land and that acts of violence against Dalits due to land disputes are punished under the Scheduled Castes and Scheduled Tribes (Prevention of Atrocities) Act (1989).

Questions to the Government of India:

- What positive measures has the government taken to improve access of Dalits to housing and land? What indicators is the government using to assess this? In particular, what are the legal and policy measures in place to ensure redress of social inequities of land ownership amongst Dalits?
- Of the total land area redistributed in the last ten years, what percentage of land has been allotted to landless Dalit families?

- How many cases have been registered under the Scheduled Castes Scheduled Tribes Prevention of Atrocities Act, 1989 in the last five years? Of these, how many have resulted in perpetrators being brought to trial?

LANDLESSNESS

The issue of landlessness and failed land reform continues to negatively impact the housing and land rights of people and communities that live in rural India. Over 1.31 crore (131 million) people are landless as per figures from the Ministry of Rural Development. These families do not have even land for their own habitation. The Common Minimum Programme of the United Progressive Alliance government clearly states that, "Landless families will be endowed with land through implementation of land ceiling and land redistribution legislation. No reversal of ceiling legislation will be permitted." Despite this, the Urban Land (Ceiling and Regulation) Act 1976 has been repealed in many states.

Land distribution in India is highly skewed. The NSS Survey of the 55 Round shows that among rural households, 5.67 per cent are landless, 66.05 per cent own less than one hectare of land, and 13.71 per cent own land between one to two hectares. Land ownership is also directly related to poverty. There is a near inverse relationship between landholding and the poverty ratio. It is thus clear that amelioration of rural poverty is contingent on redistribution of land and provision of incentives in the form of ownership rights to farmers, including women farmers and tenants through land reforms.

While the Government of India report to the Committee mentions the phenomenon of landlessness and achievements in land redistribution, the effective implementation and benefits of land and agrarian reform in order to promote social equity are still to be witnessed in most parts of the country. This is even more critical given the crisis of farmer suicides in the country. What is needed is a much stronger political will and an effort to regularise land ownership, implement land ceiling laws, and redistribute surplus land to the poorest and most marginal communities.

Questions for the Government of India:

- What concrete measures is the government taking to rectify the highly inequitable pattern of land distribution in India?
- What is the legal authority of the newly constituted National Land Commission under the aegis of the Prime Minister, to make decisions and implement land reform measures across different states?
- How much of acquired surplus ceiling land has actually been redistributed and how much of it is held up in pending legal cases? What measures is the government taking to ensure speedy resolution of land related litigation?
- How many hectares of surplus ceiling lands have been vested and

distributed to landless families in the last ten years? Of the recipient families, how many have received secure legal titles over the land?

Recommendations for the Government of India:

- The government needs to prioritise land reform on the political agenda. Even though land is a state subject under the Indian constitution, the central government should play a greater role in its administration and regulation.
- The National Land Commission set up by the Prime Minister should play a lead role in implementing equitable land reform measures and prioritising needs of marginal farmers and other land-dependent communities.
- Special land courts should be set up to expedite litigation related to land.
- Surplus ceiling land should be distributed to landless families. Secure titles, in the name of women, should be given over all redistributed land.

DISCRIMINATION AND DENIAL OF WOMEN'S EQUAL RIGHTS TO ADEQUATE HOUSING, LAND, PROPERTY AND INHERITANCE

Despite the existence of laws that protect women's rights, women in India continue to suffer discrimination with regard to their rights to adequate housing, land, property and inheritance.

The impacts of inadequate living conditions, forced evictions and homelessness are greater on women. Overcrowding and precarious housing threaten women's rights to security of the home and person, and the right to privacy, and leave them vulnerable to violence and ill-health. Violence within the home is one manifestation of women's particular vulnerability in relation to housing rights. In this context, *The Prevention of Women from Domestic Violence Act 2005* is significant and holds promise, if implemented appropriately.

In review of India's progress in fulfilling its CEDAW obligations, the Committee on the Elimination of Discrimination against Women stated that denial of inheritance rights in land result in gross exploitation of women's labour and their impoverishment. Time-use data and agricultural census figures indicate that women perform well over 50 per cent of all agricultural work in the country.

Nearly 20 per cent of rural households are now women-headed. However, less than two per cent of women hold titles to land and have access to independent agricultural credit. The impoverishing impact of landlessness is exacerbated by social exclusion and discrimination for Dalit women. An existing Government of India directive (issued in 1992) on joint registration of land distributed under government schemes in the name of both husband

and wife is neither enforced nor monitored. Recent amendments to legislation on Hindu women's property rights (*Hindu Succession Amendment Act, 2005*) have mandated equal inheritance rights for men and women in agricultural land and family property, including dwellings. However, these amendments do not apply to non-Hindu women. The extent to which Hindu women will be able to take advantage of these provisions in a milieu where dowry is still prevalent, remains to be seen.

Questions for the Government of India:

- Does the government have any data on the number of states with legislation (or Government Orders/ Regulations) recognising women's individual and collective rights, and on registering land/ housing/ property in the name of women or jointly?
- What percentage of housing units distributed under government schemes in the last ten years has been registered in the joint names of husband and wife and in the names of single women? What measures have been instituted to enforce directives in this regard?
- Have there been any attempts to monitor the implementation of the *Prevention of Domestic Violence Act 2005*, in particular the number of cases in which women have retained their right to continue living in their place of residence?
- What percentage of redistributed surplus ceiling lands has been registered in the names of women or men and women jointly? What measures have been instituted to enforce directives in this regard?
- What efforts has the government taken to implement the Concluding Observations of CEDAW to, *inter alia*, study the impact of mega projects on tribal and rural women and to institute safeguards against their displacement and violation of their rights as well as to ensure that surplus land given to displaced rural and tribal women is cultivable?

Recommendations for the Government of India:

- The Government of India needs to adopt and promote a gender-equality approach based on principles of substantive equality and intersectionality in all national and local laws and policies, including the draft *Rehabilitation and Resettlement Act 2007* and the draft *National Housing and Habitat Policy 2007*.
- The Government should take immediate steps to implement the Concluding Observation 83 (2000) of the Committee on the Elimination of All Forms of Discrimination against Women wherein, "it calls upon the Government to review laws on inheritance urgently and to ensure that rural women obtain access to land and credit," and Concluding Observation 47 (February 2007): "The Committee urges the State party to study the impact of mega projects on tribal and rural women and to institute safeguards against their displacement and violation of their

human rights. It also urges the State party to ensure that surplus land given to displaced rural and tribal women is cultivable. Moreover, the Committee recommends that efforts be made to ensure that tribal and rural women have individual rights to inherit and own land and property."

- The government should consider implementing the recommendations for state action contained in the numerous resolutions and reports of the UN on women's rights to land, housing, property and inheritance.
- The central government should undertake periodic surveys and provide disaggregated data on indicators related to women, housing and land.
- The collective and individual land rights of women to adequate housing, land, natural resources, property, and inheritance should be legally recognised and promoted.

INADEQUATE REHABILITATION OF TSUNAMI SURVIVORS

The 2004 tsunami affected the coastal areas of Andhra Pradesh, Kerala, Tamil Nadu, Andaman and Nicobar Islands and Puducherry, affecting over 28 lakh (2.8 million) people and leading to loss of life and property. Post-tsunami rehabilitation, however, despite the passage of three years, continues to be fraught with delays and inadequacie s in restoring permanent housing and livelihoods to the survivors. The Public Accounts Committee in its 2007-08 report on "Tsunami Relief and Rehabilitation" divulges that the affected State and Union Territory governments had diverted funds and committe d other irregularities in the amount of ₹228.58 crores (₹2.285 billion). It also mentions that the government has "failed to provide much needed relief" to the victims even after three years.

While most families have been allotted alternate housing in the state of Tamil Nadu, several families in Chennai and Thiruvallur districts, are still awaiting housing. Some of the permanent housing that has been provided, as in Thondiarpet, violates standards of adequacy in terms of size, location and design. Though the Indian Supreme Court, as mentioned in the Government of India report too, defines an adequate house, most of the houses constructed for the tsunami affected do not meet these criteria. In Chennai, most of the houses are located far from the city and are not connected with proper roads and transportation facilities.

The three-story houses given to survivors in Thondiarpet do not cater to the specific needs of the fishing community, and do not take into account the size of families or needs of women and persons with disabilities. All families, irrespective of number of family members, have been allotted flats that have an inner plinth area of the house of just 160-170 square feet. The houses have just one room with a partition for kitchen and an attached bathroom that is just 30 square feet. As is evident in the case of the tsunami, the impacts of natural disasters and failed rehabilitation are felt most strongly by women and children. Relocation of families in the middle of the academic year has resulted in an increase in dropouts from school, especially of girl children. In Okkiyum Thoraipakkam in Tamil Nadu, 43 school going children have dropped out due to the increased distance from the relocation site to the school. Two women in the same relocation site were forced to give birth on the road, as they were unable to reach the hospital on time; the hospital is more than 20 kilometres from the site. Two people have died because of delay in transporting them to hospital.

There are no public health centres and Integrated Child Development Service (ICDS) centres. Though the Government of India report states that the Indira Awas Yojna is applicable to construction of houses for victims of a natural calamity, in the coastal areas of Chenna i and Thiruvallur as well as in other urban mainland slums, all housing is under the aegis of the Tamil Nadu Slum Clearance Board (TNSCB) and the design, size and location of the housing is inadequate. TNSCB is also responsible for several demolition and relocation projects related to redevelopment across Chennai.

A common complaint across tsunami sites has been the lack of consultation with survivors. The discriminatory nature of rehabilitation for fishing and non-fishing communities has also been proble matic. From Chennai District alone, there were 7342 people who were relocated to resettlement sites that were far from the coast and the city where their livelihood thrives. The people who were relocated were predominantly Dalits and other minorities who were considered to be non-fishing communities.

In the Andaman and Nicobar Islands, only 298 houses have been provided of the 9797 houses that the government has agreed to build. This list, however, has left out several hundred families who are still await ing news on whether they will receive government housing or not. While the government plans to complete construction of housing by December 2008, the majority of people (9500 families) are still living in intermediate tin shelters in highly inadequate conditions. In order for rehabilitation to be adequate, it must be grounded in human rights principles, and must especially incorporate a gender-equality approach.

Questions for the Government of India:

- Why is it that even three years after the tsunami, thousands of families are still awaiting permanent housing in Tamil Nadu?
- What steps is the government taking to ensure that housing is provided for those whose names are left out of the housing lists – in both Tamil Nadu and the Andaman and Nicobar Islands, including tenants?
- Why are the majority of tsunami survivors still living in intermediate tin shelters in the Andaman and Nicobar Islands?
- Does the government have a clear timeline as to when permanent

housing will be completed for all tsunami survivors in all the affected areas?

- How does the government justify the finding of the Public Accounts Committee (PAC) in its 2007-08 report that states and Union Territories have diverted ₹228.58 crores (₹2.285 billion) at the cost of beneficiaries?

Recommendations for the Government of India:

- The right to relief and rehabilitation, as well as the right to disaster prevention must be recognised as human rights, and the Government of India must take measures to ensure the adoption and implementation of human rights standards in all aspects of disaster management and post-disaster response.
- As also requested by the Committee in its List of Issues, the government should provide detailed information on the post-tsunami rehabilitation process, including in terms of housing, education, and livelihood restoration in the affected districts in Tamil Nadu.

PLIGHT OF INTERNALLY DISPLACED IN GUJARAT

Six years after the 2002 communal violence in the state of Gujarat, in which more than 2000 people were killed, survivors continue to face discrimination in housing as well as serious challenges and obstacles in securing justice. An estimated 250,000 individuals were displaced as a direct result of the 2002 violence against the Muslim community in Gujarat. The vast majority of them has reportedly left the state or has moved to other, mostly Muslim, localities within the state.

An approximate 5,000 families are still living in what are being referred to as "relief colonies" in four districts of Gujarat - Panchmahals, Sabarkantha, Dahod, Anand, and in the cities of Ahmedabad and Vadodara. An independent survey conducted by *Citizens for Justice and Peace* for a public interest litigation in the Gujarat High Court, fear and terror continues to affect rehabilitation and return of these families from the camps to their original and ancestral habitats. Reasons are varied but the single reason cited in this survey conducted in over 24,000 homes is that the affected displaced persons are threatened by the perpetrators not to return.

Over the last six years, these camps have become permanent places of residence for those who are too frightened to return home. Most of the survivors living in these colonies lost land, housing, cattle, agricultural implements and other means of livelihood, and have not received adequate compensation or restoration and reparation of their human rights. A survey by *Citizens for Justice and Peace* conducted for a Member of Parliament Delegation and also presented to the National Commission for Minorities on November 30 2006, all relief colonies are run and maintained by community groups and NGOs, none supported by the state. These colonies do not have basic amenities, nor are they officially recognised by the Government of Gujarat. Victim survivor groups have consistently complained to the administration and the authorities abut the inadequate living conditions in camps. In Citizens Nagar, Bombay Hotel area, and Faizal Park area, the lack of potable drinking water and sanitation is making life difficult for displaced persons. In early November 2007, a 13-year old boy Riyaz died of kidney failure – attributed to high salinity in the water supply in Citizens Nagar.

In October 2006, for the first time in five years, India's National Commission of Minorities (NCM) visited these relief colonies. The NCM's findings contested the Government of Gujarat's claim that all those displaced by the violence had been adequately rehabilitated. The report also asserted that the Gujarat government had failed to provide a safe environment for these people or facilitate their return to their homes. This includes the failure to adequately recompense those families whose houses were partially or completely destroyed during the 2002 violence.

The People's Union for Civil Liberties (PUCL) filed a Right to Food petition for survivors in the Supreme Court of India in March 2007. In the course of the hearing of this petition, Court Commissioner, NC Saxena filed a report, scathing in its findings of the position and plight of Gujarat's internally displaced persons. The report states that 4,545 families comprising around 30,000 persons still live in very difficult conditions in 81 relief colonies. The response of both the Government of Gujarat and the Government of India to the plight of the internally displaced, in particular the lack of attention or action, has been disconcerting.

Questions for the Government of India and the Government of Gujarat:

- How does the Government of Gujarat justify the fact that six years after the 2002 communal violence, thousands of affected families are still living in relief camps in adequate living conditions without any state assistance?
- Despite strong recommendations by the NCM and recently by the Saxena report, why has the Government not taken any concrete measures to ensure the safe return of displaced Muslims to their original homes and habitats?
- What measures is the Government taking to improve the housing and living conditions of the internally displaced familie s in Gujarat? What standards/benchmarks is the Government using to monitor living conditions in resettlement colonies?

Recommendations for the Government of India:

- The Government must act on the recommendations of the NCM, in particular, to provide a special economic package for the rehabilitation of those families living in camps; ensure that basic amenities are provided in the camps; formally recognize those displaced as a result of the violence as internally displaced persons; and to draft a policy to deal with the displacement of individuals as a result of communal as well as other types of conflict.

- Both the Government of India and Gujarat must implement the recommendations of the Saxena report, which include, *inter alia* that:
  - Contempt of court notices are issued to the chief secretary and other officials of the government.
  - Antyodaya cards are given to all families who continue to live in relief colonies
  - Primary schools with midday meals and ICDS centres should be opened in all 81 relief colonies.
  - Public Distribution System (PDS or ration shops) should be opened in all colonies where these are not available within a distance of three kilometres.
  - Issue job cards under the National Rural Employment Guarantee Act (NREGA) to all residents of relief colonies who are desirous of these.
- Document the number of families living in relief colonies and their living conditions, and submit periodic action taken reports describing steps to facilitate their return to their original habitats.

9

Dalit Rights and Caste Discrimination

Caste discrimination and Dalit Rights over natural resources is one of the most complicated issues that the country is today faced with. As such this is not a new question; however the current format is a relatively newer one. There are specific reasons and compulsion for raising this question at this juncture of history as the betrayal of the betrayed continues for centuries unknown till today. Raising this issue would unfold the conspiracy of the upper caste rulers of this country to which they may be obliged to answer. Caste system is to be understood in two parts *viz.* the material and ideological-culturalspiritual one.

The material base of caste system systematically took away the control over property (the entire resource base), operationalised division of labour, income distribution and surplus appropriation. In the second part the geo-centric culture, history, ideology and spirituality was replaced with an alien one consisting of slavery, subjugation, made the indigenous communities realise that such culture is substandard, subjected them to inhuman suppression as the caste (jati) and birth determined it to be their destination. Therefore everything was centred on 'birth'.

The indigenous communities were forced to culturally, ideologically and spiritually forced to apply all energy and efforts on the revival of their 'birth' from the present lower caste background to a higher ladder. This elevation of status – as per the '*shastras*' – was only possible through tireless service of the upper caste lords in the present birth thereby avoiding the traumas in the next birth.

This traditional order was not merely an ideological construct but an economic and political structure too. It articulated and encapsulated an entire system of production that existed over centuries with only minor alterations within its confines. The economical and political realities of inequalities were justified, defied and glorified through religious pronouncements based on the purity - pollution divide. Traditionally, ritualistic compulsion and coercive oppression ensured their compliance in providing virtually free labour for the upper caste land owners. The fact that they had been denied right over land or territory only compounded the matter by making them completely dependent upon the owners and controllers of the means of production and livelihood. The subsequent consequences had been drastic. All forms of resources, (both productive and natural) including land, water, forests and other sources went out of the hands. The belief system that evolved over the course of time told the indigenous people time and again that they were not supposed to owe any property, lest lay claims over it. They were reduced as slaves and labouring class on their own land. Land and forest turned to be alien to the Dalits. Yet the cultural history speaks volumes about their closed relationship with nature and natural resources and its mutuality with human beings. There are traces of Buddha's Sanghas in several forestlands which was mostly inhabited by lower caste people. Many untouchable communities had been living in forest areas and forest fringes for hundreds of years as weavers, bamboo weavers/workers, yet they haven't been recognized as the original inhabitants in most of the cases.

Today land, forests and other natural resources are not free from public debates. However with caste become the key constituent and the centre of power it also developed as a social system in resource control and management. The very character of control and management shifted from a community oriented *"sangha"* to production, accumulation, surplus and so on. As relation of property in the means of production drifts, the nature of relations among people in the process also alters. The fact that Dalits have been denied any permanent right over any land or territory has only compounded that matter by making them completely dependent upon the owners and controllers of the means of production and livelihood. It is an undeniable fact that Dalits have suffered displacement from land through the ages. The land occupied by them has always been seized at the flimsiest excuse, forcibly or through economic strangling. The right to hold land - even homestead land - of these groups, has always been tenuous at best.

The continuous process of expropriation of resources, particularly land, from these sections takes on a new dimension today. The pasture and fallow lands were developed by the labour of particularly the Dalit toilers in the hope that they would at last acquire a piece of land to call their own. However, once the land is developed and made cultivable, however, they are forced off it through various measures, covert and overt, legal and illegal, economic and extra-economic. Debts and mortgages, denial of other vital resources like water and agricultural implements and inputs, social boycotts, upper caste violence, rapes, mutilations and killings throw them off the land. Their labour invested in the development of land is expropriated, at best at a pittance.

AGRARIAN REFORMS, ITS FAILURE AND DALIT

The owners of the land are today landless; that is Dalits. In most part of the country Dalits are either landless or marginal farmer. Analysing it from the historical viewpoint they are the first plebeian community of the country. Due to caste discrimination and high skewed landholding, it created the paucity of land right of the marginalised sections. During the pre-independence period the question of Dalit land came up time and again, which was mostly centred on two types of questions. One was the demand of land rights as the Dalits were mostly working as bonded labourers to their caste lords. Second was related with independent agricultural rights of the cultivators. This discourse gave birth to the slogan "land to the tillers".

In several parts of the country it came up as a mass movement particularly in areas where the sizeable majority had been the landless or agricultural labourers. Despite severe resistance of the landed upper caste section, the mass character of the movement compelled the government to address the questions of land reforms as well as agricultural reforms. There had been controversies on land reforms to the verge that any such steps would enrage the upper caste zamindars to topple any government.

The majority of Dalits being part of the rustic labouring class with some openings of upward mobility via positive discrimination, the impetus created by the peasant movements and ideological pressure by left for land redistribution altogether led to the emergence of certain concerns for the rural landless poor – compelled a step towards agrarian reforms. Notwithstanding the social and political influence of the landlords sought to maintain their traditional hold over the land and agrarian system and structure. As a result of this, even after independence there were no radical agrarian reforms. Although in the post independence period, government abolished the zamindari system and enacted the Tenancy Regulation Act to be implemented by the various states, it failed to address the question of land-to-the tiller whereby large sections of the rural poor especially Dalits were deprived of land.

A close examination of various land reforms laws has shown that the present legislative measures have become so complex that a graduated or phased programme of implementation according to priority attached in each problem in various areas was what was really absent in it. Beneath the undercurrents of the dominant landholding system of Zamindari, land reforms and land distribution become more harsh and formidable in the newly arisen socio-political context. One of the classic instances of this is the countrywide struggle on the question of land distribution between the rich landholders and the landless poor across the country.

The failure of the land reforms can be judged by the fact that 86% own small tracks of land, not enough for sustenance, forcing Dalits to work as agricultural labourers. Besides, there was the so-called Dakathia system, in Central Bihar, that had evolved by the upper caste to perpetuate their control over the Dalits. A landlord gave 10 katha (a little less than half acre) of land to a labourer who cultivated it and keep the harvest. In return, he had to be ready to work for the landlord at a standard rate of 2 kgs of rice and half a kg of sattu (flour of Bengal gram). Often 10-15 persons in the rural areas depend on such land for survival. If the Dalits wish to migrate the land is confiscated along with the standing crop and if harvested he is forced to pay the rent for the whole year which the Dalits cannot afford. Hence they are bound to that system and the land for generations.

The redistribution of surplus land was initially a voluntary step through the Bhoodan movement which arose in response to the revolutionary uprising of the peasantry in Telangana. Distribution of 'surplus' land donated by the landlords to the landless to prevent a revolutionary uprising was the driving impetus for this campaign. With the adoption of land ceiling, redistribution of land found acceptance in some states.

The implementation of this measure was however, haphazard. The redistribution was extremely conditional. Commercialisation of agriculture necessitated intensive cultivation of food grains. This was in direct contradiction with the policy of assisting a subsistence level of existence to the rural poor who had been distributed wasteland. The land distributed under the land reforms as well as the bhoodan movement was economically nonviable and to a large extent of inferior quality. (The land less labourers got on an average one acre of land per household which was insufficient for their sustenance which forced them to seek opportunities for work as labour elsewhere). They also did not posses the required capital for seeds and fertilizers. In certain areas where the co-operative movement was strong they were able to sustain by taking loans. To convert a landless agricultural labourer into a subsistence farmer in an age when subsistence farming is non-viable due to rise in the cost of production and marketing is problematic. This has given rise to the sale of lands.

The Bhoodan movement did not actually reduce the landlessness among the dalits. Instead, the opposite trend can be observed for non SC/ST rural communities. The percentage of households with land increased and percentage without land decreased during the same period. The land reforms and the Bhoodan movement were necessarily limited in their scope.

They promoted further commercialisation, and capitalisation of agriculture, paving the way for the creation of a relatively new class of surplus producing owner-cultivators relating to the market, the potential capitalist peasantry in the country. In caste terms, the measure immensely aided the middle castes economically and hence socially and politically to dominate the Dalits agricultural labourers. The agricultural labourers were left untouched in these reforms. The percentage of rural Dalit labour households with land declined from 44.38% in 1974-75 to 35.05% in 1993-94. On the other hand, the percentage of rural labour households without land increased from 55.65% in 1974-75 to 64.95% in 1993-94. Many of those displaced have ended up as daily wage labourers in the Public Works Department, working on national highways, suffering from poisonous fumes, heat and dust, and earning less than ₹ 45 per day.

FOREST, FORESTLAND AND DALITS

For sometime the question of forest, forestland and people – particularly Dalits and Adivasis – have been striking our ears every now and then. Predominantly the general opinion is that Adivasis are only connected with forest and forestland. It is unchallengeable that Adivasi history, life, culture and identity has been so closely linked with the forests that it cannot be separated into watertight compartments such as social, economic, religious, administrative and political. However it cannot be denied that the ex-untouchable were never in close interaction with the forest eco-system. The symbiotic relationship with forests wasn't only maintained by the Adivasisi but also the ex-untouchables – the Dalits. There are several examples of Dalit being part of the forest ecosystem for generations unknown. Even today there are several worship orders which is geo-centric in which they worship the bhumidevi, matidevi, vandevi which indicates that they had been living in close association with forest, forestland and forest resources.

Any system in harmony with the traditional system, therefore, has to be designed around this holistic perception of life of the not only Adivasis but also Dalits. There should be no doubt that the historically broken and scattered Dalits are also part of the larger indigenous family in India. The problem is not whether the Adivasis consider Dalits as indigenous. The problem had been that independent India continued with the British legacy – the huge and bureaucratic forest department and the Indian Forest Act of 1927. In 1980, the Central government centralized its powers further. It is interesting to note that the forest department is the biggest landlord in India today with 76.5 million hectares (23% of total land mass) as forest lands, though not necessarily under tree cover (which is 62.4 million ha. only).

The biggest dilemma is that almost 75 years after independence, today in forest regions Indian state continues all anti-Dalit juxtaposes, strengthens caste system, defends and sustains the British-India's draconian acts and laws quite uninterruptedly, without leaving the minimum breathing space at all. Despite the change of governments under the auspices of different political parties it has almost failed to address this issue of Dalit rights over forest resources in any manner. This raises an array of question on the very character and approach of the state, rather the ruling class towards the forest based communities of the country.

Ironically without taking such aspects into consideration and without even consulting with Dalit NGOs, movements and organizations, the process was carried forth in drafting of the Scheduled Tribes and Other Traditional Forest Dwellers (Recognition of Forest Rights) Act, 2006. No doubt it is a result of the protracted struggle by the Adivasi and marginal communities of the country to assert their rights over the forestland over which they were traditionally dependent. This Act is crucial to the rights of millions of Adivasis and other forest dwellers in different parts of our country as it provides for the restitution of deprived forest rights across India.

The rights which are included in section 3(1) of the Act are:

- Right to hold and live in the forest land under the individual or common occupation for habitation or for self-cultivation for livelihood by a member or members of a forest dwelling Scheduled Tribe or other traditional forest dwellers;
- Community rights such as nistar, by whatever name called, including those used in erstwhile Princely states, Zamindari or such intermediary regimes;
- Right of ownership, access to collect, use, and dispose of minor forest produce which has been traditionally collected within or outside village boundaries;
- Other community rights of uses or entitlements such as fish and other products of water bodies, gazing (both settled or transhumant) and traditional seasonal resource access of nomadic or pastoralist communities;
- Rights including community tenures of habitat and habitation for primitive tribal groups and pre-agriculture communities;
- Rights in or over disputed lands under any nomenclature in any State where claims are disputed;
- Rights for conversion of Pattas or leases or grants issued by any local authority or any State Govt. on forest lands to titles;
- Rights of settlement and conversion of all forest villages, old habitation, unsurveyed villages and other villages in forest, whether recorded, notified or not into revenue villages;
- Right to protect, regenerate or conserve or manage any community forest resource which they have been traditionally protecting and conserving for sustainable use;
- Rights which are recognized under any State law or laws of any Autonomous Dist. Council or Autonomous Regional Council or which are accepted as rights of tribals under any traditional or customary law of the concerned tribes of any State;
- Right of access to biodiversity and community right to intellectual property and traditional knowledge related to biodiversity and cultural diversity;
- Any other traditional right customarily enjoyed by the forest dwelling Scheduled Tribes or other traditional forest dwellers, as the case may be, which are not mentioned in clauses-1 to 11, but excluding the traditional right of hunting or trapping extracting a part of the body of any species of wild animal

These rights can be summarized as:

- *Title Rights: i.e.* ownership - to land that is being farmed by tribals or forest dwellers as on December 13, 2005, subject to a maximum of 4 hectares; ownership is only for land that is actually being cultivated by the concerned family as on that date, meaning that no new lands are granted;
- *Use Rights:* To minor forest produce (also including ownership), to grazing areas, to pastoralist routes, etc.;
- *Relief and Development Rights:* To rehabilitation in case of illegal eviction or forced displacement and to basic amenities, subject to restrictions for forest protection;
- *Forest Management Rights:* To protect forests and wildlife.

The preamble of the Act shouts loudly in this fashion. *"Whereas the forest rights on ancestral lands and their habitat were not adequately recognised in the consolidation of State forests during the colonial period as well as in independent India resulting in historic injustice to the forest dwelling Scheduled Tribes and other traditional forest dwellers…"*. Unfortunately the conditions laid for the fulfilment of accessing these rights for the Dalits and other non-Adivasis have become almost impossible. This has given rise to serve conflicts in several states, where Dalits live on forest land for several generations. However there is a huge paucity of records due to various practical reasons due to which the records of Dalits couldn't be submitted for claim.

It is very difficult for 'non-adivasi' forest people to prove 75 years of existence on the land before they can claim rights to it under the FRA. The state agencies – especially the forest and revenue departments – don't want to see the FRA implemented in letter and spirit because it will undermine their control over the resources. So these agencies, along with some NGOs and feudal lords, have been spreading misinformation about the Act to create confusion and conflict. This situation has created a direct confrontation between the Dalits and Adivasis on their rights over land. In several states like Chhattisgarh, Odisha, Jharkhand, Maharastra, Uttar Pradesh and others there is a war-like situation. Recently there was a case where a Dalit was arrested in Odisha for raising the question of rights over forestland.

THE CASE STUDY OF ORISSA

An intense conflict over forestland rights has caused a face-off between two neighbouring villages in Bolangir district of Odisha. As a result, villagers in Kuiminda (with seven adivasi and three dalit families) now live in absolute fear of being thrown off their land and out of their homes. In November 2009, they were attacked by hundreds of people from the nearby Bharuamunda village (mostly inhabited by non-adivasis) and their houses destroyed. All the men fled in fear, so the women had to face the abuse and blows of the angry mob. All this happened in the presence of policemen, government officials, and members of an NGO. Since then, the men in Kuimunda go into hiding the moment they sense trouble. Bharuamunda is one of the villages misinformed about the FRA. They have been told that the FRA is a menace, that it will usurp the lands of the non-adivasis and distribute them among the adivasis, that the forest department will clear all the forests they have been protecting and turn them into farmlands for the Adivasis. So while the villagers of Bharuamunda rant and rave and the villagers of Kuimunda cower in fear, the forest is being clear-felled right under the noses of those who are accountable for the implementation of the FRA process.

The conflict erupted soon after a couple of Adivasi families received *pattas* (land titles) for some tiny pieces of land under the FRA last year. Bharuamunda villagers suddenly started alleging that some people of Kuimunda had moved in after December 13, 2005 only to avail of these *pattas*. The allegation clearly stems from some rumour-mongering. To add to Kuimunda's woes, the watershed department is now planning a watershed project on the lands of Kuimunda villagers, which means the whole village, will have to move out. Besides the attacks on Kuimunda village, several (false) criminal cases were filed against some villagers, especially against Rabi Bagh a Dalit with some knowledge of the general state of affairs and helped other Dalits in filing FRA claims.

On the one hand, he has been alleged to be acting as an 'agent', hand-in-glove with the forest department, to get his fellow villagers *pattas* in exchange for money, and on the other, he and other villagers of Kuimunda have regularly been summoned by both the forest department and the police, and terrorised. On the morning of July 21, 2010, Rabi Bagh along with his wife was on his way to the weekly market in nearby Lathor when he was again summoned to the Lathor police outpost. There, he was forced to sign on a blank sheet of paper, was told that he had been arrested, and his wife forced out of the office. Rabi was then taken to the Patnagarh court.

This is yet another unfortunate illustration of how the FRA, dubbed an instrument to correct the 'historical injustices' meted out to forest communities, is instead being used as a tool of oppression and intimidation for raising the issue of forest rights. In a similar case, Trilochan Punji – a leader of the Odisha Jana Adhikar Morcha (OJAM) of Bolangir district and also a state committee member of OJAM – has been subjected to harassment by state agencies. Trilochan has been creating legal awareness, along with Rabi Bagh and others, on the FRA in the district mainly because the state agencies assigned to do so are actually spreading misinformation. He has also organised a series of protests highlighting provisions in the FRA about 'community rights' and has become an enemy of the administration. The cases registered against Rabi Bagh have now also been registered against Trilochan Punji. And Trilochan fears arrest at any moment. Thus the conflict between the forest-based Dalits vis-à-vis the non-Dalits have engulfed. This is not only the case of Odisha but a similar situation does exist in almost all states. This is not the singled out case of FRA, there are many other similar issues related with Forest Conservation, Wildlife Conservation, etc. where the Dalits are thoroughly betrayed.

INDUSTRIAL ACQUISITION, LAND QUESTION AND DALITS

Industrial revolution, which made a colourful and dreamy entry, is turning out to be the worst form of human development. The steady economic growth of industries with active support from the state machinery is directly proportional to the unchecked exploitation of masses. Most of them belong to marginalised communities such as Dalits, Adivasis, women, working class, etc. Displacement, migration, repercussion of workers, loss of land and livelihood, pilfering state revenue, forest resources, etc. has outgrown to monstrous level.

With the concept of Planned Development, planned mining was introduced in 1951. The Private Sector and the Public Sector were clearly demarcated giving the Public Sector a bigger role in India's mineral wealth. There was spectacular progress in Indian Mining Industry from 1947 to 1985 when mineral production grew by about 120 times. The Indian peninsular has had a varied and complex geology, as a result of which rich mineral endowments covering a variety of mineral types are found. All Five Year Plans have focused on mining to achieve 'development', demanding the forfeiture of people's lands for 'national prosperity'. Most mineral and mining operations are found in forest regions, habituated by Adivasi and other indigenous communities. Mining projects vary from rat hole mining, small-scale legal and illegal mining, to large-scale mining – most of which has been historically managed by the public sector. Since the introduction of private sector participation in the 1990's, a number of mining related community conflicts have arisen with far reaching consequences.

Mining industry gives employment to a large proportion of the industrial workforce. But are the developments in the mining industry in keeping with national interests? This draws a lot of controversial aspects, which flouting the Constitutional and other rights of the people in mining areas is a matter of grave concern.

MINING AND THE QUESTION OF LAND – THE CASE STUDY OF CHHATTISGARH

Chhattisgarh is the richest State in terms of mineral wealth, with 28 varieties of major minerals. Chhattisgarh, along with two other Indian States has almost all the coal deposits in India, and with this the state has planned the power hub strategy. All the tin ore in India is in Chhattisgarh. A fifth of iron ore in the country is here, and one of the best quality iron ore deposits in the world is found in the Bailadila in south Chhattisgarh, which is exported to Japan. Rich deposits of Bauxite, Limestone, Dolomite and Corundum are found in the State. The State has large deposits of coal, iron ore and limestone too. All doors for private participation in the mining sector are widely open in the state. The State's Mineral Policy, 2001 has created conducive business environment to attract private investment in the State, both domestic and international. Procedures have been simplified. At the same time the state is willing to provide resources and manpower having trained in tailor-made programmes in geology, geophysics, geochemistry, mineral beneficiation, mining engineering, etc.

The State is ensuring a minimum lease area with secured land rights so that investors can safely commit large resources to mining projects. For surmounting the long-drawn out process of getting mineral-related leases, at the State level, quick processing of applications is given top priority. For major minerals under the Minesand Minerals (Development and Regulation) Act, where approvals are required from Government of India, the State Government is helping in strong advocacy to get such approvals quickly.

Sarguja, Raigarh and Bilaspur districts are the coal zones in Chhattisgarh. It is estimated that more than 72 thousand acres of land have leased out to SECL for coal mining, by which hundreds of villages have already been affected. Bastar and Durg districts have some of the rare quality of steel in the world. Nearly 20 thousand acres of land have been occupied for mining steel in Bailadeela and Dalli Rajhara area of these districts.

Heavy deposits of limestone are also found in Chhattisgarh region. In an area of three districts itself, *i.e.* Raipur, Durg and Bilaspur, there are 12 big factories of all big industrial houses and with many more small ones and its auxiliary units. Most of these have been established in the last 20-22 years. Huge diamond deposits in Devbhog (Raipur) and Bastar are also in the eyes of the MNCs. In all for cement industry 6990 acres, 14530 acres for rice mills, 14665 acres for steel industry, for ferry alloys 940 acres and 285 acres for re-rolling mills have been already acquired in the area. Apart from these 18652.377 acres of lands has been rendered on lease for other mining purpose. Therefore land acquisition followed by the adverse impact on the people is a major issue in Chhattisgarh.

In Janjgir-Champa district alone, 52 new MoUs, mostly for power plants have been signed by the state government. An approximate estimation of 140000 acres of land is required for these, which includes establishment of plants, establishment of ancillary units, dumping space for overburden, fly-ash, colony development for staff, etc. For all these projects coal will be brought from Jashpurnagar, Raigarh and Korba districts. Water would be drawn from Mahanadi, Maand, Sheonath and Kelo rivers.

Between 2005 and 2007 Jindal alone had applied for the prospecting licence (PL) and mining licence (ML) for 6110.95 sq km and another 1559.172 hectare (3852.66 acres) in Dantewada, Bijapur, Narayanpur, Rajnandgoan,

Bilaspur, Janjgir-Champa, Raigarh, Jashpur and Surguja districts. The minerals in this area are iron ore, limestone, dolomite, coal, diamond, precious and semiprecious gemstone, etc. Most of the regions and districts where Jindal has applied for mining licence falls within forests areas.

It also means several hundred million tonnes per annum of solid wastes and fly ash will be indiscriminately dumped on land. These would contain heavy metal constituents that will eventually leach into both surface and ground water regimes over the years, making the water unfit for human and animal consumption as well as damaging to all other forms of life. Health consequences will inevitably follow; they will now have started, since it takes a number of years for the lactates to penetrate fresh water sources. So far the people are concerned the situation is grim. They are pushed beyond the margins and the space is further withering. Usurpation of thousands of acres of land is a usual phenomenon of all mining and industrialisation process. Women are the most pretentious in this process, as they bear triple burden. They remain as the unobserved recipient of all these misfortunes. Due to automation and mechanisation even the employment opportunity provided by these industrial houses disappeared in the course of time. Health in general in these areas and more specifically occupational health is another area of severe concern. Education for the children of the already battered strata has become a distant dream.

RIGHTS OF MINEWORKERS

Five years back a survey of Vedanta's bauxite mines in Mainpat and Daldali was done. At Mainpat, the biggest single bauxite mining complex in Chhattisgarh, the research team met with thirty Adivasi workers, un-helmeted, clad in shirts and sarees under the blazing sun, as the lateritic overburden was blasted. They then moved in with a few iron rodes and hammers, to break and sort the ore before loading it by hand onto waiting trucks. The same story is that of the workers in the Daldali mines of Vedanta.

Virtually all Vedanta's bauxite miners are contract labourers. The labourers at Mainpat informed that, on a good day they can earn just over 60 rupees (less for women), for delivering one ton of ore. In Daldali it is different story since the rates are different for different group of people. Those who could bargain better rates get better and those who couldn't bargain it to their level are the lost ones. Particularly the Baigas (a primitive tribe) couldn't bargain to the extent of the Gonds (a much better tribe). However it won't be more than 60 rupees per person per day in either case.

In Mainpat their habitations are small thatched hovels, perched over the quarry, deprived of electricity and adequate water. "There's only one hand pump to serve 150 families," a young Adivasi woman worker, Mati Shahu, told us. "The company provides no medical facilities and if someone is injured we have to take them ourselves by taxi down to the plains", continued Mati.

Villagers at another site complained that, day and night, the silica-laden dust from the mining blew into their windows, covering walls and floors. In Bodai-Daldali of Kabirdham district, which again is another of the mining areas of Vedanta, in typical fashion, Baigha inhabitants from the first of four Adivasi settlements in the project's pathway have been ejected from their homes, without due legal process, and dumped on the plains in the heart of a nonAdivasi community. They had to leave behind their crops.

In June 2005, Vedanta's contract labourers at Mainpat went on strike against the appalling conditions to which they are subjected. On July 18 2005, another 2500 contract workers at the Vedanta's Korba expansion project 200 km further north, went on strike to protest a worker's death on duty. They reportedly smashed the windows of three vehicles and set a company ambulance on fire, accusing the management of being casual in their demand for security equipment. A Centre of Indian Trade Unions (CITU) leader claimed that eight workers have died at Vedanta's expansion work site during the previous 12 months. On July 19th 2005, police baton charged the striking workers, injuring seven, instead of consoling the family of the deceased that has four children.

Employment issues are of deeper concern in mining areas. Dalli-Rajhara is an iron oremining town. It meets the total iron ore requirements of the Bhilai Steel Plant. In Dalli- Rajhara, since 1958 onwards mining activites has been continued. The preparations for mechanizing the Dalli mine began in 1977. By 1978 the situation of mechanization became even more clear and lucid, when at deposit no. 5 in Bailadila mines, 10000 labourers were rendered jobless at one stroke. All resistance was crushed. Hundreds of huts were burnt down, numerous women raped, and labourers fired upon. The orgy of mechanization forced nearly 10000 labourers to face the desperation of hunger. A growing argument was that machinery in question was produced in Russia and was therefore socialistic, progressive machinery – however it did not mitigate the grim fate of these labourers.

ECOLOGICAL CONCERNS

Chhattisgarh, carved out of Madhya Pradesh, is both rich in forest and mineral wealth. The state has heavy deposits of iron ore, coal, limestone, bauxite, dolomite, tin ore, gold, etc. and is also rich in the deposits of precious and semiprecious stones like diamond, corundum, alexandrite, garnet, etc. The main bauxite producing areas are Phutka Hills, Main Pat, Samri Pat, Keshkal valley and Maikal ranges. The state is also a huge producer of limestone and dolomite and is being targeted for diamond prospecting and mining in a big way. Diamond are reported from in Payalikhand and Behradih villages of Deobhog area of Raipur and Tokpal of Bastar district. These are present in the form phenocrysts in kimberlite-like volcanic rocks. The main coal producing areas are: Korba Colliery, Hasdo- Rampur Colliery, Mand-

Raigarh Colliery, Vishrampur Colliery, Lakhanpur Colliery, Tatapani-Ramkola Colliery, Jhilmili Colliery, Sonhat Colliery, Jhagrakhand Colliery, Chirmiri-Kurasiya Colliery.

The following areas within the state containing different minerals are being looked at for future exploitation: Deobhog in Raipur district and Tokpal in Bastar district has been identified for the exploration of Diamond; Bijapur in Bastar district for Corrandum; Saraipali of Mahasamund district for Gold and Tin (Cassiterite); Bailadila, Raoghat and areas in Rajnandgaon district for iron ore; Jhanjhar, Meru, Durg, Bhaupratapur, Kondal area of Kanker district for gold; Renger, Markanar, Vasanpur area of Dantewada district for tin; Chhirahi-Newari, Saradih, Garrabhata and Patharkundi village of Raipur district and Sakti area of Janjgir district for limestone.

In addition 500 lakh tonnes of high grade dolomite has been found in Lagra-Madanpur in Champa-Janjgir district; 5 lakh tonnes of metal grade bauxite in Dorima (or Barima) of Surguja district; 220 lakh tonnes of coal has been identified in Hardi Bazar-Kertali in Korba district; 170.4 lakh cubic metres of flagstone having different shades and colours has been demarcated in revenue land of Chitrakot and Matkot area of Bastar district; clay and Banded heamatite quartzite (BHQ) in the Balod area in Durg district. The entire ecological balance being evolved by the people of these regions over several millenniums will get destroyed in very short period with any reason.

LAND ACQUISITION VERSUS LAND PURCHASE

In recent time a new tendency is observed among the corporate houses to appropriate farmland. Instead of engaging the state in acquiring land, the corporate house has started buying land directly from the farmer. This trend is widely seen in parts of Janjgir-Champa district where the corporate house directly bought land from the farmers. In fact the latest amendment in the LAA bill also speaks about these aspects. The amendment says that land acquisition wouldn't be the responsibility of the government. 70% should be directly either acquired or bought by the company itself. State's responsibility would only be limited to provide 30% of land either through acquisition of public land or by transferring government land in favour of the company.

MINING ON FORESTLAND

The mining areas have a huge overlap with the forest and Adivasi-Indigenous land in the state and the increasing mining activities and allied industries have had a tremendous negative impact on these. An ongoing study by the Forest Survey of India (FSI) looking at 'Forest cover in metal mining areas' shows some revealing statistics. In the Bastar district, one of the biodiversity rich areas of Chhattisgarh, out of the 13,470 ha area under leases for iron ore mining, 11,657 ha is covered by forests. This of course indicates the forest within the actual lease, but the impact on the forests, biodiversity and the communities dependent on this region due to ancillary impacts of mining extends far beyond the actual lease area. Conflicts over industrialization and particularly mining in Chhattisgarh have existed for more than five decades in different forms. In earlier days it wasn't taken to be conflicts as such, but only as immediate questions related to the question of inadequacy.

The standpoints of trade unions were also only one-dimensional related to increment in wages or related matters of labourers. It could never address the entire questions mining in totality. Moreover mining has been strongly presupposed as a major means of industrial development contributing to the state economy. So how a means of development could be understood as a conflict is another point. Over the course of time the very definition of state and its economy has changed.

DEVELOPMENT, DISPLACEMENT AND DALITS

For some time the question of development, displacement and Dalits have been striking our ears every now and then. Whenever there is a new development, particularly a new project being launched by the state in connivance with international agencies such as the World Bank, ADB, or the corporate sector, such debates becomes inevitable. Displacement in the name of dams, reservoirs, forest conservation, protection of forests and wildlife has become a common feature to the forest based communities. In many places one could find lots of cases of multiple displacements as well. This could be widely observed all across India, particularly after the interim order in the case of Godavaraman Thirumalpad vs Union of India. This case has given a new turn to the conflict situation.

Today forests, the nurturer of thousands of Adivasis, Dalits and other forest based communities, are also under nose of the corporate investors. Currently the situation is that almost 17 lakh acres of land has been demarcated as protected area for the sake of wildlife conservation, where people face the threat of eviction. According to government sources there are more than 250 villages in Chhattisgarh with a population above 35000 standing at the brink of dispossession. The majority of them are Adivasis, Dalits and other unprivileged strata. The indigenous people living inside the forest are almost bonded labourers of the forest department.

As per 2000 records in Chhattisgarh 10 major projects have already been completed, for which 257032.585 acres of land have been lost. In all 238 villages have been affected by these dams and their rehabilitation has not yet been done.

Another major reason of destruction is the mass felling of trees for commercial purpose. In many areas of Chhattisgarh there are cases of coop felling of trees and this happens through the forest department. Powerful lobbies of timber contractors, politicians, bureaucrats are actively operating the illegal felling. One major case of similar character in which the Adivasis were deceived was exposed in Bastar through the Supreme Court intervention in the Malik Makbooja case. This case drew a lot of attention and a CBI investigation was ordered. Due to the positive intervention of the court some of the government officials were also suspended.

WATER WAR

All water sources originate from the indigenous land and the indigenous people have no say in the entire question of rights over water. Clearly, the intentions are to establish market principles in the operation of the water, depoliticizing the sector by creating an independent tariff regulatory body. The country needs to urgently recognize that so long as we persist in spreading Green Revolution-type agricultural development to all regions, there will be no relief from the growing water crisis.

In the last 15-20 years, there have been several developments that aided the privatization of water. Bottled water became easily available in local markets. A NGO An exposed the bottled water defaulting on the requisite quality standards, thus bringing into the open the darker side of privatization. The entry of global corporations brought a fundamental shift in the nature of water utilization and management. The players are mainly multinational corporations who wield enormous influence over governments and policy-makers.

The private players are therefore in a position to control whole cities and whole sections of the rivers. There are many cases where the water is being taken off the public domain and being deployed into the hand of corporate sectors in states like Chhattisgarh, Orissa, Jharkhand, Kerala, etc. Officially, 19 water privatisation projects are in different stages of implementation in India at present but unofficial accounts put the figure at 40. The 19 projects under implementation are in Chhattisgarh, Tamil Nadu, Maharashtra, Karnataka, Kerala, Himachal Pradesh, Manipur, Rajasthan, West Bengal, Andhra Pradesh and Sikkim. While eight of them are being run by French corporations, the others are by Japanese and Australian concerns.

The Indian market is estimated to be worth over $2,000 million. Major global corporations including the top three global water giants Suez and Vivendi of France and RWE-AG of Germany, have shown interest in the Indian market. These three corporations control over 70 per cent of the water systems in Europe and North America. Vivendi has operations in 90 countries around the world, and Suez in 120. Together these water corporations are targeting four areas within the water sector: water and waste water services, water treatment, water-related construction and engineering, and innovative technologies. An obvious case is Rajasthan where water will be supplied to the towns of Jaipur and Ajmer from the Bisalpur dam. The ADB, which is involved in the project, has absolved itself of all responsibility by telling the affected communities living near the dam site that it is not funding the dam but only taking the water and supplying it to the cities. While the ADB encourages full cost recovery and managerial efficiency for water resources, experts in developing countries warn of the consequences for the poor, who are already squeezed by the vagaries of an inflationary economy. Much of this privatization spree has been facilitated by the Urban Development Ministry, which released a set of guidelines for the State governments encouraging them to move towards "private partnerships". These guidelines are in tune with half a dozen reports produced by State governments and the World Bank that outline the blueprint for privatizing the country's water.

While the Water Policy has *de facto* redefined water rights and undermines the community's rights of people, this has never been debated in Parliament, which is the only body, which can legislate on resource rights. The Water Policy is therefore a subversion of the Constitution and a hijack of the peoples' natural rights to water as a vital resources needed for sustenance. This is a surreptitious attempt to establish the Principle of Eminent Domain in water, which was always peoples' resources, in place of the Public Trust Doctrine that define the role of the state with respect to natural resources, the collective wealth of the people. Creation of an El Dorado orbits around the industries in India.

PRIVATIZATION OF WATER AND DEPRIVATION OF RIPARIAN RIGHTS IN CHHATTISGARH

In Chhattisgarh as per quick estimates, the state would require a hefty investment of ₹9,651 crores to fully develop the estimated 43 lakh ha of its irrigation potential as against the existing irrigation potential of 13.37 lakh ha. A similar situation exists in the urban water sector also. For example the Municipal Corporation of Raipur has proposed an urban water scheme costing ₹397.42 crores to meet the water requirements of the city till the year 2031. Chhattisgarh is the first state in India where the erstwhile Madhya Pradesh government had leased out 23.6-km stretches of the Sheonath River near Durg town, to Kailash Soni, a businessman, on a 22-year renewable contract in 1998.

Soni prohibited local people and fishermen in the area from using that stretch of the river in order to supply water to his big clients - the waterintensive industries in the region. Given the manner in which the contract was formulated, Soni could get away by saying that he had not privatized the river but was providing a service to the people. The former government headed by Ajit Jogi however, decided in April 2003 to cancel the contract with Soni's Radius Water Company. However the Radius Water Company threatened to file a suit against the government in the international court after which the decision was taken back. Though undeclared almost in a similar fashion the government has leased out part of Kelo to Jindals in Raigarh. A similar plan is well set on card to deal with industrial water demands by carving out small length of other rivers such as Mahanadi, Maand, Kharun and other extents of Sheonath.

MODERN TRENDS IN FARMING

While discussing on land rights and land related issues it is also essential to investigate the modes and means which in some form or other has outgrown in recent times. A quick recap of what has been happening in Chhattisgarh would also draw our attention to the national picture too. India being agriculture based economy and a country where almost 70% of its population depends for its subsistence, the utilization of land under the genetically modified formula of crop production has also evolved a culture of monocrop cultivation too. This has developed a dangerous trend among the different layers of farmers. Further it also challenges the very foundation of sustainable agricultural economy.

Sustainability is a process by which a community lives in close contact with the nature and preserves the harmonious relationship among human being. In all the cases we would find that the most important aspect is that there are some basic values that sustain the mutuality within the community and that of life. That is the most important aspect of life. Sustainability of any community depends upon the strength of mutuality. This in fact gives birth to the process of harmonious development. In developmental terms this gives rise to the concept of containing food sovereignty, which again is yet another means of sustaining the community life and spirit. Food sovereignty goes beyond the common concept of food security, which merely seeks to ensure that a sufficient amount of safe food is produced without taking into account the kind of food produced and how, where and on what scale it is produced. It encompasses of sustainability and sustainable development practices.

Hypothetically food sovereignty involves the following:

- Prioritising local agricultural production to feed the population and the access of women and men to land, water, forests, seeds and credit.
- Production is need-based for local consumption not for market.
- Sustaining the traditional systems of community life in an organic manner with rights over resources. Since land belongs or belonged to indigenous poor who had worked on it, they have a legitimate right on these resources.
- The right of peasant to produce food and the right of consumer to decide what they want to consume and how and who produces it.
- Essentially involving people's participation in the definition of agrarian policies, right from land development to crop choice.
- Envisioning and ensuring discrimination (caste, colour, gender)-free social relationships in order to enhance appropriate human

relationship that is closed associated with the production pattern.

- Acknowledging the right of women peasants who play a key role in agricultural production.
- Drawing most of our financial resources for development from within rather than relying on foreign investment and foreign financial markets.
- The right of all nations to protect themselves from excessive and cheap agricultural and food imports (dumping).

Little by little the entire agriculture land in the state has and is being converted into non-agriculture land, for industrial purpose. The cultivation pattern that has evolved in the last two decades has raised serious questions on farming. Much of the farmers are left without water for cultivation, while the government is busy leasing out portions of the rivers to industrial houses. Non-availability of water is denial to cultivation. Denial of cultivation leads depeasantisation of community. This is happening at an elevated pace.

Peasantry in Chhattisgarh have been encountering the fact of denial to cultivation and that is why in most of the villages they have lost their attribute as a peasant. Thus they are more inclined towards migrating out as they find it as the best alternative of earning money. This adds impetus and strengthens is the process of depeasantisation. However in the same area big farmers find it easy to adopt the hybrid varieties of paddy. Some of them are also of the option to go for GMOs although they don't understand what it is all about.

In the last one decade the government of Chhattisgarh had been consistently propagating new farm model. On one hand the state is promoting alien plantation culture and on the other hand they are advocating of crop rotation. Massive plantation of *saffed musli* and *jetropha* was promptly endorsed in the whole of the state. While *saffed musli* is said to be for the promotion of herb culture in the state, *jetropha* is meant for extracting fuel. In Bastar district itself nearly 1500 hectares of paddy farmland was turned into *musli* farmland. Many other individual landlords had adapted to this pattern and they say it gives more returns than rice paddy cultivation.

Resembling to this is the case of *jetropha,* which is upheld under the pretext of alternate fuel generation. Scientific studies say that *jetropha* is highly destructive to the surrounding environment as well as for the despoliation of soil. Many specialists are of the opinion that the seeds of *jetropha* was first sent to India in late 50s and early 60s along with wheat from US and European countries as part of their aid package to combat the severe famine. Since then the seeds began to breed in every part of the country wherever the aid was provided. Ironically in US and most of the European nations it has been banned after reaching a scientific conclusion of its inimical impression on human habitation. Currently crop rotation has now become a common parlance among development experts at the national level. In Chhattisgarh the former government was of the opinion to promote sugarcane production instead of rice. It was advocated through the entire government machinery that rice is less productivity and of lesser market value and contrary to this the sugarcane is high yielding as well as high market value. The prime intention was not do any good for the people but the introduction of sugar industries and sugar lobby in Chhattisgarh. Rice mills and rice market has so far saturated in Chhattisgarh. However people in the rural areas resisted this move bravely. Nevertheless this is still on cards.

Contract Farming is another aspect being established through this process. In fact many *dalals* (middleman) are already moving across the rural areas to buy land in order to promote corporate contract farming. Strings of such processes were already on the rise during the last one decade. Land mafias become very active in the past one decade buying and selling large plots of land. Most of the land had been appropriate with this purpose of establishing private farmhouses. This sprouted the monoculture cultivation pattern stubbing all existing sustainable production practices. Monoculture along the line of profit generating economics is the role model to the marginal farmer or even the landless labourers who bank on sharecropping (*adhiya*), contract farming (*regha*) and other similar systems. Hence a transformation of agriculture into agri-business even among the landless labourer is what is happening.

CONCLUSION REMARKS

It is under this context that we need to develop a wider understanding and proper perspective about the diverse dynamics of Dalit rights over natural resources. To understand the dynamics of the problem in the totality, one needs an understanding of the logic of the underlying forces that govern the current pattern of ownership. The specific economic form in which unpaid surplus labour is pumped out, determines the relation of the rulers and the ruled. Hence the crisis of Dalits and rights over natural resources has to be understood in its historical perspective. Historical evidences are ample to prove the conception of depeasantisation as a net result of the uneven structural changes, land holding patterns that have taken place from time to time due to the commoditization of the economy in which land plays a critical and predominant role.

It is beyond all doubts that industrial land acquisition and free market economy goes hand in hand. The mechanism of compensation and rehabilitation is a supportive kitty of the corporate sector; this only pauperises the poor than a change in their destiny. The principles of compensation never estimates or often forgets that on the very first day of reaching a rehabilitation colony, a poor family has to buy firewood, which they procured free from the Common Property Rights (CPR). The tripartite of politicians, bureaucracy, and capitalist ruled by Brahminical Social Order raise a whole range of questions. The hire and fire formula of the capitalfascist brigade, the coherence of world capital with Hindutva fascism has permeated fast across. The state should become more responsible and accountable to the masses. In the globalised era, the sweeping changes in political structures, coupled with the disempowerment of state, it won't be so easy for the people to survive.

Ambedkar's dream of a 'welfare state' has disappeared in the whirlwind of continued caste discrimination, planned development and further with the outgrown with the globalisation liberalisation policies. Only the people's rise with acute political clarity can save them from this trauma.

10

Economic, Social and Cultural Rights for Dalit in India

INTRODUCTION

Economic, social and cultural (ESC) rights form an integral part of the Universal Declaration of Human Rights of 1948 and in the 1966 International Covenant of Economic, Social and Cultural Rights (ICESCR). However, since their inclusion in these treaties, they have received little attention from states and human rights organizations. In fact, many are not even aware of the existence of ESC rights, believing human rights to be comprised only of civil and political rights. This limits the prospects for systemic changes, reduces knowledge of individual and group entitlements, and reduces government accountability to international agreements.

Fortunately, both human rights and development organizations are slowly beginning to recognize the importance of ESC rights. However, not all organizations have arrived at this conclusion, and for those that have, they have yet to move beyond mere recognition. This needs to change. It is time that organizations reassess their current approaches, change their perceptions regarding human rights and begin to use a comprehensive human rights framework to reduce and eradicate poverty.

We present a case study that exemplifies a situation in need of a human rights approach that incorporates ESC rights: that of Dalits in India. For centuries, Dalits have been victims of gross human rights violations. This has led to their current low social and economic status within Indian society. All of this has occurred in a country in which the government has not only signed numerous treaties pledging respect of human rights, but has also incorporated human rights into its Constitution. Thus, India presents an interesting case in which commitment is evident on paper but is not exercised in practice. Within this case study, we examine how India has violated one fundamental ESC right: the right to education. To further support this claim, we take the specific example of violations of the right to primary education in rural villages in Gujarat. We then offer recommendations aimed at improving this particular situation, as well as recommendations that address the more global problem – the lack of full recognition of ESC rights in the human rights dialogue.

ECONOMIC, SOCIAL AND CULTURAL RIGHTS

Economic, social and cultural rights have been enumerated in a number of international treaties, such as the International Covenant of Economic, Social and Cultural Rights (ICESCR). These rights include, among others, the right of self-determination (Article 1), the right to work (6), the right to just and favourable conditions of work (7), the right to form and join trade unions (8), the right to social security and social insurance (9), the right to an adequate standard of living (11), and the right to education (13 and 14). In practice, however, ESC rights have never received a great deal of attention from the 137 states that signed the ICESCR or human rights organizations. While there are reasonable explanations given for this neglect, they are not substantial enough to prevent the inclusion of ESC rights into a human rights approach – especially after one considers the benefits resulting from such inclusion.

REASONS FOR NEGLECT

ESC rights have not only suffered from lack of implementation, but also from lack of recognition. According to the Center for Economic and Social Rights, one reason for this neglect is that addressing ESC rights would mean, "addressing the enormous and growing inequalities at all levels of human society, from local to global." So far, the international community has not been willing to take on such a monumental task.

The other explanations for this neglect can be divided into two categories:

1) Predominance of civil and political rights,
2) Lack of clarity regarding ESC rights.

Civil and Political Rights

Simply put, for the last 50 years, human rights organizations and states have focused their attention almost solely on civil and political rights. This preference can be attributed to a number of different causes. First, during the Cold War the United States used its relatively good record on civil and political rights to condemn the gross civil and political rights abuses that were occurring in communist countries such as China and the USSR.

Second, some believe that there is an implicit ranking system for human rights and that civil and political rights must first be met in order to enable a struggle for ESC rights. For example, Josh Rubenstein of Amnesty International asserts, "the dirty little secret is that [the human rights movement] really does believe that if you don't have the right to say what you want, you're not going to get what you need. It comes down to the fact that you have to protect civil and political rights first, if only as a vehicle to assert ESC rights." Lastly, many view civil and political rights as negative rights, while ESC rights are viewed as positive rights. Negative rights are those that do not require state resources and the actual obligation of the state is *not to do something, i.e.* not to subject an individual to torture or not to carry out arbitrary arrests. Positive rights, on the other hand, require state resources since they are seen as obligations *to do something, i.e.* to provide free education. Presented in this manner, it is easy to see why states have been more receptive to implementing civil and political rights and thus why NGOs have chosen subsequently to focus their efforts on this set of rights.

Ambiguity Surrounding ESC Rights

The other main reason for neglect stems from the general ambiguity surrounding ESC rights. A training resource on ESC rights asserts, "as a result of the relative inattention paid to ESC rights over the past several decades … the content and meaning of most ESC rights remain relatively ill-defined." This lack of clarity as to what exactly constitutes an ESC right has served to complicate and deter efforts of human rights organizations to address these rights.

There is also a high degree of vagueness regarding what the actual obligations of the state are.

This can be attributed to Article 2 (1) of the ICESCR, which states:

- Each State Party to the present Covenant undertakes to take steps, individually and through international assistance and co-operation, especially economic and technical, to the *maximum* of its *available* resources, with a view to achieving *progressively* the full realization of the rights recognized in the present Covenant by all appropriate means, including particularly the adoption of legislative measures.

Without having a sound notion of the exact nature of state parties' obligations, individuals and human rights organizations are given very little room to either accuse states of being violators or to pressure them into living up to their commitments. Furthermore, the state itself is unsure of its exact obligations. Thus, they might not be fulfilling them for lack of knowledge, rather than lack of desire.

THE HUMAN RIGHTS FRAMEWORK

Even after considering the challenges, using a human rights framework that incorporates economic, social and cultural rights to confront poverty and inequity is still desirable.

States' Obligations – Changing the Perception

ESC rights, such as the right to an adequate standard of living or the right to work, are not generally seen as rights, but rather as benefits given by the state. They are also commonly viewed as aspirations that the state would one day like to fulfill. The human rights framework radically alters this perception by presenting ESC rights as obligations of the state.

As stated by the Committee on Economic, Social and Cultural Rights:

- When a State ratifies one of the Covenants, it accepts a solemn responsibility to apply each of the obligations embodied therein and to ensure the compatibility of their national laws with their international duties, in a spirit of good faith. Through the ratification of human rights treaties, therefore, States become accountable to the international community, to other States, which have ratified the same texts, and to their own citizens and others resident in their territories.

Governments therefore have a duty to fulfill, respect, promote and protect all of the rights of their citizens. Governments that fail to do so should be held accountable for their behaviour. A comprehensive human rights framework utilizes this obligation, equipping non-governmental organizations and citizens with a powerful new tool. This tool can be used to pressure governments to both provide the basic social services addressed in the ICESCR and to reevaluate their policies to ensure that they are in-line with the international human rights norms and treaties to which the governments are parties.

Empowerment Tool

At a local level, changing the view of ESC rights would have significant impacts. As individuals begin to regard ESC rights as entitlements, not handouts, they would no longer tolerate the inaction or neglect of their governments on these social issues. They would start to mobilize and demand that their governments fulfill their obligations to their people.

A Complete Approach

Any human rights approach should be comprehensive, stressing the importance of all human rights, be they civil and political or economic, social and cultural. This approach not only recognizes the equal value of each right, but it is more realistic. Rights are inextricably intertwined with one another: the full enjoyment of one right often requires the full enjoyment of another. Nowhere is this more evident than with the right to education.

FOCUS ON THE RIGHT TO EDUCATION

The right to education can be found at the intersection of economic, cultural and social rights with civil and political rights. An undereducated person will face limited employment opportunities, thus making him economically vulnerable. This vulnerability could result in his conscious decision not to exercise other rights, such as the right to join a trade union or the right to freedom of speech, out of fear of possible reprisals. An undereducated person might be unaware of the rights to which he is entitled or may not fully comprehend their meaning. An undereducated person may not be able to effectively participate in the political arena. In sum, without adequate education a person is not able to fully enjoy or assert his human rights. The right to education serves not only to unlock other human rights, but also a number of other vital functions.

First, being educated itself has important intrinsic value. Second, greater literacy and educational achievements of disadvantaged groups can increase their ability to resist oppression, to organize politically, and to get a fairer deal. Lastly, education is an empowerment tool by which "economically and socially marginalized adults and children can lift themselves out of poverty and obtain the means to participate fully in their communities."

DALITS

- Despite the fact that "untouchability" was abolished under India's constitution in 1950, the practice of "untouchability"—the imposition of social disabilities on persons by reason of their birth in certain castes— remains very much a part of rural India. "Untouchables" may not cross the line dividing their part of the village from that occupied by higher castes. They may not use the same wells, visit the same temples, drink from the same cups in tea stalls, or lay claim to land that is legally theirs. Dalit children are frequently made to sit in the back of classrooms, and communities as a whole are made to perform degrading rituals in the name of caste. Most Dalits continue to live in extreme poverty, without land or opportunities for better employment or education. With the exception of a minority who have benefited from India's policy of quotas in education and government jobs, Dalits are relegated to the most menial of tasks, as manual scavengers, removers of human waste and dead animals, leather workers, street sweepers, and cobblers. Dalit children make up the majority of those sold into bondage to pay off debts to upper-caste creditors. Dalit men, women, and children numbering in the tens of millions work as agricultural laborers for a few kilograms of rice or ` 15 to ₹35 (US$0.38 to $0.88) a day. Their upper-caste employers frequently use caste as a cover for exploitative economic arrangements: social sanction of their status as lesser beings allows their impoverishment to continue.

This is the reality faced by the more than 160 million Dalits living in India today. As this description shows and as the National Campaign on Dalit Human Rights asserts "India's version of apartheid and racism, caste discrimination and "untouchability" affect every facet and dimension of Dalits' daily lives – economic, social, cultural and political." Thus, the need to address this situation through a human rights lens that incorporates ESC rights is vital. Centuries of this "hidden apartheid" that has perpetuated discrimination and denial of their human rights, has resulted not only in Dalits representing a disproportional amount of the poor in India, but also in the creation of numerous other obstacles that hinder Dalits' ability to change their situation.

VESTIGES OF UNTOUCHABILITY

Caste separation is manifested in many ways. It is common place in rural villages for there to be an area called "Dalit Street." This is the only area in which Dalits are allowed to live. As such, it is often the site of neglect as services can easily be diverted away from it or never brought to it. Dalits are often expected to carry out traditional roles for which they receive no compensation. For example, they must play the drums in religious ceremonies and must remove dead animals. Their participation in such acts only works to perpetuate the discrimination against them. Finally, overcoming one's status as a Dalit is incredibly difficult. When a qualified Dalit applies for a job, interviewers often enquire as to the applicant's caste. Once this is known, his prospects of getting the job are greatly diminished.

EMPLOYMENT OPPORTUNITIES

According to the National Campaign on Dalit Rights, Dalits constitute the majority of the bonded and child labour in India. Agricultural work is done mainly by Dalits, and many Dalit women are forced into ritualized prostitution. In many villages, the practice of manual scavenging, the removal of human excrement, is only undertaken by Dalits. Added to this is the fact that Dalits are often paid less than the minimum wage or not at all, instead receiving payments-in-kind. The reservation system, which was specifically designed to provide employment opportunities to disadvantaged groups within India, has only benefited a small number of Dalits. This is partly because the system only applies to the government sector. More generally, it is because this system has proven itself to be flawed, corrupt, and lacking full implementation, as numerous positions go unfilled.

Entrepreneurial opportunities for Dalits are extremely limited. First of all, Dalits lack both the capital investment for such a venture and the collateral to secure a loan to obtain it. Moreover, even if they were to open a business, it would almost certainly be doomed to fail. This is because non-Dalits would not frequent it, preferring instead to frequent a non-Dalit store. Thus, its success would depend entirely on the Dalits in the village. Given that they generally constitute a very small minority in villages and that they have very little money to spend, the prospects are not very encouraging. Other economic opportunities are also scarce for Dalits as India suffers from a limited amount of jobs and resources. The small amount that does exist largely goes to those already in power, exacerbating the gap between poor and rich.

MIGRATION

In order to survive, Dalits often must migrate in search of work. The main cause of this migration is lack of land ownership. Without their own land, Dalits are unable to produce crops for their own consumption or for sale in the market. This combined with the limited employment opportunities available in their small villages forces them to leave their village in search of work elsewhere.

Another cause of migration is general economic hardships, such as droughts. Dalits do not have the resources needed to get through such periods, as they are often refused loans even after agreeing to exorbitantly high interest rates and are unable to turn to their equally challenged Dalit neighbours for help. Lastly, Dalits prefer migration to permanent establishment in new communities since such an endeavor would require vast resources and would result in the loss of their existing social networks.

INDIA

THE ECONOMIC AND POLITICAL SITUATION IN INDIA

India, in particular, presents an interesting case study for further examining the recognition and implementation of ESC rights. Like many developing countries, the economy is driven by agriculture, with one-third of national output and two-thirds of employment being accounted for by this sector. In the economy there is divisive income inequality, and a full twenty per cent of the urban population and thirty per cent of the rural population live below the poverty level.

An expanding population of more than one billion further compounds economic problems. India, also however, exhibits many characteristics associated with developed countries. It continues to be in transition from a largely government-controlled economy to one that is largely market driven. It has a comprehensive Constitution supported and upheld by a well-established legislative and judicial system. However, in India there remains a momentous divide between commitment to making law and enforcing full implementation of such laws.

There is conflicting evidence on India's commitment to ensuring ESC rights.

In a speech addressing India and human rights Prime Minister Atal Bihari Vajpayee said:

- The more we enforce the rule of law, the better we promote human rights...In a developing country like India, the task of advancing human rights is integrally linked to speedy and balanced socio-economic growth. Poverty is one of the worst violators of human rights—and so also is the society that allows poverty to persist. India has all the human and natural resources needed to provide decent living standards to all our citizens. This, however, can be achieved only by removing the shackles on India's all-round economic progress. This is the true purpose of our economic reforms. Our reforms have a human face because they are designed to promote economic and social justice for all our citizens, especially the poorest and the most deprived.

India is committed to legislating ideas of civil, political, economic, social, and cultural rights as well as legislating against human rights violations. To help overcome the problems of historic discrimination of caste and gender, India legislated and created a stringent reservation system to allow for increased opportunity. However, while there have been successes as a result of the system, there is not complete commitment to implementation and support of the system. The intended recipients are still unable to be equally educated or to be hired for the reserved government jobs. They do not have the authority positions to make changes. Instead, this motivation must come from those who are upper caste and upper class, and there is simply a lack of political will at any level to implement the laws and realise such advancements towards human rights.

India has also ratified several international covenants focusing on varying aspects of human rights, including the Universal Declaration of Human Rights as well as ICESCR. It has enacted many laws that support the spirit of the Declaration and the Covenant, as well as laws that provide precise rights and obligations beyond the vagueness of the international documents. Along with 188 other countries India has committed itself to eight Millennium Development Goals that aim to eradicate extreme poverty and improve the welfare of all peoples by the year 2015. The second development goal has been coined "Education for All" with the goal being to "achieve universal primary education" with the specific target of "ensuring that, by 2015, children everywhere, boys and girls alike, will be able to complete a full course of primary schooling." As one of the largest countries, and with large amounts of children failing to complete primary school, improvement in India is crucial to the United Nations and the world meeting this second goal.

INDIA AND EDUCATION

The Constitution of India goes well beyond the UN's primary education mandate (defined as completing fifth standard). Article 45 of the Constitution states that:

- "The State shall endeavor to provide within a period of ten years from the commencement of this Constitution, for free and compulsory education for all children until they complete the age of fourteen years." The next article certifies that "the State shall promote with special care the educational and economic interests of the weaker sections of the people, and in particular, of the Scheduled Castes and the Scheduled Tribes, and shall protect them from social injustice and all forms of exploitation."

However, government reports estimate that only two-thirds of children in India complete their primary education; this translates into a conservative estimate of 20 to 30 million children not being in primary school or twenty-five per cent of the estimated 120 million primary-aged children not in school worldwide. Activists consider this to be a vast understatement of the number of unenrolled children. It is also estimated that ten per cent of children in India never begin primary school; these children are disproportionately comprised of children from rural areas, those from scheduled tribes and scheduled castes, and girls.

Quality of Education

Even when children are able to attend school the quality of public education in India is inconsistent and often inadequate. Quality varies dramatically across states and districts as well as between urban and rural areas. The poor quality of schooling in India can be attributed to many factors. First, the physical infrastructure of the schools has historically been inadequate. Schools are often in poor condition or are too small to serve the number of kids in the district. Children are often in classrooms upward of sixty people. Even if a teacher is actively attempting to teach the students, he or she is unable to spend time on individual instruction. There is a more significant issue given that students are often well below the competency required of their current grade level.

On one side, there are reports that teachers do not "teach" enough. Many times they show up late or simply do not even show up at all. Such a situation occurs partly because teachers are not accountable to the local community. They are often not from the community in which they teach and their salaries are controlled by the state. Conversely, teachers feel that their work conditions are not conducive to better teaching methods. For instance, teachers are often compelled to teach more than one grade at a time. Together, the weight of these simultaneous conditions all serve to weaken the quality of the schools.

Government does provide many schemes to attempt to improve both access and quality of education. Currently, there are 130 such schemes with the largest being the *Mid-Day Meal* scheme that provides a cooked meal to all students in primary school, as a way to encourage poor-child enrollment. Other programmes include *Operation Blackboard* to improve school facilities; there are also several schemes specific to the needs of districts or even an entire state. The government is also designing schemes to meet their commitment to the goal of universality of elementary education (UEE). These programmes include reducing the costs of textbooks and exercise books to removing systematic deficiencies towards primary education for all. The expansion of these programmes shows a certain level of commitment by the Indian government. However, the question remains whether India's current commitment level to primary education is enough. As is often the case with education statistics in India, data aggregated at the national level do not reveal the disparities that are central to ensuring quality primary education across districts and states, rural and urban areas, as well as socio-economic levels. Furthermore, despite the supposed effort, the primary education completion rate has only risen from 75% in 1990 to 76% in 1999. Again, this is due to the lack of political will in both administration and implementation.

India does not allow (and therefore does not recognize) that there are byproducts of caste discrimination in the education system. The district administration officer in Gujarat acknowledges that while there may be discrimination between teachers and the village or between teachers and teachers that discrimination between teachers and Dalit students is nonexistent. This is in clear contrast to what we heard from the Dalit people. This failure to admit such discrimination prevents government officials from attempting to truly improve the situation.

DALIT EDUCATION IN INDIA

Dalit children, being disproportionately poor, most heavily suffer the ills of an inequitable and ineffective education system in India. The Indian constitution pledges to provide free and compulsory education for all children up to age fourteen. However, in 1993 only 16.2% of primary school age Dalit children in were enrolled in school as compared to 83.8% of primary aged children from non-scheduled castes.

According to the India Education Report, school attendance in rural areas in 1993-94 was 64.3% for Dalit boys and 46.2% for Dalit girls, compared to 74.9% among boys and 61% girls from other social groups Dalits lagged behind the general population by as many as 15 percentage points in literacy, barely 24 per cent of Dalit women were literate.

Statistics also show that Dalit children are more likely to drop out than their non-Dalit counterparts, particularly in the early elementary stages. Education represents one way to break out of cycles of poverty and distress, but it is also a by-product of such economic conditions. Even when Dalits are allowed access to school, Dalit students face substandard conditions. Ninety-nine per cent of Dalit students come from government schools that lack basic infrastructure, classrooms, teachers and teaching aid. In contrast, it is common for non-Dalit children to seek private tutoring or to access private education of generally better quality.

The motivation to do so comes from the fact that most primary government schools are considered low quality. Few Dalits are able to access such supplementation to their education; this furthers the education gap. Once enrolled, discrimination continues to obstruct the access of Dalit children to schooling as well as to affect the quality of education they receive. Case Study of the Violation of the Right to Primary Education in Gujarat Like civil and political rights, ESC rights can be broken when inadequate protection is taken.

We address the issue of the violation of ESC rights, defined in the following international agreements to which India is a party:

- The Universal Declaration of Human Rights (UDHR);
- The International Covenant on Economic, Social and Cultural Rights (ICESCR); and
- The Convention on the Rights of the Child (CRC).

From these texts, we have found four main themes of direct relevance to the condition of Dalit school children in Gujarat,

(1) Namely de facto discrimination,
(2) Failure to promote human dignity,
(3) Hindrances to the enjoyment of education
(4) Failure to foster the full development of children.

We offer illustrations of the violations of ESC rights as told to us by children, parents, teachers and organizers on our field visits throughout rural Gujarat.

DE FACTO DISCRIMINATION

Practices at local levels intended to keep castes separate or reinforce caste distinctions result in instances of discrimination. The informational report from Article 13, point 37 of the ICESCR states that "parties must closely monitor education - including all relevant policies, institutions, programmes, spending patterns and other practices - so as to identify and take measures to redress any de facto discrimination."

De facto discrimination in rural Gujarat occurs in myriad ways. From our visits to villages, we heard stories regarding the explicit discrimination of Dalits in the arenas of classroom seating, permission to participate in class activities and the receipt of lower marks for high quality work. Similar issues in discrimination are addressed in later categories.

Classroom Seating

Perhaps the most widely discussed violation regarding children is the requirement of some non-Dalit teachers for Dalit students to sit exclusively in the back of classrooms. This was a common complaint in many of the villages we visited. In each instance of violation, the teacher was a non-Dalit who was either the only teacher for the village or among a non-Dalit teacher majority.

- Visiting with Dalit rights organizers in the taluka of Sami, we were told that this practice occurs in the majority of the schools in the 34 villages that comprise the taluka.
- The village of Sahpur has about 2000 residents and a Dalit minority of 100. Students in this village told us that they are required to reserve front seats in the classroom for non-Dalit children.
- The village of Dodar has about 3500 residents, 600 of whom are

Dalit. One young girl named Sonar told us that she likes school, and that she one day hopes to become a doctor or teacher. She told us that Dalit children in her school are required to sit in the back of the classroom and are required to remove their shoes in the classroom. Non-Dalit children, she said, are not subject to the same requirements.

Access to Participation

Forced seating in the back of the classroom expressly limits student access to participation in class. Class sizes in rural Gujarat average 60 students. The vast overcrowding of Gujarati classrooms limits teacher capacity to interact with students; sitting in the back further minimizes interaction with and support from teachers.

- Dalit children in Sahpur said that they are not called on to answer teacher questions or invited to write on the board as frequently as non-Dalit children. These students told us that this is a source of embarrassment, and is a reason why non-Dalit children mock them.
- Sonar from Dodar told us that her teacher often calls on students, but only calls on those sitting in the first through fourth rows. The vast class size in her village and her status as a Dalit keeps her far from even the fourth row.

Grading

The receipt of unjustifiably low marks is a common concern we heard from children in rural Gujarat. Dalit Organizers say that there are many reports from villages throughout the state that non-Dalits receive higher marks while Dalits fare relatively poorly. Local organizers in the taluka of Sami have received numerous complaints from students regarding grading in their villages. These complaints have come from even the top-scoring Dalits who feel their work is of equal or better quality to the work of the best non-Dalits.

- In Sahpur, a young girl named Sangeetha believes she was kept in the third grade for three consecutive years because she is Dalit. She considers herself a hard-working student who does well in class. However, she believes that her teacher intentionally makes her and other Dalit children fail by falsifying grades. She told us that it is frustrating to do the same work year after year, work she claims is easy. She said it makes her not want to go to school at all.

FAILURE TO PROMOTE HUMAN DIGNITY

An issue closely linked to de facto discrimination is the failure to promote human dignity. ESC documents explicitly address the issue of human dignity, asserting that equality is a trait that should be both engendered and upheld. Article 29 (1)(d) of the CRC states an education is to be "the preparation of the child for responsible life in a free society, in the spirit of understanding, peace, tolerance, equality of sexes, and friendship...." Article 13 (1) of the ICESCR further states that "education shall be directed to the full development of the human personality and the sense of its dignity."

With regard to the achievement of full human dignity for and within the Dalit community, actions of some schools demonstrate that this aim is not always taken seriously. Explicit reinforcement of caste lines exacerbates inequality. This is evident in the relegation of Dalit students to the backs of classrooms, the separation of children and even teachers for water and food consumption, the exclusive assignment of Dalit students to custodial duties, and verbally abusive statements directed to reinforce inequalities.

Sitting in the Back of the Classroom

Forcing Dalits to sit in the back of the room limits their learning potential. Moreover, it reinforces inequality among the students, creates tiers within the classroom based on caste and instills a feeling of inferiority within Dalit children. We met children who, despite being forced to save front row seats for non-Dalit children, have internalized the separation, accepted it as a way of life, and do not believe their own human dignity demands equality in the classroom.

- We met with a group of Dalit teachers outside of Ahmedabad who say that even when seating is not assigned, Dalit students will gravitate towards the back of the classroom. They said this is most likely a result of previous experience with non-Dalit teachers. The students may have been told at some point to sit in the back and threatened with punishment. The teachers told us that Dalit students have been conditioned to be afraid of sitting in the front, fearing punishment from the teacher and/or ostracizing from non-Dalits.
- A young girl in Sahpur told us, "we are Harijans, so we are obliged to sit in the back."

Food and Water Consumption

Caste divisions and inequalities are reinforced with historic caste taboos regarding food and water consumption. Notions that Dalits are "dirty" or "impure" are pervasive in some villages, and teachers systematically seek to have students internalize and accept these derogatory terms.

- In the village of Tara Nagar, Dalit children told us that their teachers forbid them from sitting with non-Dalit children, either in the classroom or during lunch hours. These children also told us that they are explicitly forbidden from touching the plates of non-Dalit children.
- Jagruti, a 12 year-old girl from the village of Sahpur, told us that if Dalit children want water they are required by the teacher to wait

until a non-Dalit is available to pour water from several feet above them into either their hands our their mouths.

- According to Sami Dalit organizers, six schools in the taluka have requirements that keep Dalit students separate from non-Dalit students at lunchtime.
- Dalit teachers are not excluded from such discriminatory behaviour. In the village of Kumbhana, a Dalit teacher named Jignasha was told by her principal to keep her water pot separate from the water pots of other teachers.

Custodial Duties

The human dignity of Dalit children is further hindered in schools in which Dalit children are exclusively required to take on additional custodial duties. In instances of this violation, Dalit children were as a group required to take on additional cleaning duties, while non-Dalit children were not.

- In the village of Sahpur, despite not being allowed to get their own water from the school's supply, Dalit children are required to clean the water tank on behalf of non-Dalit children and the non-Dalit teacher.
- Bankje, a young boy in the same village, told us that Dalit children are required to arrive to school early in order to clean the school before the non-Dalit children arrive. When late for cleaning, Bankje said, students are scolded.
- In the village of Dodar, Dalit children are also made to clean. A young girl, Jusna, this cleaning can include both the school and the outdoor garden.

Verbal Abuse

Specific instances of verbal abuse on the part of teachers illustrate the reinforcement of caste prejudices and inequalities.

- Jagrathi, a boy in his final year of primary school in Sahpur, spoke of an incident at school. The teacher asked that students planning to go on to secondary school raise their hands. Jagrathi and one other Dalit child raised their hands. The teacher approached the two, and told them that they are Dalits, that they were never going to go to secondary school and that they should lower their hands.
- The father told us that his young daughter came home after school one day and asked him, "Father, are we daed?" He asked her who told her that they are daed. She replied, "my teacher."

HINDRANCES TO ENJOYING EDUCATION

Constraints that are especially felt by the Dalit community hinder the access of Dalit children to educational opportunities. The informational report on implementation of Article 13 (47) of ICESCR requires "States parties to avoid measures that hinder or prevent the enjoyment of the right to education." It goes on to require that "[s]tates ... take positive measures that enable and assist individuals and communities to enjoy the right to education."

Issues of land-ownership, generational repetition of under-education and limited social networks compound to render the Dalit community particularly vulnerable. These characteristics are common in poor communities throughout the world, but the Dalits of Gujarat and of India experience them more so than other caste groups. They especially effect primary school age children through migratory laboring.

Migratory Labour

Though the problem of and the problems deriving from labour migration are not unique to the Dalit community, we found them to be especially pervasive among Dalits. Migration serves as a hindrance to the education in that parents generally take their children with them while searching for labour. Young boys and girls are often expected to work alongside their parents in day laboring jobs and young girls are often made to care for younger siblings. Permanent migration is not always a preferred option for families, as much weight is put on extended familial connections and ritual obligations such as marriage. Migratory spells generally last four months and are most common during the dry season.

Once students have missed 18 days, children are no longer allowed to advance with their class:

- In the village of Gadthal, the parents of 35 Dalit children have left in search of labour and taken their children with them. Very few non-Dalit children are effected by migration in this village as most non-Dalits own land. Only a small minority of Dalits own land there. Families travel up to 200 km to find work.
- In the village of Nani Kathechi, the parents of 29 of the village's 44 Dalit children have left in search of labour, and taken their children with them. Though most return about every four months, the 29 children are not able to keep up in school, and many simply drop out.
- Some migrant laborers are doing their best to stop history from repeating itself. A man in the same village, who is temporarily back from his time as a migrant laborer in Jogar, told us that he leaves his son in the village with older relatives so that he can attend school. When asked why he makes this a priority, he said that it is indeed difficult, because he could use his son's help. However, he told us that his father too was a migrant laborer, and he had to go with his father and drop out of school. He does not want his son to live the life that he has had to live.

FAILURE TO FOSTER THE FULL DEVELOPMENT OF CHILDREN

The full development of children is a standard component of ESC rights documents. Article 29 (1)(a) of the CRC requires that the education of a child be directed "to the development of the child's personality, talents and mental and physical abilities to their fullest potential." Article 26 (2) of the UDHR states that "education shall be directed to the full development of the human personality and to the strengthening of respect for human rights and fundamental freedoms." Article 13 (1) of the ICESCR further reinforces its predecessors, stating that "education shall be directed to the full development of the human personality and the sense of its dignity, and shall strengthen the respect for human rights and fundamental freedoms."

Achieving the full development of children requires significant resources. Understanding that resources are greatly constrained in a developing country, we seek to evaluate Gujarat in its specific context. We identify the violation of rights based on the pursuit to provide means towards full development to one group while explicitly excluding another. We heard of instances of such violation with regard to school activities.

School Activities

We met young children who told us that they are not allowed to participate in various school activities simply because they are Dalits.

- In the village of Sahpur, a young girl named Jagneth told us that Dalit children are routinely excluded from participation in school activities, such as cultural programmes. Students are told that only non-Dalits can participate in events.
- A young Dalit boy in the same village, Nitesh, told us that he was recently not allowed to participate in a picnic, as it was restricted to only non-Dalits.

CONCLUSION AND RECOMMENDATIONS

Dalits face a cultural and normative history entrenched in discrimination. Despite efforts to codify human rights into state legislation, the violation of many ESC rights is visible throughout India. Discrimination is indeed deeply rooted, and efforts must be taken to realise the international commitments to which India is subject. Both the Indian government and the NGO sector can advance the condition of Dalits concerning ESC rights.

RECOMMENDATIONS TO THE INDIAN GOVERNMENT

The discrimination that exists in India has serious ramifications in the realm of education. The caste-based statements made by teachers damage children. School and classroom rules regarding the separation of students by caste and reinforcement of taboos result in the maintenance of centuries-old divisions and minimize other public efforts to fight discrimination. Beyond mere legislation, the Indian government can make a difference in the classroom.

Actions include the following:

- *Reverse the current trend of decreased spending on education and work towards meeting international spending norms.* In 1990, India's public expenditure on education was 3.9% of its GNP. In 1997 this proportion had dropped to 3.3%. India must not continue to cut spending. Instead it should increase spending on education to at least 5% of its GNP, which would bring it within the range of the world average. It could do so by prioritizing spending and shifting obligations within the federal budget. For instance, India currently spends a large amount of tax revenue on the government sector, but a small amount on education. By increasing spending, the government will be able to improve the quality of education by providing more schools and teachers (thus, reducing class size), higher salaries for teachers, better teacher training and increased availability of school materials.
- *Incorporate ESC rights education into teachers' training curriculum.* This will inform teachers of both their rights and those of their students. Moreover, by providing such education, teachers can then be held more accountable for any violations they may commit.
- *Provide teachers with sensitivity training.* This would go one step beyond basic human rights education in that it would equip teachers with the skills needed to effectively address inequalities in their classrooms. First, it would focus on the teachers' belief system and would try to get teachers to recognize any prejudices they may have. It would then discuss ways for teachers to deal with and ultimately overcome these prejudices. Second, it would look at Dalit children, in particular at their internalization of discrimination and at their economic and social condition. It would discuss how both of these have significant effects on the way Dalits' participate and perform in school. It would then offer ways for teachers to encourage greater participation by Dalits. Lastly, it would concentrate on the mentality of non-Dalit children, recognizing that they too carry prejudices that need to be addressed. It would offer ways to deal with these prejudices, such as promoting dignity and equality among all students.
- *Random monitoring to ensure compliance.* In order to ensure that teachers are not forcing Dalits to sit in the back of classrooms, restricting them from passing out food and requiring them to clean the classrooms, the government should make unannounced visits to schools. During these visits, the officials could also speak with Dalit and non-Dalit children, as well as parents and teachers in the

village to assess the situation. If violations are taking place, the officials should take immediate action to stop them.

- *Punishment for non-compliance.* If a teacher is found to be violating any student's rights, regardless of their caste, then he should be given a strict penalty, such as suspension without pay.

As important as these recommendations are, it goes without saying that they only scratch the surface of the challenges that India face. In order to have a real impact, they need to be accompanied by an integrated commitment to ESC rights and to an elevation of the status and economic situation of Dalits by the Indian government. For example, the government needs to look for solutions to the migration problem, such as providing the poor with productive land or providing more economic opportunities for people in villages. It must also look for ways to end the segregation of Dalits in villages.

RECOMMENDATIONS TO LOCAL AND INTERNATIONAL NGOS

Unfortunately, the prospects for self-initiated change within the government are very low. In the past, India has done a great job of creating legislation, but has not been able to effectively implement it. Added to this is the fact that Dalits have traditionally been overlooked, thus making it even more unlikely programmes designed to specifically help them will actually see fruition. Therefore, local and international NGOs must simultaneously seek out independent solutions for improving this situation.

Such solutions may include:

- *Pressuring the state to fully comply with its ESC obligations.* One way to do so is by using the human rights framework, and in particular the ICESCR. They must remind the state of the obligations it assumed when signing the various international human rights treaties. They may also turn to other governments or international organization such as the United Nation High Commissioner for Human Rights to help in applying pressure.
- *Educating people of their rights.* Once educated, people will be more likely to mobilize and demand that the state honour its obligations.
- *Taking immediate action and filling the gap themselves.* It is evident that in many areas, Dalits are receiving a substandard education relative to their non-Dalit counterparts. Mobilizing the state to radically improve the public education system will take considerable time. In the meantime, whole generations could be left under-educated. Religious organizations, particularly Roman Catholics, have helped some of the poorest in Gujarat by giving providing a quality education to many Dalit children at private schools. Other non-state organizations could also step in and provide alternatives to public schooling that would better ensure small class size, caste-blindness in the classroom and support for human dignity. Creating a

generation of well-educated Dalits, prepared in quality schools to be competitive on the job market, could alter the assumptions of many non-Dalits. These well-educated Dalits will be better prepared to articulate their concerns to the state, and increase the movement exponentially. Furthermore, the high quality of these non-state schools may "shame" the state into improving public schools for those non-Dalits left behind.

- *Public informational activities.* In our travels in rural Gujarat, we were amazed at how unfamiliar discussions of caste were to people, especially the non-Dalits. A system that controls their communal existence to such a degree is rarely discussed openly or examined critically. Public informational activities could work to render Indians, regardless of caste, better aware of the ancient feelings of discrimination they hold. Such activities might include role-plays or skits. While NGOs should offer ways to combat these feelings, such as through education, they should also elicit suggestions from the participants. This is an extremely important venture as educating children in schools about the need for equality has severe limitations. Once they leave school, they return to parents and a society rife with discrimination. Thus, NGOs must undertake projects such as this in an attempt to fight for more comprehensive social change.
- *Seek to change the existing power structure of India.* At the heart of the persistent caste system is a division of power. This division renders one group as subjugated to another, and is seemingly authorized by religious and historic mandate. Efforts must be taken by the NGO community to chip away at this rigid balance. NGOs should provide public service announcements regarding valid criticisms of the caste system. For example, Gandhi considered the caste system to be the shame of the Hindu religion. NGOs must also seek to advance the general economic condition of Dalits throughout India. In many villages that we visited, stores were rarely owned by Dalits. NGOs should provide greater assistance to Dalits in need of loans to build their own shops or to advance new ideas for commerce and trade. Lessening dependence on non-Dalits renders Dalits increasingly powerful and more capable of assuming their ESC rights.

Indeed, change will not come about overnight. The caste system has endured for centuries, and the descendants of the original high caste members continue to exploit artificial caste lines, despite the better sensibilities of existing international and state legislations. Like any great social change, this one will require time and the cooperative efforts of individuals at all levels – local, state, and international. As Macwan told us in Gujarat, "We do not seek to change the system in the blink of an eye. That would be unrealistic. What we are committed to here is a *movement*."

This movement to which Macwan and numerous other progressive individuals commit themselves also requires new approaches, as past ones have sadly proven insufficient. The case of primary school children in rural Gujarat shows that the protection of human rights demands more than civil and political rights. Beyond expressed exclusions are more subtle violations. Indeed, the violation of ESC rights results in identifiable instances of discrimination and the denial of simple human dignity. Attention to ESC rights allows us to do more than just write legislation – it allows us to pursue systematic change.

11

Dalit Rights to Political Participation

Direct political participation of Dalit women in local governance (Panchayati Raj) is a central human right in itself and enables the realisation of a host of other human rights. Political voice and decision-making power concerning basic services, economic development and social justice are critical factors in challenging and transforming structural caste-class-gender discrimination, and enabling Dalit women to realise their fundamental rights. Political participation also demands accountability from state and non-state actors to guarantee and respect these women's equal political voice and development. This requires a transformation of power relationships both within institutions of governance and in the women's social environment.

Recent legal and policy reforms in India to ensure the representation of marginalised social groups in decentralised governance, including Dalits and specifically Dalit women, through constitutionally mandated reservations in Panchayati Raj institutions bring these issues to the fore. They demand analysis to determine how Dalit women are enabled to claim their right to political participation in local governance, and the extent to which this participation is an effective tool for empowerment and realisation of human rights for excluded social groups. Annammal calls on Dalit women to persevere with the 'social revolution' that the panchayat system and reservations therein have started in India. At the same time, the more tempered words by the Dalit women panchayat representatives from Ahmedabad district are an assessment of the present political situation and indicate where change is required: formal authority does not equal political power.!

Key questions therefore posed in this research are:

- Are Dalit women able to access panchayat posts and, once elected, exercise freely political power and authority for the welfare of their constituency, Dalits and women in particular?
- What factors and structures facilitate or inhibit Dalit women's access, participation and impact in Panchayati Raj?
- What is the role of various state institutions in preventing and responding to obstructions against Dalit women in Panchayati Raj?

ACCESS TO PANCHAYAT POSTS

Only a minority of the 200 Dalit women in this research, approximately one-third, were able to act with independence and freedom to win the panchayat elections. Both personal factors such as education, experience on social issues, motivation to bring development to their community and others, prior performance in panchayats, political negotiation skills, as well as external factors including family support, good relations with other villagers, economic stability and family's political contacts, all played a supportive role in enabling women to access panchayat positions. Given the low social, educational, economic and gender status of these women, however, they could be challenged and overpowered relatively easily by dominant forces.

For the majority of Dalit women, the panchayat election process masks strong, caste-based patriarchal control over them and the enjoyment of their rights. Around 85% of Dalit women were pushed into panchayat politics primarily by dominant castes or their husbands, the former often working through the women's husbands. Dominant castes also for the most part sought to directly engineer elections by consensus, thereby making the reservation policy redundant. The primary tool for this, and the most significant factor drawn from this research, was *benami* or proxy politics.

TACTICS OF CONTROL

The effective use of proxy candidature provided legitimised political space for primarily dominant caste men and secondarily Dalit men to exploit Dalit women, and reinforce their own interests and the suppression of these women. At the same time, this denied Dalit women's right to independent and empowered participation in local governance. For example, a dominant caste man in Anand district in Gujarat named Dalit woman Gangaben a consensus candidate for the panchayat President's post, alongside determining the entire panchayat membership and making his wife the Vice President. The night before the news of this consensus panchayat became public, the man came to Gangaben's house to tell her that she had been elected President while threatening to stop her husband's work if she did not allow him to control the panchayat administration through her.

To ensure success in proxy politics, various strategies were employed drawing on Dalit women's vulnerabilities: their low gender status in the family (as economically dependent and bounded within marital and kinship relations); their low gender, caste and class status (as woman and Dalit, as illiterate and labourer) in society; their old age or widowhood status; exploiting and deepening intra-Dalit divisions through supporting one sub-caste against another, often to prevent a more assertive or vocal sub-caste member from being elected. Livelihood dependency and lack of sufficient financial resources to meet election expenses also made the women vulnerable to proxy politics especially from dominant castes and political parties (dominated by dominant castes). Further, traditional, and in Gujarat state supported, consensus politics was used to uphold the caste-class-gender hierarchical status quo. Dalit women elected representatives in Ahmedabad district in Gujarat, *"Consensus candidates who get selected are usually illiterate, poor people who are influenced by dominant castes on whom they depend for employment. Whoever becomes President through consensus always has to act as a pawn of the village."* Similarly, Dalit women elected representatives in Cuddalore district in Tamil Nadu stated, *"It is completely wrong to be elected unopposed or unanimously. This way of election is an instrument to strengthen the power of the dominant castes. Not only this, it is against democratic rights, freedom and equality. This is another kind of violence that dominant castes use against us."*

ACTIVE OBSTRUCTIONS DURING ELECTORAL PROCESS

Control over the election process was also achieved through other means, aiming to prevent or discourage the Dalit women from filing nominations (experienced by 12.5% of the women), or to force or push them to withdraw their nominations (14.5% of the women). This included pressure in the forms of caste and sexually-based abuse, allegations of immoral behaviour, threats, bribes and vilifying campaigns against women's capacity to govern, physical assaults and property destruction. It further included restrictions on freedoms through social norms preventing movement outside the home for campaigning, livelihood demands and compulsions of household responsibilities.

Obstructions also arose as a result of Dalit caste or sub-caste assertion, with identity politics playing a major role in the electoral process. A clear example was when dominant castes put up candidates from a smaller Dalit sub-caste, or divided the Dalit vote by supporting multiple candidates from one Dalit sub-caste to contest. This was done in order to obstruct independent and active Dalit women supporting Dalits' interests from nominating for panchayat posts, thereby challenging the norms of dominant caste authority and control. As a result of mainly dominant caste efforts, therefore, 34 women failed to secure a panchayat seat. Likewise, rival Dalit women candidates and their families sometimes obstructed women in their efforts to secure the reserved seat for their own sub-caste or other interests, or to ensure that Dalit interests were represented in the panchayat rather than dominant caste interests through proxy Dalit candidates.

The obstructions 10.5% of the women faced – primarily from dominant castes and other Dalit candidates/families – were heightened on the election day, when widespread breaches of the rule of law and electoral process were evident. Illegal voting practices included threatening or physically preventing the women candidates or other Dalits from voting or entering the election booths, attempted bogus voting, bribes given to voters to vote for rival candidates, and harassment or assault against the women. Further, 15.1% of

Dalit women also faced problems following the release of election results, thus being denied their right to post-election safety and security. Overall then, out of the 200 Dalit women interviewed, 166 women (83.0%) entered into the panchayats as either presidents or members. Out of these women, 83.7% did so through elections, 13.9% were nominated as consensus candidates and 2.4% were elected unopposed. The predominance of Dalit women entering through seats reserved specifically for them (SC women reserved) worked on the caste and gender biased assumption that general women reserved seats are for dominant caste women and SC reserved seats are for Dalit men. Dalit women then are effectively ghettoised into those seats specifically reserved for them.

PARTICIPATION IN THE PANCHAYATS

Once elected, dominant caste male control over panchayat resources and ingrained discriminatory attitudes continued to govern to a large extent the experiences of Dalit women panchayat representatives. At least three-quarters of these women were either proxies or faced strong opposition and obstructions while attempting to work for the benefit of their community. The study findings confirm the Concluding Observations of the CERD Committee on the Indian Government's Report in 2007 that: *"Dalit candidates, especially women, are frequently forcibly prevented from standing for election or, if elected, forced to resign from village councils or other elected bodies or not to exercise their mandate."*

FULFILMENT OF PANCHAYAT ROLES

Only one-third of 119 Dalit women presidents were able to discharge their official responsibilities with freedom and independence. Taking three basic presidential roles, only 35.3% of women called panchayat meetings, 31.9% chaired them, and 27.7% voluntarily signed resolutions. Only 26.1% of women voluntarily authorised panchayat payments (or monitored the panchayat administration and supervised the work of the BDOs/TDOs or DDOs as per their role at taluka/union or district levels).

Similarly, only 23.5% of women approved contracts for panchayat development works (or reviewed them as per their role at taluka/union or district levels). Instead, a number of women spoke of rubber-stamping panchayat decisions and signing cheques at the behest of others. The motive for these actions by dominant caste panchayat members, according to a group of Dalit women villagers in Madurai district in Tamil Nadu, is: *"They think that if they allow [the Dalit woman President] to function in the panchayat, she will work for the welfare of Dalits. And if they allow this once, it will become a tradition in future, so she should continue to be subjugated under them. Thus they take away all responsibilities from her."* Power politics thus meant that dominant caste males, and to a lesser extent Dalit males and political parties controlled by dominant castes, were the real authority bearers in the majority of Dalit women headed panchayats. Data on proxy representation reveals that a little less than onefifth of elected Dalit women functioned as proxies for their husbands and/ or male relatives out of a total of 59% proxy representatives, as compared to the one-third of elected women who were proxies for dominant castes and less than one-tenth for others including political parties. Thus the generally accepted assumption that Dalit women are mostly proxies for their husbands, like other caste women, was disproved through this research.

Further, while over half (52.4%) of the 166 elected presidents and members attended many or all of the panchayat meetings held during their term in office, only around half these women were vocal in terms of raising development-related and other issues in meetings. The remainder, most of them presidents, did not raise any new issues during meetings. For just over half of the 90 Dalit women who raised issues in panchayat meetings (52.2%), however, their issues were never or only a few times discussed and approved. Moreover, what must be borne in mind is the number of women directed by dominant castes or their husbands as to what issues to discuss in meetings, essentially serving others' interests. Otherwise, especially Dalit women panchayat presidents often faced opposition and had to struggle to get their proposals discussed and approved.

ACTIVE OBSTRUCTIONS AND OTHER DISABLING FACTORS FOR PARTICIPATION

Around one-quarter of Dalit women elected representatives (23%) were restricted by others from active participation in panchayat council meetings. For example: they were prevented from attending; their right to speak was opposed; others spoke in their place; they faced caste or sexually charged abuse; others reinforced gender and caste norms on them (eg: that women should remain in the home, that Dalit women should not speak in front of dominant castes) in order to restrict their space for participation. Women who asserted their right to freely express their views in meetings were often negatively labelled as 'outspoken'. Dominant castes and men also refused to share knowledge that would enhance the women's administrative capabilities. This was what a dominant caste Clerk did to village panchayat President Kowsalya from Coimbatore district in Tamil Nadu, in addition to which he wrote caste abusive words against her on the walls of the panchayat office, and along with dominant caste panchayat members tried to silence her in the panchayat.

More internal reasoning for low participation of the women elected representatives, mentioned by 120 Dalit women elected representatives (72.3%), concerned a number of interconnecting factors: their proxy status, fear, lack of self-confidence and knowledge connected to their poor educational status, and compliance with imposed traditional caste and gender roles. Less than one-third of women came from families with prior political experience in panchayat governance (30%) and very few had previous personal experience (16%). Viewed in light of the rotation of reserved seats, especially in Gujarat where seats rotate with every panchayat term, the implications are to limit rather than encourage active political participation; that is, Dalit women often were offered little chance to develop their political skills over a longer period in office.

As little as 44.6% of the women had never attended government organised trainings, while 75.3% have never attended trainings organised by NGOs. Hence, only between 10% and 20% of the elected representatives had solid knowledge of their own responsibilities, development programmes, officials responsible, funding issues and redress mechanisms. Further, 37% of women presidents reported direct obstructions while undertaking their panchayat responsibilities, driven primarily from dominant caste men within or outside the panchayat. Note that the above percentage excludes the significant number of proxy presidents whose role was entirely appropriated by others. The obstructions referred to by the women included: being silenced or ignored; caste and sexually-based abuse; having bribes demanded of her; no confidence motions; denial of information on panchayat activities; harassment, threats and assaults on the women or their family members; etc. Village panchayat President Leela in Madurai district in Tamil Nadu was pushed to contest the 2006 elections as a proxy for the dominant castes.

After the elections, they demanded that she submit title deeds to her house and land to them, to ensure that she would remain under their control during her term in office. Further, her panchayat powers were auctioned off to the highest dominant caste bidder. While eventually government officials intervened to arrest those participating in the auction, no further action ensued and Leela continues to be a proxy President for the dominant castes.

DISCRIMINATORY PRACTICES

- "As we are Dalits and women, we are forced to bear the brunt of double discrimination unlike our male counterparts... Other members of the panchayat do not give respect to us because we are born Dalit and female; they will even go to the extent of working against us. The dominant caste men do not let a Dalit woman function because of their wrong view that women are good for nothing, that they are simply proxies, that they cannot be permitted to involve in public life and if they do, then they are immoral women. They subject us to such discrimination precisely because they cannot bear the sight of a Dalit woman occupying a position of governance over them... In general we can say that Dalit women are forced to encounter more problems and more opposition than Dalit men, dominant caste men and women. That is to say, for a dominant caste woman, it is only her husband or a male member of her caste who can be a source of irritation, pressure and obstacles. But for a Dalit woman, such opposition comes from Dalit men, dominant caste men and women. She has to encounter three sources of obstructions. What is the reason? It is simply their anti-Dalit woman mindset; that is, these three sets of people are of the view that a Dalit woman is someone who need not be given any importance on any matter and hence can easily be dispensed with, who is incapable of asserting herself, who is ever submissive and patient, whatever is done or happens to her." — Dalit women elected representatives in Thirunelveli district, Tamil Nadu

The fundamental right to equality and non-discrimination enshrined in *Article 15* of the *Indian Constitution* notwithstanding, 89.8% of Dalit women elected representatives felt they were treated differently from other elected representatives in their panchayats. These 149 women attributed this primarily to their status as women (90.6%) and Dalits (84.6%). Additional identities with negative connotations, such as widows or separated women, exacerbated discriminatory practices. A TDO's statement in Gujarat substantiates this data: *"Dalit women elected representatives confront problems of traditional gender and caste practices. They have to face all these challenges at the time of election and even after election as well. The caste system is an obstacle which exists at all the panchayat levels in many different forms."* Even the Assistant Development Commissioner in Gujarat openly stated that Dalit women faced a number of problems because *"no elected representative supports Dalit women directly."* ! This was confirmed by a dominant caste village panchayat Vice President from Kheda district in Gujarat, in whose opinion *"it is impossible for Dalit women to become capable elected representatives. If I make her capable, then she will go against me, so better not to make her capable."* Contrast all this with the statement of the Assistant Director of Panchayats in Tamil Nadu that *"Dalit women do not face any problems at all."*

Aside from the caste or sexually-based abuse which over one-third of the women faced in carrying out their panchayat responsibilities, complex segregation methods surrounding seating arrangements as well as discriminatory practices related to water, tea and food were prevalent in the panchayat offices. These to a large part mirrored socio-cultural practices of untouchability prevailing outside the offices. Thus 38% of women stated that they were not allowed to sit on chairs alongside other elected representatives in the office.

The extent of enforced segregation in seating is evident from the case of village panchayat member Rajniben from Ahmedabad district; in her panchayat there were two chairs for the President and Vice President, two mattresses for other panchayat members and a sack on the floor reserved for her. Over two-thirds of women (67.5%) still stood up when dominant castes entered into the panchayat office in deference to the latter's 'higher' caste status. Discriminatory practices related to water, tea and food in the panchayats were also manifested in a number of ways: 64.5% of Dalit women reported that they were not able to drink water from the same container used by other elected representatives; 53.6% mentioned that they could not drink tea from the same cups used by other representatives; and 38.0% said that they could not eat food/snacks with the same plates/utensils used by the others while others indicated that food/snacks were not served in their panchayat offices.

DEVELOPMENT AND SOCIAL IMPACT

- "Women's participation, Dalit women's in particular, in the panchayats is necessary so that society can develop. Only women will think about women's issues. Only Dalit women can respond to and take a stand on Dalit issues and particularly on Dalit women's issues. In as much as Dalit women's participation is required, they also need to be given support and guidance. Then only can they become capable representatives... Nothing is attainable without exercising authority, and my desire is to increase the confidence of Dalits to fight and gain authority and power in society for their development."—Ramilaben, taluka panchayat President, Vadodara district, Gujarat
- "Dalit women's political participation is necessary for the Dalit community and its development, because if a Dalit woman comes then she will work for the Dalit community and Dalit women. Other castes will never work for the Dalit community. Moreover, they will eat up the money which comes under Dalit grants."—Jasodaben, village panchayat President, Surendranagar district, Gujarat

Few Dalit women elected representatives were able to exert any substantial influence in the panchayats to ensure development benefits for their communities, though many did put forward Dalit interests. Only 18.5% of Dalit women presidents felt that they had a significant say in the distribution of development schemes. At one level, the positive development outcomes for Dalits and women that some Dalit women elected representatives achieved took the form of primarily small projects for basic amenities – roads, housing, drinking water, etc. – rather than projects that would challenge existing gender-caste inequalities such as land distribution or alternative employment opportunities for Dalits. According to a dominant caste union panchayat President from Coimbatore district, Tamil Nadu: *"To be able to function in a way that ensured distribution of resources/funds to all sections of the panchayat community, as President I saw to it that development projects were distributed to each section. However, to prevent disaffection from the dominant caste communities, prior allotment went to them, and then only to the Dalits. It also happened sometimes that one section of the dominant caste community returned for another allotment or wanted to enjoy the allotment meant for the Dalit community, thereby making the latter forego its due share..."*

IMPACT ON PROCESS OF RESOURCE ALLOCATION

The second level of outcomes relates more to changing institutional rules and resource allocations in favour of Dalits and women. On this front, there was little success. The women's ability to generate development outcomes remains significantly limited by government resistance in practice to the implementation of the Panchayati Raj system, including the full devolution of functions, powers and resources. Within this context, there was little evidence to suggest that the Dalit women panchayat representatives were able to significantly increase attention and resources to address the critical livelihood needs of Dalits or women. This was made apparent by their low participation in decision-making on the use of panchayat revenue, development and welfare funds, as well as in dominant caste male monopolisation of panchayat resources and benefits.

ACCOUNTABILITY IN GRAM SABHAS AND FINANCIAL REPORTING

Lines of accountability to one's panchayat constituency through the *gram sabhas* (local village assemblies) were disrupted most clearly in the case of proxies, where Dalit women elected representatives played no major role in convening these meetings and directing discussions on panchayat development works for the people. At the other end of the spectrum, a small number of active elected representatives stated that they were able to convene and preside over *gram sabhas*. In terms of financial accountability for funds received and disbursed for panchayat schemes, a large 59.6% of women (mostly proxies) could not review how funds were spent, either by monitoring accounts or the implementation of development works. The remaining roughly onethird of women elected representatives personally monitored development works, or checked the accounts to ensure that receipts reflected the funds paid out for actual work done, or took concrete action when they saw people misusing panchayat funds.

OBSTRUCTIONS TO DALIT DEVELOPMENT

Many Dalit women presidents/members indicated the following factors behind low development outcomes for Dalits: others' influence over their decisions regarding development schemes to the detriment of the Dalit community (54.8%); the panchayat did not prioritise Dalit development needs (21.1%); their lack of knowledge of development issues and panchayat schemes (24.7%); active obstructions by others affecting development outcomes (29.5%). Obstructions included blocking approval of development projects; delaying the release of or misappropriating development funds; obstructing or not allowing approved development projects to be implemented; offering or demanding bribes, commissions or panchayat contracts; damaging or destroying panchayat property the women had seen built; caste and sexually-based verbal attacks on the women's personal character and performance, etc. Consequently, dominant caste economic control was maintained through the panchayats by channelling development benefits towards their communities as well as securing development contracts. As Dalit woman elected representatives shared in a group interview in Kheda district in Gujarat, *"At least we [Dalit women] get our seat due to reservation. But still we don't have any say in the panchayat because the dominant caste panchayat members, including the Talati, take away most of the ongoing work in the village as well as schemes available at the taluka level."*

Dalit women elected representatives who accomplished development gains for their communities, therefore, did so either individually amidst frequent opposition, or in several cases with the help of others. This included support from Dalit panchayat members, use of political party connections and support base in the panchayat, or negotiation with other caste panchayat members.

SOCIAL IMPACT ON STRUCTURAL INTERESTS

Research data showed little evidence of the third level of change envisaged by Dalit women's active political participation, that is, the restructuring of gender and caste social relations towards social equality and justice. What changes occurred were mostly at the personal and family levels. Examples of personal changes were: greater self-confidence (55%); greater social contacts (37.5%); greater freedom of movement (31.5%); increased leadership skills (31%); and heightened awareness of socio-political problems in society (29.5%). The most common changes at the family level for 66 women (39.8%) were that families shared responsibilities in looking after the children while the elected women were fulfilling their official duties, consulted these women more on important family matters, and allowed them greater decision-making power in family affairs. Overall, greater freedom of speech in both the family as well as public spaces emerged as one of the most significant influences of active Dalit women's political participation. Further benefits included greater public participation and freedom of movement.

Changes to Dalit women's 'low' social status, however, were rare, reflecting entrenched caste and gender interests linked to dominant caste exercise of socio-political power and control over resources. Hence, while over half the Dalit women elected representatives (58.4%) felt they were more respected as a result of their position in the panchayat, few could exercise actual sociopolitical power and effect longer-term changes in social status. Village panchayat President Jasodaben from Surendranagar district in Gujarat was forthright in stating: *"because I was President and useful to them, both Dalits and non-Dalits respected me, but they never supported me as an individual. That was also because of reservations; otherwise who really respects Dalits?"* According to 34.3% of Dalit women elected representatives, their political participation had generated some change among women, mainly that some women were able to speak up in their households and *gram sabhas* more freely. Other Dalit women also increasingly recognised their own capacities for leadership and expressed greater willingness to contest panchayat elections. By comparison, only 28.9% of Dalit women elected representatives indicated change in attitudes towards them from the Dalit community, mainly in terms of Dalits now approaching these women to represent their developmental problems to government officials; Dalits now settling disputes among themselves under the women's leadership; and other Dalits now feeling that they too had the capacity to play leadership roles in village administration. Some also noted greater confidence exhibited by Dalits (32.5%) as well as increased unity among them (22%).

The majority of the women witnessed little transformation of caste prejudices or reduced discriminatory practices either towards themselves or their community. Only 21.1% of Dalit women elected representatives mentioned some change, mainly in terms of greater ability to interact with dominant castes as a result of their public office, greater freedom to walk along dominant caste streets in the villages, and being able to wear shoes while on official panchayat duties. To be noted, though, is that changes in support patterns, respect and attitudes of dominant castes towards Dalit women panchayat representatives that did occur did not include recognition of Dalit women's power and authority, especially as panchayat heads. This was most clearly highlighted through dominant caste support that was withdrawn following the women's support for Dalit development needs or assertions of independence. In the case of Kamachi, twice-elected village panchayat President from Coimbatore district in Tamil Nadu, she faced constant opposition from dominant castes during her tenure as President. Then, after her defeat in the 2006 election, her chair was removed from the office and the dominant castes performed a *pooja* (religious ritual) to 'purify' the office. Only after this did the next dominant caste President come and sit on the president's chair in the office.

By contrast, negative consequences included the reinforcement of gender and caste hierarchies and dominance, thereby helping to preserve the inequitable political status quo and deter Dalit women from active political participation in future. These included fear and insecurity of life caused by harassment, threats and violence, and decreased self-confidence among the Dalit women. In the case of Reshmaben, in addition to an attack on her and other Dalits after she won the election to the village panchayat member's seat in Ahmedabad district in Gujarat, her subcaste was socially boycotted by the main dominant castes. The instigation of Dalit sub-caste divisions by dominant castes in order to control the exercise of Dalits' political power also raises serious concern, as mentioned by 22.5% of the women. This reality contrasts sharply with the recent statement of Prime Minister Manmohan Singh on the impact of reservations for women in local governance, which he asserted *"constitutes a historic measure for gender equality. It has brought about a significant shift in public policy and in social attitudes towards women."*

RESPONSIVENESS OF THE STATE

- "I did not take other problems concerning the Vice President's cheating behaviour to the police. I was well aware it would mean more expense and no action would be taken against the dominant caste man. I suffered it all within ... Ever since I decided to enter the panchayat, I am fighting against injustice and atrocities ... Be it a Dalit or non-Dalit woman, their participation in the panchayat administration is never appreciated in this patriarchal country. Then what is the value of social justice here?"—Pushpa, village panchayat President, Thirunelveli district, Tamil Nadu, after facing police inaction following her numerous complaints of obstructions during the election process

Overall, the Indian law enforcement machinery and district administration repeatedly failed in their national and international obligations to both prevent and respond to obstructions that Dalit women experienced while asserting their right to political participation. This denied the women their right to an effective remedy. These officials repeatedly failed to ensure the implementation of laws and to ensure access to justice for legal violations in relation to Dalit women's political participation. This demonstrated disturbing signs of impunity – impunity exercised in the name of caste power, leaving dominant caste and male perpetrators free from accountability. Dominant caste power therefore remained entrenched both within the state governance and law enforcement systems as well as the local social system.

WOMEN WHO DID NOT SEEK REDRESS FOR OBSTRUCTIONS

Given their socio-political situation, the majority of Dalit women kept silent in 71.3% of instances of obstructions: most felt unable to oppose caste-class-gender norms and discrimination (32.5%), or feared dominant caste reaction (16.3%), or felt it futile to raise protest (14.7%), or ignored or tried to resolve the problem with the support of their families (11.8%). For example, Sareekaben, a village panchayat President in Surendranagar district in Gujarat, while taking strong action in response to violations at various times, also let many go by without action. This was because: *"they [dominant castes] have money and contacts with the police station, bank, taluka and district panchayat, right up to the State Assembly. In such a situation, any person – no matter how courageous or determined – becomes tired of fighting and loses hope. ....the [dominant castes'] influence is everywhere."*

WOMEN WHO DID SEEK REDRESS FOR OBSTRUCTIONS

Dalit women who did seek redress found more often than not that justice was not accessible for them. The women rarely approached non-state actors, especially from their community, with their complaints (only for 1.3% of obstructions). This may be explained by various reasons, including the women's understanding that it was the government officials and other formal actors that were actually responsible for taking action to remedy violations faced by them, or the pressure on Dalit village elders to conform to dominant caste interests out of fear, or simply because of the women's lack of faith in the elders' responsiveness. Overall, therefore, just over two-thirds of non-state actors – mainly Dalit elders, traditional panchayat elders, political parties, NGOs, and family members – approached by the women regarding obstructions did not support Dalit women to achieve effective redress.

The most common recourse for those women who did take action regarding 28.7% of obstructions, was to approach mainly government officials linked to the panchayats or the police. Just over half of responses from state actors – the police, administrative and judicial courts, government officials and government related bodies – also suggest a breach in duties. A total of 24.7% of responses from state actors involved further obstructions to the women's efforts, such as chasing the women away, taking no action, demanding a bribe, and refusing to provide any assistance. Pressure or advice not to file any complaint, or pressure to enter into a compromise comprised another 17.9% of state actor responses. Finally, 13.7% of complaints led to registration, but state actors refused to investigate the matter or file a charge sheet, and 1.4% of FIR cases went no further than investigation. This may be due to both compromises outside of police engagement or police refusal to take the matter further. Far from the norm were the experiences of state officials being responsive to Dalit women – 5.5% of state actors advised the women on how to approach the problem; 16.4% investigated and resolved their problems; and 11.0% filed the women's complaints, investigated the matter and helped the women to reach a compromise or solution. For instance, the District Collector helped Janaki, a village panchayat President in Cuddalore district in Tamil Nadu, by pacifying the Vice President who opposed her, and ensuring the construction of the road she had planned.

Finally, a small number of cases went to the stage of judicial proceedings, with 8.9% of state responses leading to court proceedings. Breaking down these cases, 4.8% are still pending (seven through police action and one through a woman filing a petition directly with the court), 3.4% had verdicts in favour of the Dalit woman (four cases initiated directly with the court and one filed through police action) and finally, in one case Shiviben, village panchayat President in Kheda district in Gujarat, lost against a no confidence motion brought against her when a witness turned hostile during the judicial proceedings.

INTERACTIONS WITH GOVERNMENT OFFICIALS

Government officials were often complicit in reinforcing dominant caste male power by adopting the role of neutral facilitator regarding Dalit women's political participation: that is, they failed to intervene when witnessing proxy representation and discrimination, or pleaded lack of power to take action. A BDO in Tamil Nadu stated, *"During my tenure [as BDO], many Dalit women members and presidents sought my help. When they come to speak about their problems, their husbands accompany them and they only speak."* In fact, some government officials suggested that their sole jurisdiction over issues Dalit women elected representatives brought to them concerned only development schemes and funds. As an Assistant Director for Panchayats in Tamil Nadu emphasised, *"There could have been caste discrimination or violence [in the panchayat]. But the panchayat representatives give more importance to administrative problems and not to any discriminatory practices. We cannot go and force them to talk about such problems... And it is not our duty or responsibility at all to respond to caste problems. We monitor only Dalit women's administration."* The aforementioned BDO similarly pointed out that officials had no duty to take action on complaints of caste or gender based discrimination. This was confirmed by a TDO from Gujarat, who while noting the problems Dalit women elected representatives faced due to caste and gender discrimination, insisted that government officials cannot intervene in these practices as these are *'very sensitive and emotional issues for the community'*.

Thus, while constitutional provisions render illegal discrimination on grounds of caste or gender, and reservations in the panchayats aim to correct structural discrimination against Dalits and women, government officials expect those affected by discrimination to deal with such problems. The only conclusion to be drawn is negligence by these officials in the execution of their legally mandated supervisory roles over the panchayats. For the 117 Dalit women elected representatives who visited government and other officials in connection with their panchayat responsibilities, positive indications are that 39.3% of women had their invitations accepted by officials to visit their panchayats; 36.8% mentioned how officials implemented schemes requested by them or otherwise supported them in implementing schemes; and 34.2% stated that officials took prompt action on the women's requests or complaints. On the other hand, officials also harassed Dalit women elected representatives by making them frequent visit government offices to deal with the same matter, or delayed in implementing schemes despite repeated requests from the women, as mentioned by 23.1% of women.

Linked to this, 17.9% of women had to wait for a long time to meet these officials to discuss official panchayat matters. A further 2.6% of women also mentioned how government officials expected bribes in order to render any service to the women. Further, as noted by Jasodaben from Surendranagar district in Gujarat,: *"Whenever I approached government officials, they never responded immediately and they didn't do work fast. Only if they [dominant castes] approach do government officials respond quickly."* Another 6.0% of women experienced government officials taking little or no action on their requests. Finally, in the case of four women, they experienced overt forms of discrimination from government officials based on their caste and gender. Government officials also generally failed to adequately monitor the reserved panchayats, displaying a lack of accountability including turning a blind eye to corrupt practices such as the diversion of funds meant for Dalit development.

The Indian state, therefore, appeared to limit its obligation to providing free access to panchayats, vis-à-vis specially protected groups such as Dalit women, via the reservation of panchayat seats. This stops far short of ensuring that the women enjoy the benefits of this policy in its implementation – that they enjoy free and independent political participation. In a complex society structured along highly unequal caste-class-gender lines, to place the entire burden of safety and security in accessing political participation on the shoulders of Dalit women who are traditionally excluded from enjoying this right, and to expect them to act with freedom and independence in the electoral process, suggests abdication of state duty.

KEY RECOMMENDATIONS

- "Our challenge today is to institutionalise this system of local self-governance, but also to make it the world's most representative and participatory democracy."
- Prime Minister Manmohan Singh, inaugural speech, Conference of Chief Ministers, New Delhi, 29.06.04

The institutionalisation of the Panchayati Raj system – with all its aims and ambitions – must be further revisited on the basis of the core issues elaborated in this research. There are major weaknesses in the current interpretation and implementation of reservations in Panchayati Raj, as well as in broader strategies to transform a society pervaded by caste-class-gender discrimination. At present, these dramatically limit the ability of the panchayats to fulfil their core objectives of equitable development and social justice. Specifically, they impact negatively on the space for Dalit women to create development and social outcomes in line with these objectives. Essentially, required reforms must recognise that political participation cannot be viewed in isolation: efforts to realise other enabling rights – especially the rights to education and information, to free employment, alongside the right to equality within the family and in society – must be integrated with efforts to ensure Dalit women's enjoyment of their right to political participation. Sustained systemic change requires multiple state and non-state actors at the state and national levels working together to influence formal and non-formal local institutions of power and to strengthen Dalit women's sense of confidence, skills, power and support networks. Creative ways must be explored, with Dalit women as well as Dalit men and non-Dalits, to capitalise on the success stories of Dalit women's political leadership, and cultivate their growth. Inspiring examples of Dalit women elected representatives speak of the great potential for further political and social reform through active participation in panchayat governance. Ultimately efforts must lead to a supportive environment for these women's political participation in order to transform access to and control over resources and benefits in society, as well as promote a human rights culture that itself demands accountable governance and equality for all.

TO THE GOVERNMENT OF INDIA, GOVERNMENTS OF GUJARAT AND TAMIL NADU: PANCHAYAT STRUCTURE AND SPECIAL SUPPORT MECHANISMS

- Effectively enforce the reservation policy by ensuring the rights of Dalits to freely and safely vote and stand for election and to exercise their full mandate if elected to their reserved seats. This includes adequate police and government official monitoring and protection of Dalit candidates as well as elected representatives.
- Devolve greater functions, funds and functionaries to the panchayats so that they have effective political authority and discharge their duties and functions as local institutions of self-government within the meaning contemplated by the *Indian Constitution*. This includes lessening bureaucratic control over panchayat programmes and making bureaucrats more accountable to the panchayats, especially as regards abiding by panchayat decisions.
- Institute quotas in the lower level bureaucracy for SC women and men, ST women and men, and women in general as per panchayat quotas, to ensure that government officials, especially BDOs/TDOs, are representative of these sections of the population. Moreover, the reserved panchayats should come under the direction of these government officials. Similar quotas should be established in the local and district police forces.
- Establish a specific office in each district to act as a support mechanism for Dalit, Adivasi and women panchayat presidents, including providing advice, training and information as well as monitoring their implementation of duties and interventions by others such as panchayat members and government officials. These offices should mediate and resolve problems encountered by the above panchayat representatives and ensure the efficient and effective running of the panchayats. Dalit and Adivasi women and men, as well as other women, should be all represented as much as possible in each office.

Planning and Budgets:

- Facilitate a mandatory process of village, taluka/union and district panchayats preparing a scheduled caste development plan with a clear gender component, which should become a charter to work towards the economic development of Dalit women and men in the panchayats.
- *In Gujarat*: Allocate separate funds to the Social Justice Committees, which can independently decide on utilisation of these funds. These funds could be used to organise gender awareness camps and camps on the *SC/ST (PA) Act*.

Gram Sabhas:

- Give the *gram sabhas* greater powers to monitor the functioning of the panchayats and decide on budgets and the allocation of funds and other resources, as well as the identification of beneficiaries for panchayat schemes. Village development plans should be formulated by the *gram sabhas*, which would then feed into development plans at the taluka/union and district levels. Information on gram sabha meeting agendas must be publicly shared in advance.
- Establish separate quorums for participation by SC women, SC men, ST women, ST men and women in general in *gram sabhas* and *sub-gram sabhas* (*i.e. ward sabhas*).

Panchayat Administration:

- Make it mandatory for all panchayat cheques to be signed in the presence of members, for funds to be sanctioned with the signature of the panchayat president alone, and for all accounts to be compulsorily shared with members in all meetings.
- Mandate that in all government contracts related to common properties, these contracts benefit Dalits in proportion to their population.
- Announce incentives (for example, monetary resources, land, government employment or scholarships for children's education) before the period for filing nominations to panchayat seats to encourage Dalit women to file nominations for general panchayat seats, and award these to Dalit women who win these seats.

Economic Development:

- In order to improve the economic conditions of Dalits in rural areas, necessary to facilitate their political participation, develop a national perspective plan with explicit short- and long-term goals for overall development of Dalit women within fixed time-bound targets and allocate separate funding for this plan (as per recommendation of National Human Rights Commission).
- Enforce land reforms and land distribution to the landless on a priority basis and initiate a drive to remove encroachments on government lands and other common lands.

- *To the State Election Commissions:* Establish a small fund to provide limited basic financial support for election costs for Dalits, Adivasis and women in general falling within stipulated low household income brackets.
- Establish a minimum salary system for all panchayat president posts and members' posts at the higher tiers, with increased travel allowance, dearness allowance and sitting fees considering their powers and duties, to encourage less corruption and more transparency in the panchayat administration (as per recommendations of Tamil Nadu Women Panchayat President's Federation).

Monitoring and Accountability Mechanisms:

- Establish an autonomous statutory Directorate for all reserved panchayats at the state level to be headed by a Dalit/Adivasi woman IAS officer, and Assistant Directorates at the district level to function under the Directorate and to be headed by a Dalit/Adivasi woman officer below the rank of IAS. These two institutions should fall under the jurisdiction of the Legislative Assembly through the Governor, to perform such responsibilities as monitoring and reviewing the pre- and post-election performance of the reserved panchayats, and prepare annual reports to the Legislative Assembly. *Gram sabhas* as well as local non-governmental organisations focusing on Panchayati Raj should be made part of the monitoring mechanisms appointed by the Directorate in consultation with the Assistant Directorates, and the monitoring reports should be made publicly available to villagers in the *gram sabhas*.
- Make it mandatory for government officials in charge of Panchayati Raj to pay monthly visits to the panchayats and monitor development works in progress as well as, explicitly, issues of discrimination and other obstacles prevailing in panchayats. They should also check the panchayat accounts during their monthly visits.
- The District Collector should convene monthly meetings with all village panchayat presidents, and a separate meeting with presidents in the different categories of reserved posts – Dalit women, Dalit men, Adivasi men, Adivasi women and general women – on a monthly or bi-monthly basis, in order to understand the different needs and obstacles faced by these different groups, and to resolve their specific difficulties and problems. BDOs/TDOs attached to the respective reserved panchayats should also attend these meetings.
- Monitor regularly government training programmes to ensure women are attending and not sending their husbands in their stead, with sanctions applicable to government officials who allow this practice.

- Evolve strict government rules and programmes to eradicate the presence of proxy candidates, by ensuring that: at all panchayat tiers only elected representatives attend panchayat meetings and meetings with government officials; panchayat funds are sanctioned with the signature of the president alone; mechanisms for closer monitoring of panchayats with Dalit, women and Adivasi presidents; educational programmes for all Dalit, Adivasi and women presidents and members with little or no literacy skills; comprehensive mandatory training at the commencement of the term for Dalit women, Adivasi women and other women on panchayat governance; establishing a rule that no two family members should contest elections for posts in the same panchayat.
- Implement strict legal sanctions against government and police officials who neglect to respond to complaints by persons who have filed nominations for panchayat posts or by elected panchayat representatives in reserved panchayats.
- Every five years, evaluate the performance of the panchayat institutions, with specific evaluation of all reserved panchayat posts, both presidents and members, and provide gender-and-sex data on the numbers and functioning of elected representatives, numbers of no confidence motions initiated and ending with dismissal, etc. (as per recommendation of Rajiv Gandhi Chair for Panchayat Studies).

Policy and Legal Amendments:

- *In Gujarat*: Immediately withdraw the government Samras Gram Yojna policy (consensus panchayat scheme) and ensure that all panchayat posts are established through regular, democratic elections.
- *In Gujarat:* Promulgate a Government Order with a new rule to the *Gujarat Panchayats Act 1993,* to stipulate that reserved panchayats rotate after every two terms – *i.e.* ten years.
- Amend both the *Gujarat* and *Tamil Nadu Panchayat Acts* to ensure that where it is a SC women or ST or general women reserved panchayat, the Vice President and Talati/Clerk are from the same reserved category.
- Amend both the *Gujarat* and *Tamil Nadu Panchayat Acts* to impose an additional burden of proof on panchayats which dismiss presidents from office using no confidence motions. In addition, the use of no confidence motions against Dalit, Adivasi and women presidents should be strictly monitored by government officials, and timely investigations carried out in all cases to ensure that these presidents are given an equal opportunity to serve out their entire term. In this regard, in Tamil Nadu *sec. 205 Tamil Nadu Panchayats Act* should be repealed so as to remove the discretionary powers of the District Collectors to remove panchayat presidents.

- Amend the *SC/ST (Prevention of Atrocities) Act 1989* to include offences related to interference with Dalits' political participation: that is, any person not being a member of a scheduled caste or scheduled tribe forcing, intimidating or bribing a member of a scheduled caste or scheduled tribe to function as a *benami* for them; and any person not being a member of a scheduled caste or scheduled tribe instigating false or malicious no confidence motions or complaints against panchayat presidents with the intention to remove them from office. The latter offence could be created through a suitable amendment to *sec. 3(1)(viii) SC/ST (PA) Act* – instituting false, malicious or vexatious suit or criminal or other legal proceedings against a member of a scheduled caste or scheduled tribe – to include no confidence motions in the panchayats.
- Mandate the National and State Scheduled Caste, Scheduled Tribe and Women's Commissions with sufficient powers, funds and staff to specifically enquire into acts of political obstruction or violence committed against Dalit women, Dalit men, Adivasi women, Adivasi men and other women elected representatives.
- Provide free legal aid for Dalit women panchayat representatives who seek access to judicial redress for obstructions in the performance of their official duties, and review the reasons why Dalit women are unable to access legal aid in many cases.

Capacitation and Support Measures:

- Conduct open information sessions in all panchayat union/taluka headquarters immediately after the announcement of panchayat elections on election procedures, the importance of reservations and Dalit, Adivasi and women's political participation.
- In addition to regular panchayat trainings for all panchayat representatives, devise and conduct special trainings for Dalits, Adivasis and women elected representatives, as closely as possible to the start of their term of office, in order to specifically capacitate them for their panchayat duties. All trainings should include a gender and caste perspective, as well as legal sanctions which apply to those who block Dalit women's political participation.
- Integrate gender and caste awareness training into all trainings for panchayat representatives, including methods of recourse in cases of discrimination and other rights violations towards Dalits, Adivasis and women. These trainings should further specifically focus on promoting a culture of inclusive development, accountability and transparency in the panchayat administration.
- Form associations/networks, or strengthen existing associations/ networks of women panchayat representatives at the village, taluka/ union and district levels with specific focus on the different

experiences of Dalit and Adivasi women representatives. These should operate as both support networks to women elected representatives as well as an effective lobbying block to, among other things, restructure the allocation of resources for Dalit, Adivasi and women's development.

- Capacitate all officials concerned with Panchayati Raj, including election officers, rural extension officers and particularly lower government officials dealing with the panchayats, to understand and respond to issues of caste and gender discrimination, encourage greater information sharing and less bureaucratic control over panchayat development schemes, so that these officials are able to better monitor and support Dalit women elected representatives in the panchayats to ensure others do not coerce the women into relinquishing their powers.
- Conduct training programmes to increase the awareness and capacity of local police and the local and district courts to understand and respond to issues of caste and gender discrimination and violence, including in the panchayats. This should include awareness on national and international human rights laws, in particular legislation concerning Dalits, and implications for these officials' duties.
- Ensure the universalisation of primary education among Dalit women, and promote their further education. Current strategies for increasing the female literacy rate, especially among Dalit girls and women, must be strengthened.
- Conduct a widespread social education campaign through the media and local fora on gender and caste equality and non-discrimination in order to support broad change in social attitudes towards Dalits, Adivasis and women in particular. One specific component of this campaign should focus on promoting inclusive democracy through the free and independent participation of Dalits, Adivasis and women in the panchayats.

TO CIVIL SOCIETY GROUPS

- Build up a widespread campaign and lobby the respective Gujarat and Tamil Nadu governments as well as the national government in order to strengthen political will to implement the political reforms. This includes applying pressure through monitoring and further exposing the failure of government monitoring mechanisms for panchayat governance.
- Conduct regular trainings on public speaking, leadership and managerial skills, problem solving and how to interact with government officials separately for elected panchayat representatives as well as those aspiring to become elected representatives.
- Address the female burden of dual responsibility between

panchayats and households through greater education and economic programmes targeting Dalit women, as well as lobbying the government to implement or directly providing support mechanisms such as child care facilities.

- Initiate gender sensitisation programmes specifically aimed at Dalit men, to encourage them to extend greater freedom to women in their families and to support Dalit women elected representatives both within and outside the panchayats. Gender and caste sensitisation programmes should also be conduced separately for all male elected representatives as well as government officials dealing with Panchayati Raj.
- Initiate a political awareness campaign on the right to political participation by Dalit women and men, in order to highlight the importance of political unity across Dalit subcastes and their participation for community development. As part of this campaign, facilitate and support discussions among Dalit elders, men, panchayat members, husbands and male family members about the importance of Dalit women's free and independent political participation.
- Initiate district-level *sanghams* for women elected representatives, with a sub-group specifically meant for Dalit women, as a supportive network for all women and specifically Dalit women elected representatives. These *sanghams* should be strengthened through regular information inputs and capacitation trainings, and should then form a state-level federation. Support must be extended to the collective actions initiated by these groups, including their monitoring and taking action against government and police officials who fail to protect these women's right to political participation.
- Increasingly liaise with the media to expose discrimination faced by women elected panchayat representatives as well as highlight successful efforts and strategies employed by elected representatives.
- Independently monitor the situation of local reserved panchayats in order to ensure discriminatory and obstructive practices against Dalit, Adivasi and other women elected representatives do not take place, and if they do, are exposed and appropriate legal action taken against the perpetrators.
- Monitor the next panchayat elections, especially in reserved panchayats, in order to expose violations of the rights of Dalit and Adivasi women to access the panchayats and bring cases to the attention of the State Election Commissions.
- *Political parties:* Establish quotas on the numbers of SC women and men, ST women and men, and women in general, in their party structures, especially at higher levels of leadership.

- *Political parties:* Initiate specific trainings for all party cadre on gender and caste social norms and practices, legal rights and political participation for development, in order to foster a culture of accountability and transparency, as well as drive for local participation in development.

TO THE INTERNATIONAL COMMUNITY

- *To international human rights networks and academic institutes:* Take up the issue of Dalit women in local governance as a central concern, raising awareness of the issue in their activities with government officials, United Nations bodies, civil society actors and the general public.
- *To UN states governments:* Take up the issue of Dalit women's effective participation in governance as a focus policy area, including through support for the implementation of monitoring and accountability recommendations made in this research and support for relevant Dalit, Adivasi and women panchayat associations.
- *To the Special Rapporteur on Violence against Women:* Prepare a report on the effectiveness of and problems faced by Dalit women in local governance and foster dialogue and debate on this issue in the United Nations.
- *To the Special Rapporteur on Contemporary Forms of Racism, Special Rapporteur on Discrimination on the Basis of Work and Descent, and Independent Expert on Minorities*: Work with local Indian organisations to take up cases of violence and discrimination against Dalit women including in local governance through, among other ways, their reporting to respective United Nations bodies and in dialogue with the Government of India.

12

The Scheduled Castes and Scheduled Tribes Act, 1989

The Scheduled Castes (SCs), also known as the Dalit, and the Scheduled Tribes (STs) are two groupings of historically disadvantaged people that are given express recognition in the Constitution of India. During the period of British rule in the Indian sub-continent they were known as the Depressed Classes. The Scheduled Castes and Scheduled Tribes make up around 15% and 7.5% respectively of the population of India, or around 24% altogether. The proportion of Scheduled Castes and Scheduled Tribes in the country's population has steadily risen since independence in 1947. The *Constitution (Scheduled Castes) Order, 1950* lists 1,108 castes across 25 states in its First Schedule, while the *Constitution (Scheduled Tribes) Order, 1950* lists 744 tribes across 22 states in its First Schedule.

Since Independence, the Scheduled Castes have benefited by the "Reservation" policy. This policy was made an integral part of the Constitution by the efforts of Dr. Bhimrao Ambedkar, regarded as the father of the Indian constitution, who participated in Round Table Conferences and fought for the rights of the Depressed Classes. The Constitution lays down general principles for the policy of affirmative action for the SCs and STs.

HISTORY

From the 1850s these communities were loosely referred to as the "Depressed Classes". The early part of the 20th century saw a flurry of activity in the British Raj to assess the feasibility of responsible self-government for India. The Morley-Minto Reforms Report, Montagu–Chelmsford Reforms Report, and the Simon Commission were some of the initiatives that happened in this context. One of the hotly contested issues in the proposed reforms was the topic of reservation of seats for the "Depressed" Classes in provincial and central legislatures.

In 1935 the British passed the Government of India Act 1935, designed to give Indian provinces greater self-rule and set up a national federal structure. Reservation of seats for the Depressed Classes was incorporated into the act, which came into force in 1937. The Act brought the term "Scheduled Castes" into use, and defined the group as including "such castes, races or tribes or parts of groups within castes, races or tribes, which appear to His Majesty in Council to correspond to the classes of persons formerly known as the 'Depressed Classes', as His Majesty in Council may prefer". This discretionary definition was clarified in *The Government of India (Scheduled Castes) Order, 1936* which contained a list, or Schedule, of castes throughout the British administered provinces. After independence, the Constituent Assembly continued the prevailing definition of Scheduled Castes and Tribes, and gave the President of India and Governors of states responsibility to compile a full listing of castes and tribes, and also the power to edit it later as required. The actual complete listing of castes and tribes was made via two orders *The Constitution (Scheduled Castes) Order, 1950,* and *The Constitution (Scheduled Tribes) Order, 1950* respectively.

CONSTITUTIONAL FRAMEWORK FOR SAFEGUARDING OF INTERESTS

The Constitution provides a framework with a three pronged strategy to improve the situation of SCs and STs:

1. *Protective Arrangements*: Such measures as are required to enforce equality, to provide punitive measures for transgressions, to eliminate established practices that perpetuate inequities, etc. A number of laws were enacted to operationalize the provisions in the Constitution. Examples of such laws include The Untouchability Practices Act, 1955, Scheduled Caste and Scheduled Tribe (Prevention of Atrocities) Act, 1989, The Employment of Manual scavengers and Construction of Dry Latrines (Prohibition) Act, 1993, etc.
2. *Affirmative Action*: Provide positive preferential treatment in allotment of jobs and access to higher education, as a means to accelerate the integration of the SCs and STs with mainstream society. Affirmative action is also popularly referred to as Reservation.
3. *Development*: Provide for resources and benefits to bridge the wide gap in social and economic condition between the SCs/STs and other communities.

NATIONAL COMMISSIONS

To effectively implement the various safeguards built into the Constitution and other legislations, the Constitution, under Articles 338 and 338A, provides for two statutory commissions - the National Commission for Scheduled Castes, and National Commission for Scheduled Tribes.

History

In the original Constitution, Article 338 provided for a Special Officer, called the Commissioner for SCs and STs, to have the responsibility of monitoring the effective implementation of various safeguards for SCs/STs in the Constitution as well as other related legislations and to report to the President. To enable efficient discharge of duties, 17 regional offices of the Commissioner were set up all over the country.

In the meanwhile there was persistent representation for a replacement of the Commissioner with a multi-member committee. It was proposed that the 48th Amendment to the Constitution be made to alter Article 338 to enable said proposal. While the amendment was being debated, the Ministry of Welfare issued an administrative decision to establish the Commission for SCs/STs as a multi-member committee to discharge the same functions as that of the Commissioner of SCs/STs. The first commission came into being in August 1978. The functions of the commission were modified in September 1987 to advise Government on broad policy issues and levels of development of SCs/STs.

In 1990 that the Article 338 was amended to give birth to the statutory National Commission for SCs and STs via the *Constitution (Sixty fifth Amendment) Bill, 1990*. The first Commission under the 65th Amendment was constituted in March 1992 replacing the Commissioner for Scheduled Castes and Scheduled Tribes and the Commission set up under the Ministry of Welfare's Resolution of 1989.

In 2002, the Constitution was again amended to split the National Commission for Scheduled Castes and Scheduled Tribes into two separate commissions - the National Commission for Scheduled Castes and the National Commission for Scheduled Tribes.

DISTRIBUTION

According to the 61st Round Survey of the NSSO, almost nine-tenths of Buddhists in India belonged to scheduled castes of the Constitution while one-third of Christians belonged to scheduled tribes. Major part of scheduled castes were Hindus by religion but belonged to castes and tribes having low population. The Sachar Committee report of 2006 also confirmed that members of scheduled castes and tribes of India are not exclusively adherents of Hinduism.

Religion	Scheduled Caste	Scheduled Tribe
Buddhism	89.50%	7.40%
Christianity	9.00%	32.80%
Sikhism	17.0%	0.90%
Hinduism	22.20%	9.10%
Gond	–	15.90%
Jainism	–	2.60%
Islam	0.80%	0.50%

SCHEDULED CASTE SUB-PLAN

The strategy of Scheduled Castes Sub-Plan (SCSP) which was evolved in 1979 is one of the most important interventions through the planning process for social, economic and educational development of Scheduled Castes and for improvement in their working and living conditions. It is an umbrella strategy to ensure flow of targeted financial and physical benefits from all the general sectors of development for the benefit of Scheduled Castes. Under this strategy, population.

It entails targeted flow of funds and associated benefits from the annual plan of States/ Union Territories (UTs) at least in proportion to the SC population *i.e.* 16% in the total population of the country/ the particular state. Presently, 27 States/ UTs having sizeable SC populations are implementing Scheduled Castes Sub-Plan. Although the Scheduled Castes population, according to 2011 Census, was 16.66 crores constituting 16.23% of the total population of India, the allocations made through SCSP in recent years have been much lower than the population proportion. Table hereafter provides the details of total State Plan Outlay, flow to Scheduled Castes Sub-Plan (SCSP) as reported by the State/ UT Governments for the last few years especially since the present UPA government is in power at the,

2004–2005	108788.9	17656	2065.38	11.06	68.3	5591
2005–2006	136234.5	22111	16422.63	12.05	74.3	5688
2006–2007	152088	24684	21461.12	14.11	86.9	3223
2007-2008*	155013.2	25159	22939.99	14.80	91.2	2219

- Information in respect of 14 States/UTs only and as on 31-12- 2007

13

Human Rights of Minorities

INTERNATIONAL CONTEXT

TREATIES, CHARTERS AND COVENANTS

The world community today faces not only the question of how to ensure democratic majority rule but also the growing problem of guaranteeing respect for the rights of various under privileged minority groups. Although the existence of'Minorities' is an ancient phenomenon, it has taken its present form only during Nineteenth and Twentieth Centuries, particularly with the formation of'League of Nations' after the World Wars.

Thereafter, various international treaties, charters and covenants have come into existence as a response to the problems of different minorities (religious, linguistic, cultural and ethnic), establishing clearly that problems of the Minorities constitute one of the most burning issues on the international human rights agenda. Most of the countries, including India, are the signatories to most of the charters and covenants. In Europe, the question of ethnic minorities arose because of their importance in politics during the nineteenth century, and the rise of nationalism based upon the idea of a uniform lifestyle of the majority brought the life of the minorities into the mainstream. Such an idea was opposed by minority groups, particularly those living in the border areas in different countries.

The treaties signed between different European countries were intended to address the immediate problems of the countries in which they were made, but then they formed the basis for a positive understanding and response in future to the problems of minorities in general. Thereafter, the development of modern human rights philosophy has occurred in such a way that it passed over from the ideas of a simple majority rule and political rights for all to taking into consideration the interest of those who are distinct in some respects from the majority. Also, being in minority they find it difficult for themselves to make the bodies of power consider their special position and interest. After League of Nations, the United Nations vigorously pursued the task of dealing with the problems of minorities. The specific action taken by U.N. in this regard came first in the form of charter and covenants and then in the form of declaration and convention.

The most important amongst these are:

i. Universal Declaration of Human Rights 1948
ii. Convention on the Prevention and Punishment of the Crime of Genocide 1948
iii. International Convention on the Elimination of all forms of Racial Discrimination, 1965
iv. International Covenant on Economic, Social and Cultural Rights and International Covenant on Civil and Political Rights 1966.
v. Declaration on the Elimination of all forms of Intolerance and Discrimination based on Religion or Belief, 1991
vi. Declaration on the Rights of Persons belonging to National or Ethnic, Religion and Linguistic Minorities 1992

It is not possible here to deal with the contents of all those documents, except to quote Article 27 of the'International Covenant of Civil and Political Rights of 1966', which reads as follows:

- "In those States in which ethnic, religious or linguistic minorities exist, persons belonging to such minorities shall not be denied the right, in community with the other members of their group, to enjoy their own culture, to profess and practise their own religion, or use their own language".

Capotozti, Francesco, Special U.N. Rapporteur in his report on the implementation of Article 27 of the International Covenant on the civil and political rights formulated the definition of the minority just as to which"a minority is a group numerically inferior to the rest of the population, in a non-dominant position, consisting of nationals of the state, processing distinct ethnic, religious or linguistic characteristics and showing a sense of solidarity aimed at preserving these characteristics". The U.N. General Assembly adopted the'Declaration on the Rights of Persons belonging to National or Ethnic, Religious and Linguistic Minorities' on 18th December 1992 and reaffirmed a number of its concerns relating to the rights of Minorities. A perusal of the text clearly reveals that certain rights of Minorities are universally accepted and it is incumbent on the States to protect the existence of the ethnic, cultural, religious and linguistic identity of the minorities under their respective territories and encourage conditions for the promotion of that identity.

Moreover, the State is required to adopt appropriate legislative and other measures to achieve those ends. The U.N. Declaration spells out the following rights of all categories of Minorities in all parts of the World to be exercised individually as well as in community with other members of their group, without any discrimination:

i. Right to enjoy their own culture;
ii. Right to profess and practise their own religion;
iii. Right to use their own language;
iv. Right to effectively participate in cultural, religious, social, economic and public life;
v. Right to effectively participate in taking decisions concerning themselves;
vi. Right to establish and maintain their own associations;
vii. Right to establish and maintain free and peaceful contacts with other Minorities within their country; and
viii. Right to establish and maintain free and peaceful contacts with similar Minorities in other countries.

The Declaration also directs all the States of the World to take special measures for the Minorities to achieve the following objectives:

i. To protect the existence and ethnic, cultural, religious and linguistic identity of the Minorities and to encourage conditions for the promotion of that identity;
ii. To ensure that the Minorities fully and effectively exercise all their human rights and fundamental freedoms without any discrimination and in full measure of equality before law;
iii. To create favourable conditions to enable them to express their characteristics and to develop their culture, language, religion, traditions and customs;
iv. To let them have adequate opportunities to learn their mother tongue and have instructions in it;
v. To encourage knowledge of their history, traditions, languages and cultures;
vi. To assure them adequate opportunities to gain knowledge of the society as a whole;
vii. To enable them to fully participate in the economic progress and development of their country.

It is, thus, absolutely clear that the rights of minorities are an internationally accepted social norm. The UN Declaration is, therefore, intended to extend these rights to the minorities world-wide.

HUMAN RIGHTS AND MINORITY RIGHTS

The distinction and relation between human rights and minority rights is very important, particularly in the context where a large section of people have been expressing doubts regarding the validity of minority rights as distinct from the human right. It is, therefore, important to understand minority rights in its proper perspective. The historical context in which the concept of human rights emerged in the western countries over a long period made it more'individualistic' in nature than collective. The scope of human rights internationally is determined by the UN Declaration of 1948, which envisages respect for human rights of all without distinction on the basis of race, language or religion.

Thus, even when the concept encompasses all human beings, there has been a general feeling that in the Universal Declaration of Human Rights, the protection of minorities has been more or less integrated into the wider concept of human rights.

It is only in some of the latter major instruments of international law that a new system of human rights has been introduced and the rights of minorities recognized. The best example of these instruments is the Article 27 of the UN Covenant on Civil and Political Rights (1966). The other important international instruments have been listed earlier in this stage.

Article 3 of the Declaration of 1992 clearly specifies that persons belonging to minorities may exercise their rights individually as well as in community with other members of their group without any discrimination. Thus individual and collective rights have been accepted simultaneously.

This fact, of individual as well as collective rights as a special category has been accepted in the'Manual on Human Rights Reporting of UN', which says:

- "Human rights are formulated in a way that makes the individual human being the main beneficiary.... Some human rights combine individual and collective aspects. For instance, freedom to manifest religion or belief can be exercised either individually or in a community with others.... But there are also rights which by their very nature and their subject are rights of large collectiveness. Cases in point are the rights of minorities, comprising considerable number of persons with common ethnic, religious or linguistic ties, as well as people's rights. The latter includes the right to self-determination, the right to development, the right to peace and security, and the right to a healthy environment."

The 1992 Declaration not only recognizes both individual and collective rights; it also directs (Article 4) the member states almost protecting the human rights and fundamental freedom of the minorities. So, as it stands today,'minority rights' are enjoying a special status along-with the human rights in general.

MINORITIES-INDIAN CONTEXT

There are five religious groups in India, which have been given the official status of National Minorities, namely the Muslims, Christians, Sikhs, Budhists and Parsis. The Census of India, 1991, the percentage and population of minorities in the country is as follows:

Name of the Minorities	Percentage	Number
Muslims	12.12	101,596,057
Christians	2.34	19,640,284
Sikhs	1.94	16,259,749
Buddhists	0.76	6,387,500
Parsis	—	76,383

Thus, in total, the majority community comprises 82 per cent of the total population of the country, as per 1991 Census. There are certain other religious minority groups, which do not enjoy the official status of National Minority, but are still recognized by certain State Governments as minority at the State level. Jains are one such example, which have been recognized by the State of Madhya Pradesh as a minority, while Digambar Jains are recognized as a minority by the State Govt. of Karnataka.

The recognition of above five minorities as national minorities has been done through a notification issued by the Ministry of Social Justice and Empowerment, Government of India, under the provisions of the National Commission for Minorities Act, 1982, while recognition of State level minorities has been done by the State Governments under their respective statutes.

PROVISIONS IN THE CONSTITUTION

The Constitution of India provides special safeguards for minorities. These are general rights established in articles 14, 15, 16, 19, 20, 21, 22, 23, 24, 25, 26, 27, and 28, which are applicable to all citizens including the minorities. Besides, the Constitution guarantees special rights to the minorities under article 29 and 30.

There are also special provisions made for the linguistic minorities in the following articles of the Constitution of India:

- *Article* 350A:-Facilities for education in the mother tongue at primary stage.
- *Article* 350B:-Provision for a special officer of linguistic minorities.

The Provision in the Constitution that have a bearing on Minorities and their rights can, in no way, be regarded as'special rights'; rather they are in the form of specific provisions/safeguards for the protections of the rights of the Minorities which are even otherwise available to them as citizens of the country.

Provision for the protection of these rights has been considered imperative by the framers of the Constitution in the context of the'Democratic Polity' of the country, which we adopted for ourselves after Independence. Each provision related to Minorities in the Constitution was debated at length in the Constituent Assembly, and our experience of over 50 years has clearly shown how right was their'vision' of the situation that they envisaged in this regard. A brief review of the Constitutional provisions that are related to

Minorities needs to be undertaken here to appreciate the nature and scope of the rights of Minorities in the country. At the outset, an extremely significant excerpt from Babasaheb B.R. Ambedkar's speeches and writings is given, which gives the background of the basic understanding of the framers of our Constitution in this regard.

- "The British system of government imposes no obligation upon the Majority to include in its Cabinet the representation of Minorities. If applied to India, the consequences will be obvious. It would make the Majority a governing class and the Minority a subject race. It would mean that the Majority will be free to run the administration just as to its own ideas of what is good for the Minorities. Such a State of affairs could not be called democracy. It will have to be called imperialism".

In fact the concept of'secularism' has been the guiding factor behind various provision in the Constitution. Although the word'secular' was inserted in the Constitution through an amendment much latter, but the concept has been the deciding factor for determining the nature, scope and implications of the principles of religious tolerance enshrined in the Constitution. The concept of'secularism' in the minds of the framers of our Constitution is somewhat different from the Western concept.

Secularism is not negation of any religion. It is neither anti-religious nor irreligious. It implies positive respect for all religious, inter-religious understanding, complete neutrality of the State in all matters of religion with no support for any particular religion but equal respect to all religions. No disrespect or abhorrence to any religion, no discrimination between various individuals or communities on the ground of their religion and various provisions for this purpose have been incorporated in our Constitution at different places.

The Constitutional provisions regarding Minorities essentially revolve round the twin concept of Democracy and Secularism. All religions in the country have, therefore, enjoyed some Constitutional and legal status and all persons and communities have absolutely the same individual and collective rights. The two concepts can, in no way, be misused to establish hegemony of any particular faith in the Nation's affairs. It has, therefore, been an endeavour in the Constitution to make the Minorities an equal partner with the Majority in the task of Nation-building.

The architect of the Constitution, therefore, envisaged certain sensitive provisions to enable the minorities to enjoy freedom, effective political participation and protection of law and well-being. The provisions are intended to ensure protection of religious, cultural, linguistic and other rights of the minorities and providing widest scope to the minorities for their development and participation in political, economic, social and cultural spheres. The Constitution gave its citizens equal right and protection of religious freedom thorough articles 5, 14, 15, 16 and 25 to 30.

RIGHT TO EQUALITY, EQUALITY OF OPPORTUNITY AND NON-DISCRIMINATION

The concept of'Equality' and'Equality of opportunity' as enshrined in Article 15 & 16 of the Constitution is not only intended to end the discrimination on the basis of religion, race, caste etc., but also gives a scope for'positive discrimination', *i.e.* making of special provision for advantages of certain socially and educationally backward classes of citizens. If we look at the background history of the present provision in the Constitution regarding minorities in the context of the debates in the'Constituent Assembly', the genesis lies in the 1909 Minto Morley Reforms during the British days which introduced the system of communal electorate for Indian Muslims.

The principle of separate electorate for Muslims aroused similar demand from other minority group and consequently the Government of India Acts 1919 and 1935 had separate electorate for Muslims, Sikhs, and Christians, etc. The Advisory committee on the Fundamental Rights of Minorities set up by the'Constituent Assembly' opposed the communal reservation and agreed to reservation only for backward classes and not for religious or linguistic minorities.

The Constitution, however contains a programme for social reconstruction of Indian society based on the concept of individual nationalism and secularism. Thus, an individual entitled to equal access and equal opportunity to compete for valuable resources and opportunities in society irrespective of his religion or caste. The religion or caste can, however, be taken into account by the State for the purpose of achieving substantial equality. The policy of compensatory discrimination under Article 15 & 16 of the Constitution is, therefore, intended not to protect separate identity or integrity or religions or communal group but to reduce social inequalities and historic backwardness.

RIGHT TO RELIGIOUS FREEDOM

Impartiality of the State towards all religions is secured by Articles 25 & 26 of the Constitution. Article 25 guarantees right to freedom of conscience and the right to profess, practise and propagate religion, subject to certain specified conditions. Article 25 is thus an article of faith in the Constitution as it amounts to recognition of the principle that real face of the democracy is the ability of even an insignificant minority to find its identity under the country's Constitution. The right guaranteed under article 25 and 26 is not absolute, rather is must be reconciled into the sovereign power of the State to ensure peace, security and orderly living.

Under Article 25 (i) a person has two-fold freedom *i.e.*

i. Freedom of conscience

ii. Freedom to profess, practise and propagate one's religion.

The freedom of conscience is an absolute inner freedom of the citizen to mould his own relation into God in whatever manner he likes and to declare freely and openly one's faith and belief; to propagate means to spread and publicize his religious view for the edification of others. The word'propagate' involves exposition, without any element of coercion. Propagation is thus concerned with right to communicate belief to another person or to expound the tenets of one's religion but does not include right to forcible conversion. This rules out all conversion by fraud, misrepresentation, coercion, intimidation or even influence.

In fact, a good number of princely States in the pre-independence period enacted laws for protection against conversion activities and in many cases these laws required individual converts to register their conversion with specified Govt. agencies by filing an application or affidavit. Such agencies were also legally empowered to ascertain if conversion in any case was bonafide and wilful. Major anticonversion laws during the pre-independence period were the Raigarh State Conversion Act 1936, the Patna freedom of Religion Act 1942, the Sarguja State Apostasy Act 1945, Udaipur State Anti Conversion Act 1946 etc. After independence attempts were made, to enact a legislation aimed at checking conversion and in 1979 one such major attempt was made for official curbs on inter religius conversion, but the Freedom of Religion Bill introduced for this purpose fell. However, during 1967-68, two Indian States Orissa and Madhya Pradesh enacted local laws entitled Orissa Freedom of Religion Act, 1967 and Madhya Pradesh Dharam Swatantra Adhiniyam 1968. Arunachal Pradesh latter enacted similar legislation act. All these State laws have more or less identical provisions and prohibit conversion by force, allurement, inducement and fraud. Contravention of the act is a cognizable offence punishable with imprisonment, fine or both.

Those who convert a person by performing/participating in necessary'ceremony' are required to send an intimation of conversion to the District Magistrate of the locality and failure to do so is also a cognisable offence. The right to freedom of religion guaranteed under Article 25 of the Constitution is subject to certain restrictions as well. It is subject to public order, morality and health. Similarly, under clause (2) of Article 25, the State is also empowered to make laws for social welfare and reforms. As such, social evils cannot be allowed to be protected in the name of religion. Similarly, the regulatory powers of the State under this Article also means that the secular activities associated with the religious practices can also be regulated by State laws.

The right to practise religion and the power of the State to regulate any secular activity associated with religious practices and its power to restrict religious procedure in the interest of public order, morality and health has been interpreted in different judgements of the Courts. Courts have been taking a view that the rites and ceremonies of the religion, which were considered as essential in accordance with the tenets of that religion, should not be interfered by the State. Certain judgements in this regard have distinguished the'essential' elements of religion from other non-essential aspects. Although they remained conscious of the difficulties in determining essentiality of religious practices by secular authorities, Courts, while maintaining the distinction between'essential' and non-essential, have taken many decisions, *e.g.*

i. Validity of the law prohibiting cow-slaughter was upheld on the ground that sacrifice of a cow was not an obligatory act enjoyed by the Muslim religion
ii. Holding Friday prayers on public street was held to be a bad practice and State found competent to prohibit the use of road or any public place for praying
iii. Banning use of loud speaker for prayers in a busy and crowdy locality was held valid being detrimental to public health.

Similarly, in a recent case, the right of Hindus to take out a procession for immersion was found valid as constituting an essential part of their religion. The right to religious freedom guaranteed under Article 25 indicates the positive aspects of religious freedom. The Courts are expected to play a significant and important role in providing objective interpretations of the relevant provisions, in order that such a freedom is not unnecessarily restricted or restrained. Minorities are always alert and conscious that no uncalled for interference is made in regard to matters divine.

If no favour is to be shown to them, no discrimination is to be made either. The rights guaranteed under Article 26 are individual rights; whereas the right guaranteed under Article 26 are the rights of an organised body.

According to clause:

a. Of Article 26, a religious denomination has right to establish and maintain institutions for religious and charitable purpose. The words'establish' and' administer' need to be read together, as only those institutions which are established by the religious denominations can be maintained by them. Under Article 26
b. A religious denomination or organisation is free to manage its own affairs in the matters of religion and State cannot interfere in exercise of its rights, unless they run counter to public order, health or morality. Here again the secular activities connected with the religious institutions can be regulated by State laws. Thus, the places of worship cannot be used for hiding criminals or for carrying on anti-national activities; similarly, they cannot be used for political activities. Under clause (c) & (d) of Article 26, a religious denomination has right to acquire and own property and administer such properties in accordance with the law. Regarding administration of such religious properties the particular principle is that the State can make laws to regulate the administration of property of religious endowment, but such laws cannot take away the right of administration altogether.

CULTURAL AND EDUCATIONAL RIGHTS OF MINORITIES

Article 29 & 30 of the Constitution deals with the cultural and educational rights of the Minorities. Article 29, protects interests of the Minorities regarding their'language, script ad culture Article 30 gives the Minorities the right to establish and administer educational institutions. Article 30 in fact can be regarded as Magna Carta of the basic fundamental right of the Minorities through which they can preserve their identities as religious or linguistic communities. Article 29, though not exclusively for the Minorities, includes in its purview the Minorities.

Article 29 deals with the right to conserve the distinctiveness of language, script and culture of any section of citizens residing in the territory of India. The legalistic part of the right of Article 29 is common to Article 30, but still it is the Article 30, which gives the right to establish and administer educational institutions of their choice exclusively to all the religious or linguistic Minorities. Sometimes, it is said that the right given to Minorities in Article 30 (i) is restricted to the establishment and administration of institutions of their choice in order to conserve their'language, script or culture' only, but this is not true. This innocuous view is a result of the mixing of the contents of the Article 29, which should not happen as the two Articles are different in four respects.

- Article 29 (I) grants fundamental right to all sections of the citizens of our country, which include the majority also, whereas Article 30 (I) grants such a right to religious and linguistic minorities only.
- Article 29 deals with language, script or culture, while Article 30 (I) deals with Minorities based on religion or language alone.
- Article 29 (I) is concerned with the right to conserve language, script or culture, while Article 30 (I) deals with right of Minorities to establish and administer educational institutions just as to their choice.
- Article 29 relates to conservation of language, script or culture which can be undertaken through any means without unnecessarily establishing institutions. Similarly, institutions established under Article 30 (I) may not be for the purpose of conserving language, script or culture.

Thus Article 29 (I) and Article 30 (I) overlap but the former cannot limit the width of the latter. The scope of Article 30 is restricted to linguistic or religious Minorities, and no other section of the citizen has such a right. However, since Article 30 (I) gives the right to linguistic Minorities irrespective of their religion, it is not possible to exclude secular education from Article 30. Ever since the Constitution came into existence, Article 30 has been subject to too much debate amongst sections of the society and also in the Supreme Court.

The following aspects of Article 30 needs to be discussed in detail:

- *The right to establish*: The simple meaning of'to establish' is to bring into existence; a detailed discussion on the meaning of this expression has taken place in a well known case which came before the Supreme

Court of India in October 96. Since the AMU, Aligarh was established in 1920 through a Central Legislative Act, the Supreme Court took a view that University came into existence through this Act and, therefore, Muslims as a Minority could not have the right to administer it. It felt that'establishment and administration' must be read conjunctively and so, in real sense, it gives the right to Minorities to administer educational institutions, provided it has been established by it. Thus the right to establish means to bring an institution into being by a Minority community and it does not matter whether a single philanthropic individual funds the institution or the community at large contributes the funds

- *The right to administer*: Administration means management of affairs of the institutions. Thus, management must be free of control, so that the founders could mould the institution as they think fit and in accordance with their ideas of how the interests of community in general and the institution in particular will be best served. No part of its management can be taken away and vested in another body. This explanation to the expression'administer' has been given in case of State of Kerala vs Very Rev. Mother Provincial. In the same case the word of caution to the Minorities has been given in the areas in which Universities or Government can intervene for advancement of maintenance of standard of education. Thus prescribed syllabus of the Universities needs to be followed by Minority institutions with the freedom that they may teach special subjects, which the institution may like. To some extent, State can also regulate the condition of employment of teachers and health and hygiene of students. On the basis of various Supreme Court judgements, the rights covered under Article 30 can be summarized as follows:
  - To choose its management or governing body.
  - To choose its teachers
  - Not to be compelled to refuse admission to students
  - To use its properties and assets for the benefit of the institutions.
  - To select its own medium of instructions; hence a legislation which would penalize the institution by dis-affiliation from the University which uses a language as the medium of instruction other than the one prescribed by it, offends Article 30 (I).
- *Of their choice*: The Minorities both religious and linguistic are not prohibited from establishing and administering educational institutions of their choice for the purpose of giving their children the best general education. General secular education is, therefore, covered under the phrase'of their choice' and Minorities have right to establish such institution.
- *The right to compensation of property*: Clause 1 (A) of Article 30 was

inserted thorough Constitutional amendment in 1978 with a purpose to provide protection to the properties of Minority educational institutions. Thus no individual or educational institution belonging to the majority community shall have a justiceable fundamental right to compensation in case of compulsory acquisition of its property by the State, while in case of educational institutions belonging to the Minority Community the compensation is justiceable and part of the fundamental right.

- *Granting aid for recognition*: Under Article 30 (2) the State is under obligation to make equality of treatment in granting aid to education institutions, but minority institutions are to be treated differently while giving financial assistance. They are entitled to get financial assistance, the same way as the institutions of the majority community. The receipt of the State aid does not impair their rights in Article 30 (1) as the State can lay down reasonable conditions for obtaining grant-in-aid for its proper utilisation. But the State has no power to compel minority institutions to give up their right under Article 30 (I). Recognition is thus a fundamental right of the minorities and in fact is a necessity as without recognition no educational institution established or to be established by a minority Community can fulfil the real object guaranteed under Article 30 (1).

The minority organisations/institutions complain about the infringement of their rights guaranteed under Article 30 of the Constitution. In large number of cases, the minority institutions are not distinguished, as permission for opening the institution/granting recognition/affiliation is denied. The existing minority educational institutions also complain about denial of freedom to them to administer their institutions freely. Undue interference from the Education Department officials with scant regard for the rights of the minority institutions is reported.

In case of large number of States, the educational code of the State has no provision for the manner in which the minority educational institutions are required to be treated. There are very few States like Tamil Nadu, where a separate educational code for minority institutions exists. In a number of cases of educational codes of the States, the provisions run contrary to the Constitutional guarantees/rights given to the minorities. The Ministry of Human Resource Development, Department of Education, Government of India, formulated and notified vide letter No.F.7- 51/89-PM(DIII) dated 5.10.98, the Policy Norms and Principles for recognition of minority managed educational institutions and for regulating other matters related to the educational rights of minorities guaranteed under Article 29 and 30 of the Constitution. A text of these policy guidelines are enclosed. These policy norms are important and needs to be taken into account by civil administration, while dealing with the matters related to the minority managed educational institutions established and administered under Article 30 of the Constitution. In a recent judgement, the 11 Judges Constitutional Bench of the Supreme Court of India clarified the following issues that were earlier formulated on the basis of various Court judgements:

- Linguistic and religious minorities are covered by the expression'minorities' and since reorganization of the States in India has been on linguistic lines for the purpose of determining the minority, the unit will be States and not whole of India.
- In regard to the use of the word'of their choice' under Article 30(i), even the professional educational institutions would be covered.
- Admission to unaided minority educational institutions *viz.* schools, where scope for merit based selection is practically nil, cannot be regulated by the State or country (except for providing the qualifications and minimum conditions of eligibility in the interest of academic standard).
- In case, aid is received or taken by a minority educational institution, it would be governed by Article 29(2) and would then not be able to refuse admission on the grounds of religion, race, caste, language or any of them.
- A minority institution may have its own procedure and method of admission as well as selection of students, but such procedure must be fair and transparent and selection of students in professional and higher educational colleges should be on the basis of merit. The procedure adopted or selection made should not tantamount to mal-administration.
- In case of unaided minority educational institutions, regulatory measures of control should be minimal. Thus, while conditions of recognition and affiliation would apply, in matters of day-to-day administration like appointment of staff and control over them, the management should have freedom, without any external control. However, rational procedure for selection and for taking disciplinary action has to be evolved by the management itself.
- In case of minority educational institutions, where aid is provided by the State, regulation can be framed governing service conditions for teaching and other staff, without interfering with overall administrative control of management.
- The right to establish and administer educational institutions is guaranteed under the Constitution to all citizens under Article 19 (g) and 26 and to minorities specifically under Article 30.

SAFEGUARD OF MINORITY RIGHTS-INSTITUTIONAL ARRANGEMENT

The Government of India has provided a number of instruments to look into the implementation of minority rights and to safeguard the same. The need for this institutional arrangement was explained in the Resolution issued by Government of India in 1978, while constituting the Minorities Commission. The Resolution issued by the Govt. of India while constituting the Minorities Commission in 1978 through an Executive order reads:"Despite the safeguards provided in the Constitution and the law in force, there persists amongst minorities a feeling of inequality and discrimination.

In order to preserve secular tradition and to promote national integration, the Govt. of India attaches the highest importance to the enforcement of the safeguards provided for minorities and is of the firm view that effective institutional arrangements are urgently required for effective enforcement and implementation of all the safeguards provided for the minorities in the Constitution, in Central and State laws, and in Government policies and administrative schemes enunciated from time to time". The text of the Resolution determines the basic framework of the status of Constitutional rights of the Minorities in the country. It amounts to recognizing that minorities are increasingly feeling insecure and isolated with regard to their religion, personal safety and protection of their property. Studies on the status of various minorities show that there is an ample evidence to justify the feeling amongst the minority communities. The scope of the present reading forbids an attempt to give details about their status, particularly about their economic and educational status, their representation in services particularly in police, military and para-military forces.

THE NATIONAL COMMISSION FOR MINORITIES

In an attempt to make suitable institutional arrangements for the protection of the Constitutional and civil rights of the Minorities, the Government of India notified a Government Resolution to set up a Minorities Commission. The Resolution also said that all the Central Government Ministries and Departments will furnish to the Commission all information, documents and assistance required by the Commission. The Resolution also expected the State Governments to do the same.

The Commission was expected to submit its Annual Report to the President of India detailing its activities and recommendations. The Annual Reports of the Commission were required to be laid before each House of Parliament with Action Taken Memorandum, also explaining the reasons for non-acceptance of a recommendation, if any. Later, the Commission was given statutory status through the passage of the National Commission for Minorities Act, 1992. This Act more or less retained the provision of the 1978 Government of India Resolution. The Act empowered the Commission to exercise"all powers of a Civil Court trying a suit", while discharging its statutory functions namely,

i. Evaluating progress of development of minorities under the Union and the States

ii. Monitoring working of the safeguards for minorities provided in the Constitution and State Laws

iii. Looking into specific complaints regarding deprivation of rights and safeguards of the minorities. The word'minorities' has been defined in clause-C of Section 2 of the National Commission for Minorities Act, 1992, and it says that'Minority' for the purpose of this Act means,'a community notified as such by the Central Government'.

The Central Government, therefore, officially notified 5 communities as minorities in terms of provision of this Act. The National Commission for Minorities is essentially a human rights organization overseeing the enforcement of the human rights of a particular section of the people, *i.e.* religious minorities. This fact has also been recognized under the Protection of Human Rights Act 1993, wherein the Chairman of National Commission for Minorities has been declared as ex-officio Member of the National Human Rights Commission. The importance of the Commission and its essential nature has been recognized by the Supreme Court of India in one of its recent judgements *Viz.* Misbah Alam Shaikh Vs State of Maharashtra, wherein Justice K Ramaswamy and Justice G. T. Nanavati held.

- "By operation of Section 3 read with Section 9, it is the duty of the Central Government to constitute a National Commission, and it shall be the duty and the responsibility of the National Commission for Minorities to ensure compliance with the principles and programmes enumerated in Section 9 of the Act, protecting the interests of the Minorities for their development and working of the safeguards provided to them in the Constitution and the laws enacted by Parliament as well as the State Legislatures. The object thereby is to integrate them in the National mainstream in the united and integrated Bharat, providing facilities and opportunities to improve their economic and social status and empowerment."

The NCM Act 1992 can be perused. Section 9 of this Act specifies the functioning of the Commission. The functions are comprehensive and are related not only to the protection of the Constitutional rights of the persons belonging to minorities but also the development of minorities including conduct of studies and research on the issues relating to their socioeconomic development.

STATE MINORITIES COMMISSION

The idea of a Minorities Commission first originated in the State of Uttar Pradesh, when a one-man Minorities Commission was established in Lucknow in 1960. Later in 1974, the Commission was expanded to include a Chairman and nine Members. Similarly, Govt.of Bihar set up a Multi- Member Minorities Commission in 1971. Now a good number of State Governments in India have established State Minorities Commissions *e.g.* Andhra Pradesh, Bihar, Delhi,

Karnataka, Madhya Pradesh, Maharashtra, Rajasthan, Tamil Nadu, Uttar Pradesh, West Bengal. The Governemnt of Assam and Gujarat have established Development Board for this purpose and they have the status of a registered Society.

NATIONAL MINORITIES FINANCE AND DEVELOPMENT CORPORATION (NMFDC)

The second instrument in the Central Government, which came into existence on the recommendation of the National Commission for Minorities and which needs a special mention is National Minorities Finance and Development Corporation (NMDFC).

It was established on 30.9.1994 with the following objectives:

- To promote economic and developmental activities for the benefit of'backward sections' amongst the minorities, preference being given to occupational groups and women';
- To assist, subject to such income and/or economic criteria as may be prescribed by the Government of India from time to time, individuals or groups of individuals belonging to the minorities by way of loans and advances, for economically and financially viable schemes and projects;
- To promote self-employment and other ventures for the benefit of minorities;
- To grant loans and advances at such rates of interest as may be determined from time to time in accordance with the guidelines or schemes prescribed;
- To extend loans and advances to the eligible members belonging to the minorities for pursuing general/professional/technical education or training at graduate and higher levels;
- To assist the State-level organisations dealing with the development of the Minorities by way of providing financial assistance or equity contribution and in obtaining commercial funding or by way of refinancing;
- To work as an apex institution for coordinating and monitoring the work of the Corporation/Boards/other bodies set up by the State Governments/Union Territory Administrations for, or given the responsibility of assisting the minorities for their economic development; and
- To help in furthering the Government policies and programmes for the development of minorities.

15-POINT PROGRAMME FOR MINORITIES

Besides these two instruments, there is also a special programme known as the'Prime Minister's 15-Point programme for Minorities', which is in existence since 1983. On 11th May 1982, the then Prime Minister, Smt. Indira Gandhi had addressed a letter to the Home Minister, containing certain suggestions for immediate action by way of measures to prevent the recurrence of communal violence and improve the economic conditions of minorities.

This was communicated to all the Ministries of the Central Government and to State Governments, and are known as'15-Point Programme for Minorities Welfare' since then. The range of points covered under the programme relates to almost all important minority rights discussed pre-page. All the District level officers are expected to regularly monitor the progress on implementation of the Prime Minister's 15-Point programme and ensure that regular reports on each point are sent to the State Government where it need to be consolidated for sending it to the Ministry of Home Affairs, Ministry of Social Justice and Empowerment.

14

Agenda and Issues for Dalit Upliftment in States

COMPARATIVE STUDY OF UTTAR PRADESH AND MADHYA PRADESH

In the existing literature the concept of mobilisation is used to analyse electoral strategies employed by political parties to obtain votes from a section of the population–in this case dalits. This aspect has been extensively covered for both Uttar Pradesh and Madhya Pradesh during the 1990s. The attempt here is to understand the response of political parties to fundamental shifts in the democratic arena in the 1990s in these two states: the decline of the single-dominant party system and the emergence of narrower political formations based on identity which has created a more competitive environment.

The differential patterns of mobilisation employed by the BSP and the Congress in the two states using state power from above to put into effect programmes for dalits in order to enlarge their support base among them are examined. Historically the 'dalit question', i e, removal of discrimination, socio-economic improvement and share in political power, has occupied centre stage in Indian politics.

Since the colonial period political leaders have put forward different paths for the upliftment of this section hoping thereby to mobilise them and obtain their support. This issue was the cause of the disagreement between Gandhi and Ambedkar, which left its imprint on later political debates. In recent years dalit assertion against upper caste domination and political mobilisation of dalits has emerged as one of the most significant factors affecting politics in the Indian states. All political parties are attempting to gain the support of this social group which in some states has emerged as a 'third force' that holds the electoral balance between all-India parties in both assembly and national elections.

In the existing literature the concept of mobilisation is used to analyse electoral strategies employed by political parties to obtain votes from a section of the population–in this case dalits. This aspect has been extensively covered for both the selected states of UP and MP during the 1990s and will not be the main focus here. Rather the attempt is to understand the response of political parties to fundamental shifts in the democratic arena in the 1990s in two important states in north India–UP and MP: the decline of the single-dominant party system and the emergence of narrower political formations based on identity which has created a more competitive democratic arena.

In UP, the collapse of the Congress as a broad-based party has provided room for parties based on ascriptive identities such as the BSP representing the dalits. In MP, the Congress has been in power in the 1990s, but it has faced a constant challenge from the BSP and the BJP making the support of the weaker sections imperative.

In this context it is worth examining the differential patterns of mobilisation employed by the BSP and the Congress in UP and MP respectively, using state power from above to put into effect programmes for dalits, in order to enlarge their support base among them. It analyses the conceptualisation of a model of development for dalits by the BSP and the Congress Party while in power during the 1990s in UP and MP respectively.

Based on this, it evaluates the functioning of selected programmes for dalits in the two states: welfare programmes, the Ambedkar village programme and socio-cultural programmes in UP; land distribution, the Employment Guarantee Scheme and Gram Swaraj in MP. It is argued here that driven by both an ideological understanding of the dalit question as well as the political necessities arising out of politics, two distinct patterns of socio-political mobilisation using state power and patronage have emerged during the 1990s with important consequences for state and national politics.

In UP, emerging from a strong identity-based movement, the BSP's agenda for dalit uplift is based on the notion of 'swabhiman' (self-respect). Its leadership has argued that "self-respect is more important to dalits than material gains" and "what we are fighting for is dignity and self-respect". Dalit upliftment has been conceptualised as social justice that is both retributive in character and meant exclusively for dalits. On the other hand, no clear agenda has emerged for the economic uplift of dalits. The BSP's welfare/developmental programmes have been 'mere symbolism' to obtain support and have depleted the resources of the state contributing to its fiscal crisis, without addressing the longer-term deprivations faced, particularly by the subaltern dalits.

Despite this, there has been a steady rise in political consciousness throughout the 1990s and dalit mobilisation based on identity under the leadership of the BSP has played a central and determining role in state politics. There has been considerable political empowerment of dalits and the BSP has come to occupy a significant position in state politics. In contrast, the MP model of development places upliftment of all weaker sections including the dalits, within its overall strategy of economic development. It views dalits as a disadvantaged minority in need of state assistance whose political support they hope to gain. Dalit mobilisation has not taken place in the state as in UP against the backdrop of an identity movement. But the existence of a large dalit population made itself felt and dalit mobilisation emerged during the 1990s as a significant factor in state politics. All parties are competing to gain the support of the dalits.

In this situation, the Congress Party under Digvijay Singh, through the Rajiv Gandhi mission and the stress on human development sought to convey the message during its period in power that it was committed to ensure development for the weaker sections. It concentrated on improvement of the socio-economic condition of dalits and providing them equality of opportunity based on 'diversity' and 'democratisation'. However, evaluation of the functioning of some programmes for dalits and weaker sections, suggests that the intentions of the government were not transparent, based on political calculations, actual implementation was slow and ineffective and could not in some cases address the needs of quality and equity for dalits.

Despite it efforts the Congress Party has not been able to substantially improve its support base among dalits. It has not been able to compete for their support with both the BSP and the BJP, which has contributed to undermining of its position in the state and in national politics.

A comparison between MP and UP is of significance for understanding differential patterns of dalit mobilisation in north India. Both states are placed in the BIMARU category; and have a large, disadvantaged dalit population that until recently did not experience identity consciousness or participate in politics.

As the Congress Party was dominant in both states until the late-1980s they have a long history of dalit mobilisation through state patronage and support. The political discourse underlying the actions of the UP and the MP government during the 1990s has been similar: both tried to appropriate the Ambedkarite legacy and claimed to be following its ideals of social democracy. These similarities allow us to analyse the differential patterns of dalit mobilisation adopted by political parties to carve out a base in the increasingly competitive system that has emerged following the decline of single party dominance and the rise of narrower political formations based upon identity in the 1990s.

AGENDA FOR DALIT UPLIFTMENT

In UP and MP the Congress Party has enjoyed a long spell of dominance in the post-independence period. During this period it consistently followed an agenda for uplift of dalits in various forms. In UP the collapse of the Congress Party in the early 1990s provided room for the BSP to emerge as the party representing the dalits. In MP the Congress retained power during the

1990s, but its policies for dalits have undergone some significant changes. This section provides the backdrop against which the selected programmes are examined in the next section.

MODEL OF POLITICAL EMPOWERMENT

The BSP's model for dalit upliftment is based on political empowerment, i e, it believes that state power is the 'key' or agent to introduce social change. The party has followed a two-fold strategy: electoral and coalitional in order to widen its base and capture power. Based on identity mobilisation which led to increasing politicisation of the dalits, the BSP by the early 1990s was able to replace the Congress as the party representing them in UP. It gradually increased its seat and vote share in the state vis-à-vis both the SP and the BJP throughout the 1990s from 9.2 per cent in the 1991 state assembly elections to 10.8 per cent in 1996 and over 20 per cent in the 2003 assembly elections. Consequently, in a situation where no party had a clear majority, no government could be formed without the participation of the BSP. The formation of three coalition governments with the BJP and the implementation of a number of dalit-oriented programmes played an important role in the consolidation of dalit vote behind the party by the end of the decade.

The BSP since its inception has been very critical of the Indian state, which it is argued, has not and cannot provide economic upliftment for dalits. Since independence the state has been under the control of manuvadi leaders with brahminism as a ruling socio-cultural ideology. All leaders and political parties the country has produced, particularly the Congress with its upper caste leadership, are 'manuvadi'. All policies of the government after independence, based upon such thinking have hence, prevented uplift of the dalits.

Despite the dalit-bahujans forming a majority of the population, the continuation of the hierarchical caste system after independence has ensured that the fruits of development are in large measure, channeled to the upper and middle castes/classes, strengthening their position in the society and polity. Consequently, Dalits have remained poor and exploited and deprived of a share in political power and decision-making. Therefore the BSP holds that capture of state power by a dalit-based party, which will establish a dalit-bahujan state, is essential for their socio-economic upliftment].

A central role therefore is granted to the dalit-bahujan state and use of state power for social change by the BSP. It believes that an egalitarian order can be achieved by means of 'social engineering from above', i e, introducing developmental and welfare programmes using the power of the state rather than grass roots mobilisation and revolution from below. The main role of the state following the capture of power is to provide dignity and an alternative 'social justice' to the dalits. Social justice forms the core of the party's political tenets–a tool of mobilisation, an agenda of social and political action and the base upon which the party's programmes rest. However, social justice is conceived in a narrow manner as being exclusive, i e, meant only for the dalits and retributive, i e, to right historical wrongs. The BSP does not give importance to civil society, which is conceived as an unequal sphere in which oppression and domination of the weaker and disadvantaged sections has been taking place. The dalit-controlled state therefore has the role of protecting the disadvantaged sections against oppression, which the Indian state has failed to do.

The BSP describes itself as an Ambedkarite Party but it has a view of the role of the state in economic development that is different from that of Ambedkar. For Ambedkar it was not so much the political potential of democracy that the BSP stresses upon, as the economic functions of the state which could prove to be an emancipatory instrument for the dalits. He held that the lack of formal political equality could be made up by reorganisation of the economic structure of society.

He opposed the Gandhian model of decentralised socialism as it would merely reproduce the unequal rural power structures and preferred the more bureaucratised model of state socialism, which became the central aspect of the Nehruvian model of development. In the States and Minorities, a memorandum submitted to the constituent assembly in 1948, Ambedkar laid out the economic functions of the state in independent India.

While arguing for special safeguards against social and economic discrimination of socially deprived classes, he pointed to the need for state socialism because he argued it would, "put an obligation on the state to plan the economic life of people on lines which would lead to highest point of productivity without closing avenue to private enterprise and also provide for equitable distribution of wealth". Hence, the ideology of the BSP shares with the Ambedkarite view an emphasis on the importance of the state. But it diverges from Ambedkar in that it is much less the economic promise of state policy than its administrative and political potential that is now seen as the instrument of dalit emancipation. The BSP's emphasis is also exclusively on state structures, which, it argues, have always been the preserve of the upper castes.However, no detailed economic agenda has emerged based on this ideology.

An important reason is the view that the BSP leadership has of the problem of poverty and the means to overcome it. According to Kanshi Ram, poverty and deprivation among dalits is the result of social and political powerlessness historically rooted in the brahminical system and not an economic condition to be dealt with by economic policies. In his writings he argues that the prevailing economic inequalities such as skewed distribution of land and income is the result of the unequal caste system. For example, it is oppression by upper caste landlords, which is the root cause of the unequal relations on land, and ill treatment of landless labourers. He does not advocate re-distribution of land, as this would introduce social revolution, which he is keen to avoid. The unused lands instead could be utilised to set up large, mechanised collective farms on which the landless could work and prosper. Rather, if political power was in the hands of the oppressed, they could demand better wages and working conditions and would no longer be badly treated on grounds of their low social status. Economic power according to him is based upon political power; and political equality by attaining political power is primary as it assures freedom from social oppression and improves status In sum, Kanshi Ram's position has been that such questions are unimportant, appropriate policies of economic development could be adopted once in office, it is equality of political opportunity that is central for him.

While the need for ending poverty and introducing social change is underlined, and a number of required policies mentioned, such as land reform, nationalisation of industry, need for better wages, modernisation of industry, etc, how this will be implemented by the party has not been clarified. Thus, Kanshi Ram seems to be advocating a form of 'state socialism' though he still believes in the importance of individual property rights.

Redistribution of economic assets and provision of social justice is possible only by the state; hence capturing power is given so much importance. However, only a dalit-bahujan state is capable of implementing these measures, not one controlled by manuvadi parties headed by upper caste leaders. The BSP as an Ambedkarite party on attaining power would establish 'real' and 'substantial' democracy, which for Kanshi Ram is rule of the majority, i e, of the bahujans.

CONGRESS MODEL OF SOCIO-ECONOMIC DEVELOPMENT

In contrast, the Congress Party in MP placed the socio-economic improvement of dalits together with other disadvantaged groups such as tribal, women and the poor, at the heart of its developmental strategy. Digvijay Singh in his pronouncements claimed that his government would promote a "people-centric development policy…through grass roots democratisation, decentralised governance and community participation". This model of development was adopted when the party came to power after defeating the BJP in the 1993 assembly elections but was strengthened and given greater importance after the party won the 1998 assembly elections. Many important policy documents such as the Bhopal Agenda and the reports of the Task Force were drawn up after the 1998 elections.

Certain changes in the social base of the Congress Party made this strategy increasingly important in MP during the 1990s. The Congress as a single-dominant party had faced a sharp decline in a number of states beginning in the 1980s. However, empirical studies point to a shift in the social base of the party by the end of the 1990s: the reinvention of the Congress from a catch-all to a narrower party of the marginalised and poorer sections namely, the dalits, adivasis, Muslims and women in a number of states [Yadav 2003:66]. However, this was not true of MP where the support from the dalits for the Congress was much lower than many other states [ibid]. A number of reasons contributed to this, not the least being the presence of the BSP in the northern districts of MP. Hence, the Congress found itself in the position of competing with both the BJP and the BSP for the support of the dalits.

The BJP had performed well in the 1990 assembly elections gaining 219 seats out of 320. In 1993 it was able to gain only 117 seats while the Congress was able to win 174 seats. While it is true that the weakening of the Babri masjid issue and factionalism within the party were important reasons for its poor performance, an equally important reason, was its pro-upper caste/class policies, which made it unpopular in rural areas particularly among the tribals, peasants, OBCs and other disadvantaged groups. The Congress' victory was primarily based on votes gained from rural constituencies due to disappointment with the policies of the BJP.

Consequently the BJP, as in UP, since the mid-1990s has been trying to modify its image as an upper caste party and to widen its base among the dalits. The Congress Party under Digvijay Singh was able to win in the 1998 assembly elections gaining 41.13 per cent of the votes, while the BJP stood second with 39.28 per cent of the votes. An important reason for the victory of the Congress Party was its policies for the weaker sections initiated by the Digvijay Singh government, which were continued with greater vigour during its second term.

From the 1993 elections onwards an important contest for the votes of the dalits came from the BSP. The BSP was able to increase its tally of seats from two in 1990 to 11 seats in both 1993 and 1998; and double its vote share from 3.5 per cent in 1990 to 7 per cent and 6.15 per cent in the1993 and 1998 state elections. The BSP became a 'third force' within the two-party system, cutting votes from the Congress and the BJP particularly in the northern districts bordering UP where bulk of the dalit population is concentrated. In this situation Congress attempted to widen its base among the dalits, to meet the challenge of both the BSP and the BJP.

Though conceived earlier, the clearest enunciation of the Dalit Agenda of the Congress Party in MP emerges in the Bhopal Document (BD) of 2001. The MP government organised the Bhopal Conference held in January 2001 in which a number of intellectuals were invited to discuss strategies for upliftment of weaker sections and gave full support to its recommendations for uplift of disadvantaged sections, particularly dalits.

A Task Force (TF) with six committees was also established to work out the proposed strategies in detail. The agenda for dalit uplift in the Congress Party's model of development, which was based on the BD, the TF and other documents of the government, is discussed below. In the Congress model of development emphasis is laid on the improvement of the socio-economic conditions of dalits and not their political empowerment as in UP. The

Congress saw itself as a party committed to the improvement of all the disadvantaged and weaker sections of society, not of the dalits alone. The dalits form a small and disadvantaged group in need of help from the state who can in turn at best hope for a share in political power.

Consequently, in all pronouncements of the state government regarding dalit upliftment the emphasis was on a non-conflictual pattern of change, i e, on conciliation and sharing between castes/classes based upon the acceptance by society of notions of equity and justice rather than on mobilisation based on 'recognition of difference', 'identity' or capture of power which has created conflict in UP between the upper and lower castes. The role of the state was visualised as a 'conciliator' between the dalits and the rest of society. Economic change through the combined help of state and civil society must take place through evolutionary and not revolutionary channels. The Bhopal Document contrasts its own goals with those of UP and Bihar.

While the Congress model accords a central role to the state in the economic upliftment of the weaker sections, it must be distinguished from the earlier pattern of state interventionism on behalf of the dalits under Congress rule. First, in the post-independence period apart from providing reservations, scholarships to students, implementing welfare and poverty programmes the state under Congress governments had adopted a stance of neutrality in the economic sphere despite having the power to intervene.

Equally important, hitherto the dalit question was seen as part of mainstream development with growth percolating down to the dalit poor. Within this 'state welfarism' was based on the reasoning that the state apart from providing protective discrimination has to use available resources for scholarships and freeships; generate employment in the rural areas through schemes for improving rural infrastructure 'without realising the limitations of its resources'.

Such an approach did not improve the economic conditions of dalits who remained assetless and part of the population below the poverty line. Second, in the 1990s with the onset of globalisation the retreat of the state from economic activities has particularly affected the dalits. This requires the intervention of civil society for promoting development. Entirely state-centric economic models of development pursued so far have not been beneficial to dalits. Large numbers of them remain in the primary sector as landless labourers, few have moved into the secondary and tertiary sector. Third, while emphasising that reservation quotas in the government sector need to be better implemented, the BD recognises for the first time that there are limits to reservations.

The number of posts available with the government in the era of globalisation is shrinking and even if reservations were to be extended to the private sector, only a small section of the total dalit population could be accommodated. Therefore, multi-pronged strategies involving the state, civil society and the market are required, such as democratisation of the unorganised sector, in which 92 per cent of the scheduled caste workforce is concentrated.

Against this background the Congress model under Digvijay Singh provided a more interventionist role to the state, which it described as 'developmental activism'. More specifically, needs of the dalits were given a central place in development plans and state intervention was meant for at least three purposes: protection to dalits; economic upliftment through provision of land and state sponsored programmes based on diversity and democratisation; and education in order to provide social opportunity.

Within this model education is given central importance as it is the path by which scheduled castes can come out of traditional occupations which are related to the caste hierarchy and thereby 'enter a new phase of life' [GoMP 2002:59]. It would lead to creation of an educated and articulate middle class having representation not only within the state bureaucracy as in the past, but due to the policies of diversity in academia, arts, media, publishing, etc, so as to emerge as opinion makers. There is also stress on the fact that in the era of globalisation and increasing competition within the private sector, there is need for specialised education and not merely general education that was in the past given importance for obtaining government employment. Together with the state importance was also given to civil society institutions such as NGOs who are visualised as partners in providing development. With lessening of government employment the BD recommends the adoption of two practices in the private sector: Diversity and democratisation.

Drawing upon the US example, diversity means a commitment by private companies to providing equal opportunity to all sections of the population as well as the creation of a workforce at all levels that is broadly inclusive and draws upon the talent of all sections of society irrespective of ascriptive identities.

It also applies in the educational field to all institutions whether in the public or private sector to ensure that dalits are able to gain education of a high quality. Parallel to this is democratisation of capital that can provide an alternative to reservations by introducing new occupations and creating a class of entrepreneurs among dalits. Another feature was the use of the mission approach outside the sphere of the state. In MP the Rajiv Gandhi Mission was set up on August 20, 1994 by the Digvijay Singh government with the idea that time-bound programmes could be started which could target specific weaknesses such as low literacy, high infant mortality, lack of drinking water, etc. These would require heavy investment and would take a long time within the state sector whereas a different mode of functioning could be adopted in which the mission through NGOs could work at a faster pace to achieve targets for specific sections such as dalits. Finally, a significant feature is that a shift is visible in the public pronouncements of the Digvijay Singh government from earlier Congress governments. After paying a ritual homage to Gandhi and his attempts to promote the welfare of the dalits, government documents invoke the ideals put forward by Babasaheb Ambedkar. The Bhopal Document opens with "declaring our belief in Baba Saheb Ambedkar's ideal of Social Democracy".

The Report of the TF set up by the government recalls the struggles that Ambedkar had waged for the emancipation of dalits and points to the continuation of social inequality while providing political equality. Ambedkar's notion of State Socialism is invoked and the need for state supremacy in order to overcome the traditional society [GoMP 2003:3]. Thus, the Congress Party in MP appropriated the legacy of Ambedkar in order to meet the political challenge of the BSP, which describes itself as an Ambedkarite party.

POLICIES AND PROGRAMMES FOR DALITS

The goal of the BSP during the three short-lived coalition governments formed with the support of the BJP was twofold: to introduce welfare policies for dalits and second, to use them for further mobilisation for electoral gains. A few of the programmes for dalits adopted by the party during its period in power are analysed below.

WELFARE PROGRAMMES

In 1995 when the BSP came to power it introduced a number of welfare measures for dalits in a variety of fields. Of the funds available 21.57 per cent under the special component plan were allocated for the first time for these programmes. A major concern was education on which considerable funds were spent. A number of scholarships were initiated for children up to high school, hostels were built for dalit students especially girl students in urban areas, and ashram type schools and coaching centres were also begun.

Assistance was provided to dalit families during sickness, marriage and other contingencies. Dalit women were provided 440.59 days of labour under employment schemes and the target of the Indira Awas was increased four times. Priority was assigned to SC/ST members in cane supply to sugar mills and farmers belonging to the SC/ST community were nominated to all the cooperative sugarcane committees. A number of reserved posts were speedily filled up and the government included about 15 lower castes in the OBC category and promised them reservations.

The constitution of the SC/ST Commission was completed. Many posts at the district level such as Police Station incharge, were reserved for dalits and special courts for dalits in all the districts were set up for the first time which would try cases related to the Civil Rights Protection Act. The second and third Mayawati governments in 1997 and 2003, doubled scholarships to dalit students and grants to dalit families. A number of economic policies to ensure employment and income for dalits were adopted such as granting various types of contracts in stone quarries, cane crushing, etc. Many programmes for Muslims and OBCs were also initiated.

LAND DISTRIBUTION

Both in 1995 and in 1997 the BSP government under various schemes distributed land to landless dalit families. Under a special drive 81,500 dalits were granted ownership of 52,379 acres of land; 1,58,000 dalits were given actual possession of land, which had been granted to them; 20,000 dalits were given about 15,000 acres of Gaon Sabha land and all cases of illegal occupation of such land against them were withdrawn; all tenants of more than 10 years standing were granted bhumidhari rights, due to which many small dalit and OBC farmers benefited. A decision was also taken to recover compensation from those who had forcibly occupied lands allotted to pattedars However, the Tenth Plan document points out many instances where dalits have not benefited despite many laws passed and two BSP governments being in power. The government had implemented the Panchayat Extension Scheduled Area Act and the Land Acquisition Act in 1996.

Implementation of Land Ceiling Laws, security of tenants and consolidation of landholdings, remain a matter of serious concern in UP in the case of dalits. Bureaucratic antipathy, according to the report has placed insurmountable obstacles in the way of the dalit communities. Officials engaged in preparing the draft plan also argue that the government has shown undue haste in giving land to industrial units in Bundelkhand without making any alternate arrangements for the evictees.

They cite examples of bias against dalit communities. During the mid-1990s in Kashipur district (now in Uttaranchal) dalits won a case of landownership after a long court battle, the government has yet to take a decision in the case. However, in Chitrakoot where the case was won by the upper castes, officials were very prompt in restoring the land. Moreover, only 39.5 per cent cases of crimes against dalits connected with land have recorded completion of inquiry despite a government headed by a dalit party being in power.

THE AMBEDKAR VILLAGE PROGRAMME

The Ambedkar Village programme (AVP) was the most important programme undertaken by the BSP. Although begun by the Mulayam Singh government in 1991, its political importance stems from its enthusiastic adoption by the BSP under Mayawati when it came to power in collaboration with the BJP in 1995 and 1997. In this programme in every block in the state, villages with 50 per cent dalit population are selected and provided extra funds to carry on the existing programmes for weaker sections. The BSP government in 1995 lowered the required dalit population to 22-30 per cent thereby covering more villages. The capture of political power by the BSP, the increasing politicisation of dalits and reservations for them in panchayat bodies under the 73rd Constitutional Amendment, enabled this programme to be implemented.

Between 1991 and 1997-98 a total of 25,434 Ambedkar villages all over UP were selected. Thirty-seven developmental programmes were implemented in various villages depending on their requirements of which 11 were specially monitored and funded such as link roads, drainage schemes, drinking water, rural electrification, etc. Many of the programmes implemented under the AVP were not new. They were introduced by the Congress Party in the post-green revolution period in the late 1960s as anti-poverty programmes such as the IRDP and NREP to deal with rising discontent in the countryside due to increasing inequalities in the countryside. However, some features distinguish the BSP's welfare programmes from those of the Congress. First, many programmes were to be implemented exclusively for the dalits, and were located in villages where dalits being in a majority, could gain maximum benefit.

Second, the aim was to concentrate developmental funds spread thinly over the state, into villages where dalits are in large number so as to provide maximum benefits to them. Hence, the welfare programmes were based on the principle of compensating for failure of parties such as the Congress in the past to look after their socio-economic well-being. On assuming power in 1995 and again in 1997, the Mayawati government issued orders to stop all social welfare programmes so that funds could be diverted to the selected Ambedkar villages, and all officials were instructed to give maximum attention and priority to such villages. Government publications described the AVP as "only a matter of prioritisation and not exclusion of other villages. It was only for purposes of optimally utilising scarce resources for development of less developed areas... It was the first stage in the development of all rural areas in the state." But it was also described as a "unique programme for the development of the underprivileged classes".

The BSP used the AVP as a means of providing social justice to the dalit-bahujans, and of improving its electoral base in the countryside. Mayawati created a separate department for the programme and an attempt was made to create a sympathetic bureaucracy, most officials at the state and district level put in charge of it being from the dalit community. A series of government orders issued in 1995 by the Mayawati government directed district and block level officers to give top priority to implementation of the AVP. The programme could be implemented only in a small number of villages as the BSP government could not complete its tenure. When the Kalyan Singh government came to power in September 1997 the programme was continued but it slowed down considerably. The BJP government decided not to adopt villages with less than 30 per cent dalits in the population. During her third government, Mayawati identified another 10,000 Ambedkar villages and hoped to fund them either through the state budget or with help from the World Bank. However, more important, studies show that the benefits of the programmes within the AVs went into the hands of a small, and already better-off section of the dalits, who taking advantage of the reservation provided in panchayats following the 73rd amendment were elected as sarpanchs or panchayat members making them a new dominant group in parts of the state, creating unhappiness among the poorer sections. The programme alienated the non-dalit rural poor–the MBCs–who in some areas are poorer than the dalits. The programme met the aspirations and hopes of new capitalist and entrepreneurial tendencies that have arisen among sections of the dalits in the countryside and the BSP missed an opportunity to emerge as a party of the poor and downtrodden

Cultural Policies: During its tenure the BSP government spent considerable funds on 'cultural' policies. The aim was to use state power to adopt cultural policies to inculcate social awareness among the dalits in UP. This was done by constructing memorials, naming institutes and roads and renaming universities and districts after important leaders revered by dalits, carving out 16 new districts and naming them after saints and gurus belonging to the Bahujan Samaj; constructing 'parivartan sthal' in the parivartan chowk; a Dr Ambedkar Park in honour of the architect of the Indian Constitution and many other such landmarks.

The foundation stone for the Dr Bhim Rao Ambedkar Smarak in Lucknow, which stands on prime land in the city, was laid on August 15, 1995 during the first Mayawati government. Work on it was continued during her second term and it was completed in 2003. It consists of a number of imposing structures including a statue of Ambedkar. While ₹57 crore was spent on the main memorial buildings, ₹30 crore was spent on the lighting and main gate and entrance among other things (The Times of India, January 15, New Delhi). Other such measures have been the Dr Ambedkar Udyan and Memorial and Parivartan Chowk set up in Lucknow to commemorate the memory of those who worked for the upliftment of dalits.

It is reported that during her brief tenure as chief minister in 1997, Mayawati installed 15,000 Ambedkar statues all over Uttar Pradesh. A number of Awards named after famous lower caste leaders such as the Mahakavi Valmiki Sahitya Award, Dr Ambedkar Gaurav Award and the Sant Ravidas Memorial Award were begun. While the BSP has spent money on various occasions including Mayawati's birthday in the past, it is alleged that in January 2003, the state government spent ₹1.35 crore from the state contingency fund.

The policies of the BSP contributed to the sharp rise in the fiscal deficit during the 1990s leading to the state sinking deeper into the 'debt trap' [Shankar 2002:4902]. The three BSP governments made little attempt to raise more resources during their tenure. While it is true that today many state governments are in debt, some such as TN, Karnataka, Kerala and even Rajasthan considered a BIMARU state are making greater efforts at internal resource mobilisation. UP has singularly not tried to move in this direction. UP's own tax revenue finances by the late 1990s was only 45 per cent of its aggregate expenditure as a result of which it had to resort to borrowings to meets its ever mounting non-developmental expenditure and very little went to augment capital formation.

In the 2002-03 Budget, capital outlay was ₹4,101 crore or 7.5 per cent of the aggregate expenditure. This capital outlay was also mainly in the form of construction of several office buildings more so following the creation of many new districts and other wasteful expenditure. Due to these policies the fiscal position of the UP government during 2002 showed signs of deterioration.

An examination of the Budget for 2002-03 indicates the priorities of the third BSP government. The per capita plan outlay as well as budgetary expenditure was lowest among states, except in the case of Bihar [Shankar 2002]. An analysis of the revenue and capital expenditure reveals that the total expenditure on crucial areas such as agriculture and allied activities, rural development, special area programme, irrigation and flood control and power came to only ₹7,416 crore or 13 per cent of the total budgetary expenditure.

The share on social services, which includes education, water supply, health, etc, was reduced from 33 per cent to 29 per cent and on economic services, which includes activities such as agriculture, industry, power and transport from 16.4 per cent to 15.8 per cent. On the other hand, expenditure on general services in the Budget rose from previous years, reaching 52 per cent. Expenditure on administrative services was twice the expenditure on agriculture and allied services, more than twice that spent on irrigation and flood control and more than three times that on power [ibid]. Despite stagnation in agricultural production and the decline in per capita foodgrains production in the state there was hardly any fresh investment in the Budget for the irrigation sector. There was no new investment in the power sector apart from electrification of some villages, the funds for which will come from the central government. In the industrial sector the only new expenditure amounting to ₹92 crore was for providing interest-free loan to sick state industrial units for payment of trade tax.

Moreover there is evidence that the conditions of the poorer sections in UP–which includes a major chunk of the dalits–became worse during the 1990s. The National Human Development Report (NHDR) has pointed out the poor conditions of life in UP in comparison with many other states. The state's position in terms of Human Development Index was 29th in 1981 and has fallen to 31 out of 32 states in 2001. In terms of Human Poverty Index UP ranks 29th among 32 states [ibid:144]. Similarly the per capita consumption expenditure registered a fall in the state between 1993-94 and 1999-2000; that this is due to a drastic reduction in the consumption expenditure on food between the two periods clearly suggests deterioration in the standard of living. This downslide took place when the BSP supported by the BJP was in power in UP for the most part.

Despite the fact that the BSP has formed a government twice during the 1990s and again briefly in 2002-03 with the support of the BJP, the conditions of dalits have not improved according to the draft proposals of the Tenth Five-Year Plan (Jha, December 28, The Times of India, New Delhi, 2002). The BSP did not put forward policies for improving the socio-economic conditions of the subaltern sections of the dalits. The emphasis was mainly on political empowerment.

MADHYA PRADESH

Based on the BD and the Task Force the MP government formulated programmes for weaker sections including dalits. It sought to combine the policy framework set out by the government of India and the development of participatory institutions such as panchayati raj bodies, cooperatives and self-help groups in its programmes for dalits. Three major programmes of the second Digvijay Singh government are analysed below.

LAND DISTRIBUTION

Recognising that the large majority of the dalits are landless labourers, the MP government adopted a three-pronged strategy: distribution of land to dalits or help in buying land to make them independent cultivators; alternatively to move them into other occupations through capital formation with government assistance; and third, as many dalits are small cultivators or share-croppers, to provide them assistance through a policy package addressing seed, pesticides, irrigation and credit requirements.

On March 4, 1998 the government of MP issued an order to the district administration for redistribution of land gained by downsizing the area of 'charnoi' (grazing) land from 7.5 per cent in each village to 5 per cent, which it is estimated, can provide a surplus of about six lakh acres. This land was to be distributed among some four lakh SC/ST households. During this phase 1.54 lakh acres of land in the form of 80,470 pattas was distributed to 46,088 families.

Following this on September 19, 2001 the state government further reduced the charnoi land from 5 per cent to 2 per cent. Due to this in the second phase a total of about 6 lakh acres of land was expected to be surplus of which 3.68 lakh acres it was claimed had already been identified and it was expected that another 2.5 lakh acres more would be available. In this manner the government claimed that a total of 1,04,486 acres had been distributed to 32,082 scheduled caste families. The scheme was expected to benefit 4 lakh families.

The government pointed out that between 1972 and 1993 the total land declared surplus was only 3.23 lakh acres, but by taking over charnoi land it could provide much more land to the landless. By this in the post-divided state of MP, out of the 11.42 lakh scheduled castes, 4 lakhs or 15.35 per cent of them could become independent cultivators. Attempts were also made to remove encroachments on land allotted to dalits. According to the Land Records as of November 2001, 1,416 scheduled castes were found to be dispossessed of whom 528 were restored possession and another 888 cases were pending. A more recent report of the state government claimed that by July 2002, 2,48,000 hectares of land had been distributed among 3,03,000 landless individuals of whom scheduled castes constitute 1,99,178 to whom 1,60,194 hectares have been given. The process of identifying surplus land and redistributing it among the landless continued during 2003 in the state.

Few assessments have been made of the government's land distribution programme in MP. A recent study on distribution of charnoi lands to scheduled castes covering eight villages in two blocks–Hatta and Shahnagar of Damoh and Panna districts respectively, evaluates the amount of land distributed, and whether beneficiaries have been able to take possession of it. These blocks are situated within the 10 districts of the Bundelkhand region where dalits constitute 25 per cent of the population.

The study shows that the process of land distribution to scheduled castes has been slow though there are differences between districts. In Hatta block in Damoh district land had been distributed mainly to landless women so far, other categories, such as landless scheduled caste families, were yet to be covered. Only 4 per cent of the respondents in the former category had received land and some had yet to gain actual possession. In Shahnagar block in Panna district on the other hand, 33 per cent of the respondent households had received land from the government. Seven per cent of the respondents had bought land: 44 per cent of them had bought 1 acre, 11 per cent of them 5 acres and in 1 case a person had bought 6 acres of land.

More important, the study points out charnoi land comprises of poor quality wasteland in the village not suitable for agriculture, a fact that is well known to the government. Second, as the number of landless families is large, the process of identification of beneficiaries needs to be formalised, without which, villagers are unable to understand why some landless families were given land while others were excluded, leading to conflict. Third, the plots allotted are small, in some cases economically unviable. In Shahnagar block 21 per cent had received about 2 acres, 31 per cent had received up to 1.5 and 17 per cent had received up to 1 acre of land. Nor has the government helped the beneficiaries to cultivate the allotted wasteland, a task that would require considerable investment. In Hatta block, beneficiaries complained that they have not received any assistance from the government while in the Shahnagar block, about 12 per cent in a few villages have received financial assistance from the government. Equally important, in contravention of rules, in Shahnagar block 38 per cent of the respondents who have benefited from charnoi land distribution are not landless families. The respondents already owned land, with 5 per cent owning more than 3 acres of land and 3.8 per cent owning 2 acres of land.

A number of problems in the implementation of the scheme have rendered it ineffective. In Hatta block, at least half of the beneficiaries to whom land has been allotted complained that the district authorities had not begun the process of measuring and allotting village land, nor have they received ownership pattas from the government. In Shahnagar the situation is better with a larger number having received their ownership papers.

Opposition from the upper castes in the village to allotment of land to the scheduled castes leading to conflict is an important impediment. Respondents felt that government indifference was a major reason, which allowed the upper castes to prevent the scheduled castes from taking possession of land allotted to them. In Hatta block only 36 per cent of the beneficiaries are still in possession of the land allotted: 44 per cent never actually gained possession while 20 per cent have been deprived of the allotted land.

In Shahnagar, 20 per cent of those allotted land could not gain possession while 17 per cent are no longer in possession. The government also failed to check encroachments on the land allotted to scheduled castes. In Hatta block, 38 per cent and in Shahnagar 21 per cent of the respondents were allotted land already encroached upon by villagers. It was only with the help of the government machinery that a few of the beneficiaries were able to gain possession of the land allotted but none of them were able to obtain an ownership patta for the land allotted.

EDUCATION GUARANTEE SCHEME

While the Digvijay Singh government initiated a number of educational programmes, the Educational Guarantee Scheme (EGS) launched in 1997 was the most important. It had two goals: retention of children in the schooling system and improvement of quality of schooling, both of which are particularly important for children from the dalit community. Named as the Rajiv Gandhi Shiksha Mission it had two distinctive features: to bring a 'school to the doorsteps' for children in remote hamlets and it was based on a 'Three Way Partnership' between the community, local government (panchayat) and the state government.

Any village that did not have a school and had a minimum of 25 school-going children who belong to the SC/ST community, could raise a demand for a school and was expected to identity a teacher or guruji and provide a start-up space for the school. Based on a decentralised system the local panchayat was expected to appoint the teachers and supervise the functioning of the school while the state government had the responsibility of setting up the school within 90 days, provide academic supervision, the training and salaries for the teachers and provide inputs for quality enhancement.

The state government claimed that by July 2001, 23,854 schools had been established, 11,30,219 students enrolled and a total of 28,435 teachers employed under the EGS in the state. Of total children enrolled 92 per cent were from the SC/ST/OBC category of which 16 per cent are scheduled castes. In this context the sharp increases visible in literacy rates for males and females aged seven and above since 1991, from 58.5 per cent to 76.8 per cent and 29.4 per cent to 50.3 per cent respectively, are significant. The government of MP advertised these figures widely as the result of the EGS and other educational programmes initiated by it since the mid-1990s.

While initiation of EGS has led to much debate on the role of state and civil society institutions in primary education two studies, both based in the districts of Betul and Dewas which have a large dalit population, have analysed the impact of the EGS on dalit children.

They argue that the EGS has dramatically increased access to schooling in areas where schools did not exist or where scheduled caste children had limited access to them; but there has been little reform of the system as a result of which quality remains very low in many cases. On the first finding there is little dispute among scholars that this has been the major success of the scheme. It is on the second that there has been much criticism much of which is relevant for children belonging to the dalit community.

A major problem with the EGS has been that it was designed to raise the number of schools without a major increase in educational expenditure. The result has been as Leclercq's study points out low cost schooling characterised by low teacher-student ratios; few teachers with low salaries, little formal training, multigrade teaching leading to absenteeism, few school hours, little commitment or a new work culture; poor infrastructure and teaching inputs. In short, the EGS schools have reproduced all the well known negative features of the existing government schools. Hence the "guarantee is incomplete…the extension of the system is more notable than its reform".

Decentralisation has not introduced change in the behaviour of teachers. For dalit children the education hierarchy has remained the same: in the sample region children of different social backgrounds attend different schools. Parents, despite the establishment of parent-teacher associations, are unable to introduce change in the functioning of the EGS schools. The EGS schooling system is officially free of costs but parents find they have to spend on clothes, books, slates schoolbags, etc, a burden the poorer scheduled castes find difficult, and hence retention of children remains uncertain. Nor have the panchayats played a role as they are in many cases controlled–informally if not formally any longer–by the dominant sections of the village society. Despite the attempt to involve local communities and introduce a participatory system, the role of the state remains central. These findings are repeated in the second study of primary education under the EGS by a voluntary organisation in three villages of Khategaon block in Dewas district of MP.

It points out that every hamlet has a school and about 61 per cent of the children are admitted to school. However, the study provides a graphic description of poor infrastructure–the schools have barely two rooms one of which is used for panchayat meetings or as a store; few teachers and high absenteeism; short school hours; and quality of teaching is very poor. Based on his study Leclercq argues that the intentions of the Digvijay Singh government towards the quality of schooling hence, remain 'ambiguous'.

This is very pertinent where scheduled caste children are concerned because in the BD, the Task Force Report and in a plethora of official publications the MP government has underlined the importance of quality education for dalits so that they can compete in every walk of life and make use of the policies of 'Diversity and Democratisation'.

Thus, while it must be recognised that educational policies particularly for dalits have been more clearly defined in MP than in other north Indian states, the EGS has proved to be not very different from the 'two-track schooling facilities' that have emerged in many states in the 1990s due to lack of funds with the adoption of a Structural Adjustment Programme.

State education budgets adapted to this budgetary squeeze by a growing reliance on centrally sponsored schemes mainly the DPEP, and schemes which have the potential of increasing enrolment in a situation where no facilities exist, but do not address the needs of quality, equity and sustainability [Dreze and Sen 2002:170]. Much of the financial burden has been passed on to local panchayats, bureaucracy and parents. As a study observes due to the squeeze on funds the EGS was adopted by the NDA as a national scheme within less than two years of its adoption in MP without any evaluation, and this was followed then by West Bengal, Bihar, UP and other states who were quick to adopt their own version of the same [Sadgopal 2003:3512]. This has meant a dilution–and if made permanent, the danger of institutionalisation–of the already deep social inequities that exist within the elementary education system in the country.

GRAM SWARAJ

Complimentary to the above programmes for dalits has been the attempt by the MP government, through its scheme of Gram Swaraj introduced on January 26, 2001, to further involve disadvantaged groups in the new panchayats established after the 73rd Constitutional Amendment. It is a logical corollary of the efforts since the mid-1990s by the MP government to decentralise responsibilities downwards. Its main goal was to break the control of the locally dominant landowning castes over the panchayat and empower the village community as a whole, giving the lower castes a chance to play a role in decision-making. As Digvijay Singh remarked he did not want 'panchayati raj to become sarpanch raj'. It has been variously described: as an attempt to move from representative to 'direct democracy' at the grass roots [ibid] and as a bold experiment in local self-government which if successful would introduce a new era of local governance [Behar 2001:823]. But some have argued that it was based on a mixture of "Gandhian idealism, a concern for effective development and hard-nosed political calculations". The move was meant to serve the political interests of the MP government in a number of ways: by demonstrating that a Congress-led government is more people-oriented than other state governments led by rival parties; pleasing the party's state legislators who were unhappy with the assertiveness of panchayat leaders in their constituencies; and reducing the powers of the sarpanches in order to give a better share to the lower castes.

The Gram Swaraj programme made it mandatory for every village to hold monthly meetings with a quorum of 20 per cent, of which one-third must be women and members belonging to the SC/ST community. All decisions were to be taken by consensus failing which, voting through a secret ballot was compulsory. The gram sabha was given considerable powers and responsibilities for village development such as roads, drinking water, maintenance of wells and school buildings, and was expected to evolve into a local governing body based on the principle of inclusion of all excluded sections, particularly the scheduled castes and schedule tribes.

The rules allowed the gram sabha to involve voluntary agencies for the development of the village and not restrict itself to using the governmental agencies. Every gram sabha was to set up eight committees dealing with various developmental tasks such as agriculture, health, education, security, community welfare, etc, and more could be created if the necessity was felt. The committees are accountable to the gram sabha and not to the local bureaucratic agencies. The rules made provision for the establishment under the gram sabha for a grain bank, community labour, loan bank, etc.

The Digvijay Singh government in its publications claimed that there was increase in participation in gram sabhas by all sections, particularly of scheduled castes, scheduled tribes and women. But some studies paint a disappointing picture. They point out that following the passage of the act no large-scale attempt has been made by the government to inform the people about the very significant changes that it had introduced.

Consequently, in most parts of the state, villagers particularly the weaker sections are not aware of the programme, new powers and responsibilities given to the gram sabha and the new committees constituted. An important reason has been the lack of local leaders to initiate meaningful participation in the gram sabha [Singh 2002:4103]. A recent survey on the functioning of panchayat in MP points to poor implementation and low level of participation by beneficiaries of various government programmes. A study on the functioning of panchayats covering 12-13 gram panchayats in one district from each of the five geographical regions of the state during the period 1995 to 2000, points out that participation of women and scheduled castes scheduled tribes is increasing, but at a very slow pace and participation in decision-making remains very low. While lack of local leadership is important, a major reason is the caste hierarchy within the village, which is reinforced by the landowning structure.

THE BHOPAL DALIT DECLARATION

For the first time in the history of democratic experimentation in India, Madhya Pradesh, with the total involvement of the Chief Minister, organised a conference to prepare an agenda for socio-economic reform of the Indian state and civil society. Digvijay Singh's interest went beyond his day-to-day administrative problems. He in his a inaugural speech made it clear that he wanted to combine politics and power with socio-economic reform as that alone can transform a backward country such as India and a backward State such as Madhya Pradesh.

All these years, politicians made positive gestures towards Dalits only to win them over as electoral base, but never to set an agenda for their socio-economic transformation. The Dalit agenda of an average politician, so far, has been confined to affirming the reservation policy Ambedkar infused into the system. The process of privatisation began to dismantle the space of reservation.

The deliberations at the Bhopal Dalit conference focussed on the Bhopal document, which charted out an economic agenda for transforming the Dalits' socio-economic conditions. The meet evolved a database for critical examination of Dalit progress based on the experience of 50 years of policy and located the Scheduled Caste and the Scheduled Tribe question in terms of policy and performance of the Indian state. Though the document did not contextualise the Dalit question by critiquing the socio-spiritual institutions that evolved in India, it tried to examine the relationship between political democracy and civil-societal democracy. It was pointed out that the document should have paid more attention to the institutional causes of untouchability.

Untouchability in the spiritual realm led to social segregation of people who were not allowed to participate in agrarian capital in the feudal and the pre-feudal economy of India and also in the capitalist modernity of the nation in the present context. Dalits were not mere social untouchables but were kept out of the capitalist modernity.

The conference examined the Madhya Pradesh model of distribution of grazing land, empowering Dalits and tribals through decentralisation by devolving powers to the Panchayat Raj institutions. It c examined the process of making the tribals direct sellers of forest produce and direct buyers of necessary goods and commodities in a market where the system of middlemen from the business class was abolished. It, however, went beyond this model. This model, for that matter any model in India, had not worked out a blueprint for the full-blooded participation of Dalits in capitalist entrepreneurship and market. In other words, no model has so far created a capitalist class from the country's quarter of a billion Scheduled Castes and Scheduled Tribes. No class of contractors, businessmen/women have evolved from these communities. This does not mean there are no administrative and managerial skills among the Dalits and the tribals. Their talent does not have the seed capital required to match the labour capital they possess. The Dalit bureaucratic class and the political leadership were unable to become a class in themselves to turn it into a social capital of the community as the upper castes have done.

The conference posed two questions: one, is it possible to adopt the American model by developing diversified assets, capital, entrepreneurship and skills, as the Americans have done by giving a share to African-Americans in all kinds of national assets? The American economy grew from strength to strength with the robust participation of African-Americans in every sphere of economy-capital ownership, business, capitalist farming and so on. By applying their skills, which had many innovative abilities that the whites lacked, the African-Americans contributed a whole range of new ethics to capital growth.

Why does Indian capital not allow that kind of creative and productive di- versification with Dalit participation? Second, is it possible to create a democratic civil society, which would strengthen the political democracy, by creating conditions of social equality that become the backbone of national development? The answer to these two questions lies in the state repositioning its strategy in both economic and political spheres going far beyond the models of all schools of economic thought that the upper caste economists have so far worked out. No mainstream Indian economist has, so far, advocated active Dalit participation in entrepreneurship and capital ownership.

The Dalit intellectuals felt that Dalit entrepreneurship and capital ownership should not be seen as a dragon of the economy (as many have been seeing reservation in the job sector), but must be seen as a springboard for the whole economy. The truth in this argument can be realised if we understand that creative labour power still exists only among the Dalits and if that labour power owns the capital it has a tremendous ability to reposition the dignity of labour in India.

The innovativeness of capital grows only when we combine the dignity of labour and capital. Since capital in India is arrested in the Brahmin-Bania culture, it suffers from an enormous indignity of labour. When capital and markets operate in the larger cultural environment of indignity of labour they can never take revolutionary leaps. The Bhopal conference makes it clear that without a share in the liberalised private capital for Dalits, the state and civil society are bound to crack.

Further, the question of social democracy is related to establishing the spiritual democratic relations within all religions operating in India. Caste discrimination within the religious order structuralised the undemocratic relations within civil society, which led to a casteisation of state, land, capital and development. The state must step in though the Endowment Departments to abolish caste practice in all religious and educational institutions.

For example, Hinduism and some Christian institutions practice Casteism in temples and churches. The secular state that grants lands and other benefits cannot allow religious discrimination to be practised in the nation. Caste does not allow secularism to operate in any meaningful way because religions claim many assets from the state's collective property, which belongs to all people of that state. The Chief Minister's promise that the State shall make 30 per cent of its purchases from Dalit and tribal business establishments to begin with, starting from this financial year, is a great leap forward.

Let us not forget that many upper caste entrepreneurs and business establishments prospered because of the support of the state and nationalised banks. Ail these years the upper castes have used the national assets as if they belong to them alone. Now Dalits are asking for a share in all forms of state property and the state must understand their aspiration on the basis of citizenship. The notion of citizenship gets institutionalised only when Dalits share all forms of national wealth equitably.

The Central Government told the world at the Durban conference of the United Nations that India was working towards the abolition of caste Within its national interest. But so far the Centre has not come up with any meaningful strategy to transform the casteist socio-economic and spiritual realms. Dalit intellectuals believe that the BJP does not have any reform agenda because it evolved its ideology within the bonds of Hindu Varna dharma.

It, in fact, would negate all the fruits of socio-economic reforms that earlier Government had achieved with some belief in Gandhian and Ambedkar initiatives. The Dalit intelligentsia still seems to repose confidence in the Congress (I) and left-wing political formations as they have some agenda for social transformation on their cards. Digvijay Singh's initiative comes as a reassuring process in the context of post-Durban developments. One hopes the leaders of all parties make some effort to see the Dalit writing on the wall and evolve a national agenda for total diversification of national wealth to avoid a civil war in the 21st century.

The study analysed the 'political response' of the BSP and the Congress as ruling parties in UP and MP respectively to significant developments in the 1990s: the collapse of the aggregative single-dominant party system, shift to a multi-party system with parties characterised by narrower, sectarian bases and most important, the centrality of dalit identity politics. It examined the ideology and the programmes employed by these parties in two differing socio-economic and political contexts to obtain the support of the dalits and other weaker sections. By these programmes both the BSP and the Congress hoped to enlarge their own support bases in UP and MP in order to meet the challenge following the emergence of a more competitive political arena in both state and national politics.

In UP the BSP under the leadership of Mayawati adopted an agenda of political empowerment of dalits based on self-respect and dignity. She argued that these values and principles were more important for dalits than material gains in order to overcome social oppression and domination by the upper castes/classes, and equally important that these could be obtained only through capture of state power. Critical of mainstream parties, which had not been able to help the dalits, the BSP leadership held that this is the best route to fight poverty and deprivation because through use of state power the party could provide them political equality and social justice.

Based on this ideology the BSP during the period when it was in power with the support of the BJP implemented a number of welfare and socio-cultural programmes whose main aim was to raise social and political consciousness and consolidate the dalit vote behind the party. The party hoped thereby to meet the challenge posed by the SP and the BJP within the state, and become an influential player on the national scene.

In MP in contrast, rather than political mobilisation, the emphasis was on the socio-economic upliftment of dalits. The Congress Party under the leadership of Digvijay Singh, placed dalit upliftment within the larger developmental strategy aimed at improving the conditions of underprivileged groups. In contrast to Congress ideology in the past, Digvijay Singh emphasised on human development through state activism as well as multiple strategies involving voluntary associations in civil society and the market.

Accordingly, the state government supported the formulation of the BD, established a TF and adopted the mission approach to implement a number of programmes aimed at providing dalits education, greater participation and inclusion in the decision-making process in local bodies and opening up of new avenues of advancement through the principles of diversity and democratisation. Through these means the Congress hoped to gain the support of the dalits and other weaker sections and resume its position as a dominant party within the state capable of defeating both the BSP and the BJP. This would in turn strengthen its position vis-à-vis the BJP at the national level.

However, the significant question is what are the political dividends or capital that the BSP and the Congress have been able to obtain from agendas and the programmes adopted while in power during the 1990s. Clearly the political gains of the two parties have been differential. In UP the BSP's espousal of the issues self-respect and dignity struck a sensitive chord among dalits who unhappy with oppression and humiliation by upper castes moved towards the party despite its lack of enunciation of a clear-cut economic agenda for dalits.

The party through a series of welfare and identity-based 'cultural' programmes aimed directly and almost exclusively for dalits succeeded in raising political consciousness and enlarging its base among them over every election during the 1990s. Undoubtedly many of these programmes can be described as mere symbolism. While in power the BSP spent considerable resources on programmes such as Periyar Melas, Memorials and the Ambedkar park aimed at providing self-respect and empowerment and welfare programmes for immediate political support, which have emptied the coffers of the state without dealing with the longer-term disadvantages faced by particularly the poorer sections of the dalits. Yet, the important political position gained by the BSP is seen from the fact that no government could be formed without its participation during the decade and all parties were keen to gain the support of the dalits and overcome their image as upper caste parties. The BSP has succeeded in carving out a place for itself not only within the state but also in national politics, which is seen from the attempts by both the Congress and the BJP to form an alliance with it. In short the BSP within a short period due to its strategies of political empowerment has been able to carve out a seminal position in politics.

In MP the Congress Party under Digvijay Singh managed, after defeating the BJP in 1993, to retain power throughout the 1990s. But despite strenuous efforts the party has not been able to resume its earlier position of dominance, which was based on the support of the weaker sections particularly the dalits and tribals. The Congress remained under constant pressure from both the BJP and the BSP during the 1990s. The rising vote share of the BSP indicates that in spite of the BD, the setting of a TF with a focus on programmes for dalits, the Congress was not able to make significant inroads into the dalit vote in the 1990s, particularly in the northern districts.

The BSP managed to retain a position between the Congress and the BJP, and in the recent 2003 state assembly elections has spread into more areas in MP. In fact, the recent elections indicate that the Congress Party has not been able to successfully compete with both the BJP and the BSP for dalit votes. Our study shows that many of the programmes for dalits and weaker sections were well conceived. But their impact due to poor implementation has been slow and halting, and in some cases ineffective. The political gains for the Congress Party have not been commensurate with the efforts made for the underprivileged in the state. This will undoubtedly affect the position of the party vis-à-vis the BJP in the national arena.

Thus, our study shows that mobilisation is a tool or strategy used by parties to meet new exigencies that arise within the political arena, and at different points of time different ones meet with success. The end of the era of broad aggregative parties that attracted all sections of the electorate, and the appearance of narrower parties with sectarian bases, has introduced various pressures and pulls, which have increased during the 1990s.

As our study shows the necessities of democratic politics have been instrumental in shaping the developmental agenda of the BSP and the Congress in UP and MP. On the one hand, identity politics in UP with its emphasis on self-respect and 'difference' does not directly address the economic deprivation of dalits. On the other hand, promises were made in MP to the deprived sections in spite of the inability of the state to meet them due to both financial and bureaucratic constraints. In both cases despite the formulation of agendas for dalit upliftment the aim is to gain their political support for managing the more demanding and competitive arenas that have emerged in the Indian states.

RAJASTHAN: ECONOMIC REFORMS AND DALIT

Oppression of the 160 to 180 million Dalits, who are viewed as being too low to even be part of the caste system, is one of the most repelling, but enduring, realities of the Indian countryside. Equally oppressive is the violence perpetrated against them, especially their women. To be a Dalit today means having to live in a subhuman, degraded, insecure fashion: Every hour, two Dalits are assaulted. Every day, three Dalit women are raped, and two killed. In most parts of India, Dalits continue to be barred from entering Hindu temples or other holy places-although doing so is against the law. Their women are banned from wearing shoes in the presence of caste Hindus. Dalit children often suffer a form of apartheid at school by being made to sit at the back of the classroom.

Yet, the Dalits are resisting. In parts of the country, they are organizing politically to demand their rights. A Dalit woman rules the largest state, Uttar Pradesh. However, breaking the barriers laid down by the Hindu caste system is an uphill struggle, especially when the government does little to uphold the law of the land that prohibits discrimination on account of descent.

The Dalits of Chakwara village discovered this when they lay their claim to a common or public resource: the village pond, bathing in which is an important ritual. The pond and the steps leading to it have been built and maintained over the years with state funds and contributions raised by the entire village, including the Dalits. But Dalits have been excluded from using the common 'ghats' for decades. Caste-based "tradition" ensures that Dalits are treated worse than the buffaloes, cows and pigs that have virtually unrestrained access to the pond. The only exception is the women who have also, irrespective of caste, always been barred from the pond.

However, in December, Babulal and Radheshyam, who belong to the Bairwa group of Dalits, decided to defy the hallowed "tradition" and take a dip in the pond. Outraged, the caste Hindus subjected the Bairwas to vile abuse, threats of a "bloodbath", a nightly siege of their homes and a crippling social boycott. The Dalits could no longer buy tea or vegetables or hire farm implements. The local doctor would not treat them. The grocery shop ostracized them. The local mechanic would not repair their bicycles. Their men were stalked, their women abused. The local administration and police should have protected and supported the Dalits. Instead, they generally sided with the upper castes. In January, officials allied with the caste Hindus in breach of the law bullied the Dalits into signing a "compromise" agreement, which effectively erased their right to the pond. The agreement produced discontent and resentment that has been simmering ever since. Last month, the discontent culminated in another effort by the Bairwas to assert their rights, through a rally in collaboration with other human rights organizations.

The caste Hindus decided to confront the Dalits "physically" and gathered a mob of 10 to 15,000 men armed with sticks. The police tried to stop the men from attacking the rally, halted some distance away. Angered, the caste Hindus attacked the police who responded with teargas and bullets, and in the ensuing brawl more than 50 people were injured, including 44 policemen.

The incident has created waves beyond Rajasthan-one of India's most socially backward states. Rajasthan has a dismal record of anti-Dalit offenses, with an annual average of 5,024 crimes registered in the last three years. On average, there are 46 killings, 134 rapes and 93 cases of grievous injury every year. One of the worst killings was the massacre of 17 Dalits, at Kumher village, in 1992. However, the state administration and police have learnt few lessons. Rather than take preventive measures or prosecute those guilty of caste discrimination, they side with the upper castes. This is partly because the bulk of India's bureaucracy is caste Hindu. Although the Dalits are entitled to 15 per cent of all government jobs, they rarely get the better-paid ones in senior categories.

Of equal importance is the role that "tradition" plays in the Hindu religion. Many enlightened Hindus reject the idea of caste. Modern education persuaded large numbers of them to support a reform movement for cleansing Indian society of evils like caste-based apartheid, widow burning and dowry. But despite early gains, the reform momentum ran out of steam by the 1950s and conservative currents have taken hold since then. In the past 10 to 15 years, these have struck their deepest roots in the Bharatiya Janata Party (BJP), and critics allege that the party ideologically represents hierarchical Hinduism and casteism in its worst aspects.

Legally, the notion of untouchables and discrimination against the Dalits are prohibited under the Indian Constitution under a 1955 civil rights act and the 1989 Prevention of Atrocities, or POA, act. The act was written explicitly to outlaw physical and verbal abuse against Dalits, but hasn't had the desired effect. The Dalit struggle for emancipation from social and economic servitude faces heavy odds, but it has also acquired an international dimension since the World Conference Against Racism last year in South Africa. Casteism has come in for strong criticism from the United Nations. In August, while discussing descent-based discrimination, the U.N. Committee on Elimination of Racial Discrimination strongly condemned caste. The panel's recommendations for corrective measures are thoughtful and exhaustive. They confront India with a simple choice: systematically fight casteism or face opprobrium and possible sanctions from the world community.

DALITS OF PUNJAB AND ECONOMIC REFORMS

Diversities—religious, cultural, linguistic, economic and political— are a known hallmark of Indian society. These diversities are not confined to the upper castes, since diversities relating to the position of Dalits in India are enormous. These cover a wide range of local and regional differences in the historical evolution of caste hierarchies; in the differential impact of socio-economic changes and the state's affirmative actions; in individual and collective Dalit aspirations and coping strategies; and in the experiences of Dalit political resistance and mobilization within different regions of India. One simply cannot ignore the fact that the structure and evolution of caste and untouchability are socio-historical phenomena which are going to vary and change according to specific conditions and circumstances.

WEAK BRAHMANIC INFLUENCE

The state of Punjab has been, for example, known as a "notable exception" to the widely prevalent Brahmanic view of caste and untouchability in India. Denzil Ibbetson, who conducted the first serious study of Punjab castes in 1881, discovered that Brahmanic influence was "probably never so strong in Punjab as in most other parts of India". Scholars of ancient history noticed that Brahmanic orthodoxy had "practically abandoned" the Punjab region, probably because of a continuous influx of aggressive people of diverse racial and cultural characteristics, and shifted quite early in history to the Indo-Gangetic region.

Ibbetson thought that the influence of Islam in the Punjab may also have weakened Brahmanic influence. He observed that by religion the Punjab was "more Mohammedan than Hindu" and that "the people of Punjab are bound by social and tribal custom far more than by any rules of religion" such as ritual purity. The different material conditions of life may also have been part of the reason why the knowledge generated from the experience of life associated with the Sant tradition of North India was able to strongly contest the Brahmanic sources of knowledge (Dharamsastras, Smritis and Puranas) in this region.

The teachings of Sufi saints, Kabir, Ravidas and the Sikh Gurus, who ridiculed Brahminic knowledge and ritual, appear to have exercised noticeable influence on the thinking of the people of this region. Later, the struggle for removal of untouchability, started by the Arya Samaj and the Singh Sabhas in the last quarter of 19th century, and the provision for education and upliftment of Dalits all contributed to weakening the ideological hold of the purity-pollution syndrome. Whereas untouchability has been less of a problem in Punjab than elsewhere in India, the material base of caste division and the vested interests of the dominating landowning caste have proven to be more significant grounds for discrimination, exploitation and oppression of Dalits. Another significant feature of Dalit life in this region has been their use of the weapons of the weak to resist oppression. This is noticeable in the few Dalit autobiographies and literature in the Punjabi language, but more importantly in the distinctly Dalit-led and organized Ad Dharm movement launched in 1925.

Confined almost exclusively to the more progressive segment of the Chamar caste, the Ad Dharm (*i.e.*, original or ancient religion) developed a proud and distinct religio-political identity of pride around Ravidas as the chief deity; the use of new symbols, prayers, rituals, flag, dress, salutations; and claims for a communal share in political representation. " We are not Hindus... We are the original people of this country", it was asserted. "There was a time when we ruled India... The Hindu qaum came from outside and enslaved us." It was a tremendous boost to their claims when the Commissioner for the 1931 Census allowed them to record their religious identity as 'Ad Dharm' in place of Hindu, Muslim, Sikh or Christian. As many as 418,789 Dalits registered themselves as Ad Dharmis in that census. In the 1937 elections Ad Dharmis captured seven of the eight seats reserved for Scheduled Castes in the Punjab Legislative Council. Although the movement declined after the mid -1940s, it is believed that the early beginnings of the violent conflict that took place recently in village Talhan of Jalandhar district can be trace to the radicalization of Dalit consciousness and to the resulting conflict and confrontation with the Arya Samajist and Sikh leadership pf the 1930s.

THE RELIGIOUS FACTOR

The Punjab state has, at present, the largest proportion of the Scheduled Caste population, 28.3% according to the 1991 Census as compared to the all-India average of 16.4%. When the classified data for the 2001 Census becomes available, the proportion may have risen to above 30%. More than one fourth of Punjab's villages have an average Dalit population of ver 40% and in some villages such as Talhan, mentioned above, it is above 65%. The fact that Punjab is the home of Sikhism has also made a significant difference in the prevalence of caste and untouchability in the region.

Following the partition of the province in 1947 and the re-organization of the Indian Punjab in 1966, it became a Sikh majority state; 63% of its present population are Sikhs. Sikhism is known for the egalitarian teachings of the Gurus, the institutions of sangat (congregation for worship) and langar (partaking of free meals), and the absence of a caste-based priestly class (unlike the pervasive presence of Brahmins in Hindu religion).

It also offers no religious sanction for caste hierarchy. Caste discrimination and oppression against Dalits in the Punjab is less marked than in other parts of India. Over the centuries the Punjab has been witness to large scale Dalit conversions to Islam, Sikhism and later to Christianity. Conversion divided Chuhras and Chamars into different religious categories and even different names were used for Chuhras belonging to different religions (*i.e.*, Mussalli for the Muslims, Mazhabi for the Sikhs, Isai for the Christians, and Balmiki for those who kept to the distinctive Chuhra religion.) Only Hindu and Sikh Dalits were included in the list of Scheduled Castes prepared by the Government of India after independence. Around 40% of the Dalits are Sikh by religion and practically all the Christians in Punjab are also Dalits.

Christian Dalits were, however, kept out of the list of Scheduled Castes and were later included in the Backward Class category, creating a ground for discrimination against Christian Dalits. A good number of Dalits in the Punjab have converted to Buddhism in recent years. The boundary between Dalits who follow Hindu and Sikh religions is quite flexible and may be crossed inconspicuously. Their religious identification with Hinduism or Sikhism has been generally weak. Ramdasias are a Sikh Scheduled Caste. A section of the Ad Dharmis followed Sikh ways of worship and ritual.

However, most of them remain clean-shaven and regard Ravidas as their Guru. Kabirpanthis are both Hindu and Sikh, but the caste fellowship is more important to them than is the religion. Of late, Kabir temples and distinct rituals of worship have been developed to support a new religious identity. Dalits are mostly opposed to notions of Hindu or Sikh communal identity. The growth of religious communalism in Punjab from the last quarter of the 19th century was directly related to the extension of upper caste domination over the lower castes and the promotion of the economic and political interests of the elitein each community. Communalism thus blocked rather than furthered the Dalit search for equality.

THE ECONOMIC FACTOR

The British rulers had strengthened the economic order based on caste hierarchy through measures, like the Punjab Land Alienation Act 1901, which debarred the lower castes from owning land. This bolstered the social and political domination of theJat landlord and condemned the Dalits to live as a reservoir of cheap bonded labour for cultivation and other forms of menial service to the ruling castes. The Dalit share in cultivable land in Punjab today is abysmally marginal, just 2.4% of the total. The state's efforts to bring about land reforms were defeated. The Green Revolution changed the face of Punjab, but widened economic differences, increasing the economic and political clout of the Jat landowning class. Jat control of leadership in the Shiromani Akali Dal since 1962 that made it virtually a Jat political party has further increased fear and insecurity among the lower castes. The forcible appropriation of village common lands which traditionally had provided a little cushion for Dalit survival has become a major cause of violent conflicts in Punjab's villages. The Dalit struggle for dignity in the rural areas also involves resistance against social symbols of Jat hegemony. A recent field study of 5I villages spread over the three regions of the Punjab found separate Mazhabi (*i.e.*, Dalit Sikh) gurdwaras in 41 of these villages.

As many villages also had separate cremation grounds. The dominating influence of Sikh religionin Punjab has not meant an end to caste discrimination or atrocities against Dalits. Incidents of anti-Dalit violence and social boycott of Dalits or the stripping and rape of Dalit women by those dominant in the village community have been common. Harinder Singh Khalsa, a Sikh member of the National Commission for Scheduled Castes and Scheduled Tribes, recorded with some pain that "Punjab has no untouchability, probably because of Sikhism, but I am ashamed to say that in committing atrocities on Dalits, we do not lag behind." Poverty, which is a well known distingui-shing mark of Dalit life in general, is prevalent among Dalits of Punjab, especially among those living in the Malwa area.

However, the character of poverty is qualitatively different from what poverty is generally understood to be in states like Bihar, UP, Rajasthan, and Orissa. Jean Dreze and Amartya Sen noted that in the Punjab 21% of the general population lived below the poverty line (BPL) in 1994, less than half of India's 45% average. However, according to Government of Punjab records, 68% of the Scheduled Caste [Dalit] population belonged to the BPL category in 1991. It was rightly remarked, therefore, that "The poor (in Punjab) are the Scheduled Castes and the Scheduled Castes are the poor". Nearly half of the total Scheduled Caste population still live in unhygienic conditions in colonies on the edge of the village.

Yet it is not unimportant to note that,as the National Sample Survey Report 1990-91 showed, "there was no rural household in Punjab whose members were not able to eat two square meals a day on all the 365 days in a year." A significant factor that made a difference in the status and self-perception of the Dalits in Punjab has been their large scale migration to foreign countries for work.

It is estimated that on an average one member in every second Dalit family in the Doaba region of the Punjab had gone abroad. The remittances sent home by these migrants contribute to fine houses and other visible signs of prosperity. Migrant remittances have also contributed to the enlargement of the Dalits' religio-cultural autonomy, as some of it goes to the development of, *e.g.*, the Ravidassi Sachkhand dera of Sant Sarwan Dass at Ballan near Jalandhar. The prosperity of a section of Dalits has not, however, raised their social or caste status in the village. Instead it has made themnot only more apprehensive about insults and humiliation but also more inclined to retaliate violently to maltreatment and uncomplimentary remarks or body language by the upper castes in general and by Jats in particular. A major reason for the violent public clash between the Dalits and Jats of villageTalhan was the resentment born of the disparity between Dalit economic and social status. Economic disparities have also affected relationships between rich and poor Dalits. More serious are the hierarchies and walls dividing one Dalit caste from another, a formidable obstruction to Dalit political solidarity. The appeal of the Bahujan Samaj Party, which has registered a significant rise in Punjab's politics for over the past decade, has remained largely limited to the Chamar community.

The dynamics of change has enabled Dalits of Punjab, despite handicaps, to acquire a sense of autonomy, pointing to a "community in movement and not mired in helplessness." There is a marked tendency among the Dalits towards conscious dissociation from stigmatized occupations and practices which are humiliating to them. A field study by S. S. Jodhka shows that in the year 2000 not more than 10% of Dalits followed their traditional occupations and most have also moved away from agricultural labour which made them dependent upon Jat landlords. Although it was rather restricted and half-hearted, the spread of education, affirmative action by the state, and Dalit political participation have contributed to the first flush of awakening and empowerment of Dalits. Now, with the rising tide of market rationality under liberalization, privatization and globalization, as well as the state's decreasing inclination to protect their interests, it is feared that Dalits may be affected more adversely than other sections of society by market forces.

HARYANA

WELFARE OF SC AND BC

The Haryana Government is fully committed to promote the Welfare of Scheduled Castes and Backward Classes by implementing various schemes for their socio-economic and educational upliftment. To encourage the Scheduled Castes/Backward Classes students to get more marks in examinations scholarship ranging from ₹4000 per annum to ₹12000 per annum for different category of cources are given for rural and urban students under Dr. Ambedkar Medhavi Chhatar Yojna.

This scholarship will be given to those Scheduled Castes and Backward Classes students who are studying in recognized Govt./Non-Govt. Schools,Colleges, Insttutions and Universities. Under this scheme 12346 students were benefited during the year 2008-09 and approximately 10000 students will be benefited during the year 2009-10. Sensitive to the social needs of the disadvantaged groups belonging to BPL category the Government give a grant of ₹15000 to Scheduled Castes persons, widows of all sections of society and ₹5100 to the persons of other sections of society, as a financial assistance for marriage of their daughters under Indira Gandhi Priya Darshni Vivah Shagun Yojana. The assistance amount has been increased from ₹15000 to ₹31000 and from ₹5100 to ₹11000 w.e.f. 26.1.2010. Under this scheme 16907 beneficiaries were benefited during the year 2008-09 and approximately 19894 persons will be benefited during the year 2009-10. In order to solve the housing problem of Scheduled Castes and De-notified Tribes living below poverty line subsidy for construction and repair of house is given under "Housing Scheme for Scheduled Castes and De-notified Tribes" Scheme.

Under this scheme a grant of ₹50000 for construction and ₹10000 for repair is given to the Scheduled Castes and De-notified Tribes persons who live under BPL. During the year 2008-09 approximately 2428 beneficiaries were benefited under this scheme and approximately 7960 persons will be benefited during the year 2009-10. HSFDC The Haryana Scheduled Castes Finance and Development Corporation provides loan/benefit to only those identified Scheduled Castes families whose annual family income does not exceed ₹20000 in rural areas and ₹27500 in urban areas for various bank assisted income generating schemes such as Dairy Farming, Sheep Rearing, Piggery, Kiryana Shop, Animal Driven Carts, Leather and Leather Goods Making, Tea Shop, Bangles Shop, etc. In case of National Scheduled Castes Finance and Development Corporation (NSFDC) assisted schemes such as Purchase of Light Commercial Vehicles, Auto-Rickshaw (Diesel) etc.,

the income ceiling is ₹40000 per annum in rural areas and ₹55000 per annum in urban areas. There is no income limit under NSKFDC Schemes, only occupation is the criteria for eligibility. Under the Bank Tie- up Schemes, the Corporation provides financial assistance for various bankable income generating schemes costing upto ₹1.50 lakh.The Corporation provides subsidy at the rate of 50 per cent (Subsidy to maximum of ₹10000) and margin money at the rate of 10 per cent of the project cost and balance amount is provided by the bank. Under the Scheme in collaboration with National Scheduled Castes Finance and Development Corporation (NSFDC), the Corporation follows the unit cost as approved by NSFDC under various schemes.

The NSFDC, Haryana Scheduled Castes Finance and Development Corporation and beneficiaries contributes towards its share in the shape of margin money as per financing pattern approved by NSFDC under a particular scheme. However, the share of the Corporation is upto 10 per cent under NSFDC assisted schemes. In case of NSFDC assisted scheme, the Corporation provides subsidy in BPL cases at the rate of 50 per cent of the project cost. The maximum amount of subsidy is ₹10000.

Under the scheme in collaboration with National Safai Karamcharis Finance and Development Corporation (NSKFDC), the project cost ceiling is upto ₹10.00 lakh. The Corporation follows the unit cost as approved by NSKFDC under various schemes. The NSKFDC, Haryana Scheduled Castes Finance and Development Corporation and beneficiaries contributes towards the Scheme in the ratio approved by NSKFDC. The margin money is upto 5 per cent of the unit cost. However, the Corporation contributes its share in the shape of margin money as per financing pattern approved by NSKFDC under a particular scheme.There is no provision of subsidy under NSKFDC Scheme. During the year 2009-10, the Corporation will assist 16000 families for various income generating Schemes by providing them financial assistance of ₹86.26 crore including ₹16.28 crore as subsidy.

The Corporation has assisted 8397 beneficiaries by providing them financial assistance of ₹43.37 crore including ₹6.94 crore as subsidy for various self employment Schemes during the year 2009-10 (upto December, 2009). During the year 2010-11, the Corporation will assist 15000 families for various income generating Schemes by providing them financial assistance of ₹69.35 crore including ₹14.98 crore as subsidy.

HSBCANDEWSKN

Haryana Backward Classes and Economically Weaker Sections Kalyan Nigam is working for the economic upliftment of Backward Classes, Minority Communities and Handicapped persons. Against a target of ₹10.50 crore for providing financial assistance to 2100 persons of Backward Classes during 2009-10, loan of ₹67.76 lakh to 98 persons of Backward Classes has been given upto 31st December, 2009. A target of ₹10.50 crore is fixed for providing financial assistance to 2100 persons of Minority Communities during the year 2009-10 and the Nigam has managed to disburse loan worth ₹21.78 lakh to 40 persons of Minority Communities till 31st December, 2009.

Against the target of providing financial assistance of ₹10.50 crore to 1500 Handicapped Persons during 2009-10, ₹191.79 lakh have been given to the 331 Handicapped Persons till 31st December, 2009.

LABOUR

State Government has taken necessary initiatives and steps to promote harmonious industrial relations and industrial safety. In spite of global recession the State successfully contained its adverse impact on industrial peace and harmony. Two applications have been received for permission for closure, retrenchment or lay off from industrial units of the State but the same have been dismissed as withdrawn. The manufacturing units have revived normal production. Now the information technology units are also reviving their activities. The industrial unrest in units like Musashi Auto, Rico Auto, Sunbeam Auto and Honda Scooter and Motorcycles due to some disputes have been resolved as per law.

To make procedures transparent, users friendly and amenable to e-governance facilities of online Registration and Licensing under various enactments has been introduced. Most prominent among these relate to the Shops and Commercial Establishments and Factories Act etc. The process of online self-certification will also make Industrial Climate more progressive, client friendly and curb the Inspector-Raj. The rates of minimum wages of the unskilled workers in the State which had been revised at the rate of ₹3510 per month on 1.7.2007 have been further updated half yearly to fully neutralize the increase in Consumer Price Index relating to the working class.

At present the rate of minimum wages for an unskilled worker is fixed w.e.f. 1.1.2010 at the rate of ₹4214 per month and ₹162 per day respectively. To provide quick justice to the workers, 9 Industrial Tribunals-cum-Labour Courts are functioning in the State. Besides this, three Lok Adalats were held in the State to dispose of long time pending cases. In these Lok Adalats approximately 500 cases were disposed of. Three Rehabilitation Centers for Destitute and Migrant Child Labour at Panipat, Faridabad and Yamuna Nagar with a capacity of 50 each in a centre have been established.

The State Government has granted ₹1.30 crore during this financial year to run these centers regularly in which free boarding,lodging and vocational education is being provided. Construction of a Labour Welfare Complex has been taken up in Faridabad at the cost of ₹2.50 crore on 2 acre land for rehabilitation of migrant labour temporarily. In this labour transit centre a temporary rental facility will be provided to stay minimum for 2 weeks till they find jobs and shelter for themselves. Haryana Labournet Center which provides services of registration, healthcare, safety training, skill up gradation training, creche for younger children, and schools linkage for children above six years of age and tracking of worker to help him in getting additional or better paid work has been established.

Firstly such center has already been established at Manesar district Gurgaon. Three more Labournet Centers have been opened at Gurgaon and Faridabad with the cost of ₹1.11 crore. The facilities of shelters with civic amenities is being provided to labour at the labour chowks with availability of the land from local authorities. Construction of Labour Sheds at Yamuna Nagar and Faridabad has been started with a cost of ₹28.05 lakh and ₹20.00 lakh respectively which will be completed very soon. To stop the dropout rate of school going children of factory workers and to provide training to the eligible family members of factory workers,the Department has decided to set up 'Welfare Training Centers' in collaboration with a reputed NGO. Two such centers have already been setup at Faridabad, one at Gurgaon and one at Dharuhera with the cost of ₹20.00 lakh. The current plan budget for the year 2009-10 is ₹717.00 Lakhs, out of which ₹11.12 lakh had been spent till September, 2009.

DALITS, ADIVASIS AND NAXALITES

GOVERNMENT OF INDIA: GUILTY AS CHARGED

There is no end to the studies of popular discontent in India, and the Indian nation state is always eager to find ways to control such uprisings of discontent. That it fails strongly is a moot point, for it the main point is that it wins. It has the army, the police, the required ability to brutalise its own people and the complete lack of scruples. But after all that, New Delhi's writ still does not run in nearly one-third of the country.

From time to time, New Delhi's rulers keep setting up committees to study the Naxalite problems. And for India, the Planning Commission is one of the most reliable repository of comprehensive information. That it is also a helpless witness to the government's unpardonable apathy to its important proposals for remedying the situation all these years is a separate story.

The government however requires the Commission for hard statistical facts and figures, and understanding of what is happening at the ground level. That after all this, the GoI leaves all planning to the magnates of the market economy is also a different story. Quite rightly, the report says that poverty does create deprivation but other factors like denial of justice, human dignity, cause alienation and this results in the conviction that relief can be had outside the system by breaking the current order asunder. The story that we are to tell you is based on a report now in the possession of the WSN that was commissioned by the government to understand Naxal problem. That even such a wonderfully produced report may also end up with the usual obligatory list of remedial measures should not reduce its importance since these measures have remained unimplemented for years.

"Development Challenges in Extremist Affected Areas" is the title of the report of an expert group set up by the Planning Commission of the Government of India. Dated March 2008, the report contains meticulously collected latest facts and figures, rigorously examines the causes of the continuing economic exploitation and social discrimination in the adivasi and dalit-inhabited areas even after 60 years of independence. It is significant that this particular expert group was set up by the government in May 2006, in the background of increasing Naxalite activities in Andhra Pradesh, Chhattisgarh, Bihar, Jharkhand and Orissa.

The group consisted of a variety of people ranging from veteran ex-bureaucrats (like D Bandyopadhya who chaired it, and is well known for his implementing the Operation Barga land reform measure in West Bengal, and S R Sankaran who heads the Hyderabad-based Committee of Concerned Citizens which had been trying to bring the Andhra Pradesh government and the Maoist rebels to the negotiating table) to retired police officers like Prakash Singh, ex-director general of police, Uttar Pradesh and Ajit Doval, former director of the Intelligence Bureau. From the other end of the spectrum, we have well known activists and academics like K Balagopal of the human rights movement and Sukhadeo Thorat, chairman of the University Grants Commission and a champion of Dalit emancipation, among others. That a mixed bag of this nature, consisting of experts from different disciplines with differing opinions, could prepare a consensus report on several contentious issues and come up with a unanimously agreed set of recommendations, suggests that all is not lost. But all will be, given the Government of India's ability at remaining deaf and dumb. While the official attitude is to blame the Naxalites for violence, and call all actions "an act of cowardice", this report talks about the structural violence implicit in the social and economic system and underlines how Naxalites have indeed carried out certain socio-economic reforms in their areas of control. These are the reforms that the executive ought to have implemented. The deep shade of Red is replacing the judiciary and the police in ensuring law and order for the poor and the oppressed.

DALITS, ADIVASIS AND NAXALITES

Although the terms of reference did not specifically mention Naxalites (or Maoists), the group's brief was to identify causes of unrest and discontent in areas affected by "widespread displacement, forest issues, insecure tenancies and others forms of exploitation like usury, land alienation and imperfect market conditions...". Clearly, such areas fall in the above-mentioned five states–and significantly enough, the group organised field visits in these areas to observe the situation at first hand, on the basis of which it has come out with stark revelations that expose the culpability of the state in denying the poor their basic rights, the treachery of a corrupt bureaucracy to implement the laws, and its complicity with a trigger-happy police to suppress popular protest.

Maintaining that "the main support for the Naxalite movement comes from dalits and adivasis", the group concentrated on these two sections (termed as scheduled castes and scheduled tribes respectively in official parlance) which comprise about one-fourth of India's population, the majority living in rural areas.

Apart from the high levels of poverty, the dalits suffer from various types of disadvantages like limited employment opportunities, political marginalisation, low education, social discrimination, and human rights violation. As for the adivasi population, besides remaining backward in all aspects of human development including education, health, nutrition, etc, they have been steadily losing their traditional tribal rights and command over resources. The report points out in this connection the administration's failure to implement the protective regulations in scheduled areas, which has resulted in land alienation, forced eviction from land, dependence of the tribals on moneylenders–made worse often by "violence by the state functionaries".

Incidentally, every dalit and adivasi poor in India have not joined the Naxalite movement. There are many states with pockets of high proportion of adivasis and dalits but little Naxalite influence, as in Punjab, Haryana, Gujarat and Rajasthan. The report quite rightly points out that "poverty does create deprivation but other factors like denial of justice, human dignity, cause alienation resulting in the conviction that relief can be had outside the system by breaking the current order asunder". It adds that for such a violent upheaval to happen, there is the likelihood of the "spread of awareness and consciousness". And this is where, as the report suggests, the Maoists have played a significant role by stepping into the craters of dalit and adivasi deprivation in the five states, and organising the deprived for their rights.

Its authors situate the Naxalite movement in the historical context of the "development paradigm pursued since independence", which they assert, has "aggravated the prevailing discontent among marginalised sections of society". While explaining the current surge in Naxalite activities, they slam the neoliberal "directional shift in government policies towards modernisation and mechanisation, export orientation, diversification to produce for the market, withdrawal of various subsidy regimes and exposure to global trade" as "an important factor in hurting the poor in several ways". Following this conceptual approach, they look at the Maoist movement in a way that is different from the prevalent official attitude which primarily blames the Naxalites for the violence. Instead, the present report lays stress on the "structural violence which is implicit in the social and economic system" and which in the opinion of its authors prompts the radical groups to justify their own violent acts. The authors of the report admit that the Naxalites have indeed carried out certain socio-economic reforms in their areas of control.

It is better that India recognises this reality and legitimises the positive Naxalite contribution to the implementation of the pro-poor laws–which the state had failed to carry out. In other words, the government should negotiate a settlement that allows the Naxalites to run their administration in their pockets of control.

NAXALITES AS A SURROGATE STATE

The report brings out that the Maoists are actually carrying out the reforms that the executive ought to have implemented, and are replacing the judiciary and the police in ensuring law and order for the poor and the oppressed.

In the forest areas of Andhra Pradesh, Chhattisgarh, the Vidarbha region of Maharashtra, Orissa and Jharkhand, the Naxalites have led the adivasis to occupy forest lands that they should have enjoyed in the normal course of things under their traditionally recognised rights, but which were denied by government officials through forest settlement proceedings that have "taken place behind the back and over the head of the adivasi forest dwellers". While the government remained indifferent to the need for paying minimum wages to the adivasi tendu leaf gatherers in Andhra Pradesh, the Naxalites by launching a movement have secured increases in the rate of payment for the picking. The practice of forced labour in the same state, under which the toiling castes had to provide free labour to the upper castes, was done away with due to a "major upsurge led by the Naxalites in the late 1970s and early 1980s of the last century...". Commenting on the "peoples courts" set up by the Naxalites in their areas of control, the report observes that "disputes are resolved in a rough and ready manner, and generally in the interest of the weaker party".

The report also reveals how despite change of government, successive rulers suppress the poor and the disadvantaged. There is a design behind this continuity. The rulers, irrespective of party affiliations, are lackadaisical and sloppy in implementing pro-poor legal measures. But the moment the Maoists try to enforce those measures they are quick to use against them with extreme efficiency another set of laws–the draconian laws that have been enacted over the years (e g, Unlawful Activities (Prevention) Act; Chhattisgarh Public Security Act; Andhra Pradesh (Suppression of Disturbances) Act, etc).

Asserting that the Naxalite movement has to be "recognised as a political movement with a strong base among the landless and poor peasantry and adivasis", the experts warn the government against resorting to "security-centric" measures like setting up vigilante groups such as Salwa Judum in Chhattisgarh. Instead, they have called for "an ameliorative approach with emphasis on a negotiated solution", and urged the government for a resumption of the peace talks with the Naxalites which was initiated in October 2004, but broke down in January 2005. As for the Indian state, the experts have been rather frank.

They have shown how, in quite a large swathe of inaccessible territory, the state's writ does not run, and the Naxalites have been able to establish a parallel and alternative order that has largely benefited the poor–especially the dalits and adivasis. It is better that India recognises this reality and legitimises the positive Naxalite contribution to the implementation of the pro-poor laws–which the state had failed to carry out. In other words, the government should negotiate a settlement that allows the Naxalites to run their administration in their pockets of control–on the lines of the settlement arrived at with the Naga rebels of the National Socialist Council of Nagaland (Isak Muivah) who have not given up their arms and run a parallel government in parts of Nagaland.

Referring to the Indian government's conciliatory approach to such insurrectionary groups, the authors of the report raise the legitimate question: "Why a different approach to the Naxals?" It is for the Prime Minister to answer this, since he is the one who calls Naxalite violence the most serious internal security challenge faced by India.

ECONOMIC AND SOCIAL UPLIFTMENT OF DALIT

The caste system contains both social oppression and classexploitation. The dalits suffer from both types of exploitation in the worst form. 86.25 per cent of the scheduled caste households are landless and 49 per cent of the scheduled castes in the rural areas are agricultural workers. The dalits are subject to untouchability and other forms of discrimination despite these being declared unlawful. According to the 2001 census, scheduled castes comprise 16.2 per cent of the total population of India, that is, they number over 17 crore. The dalits are subject to untouchability and other forms of discrimination despite these being declared unlawful. The growing consciousness among the dalits for emancipation is sought to be met with brutal oppression and atrocities. The assertion by the dalits has a democratic content reflecting the aspirations of the most oppressed sections of society.

Along with the curse of untouchability, the dalits had no right to have any property. They had to eat the foulest food, including leftovers thrown away by the higher classes; they were not allowed to draw water from the common well; they were prohibited from entering temples; they were barred from the right to education and knowledge; they had to perform menial jobs for the higher castes; they were not allowed to use the common burial ground; they were not allowed to live in the main village inhabited by the upper classes; and they were deprived of ownership rights to land and property, leading to the lack of access to all sources of economic mobility. Thus, dalits were subjected to both social exclusion and economic discrimination over the centuries. In one form or the other, this continues even today in most parts of the country.

The caste system contains both social oppression and class exploitation. The dalits suffer from both types of exploitation in the worst form. 86.25 per cent of the scheduled caste households are landless and 49 per cent of the scheduled castes in the rural areas are agricultural workers. According to the 2001 census, scheduled castes comprise 16.2 per cent of the total population of India, that is, they number over 17 crore. Scheduled tribes comprise 8.2 per cent of the population, that is, they number over 8 crore. Both together constitute 24.4 per cent of the Indian population, that is, they together number over 25 crore.

The six states that have the highest percentage of scheduled caste population are Punjab (28.9), Himachal Pradesh (24.7), West Bengal (23.0), Uttar Pradesh (21.1), Haryana (19.3) and Tamil Nadu (19.0). The twelve states that have the largest number of scheduled castes are Uttar Pradesh (351.5 lakhs), West Bengal (184.5 lakhs), Bihar (130.5 lakhs), Andhra Pradesh (123.4 lakhs), Tamil Nadu (118.6 lakhs), Maharashtra (98.8 lakhs), Rajasthan (96.9 lakhs), Madhya Pradesh (91.6 lakhs), Karnataka (85.6 lakhs), Punjab (70.3 lakhs), Orissa (60.8 lakhs) and Haryana (40.9 lakhs).

Almost every socio-economic indicator shows that the position of scheduled caste families is awful. In many cases their plight is getting worse. Let us have a look at some of the major indicators.

- *Land:* In 1991 70% of the total SC households were landless or near landless (owning less than one acre). This increased to 75% in 2000. In 1991, 13% of the rural SC households were landless. However, in

2000 this saw a decline and was 10%. As per the Agricultural Census of 1995-96, the bottom 61.6% of operational holdings accounted for only 17.2% of the total operated land area. As against this, the top 7.3% of operational holdings accounted for 40.1% of the total operated area. This gives an indication of land concentration in the hands of a few.

- *Fixed Capital Capital Assets:* In 2000, about 28% of SC households in rural areas had acquired some access to fixed capital assets (agricultural land and non-land assets). This was only half compared to 56% for other non-SC/ST households who had some access to fixed capital assets. In the urban areas, the proportion was 27% for SCs and 35.5% for others.
- *Agriculture Labour:* In 2000, 49.06% of the working SC population were agricultural labourers, as compared to 32.69% for the STs and only 19.66% for the others. This shows the preponderance of dalits in agricultural labour. Between 1991 and 2001, the number of agricultural labourers in India increased from 7.46 crore to 10.74 crore, and a large proportion of them were dalits. On the other hand, the average number of workdays available to an agricultural labourer slumped from 123 in 1981 to 70 in 2005.
- *Child Labour:* It is reported that out of the 60 million child labour in India, 40% come from SC families. Moreover, it is estimated that 80% of child labour engaged in carpet, matchstick and firecracker industries come from scheduled caste backgrounds. The tanning, colouring and leather processing, lifting dead animals, clearing human excreta, cleaning soiled clothes, collection of waste in slaughter houses and sale of toddy are some of the hereditary jobs generally pursued by Dalit children.
- *Per Capita Income:* In 2000, as against the national average of ₹4485, the per capita income of SCs was ₹3,237. The average weekly wage earning of an SC worker was ₹174.50 compared to ₹197.05 for other non- SC/ST workers.
- *Poverty:* In 2000, 35.4% of the SC population was below the poverty line in rural areas as against 21% among others ('Others' everywhere means non-SC/ST); in urban areas the gap was larger–39% of SC as against only 15% among others. The largest incidence of poverty in rural areas was among agricultural labour followed by non-agricultural labour, whereas in urban areas the largest incidence of poverty was among casual labour followed by self-employed households. The monthly per capita expenditure (MPCE) for all household types was lower for SCs than others.
- *Employment:* In 2000, the unemployment rate based on current daily status was 5% for SCs as compared to 3.5% for others in rural and

urban areas. The wage labour households accounted for 61.4% of all SC households in rural areas and 26% in urban areas, as compared to 25.5% and 7.45% for other households.

- *Reservations:* 15% and 7.5% of central government posts are reserved for SCs and STs respectively. For SCs, in Group A, only 10.15% posts were filled, in Group B it was 12.67%, in Group C it was 16.15% and in Group D it was 21.26%. The figures for STs were even lower, at 2.89%, 2.68%, 5.69% and 6.48% for the four groups respectively. Of the 544 judges in the High Courts, only 13 were SC and 4 were ST. Among school teachers all over the country, only 6.7% were SC/STs, while among college and university teachers, only 2.6% were SC/STs.
- *Education:* In 2001, the literacy rate among SCs was 54.7% and among STs it was 47.1%, as against 68.8% for others. Among women, the literacy rate for SCs was 41.9%, for STs it was 34.8% and for others it was 58.2%. School attendance was about 10% less among SC boys than other boys, and about 5% less among SC girls than other girls. Several studies have observed discrimination against SCs in schools in various forms.
- *Health:* In 2000, the Infant Mortality Rate (child death before the age of 1) in SCs was 83 per 1000 live births as against 61.8 for the others, and the Child Mortality Rate (child death before the age of 5) was 119.3 for 1000 live births as against 82.6 for the others. These high rates among the SCs are closely linked with poverty, low educational status and discrimination in access to health services. In 1999, at least 75% of SC women suffered from anaemia and more than 70% SC womens' deliveries took place at home. More than 75% of SC children were anaemic and more than 50% suffered from various degrees of malnutrition.
- *Women:* While dalit women share common problems of gender discrimination with their high caste counterparts, they also suffer from problems specific to them. Dalit women are the worst affected and suffer the three forms oppression—caste, class and gender. As some of the above figures show, these relate to extremely low literacy and education levels, heavy dependence on wage labour, discrimination in employment and wages, heavy concentration in unskilled, low-paid and hazardous manual jobs, violence and sexual exploitation, being the victims of various forms of superstitions (like the devadasi system) etc.
- *Sanitation:* Only 11% of SC households and 7% of ST households had access to sanitary facilities as against the national average of 29%.
- *Electricity:* Only 28% of the SC population and 22% of the ST

population were users of electricity as against the national average of 48%.

- *Atrocities, Untouchability and Discrimination:* During 16 years between 1981 to 2000 for which records are available, a total of 3,57,945 cases of crime and atrocities were committed against the SCs. This comes to an annual average of about 22,371 crimes and atrocities per year. The break-up of the atrocities and violence for the year 2000 is as follows: 486 cases of murder, 3298 grievous hurt, 260 of arson, 1034 cases of rape and 18,664 cases of other offences. The practice of untouchability and social discrimination in the matter of use of public water bodies, water taps, temples, tea stalls, restaurants, community bath, roads and other social services continues to be of high magnitude.

With the onset of the policies of liberalisation, privatisation and globalisation by our country during the last decade and a half, the problems of dalits, adivasis, other backward castes and the working people as a whole have greatly aggravated. The drive to privatise the public sector has directly hit reservations for the SC/STs. The closure of thousands of mills and factories have rendered lakhs jobless and this has also hit dalits and other backward castes. The ban on recruitment to government and semi-government jobs that has been imposed in several states has also had an adverse effect. The growing commercialisation of education and health has kept innumerable people from both socially and economically backward sections out of these vital sectors.

The most disastrous effects of these policies can be seen in the deep agrarian crisis that has afflicted the rural sector. Rural employment has sharply fallen and this has hit dalits, adivasis and women the most. Mechanisation of agriculture has further compounded the problem. The real wages of agricultural workers, of whom a large proportion are dalits, have fallen in many states. No efforts are made to implement minimum wage legislation even where it exists, and periodic revision of minimum wage is also conspicuous by its absence. The dismantling of the public distribution system has increased hunger to alarming proportions. An overwhelming proportion of the malnutrition-related deaths of thousands of children in several states is from dalit and adivasi families.

To ensure a better life for the crores of dalits in our country following measures are to be taken immediately:

- *Land Refoms:* The central and state governments must immediately set in motion a process of land reforms whereby land will be redistributed to the landless agricultural labourers and poor peasants gratis. All loopholes in the present laws must be plugged. All schemes to reverse land reform legislation and give away land to multinational corporations and big business houses should be scrapped forthwith.

- *Reservations:* All the backlogs in reserved seats and posts and in promotions for SCs, STs and OBCs must be filled forthwith with special recruitment drives. The three Constitutional amendments made to correct the three OMs issued in 1997 diluting reservations for SCs and STs should be implemented. The pre-1997 vacancies based roster should be restored. A comprehensive legislation covering all aspects of reservation for SCs/STs in employment and education both public and private institutions should be enacted.
- *Special Component Plan:* Special Component Plan should be properly implemented in all the states with proper allotment of funds according to the population of dalits. A National Commission should be set up to assess the real position of dalits including reservation. The state level commissions should be set up to oversee the implementation of all schemes connected with the SCs including reservation.
- *Infrastructure Development:* Infrastructure development in the scheduled caste areas like road, water, health, culture and other needs has to be given proper importance. When allotting fund for infrastructure development, a separate allotment for scheduled caste areas should be provided.
- A comprehensive National Programme of Minor Irrigation for all irrigable but unirrigated lands of SCs and STs through wells, community wells, bore-wells, community bore-wells and tube-wells, bandheras, check-dams, lift, etc., should be immediately undertaken and implemented.
- *Rooting Out Untouchability:* All forms of untouchability must be rooted out of the country by strengthening the relevant laws, ensuring their strict implementation and most importantly, by launching a mass movement of the people.
- *Protection From Atrocities:* The Central Government should amend and strengthen the SC and ST (Prevention of Atrocities) Act 1989, providing for special courts with judges, investigating officers and public prosecutors unburdened by any other work. Social and economic boycott and blackmail should be included as substantive crimes. Full economic rehabilitation of victims and their survivors must be ensured.
- *Employment:* The privatisation drive should be stopped as it leads to loot of national assets, greater unemployment, a curtailment of reservations and also a spurt in corruption. The Central Government should enact a bill to provide reservations in the private sector, which has been a long-standing demand of SCs and STs. Special schemes to provide self-employment to SC youth should be started. The Right to Work should be incorporated as a fundamental right in the Constitution.

- *Education:* The commercialisation of education should be stopped since the massive fee and donation structure of private educational managements is something that socially and economically backward students cannot afford. For this, the central government must increase its own outlay on education to 6% of the GDP. SC/ST students should be given special scholarships to pursue their studies. The stipends in Social Welfare hostels should be raised and the quality of these hostels improved. Steps should be taken to universalise primary education and expand secondary education. Special measures to curb the drop-out rate among SCs should be undertaken.
- *Agriculture Workers:* The Minimum Wages Act for agricultural workers must be stringently implemented throughout the country. A comprehensive bill for agricultural workers is another long-standing demand and it must be enacted without delay. Homestead land must be provided for SCs, STs and agricultural workers.
- *Rural Employment Guarantee Scheme:* The National Rural Employment Guarantee Act must be strictly implemented all over the country by involving the people, their mass organisations and the panchayati raj institutions. It should be extended to all districts and also to urban areas of the country.
- *Puplic Distribution System:* The public distribution system must be universalised to ensure food to all. Until this is done, BPL ration cards must be issued to all poor families, many of whom are from SCs and STs. The grain under the BPL scheme should be made available at Antyodaya prices.
- *Credit:* Agricultural credit to peasants and agricultural workers must be made available at 4% rate of interest. For SCs and STs in both rural and urban areas, credit facilities should be expanded and the credit given at concessional interest rates.
- *Bonded Labour and Child Lbour:* The total liberation and full rehabilitation of bonded labourers must be ensured. The pernicious practice of child labour must be abolished and children properly rehabilitated and educated. Similarly, total liberation and full rehabilitation must be ensured for Safaqi Karmacharis who are engaged in scavenging.
- *Scavengers:* Ensure total liberation and full rehabilitation for scavengers (safai karamcharis), ban engagement of contract labour in safai services and other services where SC and ST numerically predominate and instead introduce necessary improvements by involving such Karamcharis; and reactivate the Central Monitoring Committee for Liberation and Rehabilitation of Safai Karamcharis and State, Municipal and District Level communities.

Index